FINDING HOME

A MEMOIR

Sir Michael McWilliam

This edition first published in 2022

ISBN 978-1-914076-29-9 (paperback)
ISBN 978-1-914076-30-5 (hardback)

Cover design by Paul Benney
Typesetting: preparetopublish.com

CONTENTS

Preface   v

Bwana Kidogo
1. Kenya Days 1933   3

Finding One's Feet
2. Cheltenham 1946   27
3. Oxford 1952   45

Back to Africa
4. Mufulira Copper Mines 1957   73
5. Kenya Treasury 1958   107

The City
6. Samuel Montagu 1962   153
7. Standard Chartered Bank 1966   173

Academia
8. School of Oriental and African Studies 1989   263

The Commonwealth Dimension
9. Royal Commonwealth Society   297
10. British Empire & Commonwealth Museum   329
11. Commonwealth Development Corporation   353

Portrait of a Marriage
12. Ruth   363

Heimat
13. From Kennington to Brimpsfield   401
14. Joining In   419

Acknowledgements   429

Index   431

PREFACE

From the age of six, I had to write a weekly letter home to my parents from an up-country prep school in Kenya and I continued the practice for the next forty years, while I lived in one country and they lived in another, until my parents finally returned to England. For some four years after leaving Oxford, I wrote regularly to Dame Margery Perham at Nuffield, commenting on the evolving political situation in what was then Northern Rhodesia and pre-independence Kenya. They were based on careful diaries, which I have retained, and I have kept a diary at other momentous periods in my life, most notably for the five years that I was chief executive of Standard Chartered Bank.[1] From the year of my marriage to Ruth in 1960, I have also maintained detailed domestic accounts and, in 2008, I turned these records into a narrative charting the changing priorities of family life as our circumstances changed. Thus, the habit of recording and reflecting on events was established over many years and it lies at the root of my deciding to write this memoir.

I have been fortunate in many ways, which prompts reflections on the role of luck as one looks back, and the extent to which one makes one's own luck – as the cliché has it. One element is recognising opportunity

---

1 My letters to Oxford are in the Perham archive in the Bodleian Library. My City diaries were made available to the recent historian of the bank, were typed, and are now in the London Metropolitan Library, together with other papers.

when it occurs and being able to seize it, which implies a degree of self-confidence and determination to reach a goal. At the age of about ten, the headmistress of Kaptagat School would talk to me quite often about aiming high, which I think imbued me with a sense of destiny.

As a new boy at Cheltenham College, I can recall articulating the ambition one day of becoming head boy. Again, in my courtship of Ruth after she had broken things off and was back in England, I set myself a goal to win her back. Although I was unsuccessful in gaining a First at Oxford, I succeeded in being awarded a coveted studentship to Nuffield. And my ambition to lead Standard Chartered was eventually realised, along with the determination to defeat a hostile takeover bid and to retain the independence of the bank.

Another dimension of luck is the role of mentors and personal contacts at critical points, whether as role models, door openers, advisers or confidants. I benefitted greatly from the influence of several remarkable women and some men. A lengthy list of Colonial Service officials would attest to the charisma of Margery Perham and to her influence on the way they approached Britain's mission in Africa. She encouraged my interest in African affairs and in writing about them, so she was quite disappointed when I eventually decided to become a banker. The artist William Rothenstein made a striking pastel drawing of Margery in her twenties in which one can deduce the idealism, intelligence and glamour of her personality. He signed it, 'With the homage of William Rothenstein, Oct. 1919'. Nuffield allowed me to have a copy of the picture, which I treasure. My complex relationship with Ruth has a chapter to itself, but in this context I merely note that it was due to her intensive mentoring that I became the winning candidate to head the School of Oriental & African Studies, after I left the bank, and it was her magnanimous initiative that saved our marriage. One man should also be included here, Dr Henry Jarecki. He came into my life as an unexpected extra when Standard Chartered bought the bullion dealer, Mocatta & Goldsmid. His intellectual brilliance and commercial acumen became legendary, but more importantly he became my closest friend and adviser during my final tumultuous years in the City and has remained so.

There is a sensitive borderline between helpful friends and contacts and what has become known as 'chumocracy' as that entails recognising a difference between knowing someone who would be suitably qualified for a particular job and proposing a person just because he or she is a personal friend or colleague. Looking back, I have been a beneficiary of and have been involved with both open competition and the 'tap on the shoulder' selection and one is conscious that procedures to ensure equal access and open competition have been greatly elaborated during my lifetime, perhaps even to the point where they have become a burden. This is especially true of smaller charities and voluntary organisations where there is often real difficulty in finding suitable persons willing to serve. The growth industry of headhunters operates in this middle ground as an essential service, but often at considerable cost.

I have been a witness to, and also a participant in, some momentous times and, as indicated above, was regularly recording my impressions of pre-independence colonial Africa and during the transformation of a very traditional bank, leading into the era of Big Bang. I also participated in the adaptation of an equally conservative university institution so it might compete in the modern educational marketplace. It was this last experience that led to my being appointed to the Order of St. Michael & St. George, 'for services to education', and to a memorable visit to Buckingham Palace.

In writing of these experiences, I became very conscious of a darker side to worldly success. The ambition and drive that is a feature of it has a personal dimension and cost. When one is in a status relationship with nearly everyone, it is difficult to forge real friendships and when the music stops, it is surprising how few remain. At the family level, there is an elephant in the room all the time arising from the demands of one's career. At the time, I thought that I was managing the tensions well, especially as Ruth was able to hold a succession of interesting jobs. But my perception was flawed, both as regards to myself and to Ruth, and the resulting crisis brought home to me the risk of a fractured marriage as an accompaniment to worldly success.

It has become fashionable to decry all aspects of colonial rule in Africa, which I find hard to reconcile with my own experiences. By the 1950s in Kenya, and notwithstanding the Mau Mau emergency, there was a mission-driven colonial administration working at social, political and agricultural reform. There was even a political movement amongst the settlers that was pursuing the chimera of multiracial politics. Everyone got their timing wrong over political independence, but it is a distorted reading of history not to recognise the motivation and some of the achievements of the period. In writing the story of the Kenya tea industry, I was able to chart one of the more singular achievements resulting from the successful introduction of tea growing by small farmers, who have helped to make Kenya the world's leading exporter. However, one has to recognise that there is a moral flaw in the very idea of colonial rule, however benign, and also that its reality for many of those subjected to it was far from positive. Most British people in the colonies led a more privileged life than their contemporaries at home, although I still recall the remark of a fellow student at Nuffield who went on to become a distinguished barrister, "Why do you want to go and splash in a smaller pond?"

The recollections and reflections in these memoirs complement several recent published histories of organisations that I have been associated with. In the case of Standard Chartered, a recent author had access to my own diaries and papers and I have enlarged upon some of the events covered by Duncan Campbell-Smith. With SOAS, I provided some papers and talked to another author, Ian Brown. With the Royal Commonwealth Society, I have charted some of the developments that I was involved with while serving on its council. I, myself, have published a history of the Commonwealth Development Corporation up until its partial privatisation. Taken together, the following pages contribute to a wider story of institutional change in the second half of the twentieth century.

In my late seventies, I had the good fortune to meet Thalia and to marry again and to put down roots in a Gloucestershire village. Good health, good neighbours, the Cotswold countryside and a challenging garden have all contributed to give us a sense of belonging and contentment that I think is encapsulated by the German word *heimat*. Looking back, it is tempting to seek patterns in one's life. A real one for me has been a sense of being uprooted from Kenya as a child and of a prolonged search for home. I commented earlier on the role of good luck in one's life story. Thalia and I have enjoyed and perhaps even have made our own good luck, so that I have been able to conclude these memoirs on a note of thankfulness.

BWANA KIDOGO

1. KENYA DAYS 1933

'I had a farm in Africa, at the foot of the Ngong Hills' is one of the more evocative opening sentences in literature. 'I had a childhood in Africa' lacks the resonance of Karen Blixen's opening line and also the experience has been shared by thousands of British children. Yet it immediately signals that the writer of such words was a participant in the imperial colonial project, probably in the middle decades of the twentieth century, for whom –as children innocent of the larger implications – growing up in Africa was both a privileged and, frequently, magical experience. It was privileged both by their status as part of the ruling power, and by the indulgence and love of children that seems to be a feature of African society. It was made magical by the freedom enjoyed by so many of us and by the ever-present awareness of the wonders of the natural world around us. As children we swapped information culled from adults on wildlife behaviour and the customs of the people around us. Before the days of national game reserves, it was rare actually to see elephant or lion, but there were plenty of anecdotes doing the rounds. On juvenile adventures into the neighbouring bush I could invent endless 'what if?' fantasies with myself as the hero.

I was born on 21 June 1933 at home in a wood-built bungalow on Cheboswa Estate, Kericho in western Kenya, where my father Douglas (or Dougal as he was called) was an assistant manager helping to plant up this new tea estate for Brooke Bond. He had come out to Kenya in 1927 to Mombasa to join Brooke Bond's marketing department which was distributing imported tea from India to local tea shops and grocers – replicating its English business model founded in Liverpool. However, the company had acquired 5,000 acres of land in Kericho in 1925 from a failed government-sponsored soldier settlement scheme (plus the lease of another 6,500 acres excised from the native reserve) and, as an able-bodied young man, my father was posted to Kericho to take part in planting up the tea estates. On his first home leave in 1930 he had married his childhood sweetheart, Margaret, who was always known as Wags on account of her vivacity.

From 1925 Kericho became the centre of the nascent Kenya tea industry as Brooke Bond and James Finlay planted up their estates in what had been a Kipsigis tribal domain. Although there were also a number of independent farms (who also began planting tea), Kericho was different from the rest of the White Highlands in that the settlers here were employees of substantial British plantation businesses, engaged in establishing a highly disciplined form of agriculture modelled on Indian practice. Elsewhere in the Highlands farming in this period was much more problematical as the appropriate seeds and animal strains had yet to be proved and many of the aspiring farmers were undercapitalised, inexperienced and not always serious. Thus, Kericho was an exceptional enclave in Kenya, both as to its relatively well capitalised form of agriculture, employing managers rather than sole proprietors, and in the society that was established there, which was more conventional and subject to corporate mores. For example, adultery was a dismissible offence, which contrasted with the popular *mot* at the time 'Are you married, or do you live in Kenya?'

The popular image of up-country Kenya settlers is heavily coloured by the numbers of English landed gentry who descended on the country, along with many ex-military veterans after the 1914-18 war. The settlers from South Africa who settled in the plateau area around Eldoret are less well known, as are the Kericho tea planters recruited by Brooke Bond and James Finlay. They followed Indian tradition with a strong preference for public school men. The traditional James Finlay recruitment interview was alleged to run: 'Do you hunt? Do you shoot? Do you fish?' Brooke Bond was different, with its background of retail distribution in England

and it tended to send out promising members of its staff, or family connections with a much more modest background. This led to the quip that Finlay men were gentlemen trying to be tea planters and Brooke men were planters trying to be gentlemen.

For my parents their life in Kenya was a genuinely transforming experience compared with their country town origins. Both of them were born in Cirencester, Gloucestershire. Grandpa Mac had come down from Scotland and established a butchery business in Cricklade Street. He married the daughter of Wakefield, the draper in the Marketplace and they produced three boys and two girls (one died in her twenties). Alan, the eldest, served in the Rifle Brigade towards the end of the First World War, was gassed and spent a year recovering in a convalescent home run by the Brooke family. Perhaps it was this that led to him becoming a tea planter. He joined the firm of Macleod & Co and went out to Assam where he remained as an estate manager until the company was sold to Indian interests after the Second World War. Alan remained a bachelor all his life; he had artistic sensibilities, enjoyed sewing, ran a beautiful home, and was probably a repressed gay. There was a tinted photograph of him aged 19 looking like Rupert Brooke, whose collected poems he owned, of course.

My father, Douglas, was athletic and mechanically minded and had a passion for motor bikes. He was working as an assistant in a hardware merchant store when Alan introduced him to the Brooke family on his first home leave in 1924, which led to the posting to Mombasa. James, the youngest brother, took over the family butchery business and married Ruth, the daughter of the other leading butcher in Cirencester, Jesse Smith, whose business still thrives.

My mother's family had deep Gloucestershire roots. Grandpa Leach was a cobbler in Dollar Street, living over the shop, and his wife was a dressmaker. They had six children. Kay married a shopkeeper and settled in Street, Somerset. Walter joined the merchant navy as a cook and never married. Ann married one of the early members of the RAF, Harry Tomlin, who never settled down after WW2 and drifted through various marginal occupations. After Margaret came Alan (known as Grog) who emigrated to New Zealand and, I think, also kept a shop. The youngest was Josephine (JoJo) who was asthmatic and looked after her widowed mother for many years before marrying a bit of a bounder, Alan

Morris, who ran a transport business. She died just after the war leaving a three-year-old son, also called Alan, who I taught to play the piano and he subsequently became a church organist.

Both parents went to Cirencester grammar school, leaving at 16. Margaret went to the teacher training college at Southampton University to become a primary school teacher, and enormously enjoyed the experience until she left for Kenya. It is interesting to reflect that in my mother's family both of her brothers left Gloucestershire to go abroad – to the merchant navy and to New Zealand, while Anne and Margaret both chose husbands who had ambitions outside the county. In my father's family, two of the three brothers made their careers in the Empire rather than in 1920s England. Although my parents had every intention of settling permanently in Kenya, they retained exceptionally strong feelings for their Cotswolds origins and, unlike several of their contemporaries, they opted finally to return to their Gloucestershire roots to Oakridge Lynch, rather than to join the dwindling band of retired whites in independent Kenya.

My parents had home leave in 1934 and my sister, Jenny, was born in October in Bath. Father was transferred back to the tea marketing side of Brooke Bond and on return from leave my parents moved to a stone bungalow on Kimugu Estate, nearer the tea factory, where they remained for the rest of his career with the company. There is a surviving photograph of my mother standing in front of the Cheboswa house, wearing a long skirt and holding me in her arms as a curly headed baby. It was probably taken to show off to the family when they went on leave. The only surviving anecdote from Cheboswa days was an incident when the house was invaded by soldier ants. At the start of the rainy season these ants would erupt from their underground nests and a column of thousands of *siafu* would strike out to found a new community. Any living thing – from caterpillars, to a dog in a kennel, to a child in a cot – was potentially a fatal victim. The ant column had marched through the house, but my *ayah* had snatched me to safety and the house was vacated until the ants had disappeared. As children we were always fascinated to come across a *siafu* column and to disrupt it with a stick and watch it re-form, and also to be taught a lesson on occasions by an outlying soldier nipping our legs with its mandibles.

The Kericho tea planting community was relatively conventional by comparison with life on the widely dispersed farms in the Highlands. Yet this was colonial Africa and a childhood in that environment has a retrospective glow to it. Specific recollections of childhood in Kericho are hard to capture; they are like a sequence of short video clips around a captured moment, often without narrative and triggered perhaps by a smell or a taste or a feeling. Press the button and peer at the passing scenes.

The Kimugu house was quite small, with a bedroom for my parents and another for Jenny and me. Early morning tea was brought at 6 am to my parents and this was the signal for us to hop into our parents' beds while they drank their tea and discussed the day ahead. Father would go to the office next to the factory after breakfast and we had the long morning ahead. The house staff comprised two male house servants (invariably referred to as 'boys' in those days) who were responsible for cleaning and laundry and waiting at table, when they donned white *kanzus* over their shirt and shorts and an embroidered cap – all derived from coastal Swahili wear. In the kitchen was a male cook, *mpishi*, assisted by a youth, the kitchen *toto*. There was a wood-fired Dover stove in which *mpishi* baked bread, cakes, roast joints, even souffles. The permanent staff lived in the boys' quarters behind a macrocarpa hedge and from time to time they received uxorial visits from home in the native reserve, between annual leave.

To one side of the house was a large expanse of tea bushes – a uniform, vivid green table three feet high and stretching up to the factory on the hill. On plucking days a gang of women and children with baskets on their backs held in place by a forehead strap would work its way over the field, singing and chattering in the bright morning sun. The skill was to pluck only the terminal unopened leaf bud and the two young leaves behind for optimum quality, but the snatch was usually more generous than that – and it filled the basket more quickly. Our garden had been excised from the forest and there was a stand of huge trees which attracted green wood pigeons in the dry weather, braying black and white casqued hornbills, copper tailed monkeys. A real cacophony heralded a six foot black tree snake. Father was a good rifle shot and he twice bagged specimens on days of memorable excitement, and the servants also killed one that had mistakenly strayed into the house.

The house was gradually enlarged over the years and especially the garden, with the help of a gang of *shamba* boys, and an easily recalled childhood memory is their singing as they went about their daily tasks of mowing and weeding, while pied wagtails scampered over the lawn looking for insects. Gardening was a great passion for both my parents in the conducive Kericho climate. The Kenya Highlands could grow most English flowers, except for the spring bulbs, and also the wonderful South African flora and shrubs from many countries. In Kericho the rich forest top soil has a stupendous depth – twelve feet and more; this, coupled with a rainfall of 70 inches over a long season, made for rewarding gardening and I inherited the parental enthusiasm. I had a large cactus bank and collected succulents from different parts of Kenya. My father enjoyed planning improvements and enlargements of the garden, while my mother was more of a plantsman and was a talented flower arranger. Every morning she would 'do' the flowers, refreshing and replacing the house arrangements. The annual flower show was a great event and my mother competed energetically for the prizes.

The other great enthusiasm was trout fishing on the rivers running out of the Mau Forest towards Lake Victoria – the Kiptiget and the Itari rivers, which were close to the tea estates. They had been stocked with rainbow trout by the Game Department which also cut a track along the river courses. A fishing licence and membership of the Kericho Fly Fishers Association was the passport to a wonderful day on the river. As small children we wore bathing costumes to splash in the pools, catch butterflies and look forward to picnic time. The approved technique was 'wet fly' – floating an Alexander or a Butcher fly down a fast run, or casting across a pool or broader channel and gradually winding in. The electrifying thrill of a fish snatching the fly, becoming hooked, and then playing it until it could be scooped into a hand net is unforgettable. Both parents, but especially my mother, liked nothing better than a day out on the river and they would walk for hours to reach favoured spots. Father became discouraged if the fishing was poor and would sit with a cigarette watching birds, but my mother was more dogged and was usually rewarded with the better day's catch.

Twenty-five years after my parents had left the house I visited Kericho as a banker, staying with the Brooke Bond chief executive, and I asked to see the Kimugu house again. It was now the home of the Kenyan company doctor. The property was fenced with an iron gate, the garden

At Cheboswa – 1933. Margaret and Douglas. Home at Kimugu. Kiptiget River. Itari River

had shrunk markedly and there was resident livestock. The house itself was instantly familiar – not least by virtue of still having some of the fittings I remembered from my childhood.

Exotic pets were common and we all had pet chameleons. We had a pet mongoose for a time, but he progressively killed our rabbits and pigeons and had to go. They break eggs by kicking them backwards through their legs against a stone or wall, which led to great entertainment with a ping-pong ball. We ran about the house and garden barefoot, although the standard Kenya kids' footwear were canvas Bata shoes, known by their Africaans name, tackies. Early snapshots from Kericho show me with Arap Chuma, the Kipsigis young man who was assigned to look after me, and to whom I became devoted. If my parents were out to dinner, taking sister Jenny with them, Arap Chuma would bring his spear and sleep on the floor by my bed. He made bows and arrows for me and took me on 'hunts' along the bush paths near our home, and this gave me the confidence later on to be allowed to go out on solo explorations to the Kimugu river and the surrounding bush carrying my father's .22 rifle in the hope of 'game'.

While husbands were out supervising work on the tea estates, Kericho wives had an active social life of their own. 'Elevenses' was an occasion for visiting each other, with any children in tow. These occasions would be triggered off by the kitchen *toto* being given the morning off and despatched on foot with a *barua* containing an invitation. Of course, tea was served rather than coffee and baking skills were on display (a cooperative effort with memsahib doing the weighing and mixing and *mpishi* in charge of the stove). It was a grown-ups' event, so there might or might not be other kids of comparable age to play with, but there was a welcome chance to explore other gardens. In any event, Jenny and I were rather shy children, to my mother's distress, and we rather enjoyed staying within earshot of indiscreet grown-ups' gossip.

While we children eavesdropped or played and explored, mothers gossiped in going-out summer frocks until it was time to drive home for family lunch and a review of the morning's intelligence. This was before, of course, the days of chatty phone calls, let alone mobile phones. The primitive telephone system was a party line, routed through an exchange in each company, with a press-to-speak, release-to-listen system that was very public to anyone else picking up a receiver, when it was working.

Solar pith helmets were still made in children's sizes in the 1930s. With the contemporary requirement for bicycle helmets for children, these helmets perhaps look less odd than once they did. But they soon gave way to cast-off felt hats with the pork pie pushed out into a pudding basis, and the more disreputable they looked the more they were treasured, serving duty equally as receptacles and as protection from the sun. Sunscreen lotions were yet to appear, and we all absorbed too much radiation for the good of our complexions; actual scorch was dealt with by liberal applications of camomile lotion – this 'pink *dawa*' was a sovereign relief for all manner of hurts.

Later, when my parents went out to dinner on neighbouring estates, or to a dance at the club, they would make up beds for Jenny and me in the back of the car. If there were several cars with children in them, a rival social event would develop amongst us children in the car park. A favourite game was to stalk the club night watchman, Arap Wassa, and then someone would come and shoo us into bed.

My father was a reserved, quiet man and seriously absorbed in his work now that he was back in tea marketing. He was not naturally convivial, yet enjoyed company and at a dinner party would usually settle down with other husbands to talk politics and local affairs. My mother was a complete contrast – bubbling and vivacious. As a couple they were much in demand in the active social life of Kericho and my mother was a popular hostess, putting great effort into the presentation of meals, the flowers and party games. Wine was not drunk much in those days; instead, there was a prolonged cocktail session before dinner, while at the meal there would be sherry with the soup, and perhaps a small glass of wine or two, then brandy and liqueurs with the coffee, and the level of hilarity built up during the evening. My mother disliked silences and would flail the air until a conversation took off:

'Now Bert, what would you do if your daughter in England wrote to say that she had fallen in love with a fellow Kikuyu student?'

'Tell me Hugh, what would you do if your cummerbund suddenly unravelled while you were dancing with Sheila.'

'And Sheila, what would you do if this happened?'

Otherwise, the form at evenings at home was to bath and change into pyjamas and dressing gowns and assemble by the crackling log fire. My parents usually had a gin and mixed vermouth cocktail until supper was wheeled in on a trolley. The signature tune of Lillebolero followed by 'London calling; this is the 9 o'clock news read by ...' ended the evening. This Kenya custom could be a social pitfall for overseas visitors, who perhaps had a different image of pyjama parties. It all added up to a happy childhood, with a vivacious mother and a kindly, somewhat reserved father

Kericho township was five miles away, where we had our personal post box No.16. In the late 1930s the main store was owned by a German refugee couple, the Heines, but they could not survive against the Indian trader network and their shop was taken over by Haridas Chaganall, who competed fiercely with Lalajee Jivanjee for custom. Everything was there from spice and vegetables, tinned goods, household appliances and even toys. There was a feeling of Aladdin's Cave on entering the shop and breathing in the smells from vegetable sacks, bolts of cloth, and Mrs Haridas's cooking in the background and peering at the crowded shelves and stands. African customers were served from a side window in those days.

Gopal the shoemaker sat cross-legged on the floor to do his work. He would draw an outline around one's foot on a piece of cardboard and a week later – with much head wobbling and smiles – he would produce a pair of approximately fitting leather shoes. On several shop verandahs there were treadle sewing machines where a pair of khaki shorts could be quickly run up by African operatives. As an important figure in Brooke Bond my father would receive gifts from the stores at Christmas time and there was much agonising over what to return as being over-the-top. Despite friendly over-the-counter relations, there was no question of a social relationship with an Indian merchant in Kenya's stratified society. My father's favourite shop was The British Hardware Store owned by Mistry, full of nails, screws and tools, and I still have a stainless steel pocket knife marked with its logo in my desk.

Social life in Kericho revolved around the Club, which had been built by Brooke Bond for its employees – with its golf course, tennis and squash courts, rugby and polo ground. Club nights were Wednesdays and Saturdays. Women were not allowed in the bar and had their own sitting room separate from the main club lounge. There was a radiogram and dancing, whist drives and dramatic shows, flower shows and an annual gymkhana presided over by Captain Tommy Darby, the senior manager for Brooke Bond – with legendary skill in managing oxen plough teams and now a race horse breeder – and his wife Lolly. Notwithstanding the fact that she had arrived from India as a divorcee with a daughter in tow and had successfully laid siege to Tommy Darby, she was queen of Kericho society. Unlike the rest of Kenya, she insisted that men wore suits and ties at dinner parties and that everyone attended club nights regularly. She kept peacocks in her garden and we children searched diligently for their feathers during 'elevenses' occasions.

Later on, during the war, the social pace became hotter. Kenya was a rest and recuperation centre for the 8th Army from the North African and Abyssinia campaigns and it was a patriotic duty to put up soldiers on leave and to give them a good time. My childhood memories of the war picture it rather as an extended party, with children being very spoilt by homesick soldiers. One of them gave me a captured Italian bayonet and Jenny was made a great fuss of. By then our house had been enlarged by building a guest cottage in the garden. First, it was just a rondavel bedroom for me, when it was decided that Jenny and I should have separate rooms, and I was escorted by torchlight to sleep there. This was quite frightening at first, until one got used to the night noises of Africa. Then it was extended to full en suite facilities, including a sitting room, so that my parents could accommodate two soldiers at a time during term time and, later on, visiting VIPs.

In 1938 my parents took advantage of the visit of the Bishop of Mombasa to Kericho to have Jenny and me christened. There was no church at the time (occasional services were held in the Club), so the ceremony took place in the sitting room of our home, with a font in the fireplace and masses of flowers from the garden. From this same fireplace I was wont to do my party piece on Elevenses mornings and to recite A A Milne's poem 'There are fairies at the bottom of our garden.'

Another home leave was due in the summer of 1939 and Kericho friends Hugh and Edith Thomas travelled with us on the Union Castle's *Majora* to Malta, and on to Marseilles and Paris, and then a daring flight across the Channel to Croydon Airport. I had my sixth birthday in a rented chalet at Durdle Door near Weymouth and the excitements included seeing glow worms and looking for bee orchids. We were staying with Granny Leach at Marshfield when war was declared and I can summon up an image of everyone huddled round the wireless listening to the fateful broadcast. We were fitted with gas masks at the local school and Jenny and I stood on the pavement to cheer passing troop movements on the main road to Bristol. It was all quite exciting, but soon we were part of a convoy back to Kenya through the Suez Canal and the start of boarding school for me.

There was no school for settler children in Kericho at that time, and in the preceding year several mothers with teaching experience had got together to organise a nursery school in the mornings at the Kericho hotel, which we attended. After returning to Kenya in October 1939 I was sent to Kaptagat School near Eldoret, about three hours' drive away over dirt roads that became treacherous in the rainy season. Kaptagat was a small mixed primary school of about 60 children that had only been going about two years. It was run by a Scottish couple who had come out to Kenya after the war as soldier settlers and whose farm had failed. M T Young was an amiable ex-officer, but his wife, Chris, was the driving force – a former teacher of great determination and charisma. The school was established on the farm of Zoe and Hugh Foster and their two sons were my contemporaries at the school. Hugh Foster and his two brothers were classic pioneers, who had originally come out to Uganda as hunters (and ivory poachers). Brother George had been killed by a lion and the other two had turned respectable and owned neighbouring farms at Kaptagat and the children needed to be educated. I am puzzled how my parents came to make this apparently eccentric choice of schools (one of many questions one failed to ask later in life), when there was a well-established school nearer at hand. But I deduce that they were influenced by a Scottish couple in the company whose daughter was my age, and the mother was a friend of Chris Young's. It meant that there could be some shared transport from time to time.

I was deposited at school one afternoon (term had already started) with my bicycle and was left to ride round the playground crying my eyes out until tea time. Actually, Kaptagat was a happy place and Jenny joined me in the following year. Another boy, Michael Templer, was already nicknamed Micky so inevitably I was called Macky, and the label stayed with me until I married Ruth. Jenny was diminutive, active and wore plaits and was nicknamed Wren, which also stuck with her until marriage. Being located in north-western Kenya, Kaptagat attracted many pupils from Uganda, such that the school readily divided into

'Ugandas' and 'Kenyas' for competitive purposes. Another brother and sister combination there was John and Jean Black, children of a Uganda medical officer, who subsequently joined P & O.

John became my brother in law, having joined James Finlay after National Service and was posted to Kericho, where Jenny was by then working as a secretary in the Brooke Bond head office.

Starting formal schooling relatively late, I still have memories of learning to read and, laboriously, to write and to do sums for the first time. The small children all had to sit together on chamber pots after breakfast until they had opened their bowels. It was a great chattering time and one could shunt around the room on one's pot, the better to engage. The stink must have been tremendous. All sweets brought to school were labelled and placed in a big cupboard and, after lunch, we lined up to select a sweet, and sometimes to trade with each other. One of the dormitories was turned into a sick room when illness struck, like chickenpox, and I recall an attack of malaria although, at 7,800 feet, we were well above the mosquito zone and we did not sleep with nets.

We learned horse riding on the Fosters' farm, and this was in many ways the most distinctive impression of our school days, as there was a morning ride before lessons. The teaching staff comprised Chris Young; her husband, M T, who taught simple maths; Dorothy Levingstone – a tough minded Irish spinster who had travelled round the world and naturally taught geography, as well as history; Sheila Brown – a young, glamorous (in our eyes) teacher who took the junior classes until she left to marry a soldier; and then a succession of temporary staff, usually with a child at the school. One such was the wife of the Barclays DCO manager, an exotic Jewess who taught us dancing and who, on special occasions, would struggle into her tutu and dance the Dying Swan. With concentration, I can still recall the ballet steps we learned for a performance of the Blue Danube for a school show. The end of year show was a great occasion: everyone had to have a part, however small, and a costume. I graduated from a rat in the Pied Piper of Hamelin to an emperor in Choo Chin Chow. We all learned to knit and embroider, making balaclava helmets for the North Atlantic sailors and napkin holders for our parents. There were Cubs and Brownies – with inspection visits from Lady Baden Powell, the widow of the founder of the Scout movement who lived in Nyeri.

Being contemporary with Robert and Francis Foster was a boon (Jenny was also contemporary with their younger sister, Mary), as it meant that at weekends one was frequently invited over to the farm. There was an extraordinary menagerie of pets: a chimpanzee, a spoonbill stork, a ground hornbill, bushbabies, dogs, cats, grey parrot and so on. Robert and Francis were crack shots with catapults and fearless tree climbers. We caught black crabs in the river with pieces of meat threaded on string, learned to smoke out wild bees, swam in a muddy swimming pool. The deep verandah was festooned with game trophies – several of them record holding. Inside was a striking series of tropical fish paintings by their mother Zoe.

Fifty years later, Robert and Francis were living as two kindly but somewhat crusty bachelors at the home their mother had built in the 1930s south of Mombasa on a bay with a fresh water spring. I picked up with them again and Ruth and I visited Sand Island a couple of times and I also went to stay during a tea research visit. The trophies and marine life paintings had been transferred from Kaptagat when the farm was sold to Nandi men of influence. There were all too obvious slave cells in front of the house as a reminder of the Arab slave trade from East Africa to Oman. The house had an eccentric architectural feature comprising the control room of a wrecked steamer that had been salvaged and manhandled to make a first-floor observation room; there was also an air conditioned annex as a billiard room. There was a paradise orchard of all manner of tropical fruit, watered from the spring. Zoe Foster had begun to write a family memoir before she died, and Francis completed the volume and published it in 2009. He came to stay with me at Brimpsfield that year and gave me a copy. There are some memorable early photographs and a story of pioneering life in Uganda around the turn of the 19th century.

One year a group of us at Kaptagat were inspired to form a 'Midnight Club', which involved taking it in turns to keep awake and then going out into the grounds with hoarded food and meeting up with some of the girls from their dormitory. The time was more likely ten o'clock than midnight and we had several exciting escapades before we were caught. For the first and only time I was given a beating by Chris Young and was greatly humiliated by the experience. She was a powerful moral force and frequently addressed us on questions of conduct. Every day after lunch she read to the older children as we lay on our backs on the floor and she introduced us to Bronte, Gaskell, Dickens and Rider Haggard. I became her favourite pupil, which may have had something to do with an unpleasant phase when I was the object of bullying, led by a sinister boy called Rusty Ishmael. When I had to go into Eldoret hospital to have my tonsils removed, Chris Young wangled her way into the operating theatre, on the grounds that she was a trained nurse, and called out encouragement to me as I struggled with the chloroform mask. And she was sitting by my bedside when I came round afterwards to give comfort in frightening surroundings. I was kept in hospital for several days, but allowed to get dressed, and I crept around the corridors to see what went on.

We were an entirely self-contained school and there was no attempt to interact with the couple of other schools within reach in Eldoret and Kitale. So, rounders rather than cricket, a bit of soccer, tennis with great enthusiasm as we got older, long walks with a teacher on the Fosters' farm, and of course the horse riding. We made grass-thatched houses, climbed trees, kept chameleons as pets, played marbles, made catapults and tried to kill small birds with them.

Most of the younger men in Kericho were called up for military service at the start of the war. At that time my father was a rising star in Brooke Bond, having been responsible for devising and managing a tea marketing scheme embracing Kenya, Uganda and Tanganyika whereby producers were each given a quota to supply tea for the domestic market (packaged and sold by Brooke Bond), before shipping the balance for export. When the Ministry of Food in London decided to purchase all East Africa's exportable tea under bulk contracts, he was appointed Tea Controller by the government to administer the scheme and, subsequently, Food Controller for the duration. He then spent long periods in Nairobi and travelling in the region. During term time my mother would join him at the New Stanley Hotel, which added some glamour to a frustrating time for her, but at least Dougal was not on active service. Margaret acquired a Boxer bitch, Belinda, for company and we all loved her. At one point my father was flown to London in a military transport in connection with his commodity control duties and witnessed the doodlebug bombing raids. It is interesting to reflect that the Allies had such domination of the air that this was possible.

We had our first holiday at the coast in 1944. The car journey took two days, first to Nairobi and then a night in the Tsavo Park at Macs Inn and a visit to Mzima Springs to see hippo but not the hoped-for rhino. Shanzu Beach Hotel comprised simple palm thatched bandas, but there was safe bathing inside a coral reef, and wonderful shells to collect at low tide, some of which I still have. We brought back a dwarf mongoose – Ricky, who became a great favourite until he discovered and murdered the pet rabbits, pigeons and the hens. The best weather – dry and hot – was at Christmas time, and this was also the best fishing weather. In 1944 and again the following year a fishing camp was organised for two or three nights. We had acquired a large army surplus tent which became our temporary home, serviced in style by our domestic staff who came with us. The days were spent fishing and at night there was a roaring log fire, freshly roasted trout, and serenading crickets and frogs.

It was also in 1944 that Chris Young had a serious dispute with the Fosters and was dismissed from Kaptagat School. She offered to see the older children through until they went on to secondary school, and we were part of a loyal group that stayed with her. In later years I failed to ask my parents what the cause of the breach was, and when I did ask Robert and Francis 60 years later, they had forgotten. Kaptagat continued as a successful up-country school for many years, before being taken over by the Africa Inland Mission. Ruth and I paid a visit there in the 1980s during a banking trip. The whole place was very much as remembered, except that it was so much smaller than in one's imagination. I could have sworn that the dormitory beds were unchanged since the 1940s.

The Youngs rented a farmhouse near Eldoret, renaming it Stanley House School, after the explorer of 'Doctor Livingstone, I presume' fame, where about a dozen of us were taught for a year. MT then got a job as manager of a sawmill at Moiben and when a house had been built for them, a rump of about six of us transferred there for a final year. In retrospect this all seems a bit irresponsible of our parents. However, it resulted in intensive personal tuition, coupled with a lot of fun. My parents had decided they could afford to fulfil a personal dream and send me to Cheltenham College, so I was coached for the common entrance exam. Latin was a problem, but my parents discovered a Dutch Catholic priest in Kericho who was prepared to give me lessons in the holidays, so I cycled the five miles into Kericho to struggle with my Latin grammar with Father Hermus.

Chris Young was one of several women who have had a great influence on my life. Although I was very average in academic terms, Chris was adamant that I had potential and she succeeded in imbuing me with both self-confidence and ambition, albeit lacking any focus at that time. On her part, she was determined to get me through Common Entrance and into Cheltenham College, and this became our joint enterprise. For many years afterwards she used to write to me at least annually, and I feel bad now that I was the one who ceased corresponding. She must have been in her forties at the time as I recall a wiry, grey haired woman with a bun and a pronounced Scottish accent talking to me, as to an adult, about world affairs, serving one's country, but she also had a mean underarm service in tennis.

I was accepted by Cheltenham – with reservations about my French and Latin papers. There followed a visit to Nairobi to have my first suit made by Ahmed Brothers. My father was able to arrange a business visit to Brooke Bond's head office and therefore to escort me to England for the start of term in autumn 1946. We said goodbye to my mother and Jenny at Lumbwa station, catching the train to Kisumu on the edge of Lake Victoria. We would next meet in a year's time when another home leave was due and Jenny would be left at Westonbirt, after a year spent at the Kenya Girls High School in Nairobi. I was relieved not to be going to the rather tough secondary school in Nairobi, or even worse to South Africa, but the several English novels I had read about public school life were not very reassuring. And, above all, there was the wrench of leaving home and my parents in Kenya – for how long?

At Kisumu we boarded a DC3 Dakota that flew a bumpy ride down the Nile to Juba (where I was sick on landing) and then to Khartoum for the night. Visiting the nearby zoo a lioness took a poor view of me and sprayed me with urine, to the delight of watching urchins. Next day to Wadi Halfa and then Cairo for a couple of nights, where I saw the Pyramids and the Great Mosque. Eventually to sooty London and a train to Cirencester to stay with Granny Mac at Grey Gables, The Whiteway, which was going to be my holiday home for the next couple of years. An early priority was to buy me a bicycle to start exploring the lanes, but also to take at college so that I could cycle the 15 miles back to Cirencester after chapel on exeat weekends for Sunday lunch, and then back again to Cheltenham after tea. Father drove me to college on the first day of term, stopping on the way in Cranham Woods with its view over the Severn plain.

'Macky, you will probably be asked what your father does by other boys. You can say that I am responsible for tea marketing in East Africa as managing director of Brooke Bond Kenya. My salary is £5,000 a year.'

He never found it easy to talk about himself and, for him, this was a major confidence. We then drove down the hill for me to be deposited at Cheltondale House and to meet my housemaster: a bluff, hearty man who had a stand full of canes inside his study door.

My parents had their first post-war leave in the summer of 1947 when Jenny was left at Westonbirt; then another leave in 1950. However, in 1949 they afforded flights out to Kenya for the summer holidays – an exciting journey by Sunderland flying boat from Southampton to Sicily, Alexandria, Khartoum and Lake Naivasha. Thus, during my five years at Cheltenham I went home once and my parents had two leave visits to England. I do not recollect being emotionally upset or homesick by these lengthy family separations, but I think they did reinforce a notion that emotions were something to be controlled, even suppressed, and that one's feelings were not a proper subject of discussion. There was inevitably a distancing of relationships, which must have been hard on my mother. Looking back, I think these inhibitions became an obstacle to frank communication when Ruth and I had problems in our marriage. It was not until I met Lisa that she taught me to articulate private thoughts and the value of emotional honesty.

Children of the Raj are a special case of the English custom of sending sons and daughters from all corners of the colonial empire, back 'home' to England to prep and public schools, and thus fracturing family links at an early age. When air travel became more commonplace and affordable other options also became available, with lollipop specials of school kids flying out every holiday, or mothers making a holiday home in England, possibly at some cost to their marriages. I had become accustomed to boarding school at Kaptagat, and I had a year to digest the prospect of going to Cheltenham. Books like *Tom Brown's Schooldays* and *Jeremy at Crale* offered a somewhat alarming glimpse of public school life, but *Stalky & Co* was more reassuring. The picture of hierarchy and ritual, the risk of bullying, the importance of achievement especially in sport, was both alarming and exciting. A mood of fatalism was perhaps a natural response, with all private fears suppressed.

All through our Kaptagat days we wrote weekly letters home, and these were responded to on a weekly basis by my mother. This tradition naturally continued in England, at school and university and on into adult life while we lived in different continents. The emphasis on both sides was to be bright, cheerful and newsy, rather than to pass on moods and concerns, so this lengthy correspondence did not really lead to a deepening relationship. I found it easier to try out thoughts about books or politics than to pin down emotional states. Much later on, my mother kept a daily diary for many years, which I now have; it is almost entirely a narrative of social life, menus and weather, and contains almost nothing of her internal life. More repressed emotions?

Can anything be distilled from a Kenya childhood beyond the fading memories that one feels has had a material bearing on one's later life? Kenya in the 1930s and 40s was an age of innocence for children, notwithstanding the great debates at that time on the future of the colony of which one retains faint echoes. The notions of a white man's country and of white supremacy were almost unquestioned amongst the settlers. My parents had liberal instincts that would later lead to support for Michael Blundell's politics of multi-racial cooperation. They exhibited no overt racial superiority and showed genuine interest in the domestic lives of their servants. Yet as children we still knew that we had the privilege of a ruling class – hence the sobriquet Bwana Kidogo, or little sir. We assumed that all Africans we met would be both respectful and helpful in need and we were therefore fearless when encountering them in the absence of our parents on walks in the bush or elsewhere. There was an additional frisson of sexuality too when encountering naked men working on the estates or women bathing in the river, or Kipsigis girls in skins and beads and provocative breasts. Unlike many white boys from southern Africa I was always completely at ease with African contemporaries in later life, so the colonial childhood did not prove to be an obstacle to working in Africa – rather the contrary.

The landscape and wildlife diversity of Kenya turns most people into amateur naturalists. My mother loved this diversity, while my father would sit and contemplate a landscape for stretches of time; I respond to both sentiments. I find a sense of being at one with nature is soul restorative, and I gain much pleasure from natural history. A childhood in Kenya with parents who had these enthusiasms has undoubtedly left

Jenny and Michael – 1948. At Mombasa in 1949

its mark, and there is still a powerful call to revisit from time to time. Were Kenya children in the 1930s and 1940s allowed more freedom than their English counterparts to pursue their enthusiasms and to take more responsibility for their actions? It is hard to say but, chasing an elusive thought through the memory garden, I think there is something about the privileged position of white children in the colonial world that gave us a sense of manifest destiny and optimism. Of course, this could have developed into arrogance and boorishness, but here the influence of Chris Young was so important. By the time I left Kaptagat for England I possessed not only the sense that I came from a special place, but that somehow I had a role awaiting me. And Cheltenham gave shape to it.

FINDING ONE'S FEET

2. CHELTENHAM 1946

I went to Cheltenham College in September 1946 and was there for five and a half years, staying on for two terms after my Higher School Certificate and my 18th birthday in order to take Oxford Science Prelims. This additional time also resulted in my being appointed Senior College Prefect in these last two terms.

After arriving from Kenya to live with my grandmother and her unmarried daughter, Jean, there was a round of shopping at school outfitters and sewing on of name tapes before being taken to Cheltondale House by my father at the start of the autumn term and to join a tea party with four other new boys and the housemaster's family. I had been allocated to Cheltondale as a result of Chris Young requesting a housemaster who would be sympathetic to a Kenya boy. Dick Jukes was a farmer schoolmaster, owning a farm about ten miles away and was married to a farmer's daughter. He was a genial, bluff man and shrewd judge of character, with a lathe in his study (rather than the grand piano of his successor) and the stand of canes, since house masters could still beat boys for serious misbehaviour. In contrast, he would sometimes take boys at weekends to help with potato harvesting and the like. In response to a letter from Chris Young, Jukes arranged for me to have access to trout fishing on the River Churn, on the land of a farmer friend.

Cheltondale had been built to accommodate 60 boys in two long dormitories. One was assigned a wood-partitioned cubicle, with a chest of drawers and a few pegs and a hard bed. I had the end cubicle furthest from the door and started to unpack. The house became uncannily silent and deserted as everyone had gone up to the college dining hall for supper. Discovered by Mrs Jukes, she detailed one of her children to rush me up College Road to the dining hall – just in time for the *Benedictus Benedicat* grace. That evening the head of house, Purves, summoned the new boys for a pep talk about the house and the importance of house spirit and loyalty. Our tribal label for such purposes as touch line support was Owenite, after the first housemaster a century before. Purves explained that it was a Cheltondale tradition to have a house wind band and each new boy was assigned to learn an instrument: 'McWilliam, a clarinet would suit you', so began a hobby that lasted until I married – playing in the college military band and the school orchestra, as well as the annual house carol band that went round the masters' houses, and eventually with the Nairobi Symphony Orchestra in 1959. The trouble with the clarinet is that there is no repertoire for the solo instrument, but I derived much enjoyment from transcriptions of the Bach violin partitas and became familiar with the wider clarinet repertoire.

Purves also explained the fagging system. Prefects were entitled to have a personal fag to do odd jobs for them – clean their boots and corps equipment, tidy their studies (known as shacks), and such like. But fags had to be paid for these services at the end of each term, so there was pocket money to be earned. Apart from this, if the prefects wanted to get a job done in the house they would stand together and shout 'Orderly!' and all the juniors had to rush to the spot, with the last few being assigned to the job in hand. I was selected as a fag by David Slater who was a nephew of one of Kenya's great pioneers, Col. Ewart Grogan. David was a spin bowler for college, the leading shot putter, and was mad about Italian opera. What with the Kenya connection, we had a very cordial relationship. The top third of the house were allocated shacks and the rest had a desk and a locker in the sweatroom, where we did our prep each evening after college supper. At 9pm there was prayers taken by the housemaster and a hymn, with one of the boys at the house piano. The juniors then went to bed after a mug of cocoa and there was a second prep period for the seniors until 10pm. Beating by prefects had been abolished during the war, so that misdemeanours were punished either by tasks, or by writing 'lines' – copying out poetry or whatever.

Cheltondale House. In uniform. Putting the shot. House prefects.

A House Man was employed to stoke the boilers for hot water and the central heating pipes; Huddy also had the task of waking everyone up in time to go up at college Dining Hall for breakfast. The first of three bells was at 6.45 and the last ('You're nearly late!') at 7.15 in order to get up at college by 7.40. The winter of 1946/47 was a severe one and I experienced chilblains for the first time. On Sundays, breakfast was an hour later and two boys could earn a bit of pocket money by getting up early and going down town to buy Sunday newspapers. On being asked what paper I wanted I asked for one that would contain news of Kenya: 'Then, you had better have *News of the World*.'

I was rather spoilt in my first year in that I became something of a house mascot – or bijou, as was the term then in vogue. Far from being bullied, as I had feared from reading *Tom Brown's Schooldays*, older boys went out of their way to be nice to me. No doubt there was an erotic undertone to all this and some masturbation, but the surface experience was quite jolly for me. There were four other new boys with me. Michael Cole was from a Jewish business family in London; he had won a scholarship and was already a budding intellectual. He had an older brother in the house, who was very left wing and musical as well. Michael and I became close friends and he had an enormous influence on me. Apart from our burgeoning musical interest, I also followed him in becoming a radical socialist and an avid reader of *Tribune*, monitoring closely the course of the revolution in China, the schisms in the Labour Party and struggling with Marxist dialectic. He also showed me how to appreciate art, and we saved up to buy Phaidon volumes and one year made a scale model of Florence cathedral for a college exhibition. I stayed several times with his family in St John's Wood and in 1949 we joined a college skiing party to St Anton in Austria, where I broke a front tooth in a fall. For several days he accompanied me down the line to Imst to have the tooth crowned and he interpreted in his budding German. Michael became increasingly disaffected with college and hostile to its ethos, whereas I was conformist and wanted to succeed. The rupture of our close relationship was quite painful. He left after a year in the Lower 6th to prepare for Cambridge from home and we never re-established contact. He went to work for the BBC and died young.

Don Walker was a Cotswold farmer's son, also with an elder brother in the house, and we were in the same forms and sets. He was good at games and was head of house just before me and was one of the escorts to Princess Elizabeth when she paid a formal visit at college in 1951. He went to Cambridge to read agriculture and became a farmer; a generation later we both had two sons at Cheltondale and we became friendly again. Sadly, there was inherited Alzheimer's in the family; first his mother and older brother died of it and then Don succumbed as well.

John Mare was the son of a naval officer who had been killed in the war. He lived in Bath and we used to see each other a bit in the holidays. He also did Russian for National Service and then modern languages and had a business career, where we lost touch. Terence McMullen was the son of the chief inspector of railway accidents and was much cleverer than me. He went to Cambridge and became a prep school headmaster. As it turned out, all five of our new boy year at Cheltondale achieved Oxbridge, which was untypical of college at that time.

On the first day of term there was assembly for the whole school in Big Classical. The headmaster read out the class lists, starting with Upper 6th Science and all the way down to the bottom form in college – Shell, where Don Walker and I had been placed. All around us on the walls were the honours boards of distinguished predecessors – prize winners and scholarship entrants and one learned to recognise the names of great Cheltenham families through several generations. Similarly, in Chapel there were the brass plaques of Old Cheltonians (OCs) who had died in all the wars of the past century, again with recurring family names. It was impossible to escape the sense of stepping into a great tradition and this was often emphasised in Sunday sermons, coupled with an enjoinder to make a contribution to the wider community. For me, this meant finding a way back to Africa. Very early on we were asked to declare our intended careers, and I said forestry to general amazement, meaning the Colonial Forestry Service. This somewhat romantic choice was a way of giving expression to my yearning for Kenya's landscapes and my enthusiasm for natural history. I was then stuck with it – destined for Sciences rather than Languages and Humanities, all the way through to Higher School Certificate and to Oxford to read Botany.

Eliot-Smith was a reforming headmaster and had been appointed early in the war from Harrow, where he had married the headmaster's daughter. He had clashed with the OC military old guard as he introduced modern teaching concepts and blew away some old traditions. He abolished the right of prefects to beat boys. Homework was organised on the basis of weekly assignments to be completed in prep and designated study periods, to teach us to organise our time. As a gesture to austerity, all boys wore boiler suits during the week to save on uniforms. He organised a menu of cultural events that were compulsory for the whole school, and an annual address from a sex expert to the different year groups; inevitably the man was referred to as 'Spermy Griffiths'. He addressed college once a week in memorable terms. In my second year the head of Cheltondale was also Senior Prefect and I still recall Eliot-Smith's encomium to Bateman-Champain when he left: the best head of college he had ever appointed, which became something of a lodestar for me. I recall vowing to myself that I would also strive to be head boy one day. In 1951 Eliot-Smith left Cheltenham to run a famous public school in Egypt that sadly became a casualty of the revolution and fall of King Farouk. I got to know the Eliot-Smiths quite well in their retirement in Eastbourne, particularly after I joined the College Council. Visits to them were challenging as Eliot had a restless, probing mind that had been put on the sidelines far too early.

Sport naturally loomed large in our lives, with formal games three afternoons a week. Apart from not being a natural athlete I had the disadvantage of not having played rugby or cricket at prep school, unlike the other boys. However, I eventually made the college 2nd XV. Inter-house matches, or Pots, aroused the greatest patriotism and it was usual to make rousing 'Once more into the breach' speeches to the team before crucial matches. Cricket was a lost cause for me and, happily, an alternative became available. One of the masters, A K Brown, had been a medium distance runner in the 1936 Berlin Olympics and otherwise taught history. He persuaded college to lay down a professional running track and athletics became an alternative to cricket in 1948. I took to this enthusiastically, focussing on the shot and discus, but one also had to attain a degree of competence in the other sports so I puffed and hurdled and high jumped for four summers and became the proud possessor of a piece of paper stating that I was Junior Discus Champion of Gloucestershire.

An interest in music that was first fostered at college became a lifelong joy. The beginning was unpromising as I could not read music and I failed the voice test on arrival to join the choir trebles. However,

I was launched on the clarinet which ensured a place in the military band on field days, and a desk with the college orchestra. When my voice broke I did join the chapel choir as a tenor and enjoyed singing in the daily chapel service as well as the Choral Society – hence knowing much of Messiah by heart. I played the Tartini Jacob clarinet concerto at at college concert in my last term – not very well, I fear. As head boy at the time I was also compering the concert, which included excerpts from Walton's Façade, which introduced me to Edith Sitwell. The most lasting legacy has been the chamber music I got to know in company with Michael Cole. He had a large record collection and my first hearings of Beethoven, Schubert and Mozart were in his company on a gramophone in an empty classroom at weekends. I started to learn the piano after taking school certificate, when my party piece was something that Mozart wrote at the age of four. Playing the piano gave much pleasure for several years as 'aunt' Gladys had one when I went to live with her. Cheltenham was home to the Music Festival started in 1945 and the Halle Orchestra used to rehearse in Big Modern, so my musical tastes evolved quickly. I had a wind-up gramophone and my first portfolio comprised: Brahms's 4th Symphony, Delius's Song of the High Hills, Mozart's Serenade for 13 Wind Instruments, Beethoven's *Razamovsky Quartets* played by the Lener Quartet, and Sibelius's 1st Symphony. Sixty years later Cheltenham Festivals became an important part of my life.

I qualified for a shack after two years – a narrow room about 10 feet long and 4 feet wide, with room for a desk and bookcases, an easy chair and pictures. I took great pride in my private space. I went back at college in the summer holidays of 1948 to redecorate it, scrounged curtains, and polished the floor. I had a music stand for my clarinet and otherwise placed on it a Phaidon art book, turning the pages daily. In a relentlessly communal environment a shack gave one a chance to develop some individuality, even eccentricity. From Uncle Alan I had learned to darn my socks and duly did so. I also acquired from him an interest in yoga and used to get up at 6.30 to have a cold shower and do my exercises. These I still do, but without the cold shower.

I had mumps in my school certificate summer of 1949 and took the exams in the Cheltondale sickroom. That holiday we flew home to Kenya for the first time. It was an exciting journey by flying boat from Southampton to Alexandria, and then up the Nile and on to Lake

Naivasha, where a motor boat whizzed up and down before the plane landed in order to scare away any hippos. The telegram of my exam results failed to show credits in French and Latin, so I had to do retakes in these two subjects in order to have a chance of Oxbridge entrance.

Our holiday arrangements had become quite a headache for my parents. Granny Mac died in 1948 soon after Uncle Alan had returned from his tea planting career in India; he and maiden Aunt Jean continued to provide a holiday home at Grey Gables for Jenny and me, except that Alan was restless and needed a job, and Jean was restless and needed a husband. Uncle Jim, the butcher, had bought the manor house at Frampton Mansell towards the end of the war and Jenny and I were invited there for part of every holiday to join our cousin Bill, who had just started at Bryanston. I suspect that he did not particularly welcome our presence and relations were polite rather than friendly. In the summer of 1948 Jenny and I had stayed for a while with Granny Leach in Marshfield and it was at this point that my mother's cousin Gladys – a spinster schoolmistress who lived in Chippenham – very gallantly offered to provide a holiday home for us, following the death of her invalid mother. Jenny and I cycled over to Chippenham to be inspected by Gladys and by Nurse Hotston– a retired nurse of strong personality who had looked after Gladys's mother and had stayed on as housekeeper, having no home of her own. Chippenham became our holiday home until we left school and Pa paid an allowance to Gladys for looking after us. I got on well with her, but Jenny was much less happy and used to spend as much as possible of her holidays with a school friend, Julia Mason, whose father was a director of ICI. They had a lovely house at Crawley to which I was also invited a couple of times. These arrangements threw us back on our resources as there was not much of a family atmosphere at Chippenham, but Nurse was glad to have a captive audience for her reminiscences.

Several Cheltenham masters left a mark on my intellectual development and evolving sensibility. Despite being labelled a scientist because of the forestry career choice, I really had more talent for the humanities. In my first year an English essay of mine was published in the *Cheltonian*. 'A River in Kenya' was an evocative piece in the style of Richard Jeffries who I much admired for his country essays. F E Halliday, a distinguished Shakespearian scholar, took an interest in me and lent me books, notably Hardy's *The Dynasts*, on which I lavished an essay. Harry Johnston succeeded Jukes as housemaster of Cheltondale and could not have been a more different personality. He had obtained a doctorate at the Sorbonne on Paul Valery, was musical and witty. He taught me in the 6th form where he made me read and write essays on Baudelaire, Aldous Huxley, Aristotle's aesthetics and Forster on the novel, and several times sent my pieces to the headmaster for commendation. I remember with squirming pride writing a short story – much praised by Johnston – based on my family in which the central situation concerned a husband who diverted a significant part of his income towards maintaining a kid sister who led him a dance, to the great distress of his wife (my mother). Perhaps fortunately, I now forget how I arranged the denouement.

The biology master who taught anatomy was also an enthusiastic collector of Japanese woodcuts and fostered my emerging interest in oriental art (yes, I was invited to his home to see his collection). In a secondhand shop in Cheltenham I bought one of Hokusai's *47 Views of Fuji* and had the excitement of going up to London to the British Museum's Print Room and being able to corroborate the find. The other biology master, Rivers-More, encouraged my interest in insect natural history; this reached its high point in the summer after I left college when I made a collection of Kenya *arachnidae* for Louis Leakey, then curator of the national museum.

Cheltenham had a close link with Oriel College and a steady flow of Cheltonians went there, especially to read science subjects. Eliot-Smith was an Oriel man and the head of science was a Cambridge contemporary of the Oriel chemistry don, Dr Hamick. The brightest scientists went to Cambridge, but I was put in for Oriel and went up for the entrance exam in autumn 1951. I got it into my head that no meals were provided in the vacation so went and bought brown bread, honey, nuts and fruit and led a monastic existence for a couple of days, revising and nibbling in my rooms in the Rhodes building. It was the custom then for the Provost and several fellows to interview all candidates during the course of the written papers, sitting at the high table in the dining hall. When my turn came, they discovered that I was head of school, that I played the clarinet and intended to read Botany. Hamick was delighted to discover a civilised scientist and I was in, notwithstanding mediocre science papers. I was encouraged to take the Science Prelims before coming up, which implied a further term at Cheltenham until Easter. It was these circumstances that gave me two extra terms at college after my Higher School Certificate – to take the Oriel entrance exam and then the Science Prelims – and so to realise my ambition of becoming Head Boy.

I was the last head boy appointed by Eliot-Smith, who left in the summer of 1951. There was an acting head when I took office in the autumn term, who I did not get on with very well, and then in the spring term I had the role of mediating the new headmaster – the Rev. Guy Pentreath. It was quite a challenge as he was generally thought to be a disaster, not least by Harry Johnston. However, this placed me in an influential position to interpret to Pentreath the customs and expectations of college in weekly meetings with him. I had a cabinet of heads of houses – the College Prefects, who had a separate table in the dining hall and a meeting room of our own. Our job was to maintain the 'tone' of college, to mediate discontents, to jump on bad behaviour and to set an example. In these last two terms I did rather little academic work – ostensibly revising for the Oxford Science Prelims. I took them in March and failed so would have to re-sit them on going up. Instead, I devoted myself wholeheartedly to making the most of the senior prefect role: participating actively in every aspect of college life, which included putting together a scratch gym team in order to lead it in an inter-house competition. As a college prefect, one was distinguished by being allowed to carry an umbrella and by being allowed to ride a bicycle around the college premises.

One episode of head boy 'leadership' is still vivid. In early 1952 college held a mock general election (following the real election of October 1951 when the Labour Government was narrowly replaced by the Tories). No boy was prepared to stand for the Labour Party so I – as a good socialist – decided to be the Labour candidate and to use my position as head boy to open up a lively political debate in the school. Naturally I was roundly defeated. On election day I conspired with the Labour voting technician in the science labs to inflate a string of red balloons with helium to which were suspended cards reading VOTE LABOUR. As everyone came out for morning break the balloons were launched over the Quad. Instead of sailing bravely over an admiring crowd of voters, the balloons were blown by a gust of wind into a huddle in a roof gutter, then two of them broke away and sailed up to the chapel roof. 'Another Socialist Disaster,' crowed the other candidates. My housemaster repeated the Shavian aphorism, 'If you are not a socialist before the age of 21 you have no heart, if you are still one after that you have no head.'

Although I messed up my Science Prelims, the extra time at Cheltenham rounded off my schooldays in a most satisfying way. The experience of being head boy enhanced my self-confidence and gave me an explicit feeling that if I set my sights on a target it could be achieved. At several key points later in life I was to recollect this feeling when coming up against a major challenge. I was now embarking on adult life with a self-conscious awareness that I had achieved the summit of schoolboy ambitions and that I could achieve similar successes in my future career. Naïve conceit though this was, it undoubtedly served to sharpen my ambitions in the years ahead.

With very few formal lessons in these last two terms, I spent much time back at Cheltondale and contrived very often to be there for morning coffee with my housemaster's wife, Morny. She became something of a surrogate mother, but also someone who could be talked to in a way that I would never have done with my own mother. I positively looked forward to the end of the holidays. In retrospect, I think Morny, who must have been in her forties, had a bit of a crush on me. I stayed in touch with the Johnstons all my time at Oxford and often went to visit them. Harry developed my appreciation of wine (and arranged for me to work at a Cheltenham wine merchant one Christmas time), and also introduced me to pink gin – taken in the nursery before dinner in order to avoid the company of the matron and under-housemaster who joined the meal every day. Morny shared the agonies of my courtship of Ruth, and Ruth was duly presented to her just before our wedding.

Morny died in a car accident with Harry at the wheel and only a mile from their home and she never knew our children. Harry rather took to the bottle after that, but I stayed in touch with him and in 1972 he arranged for Ruth and me to meet the headmaster to discuss entering our boys for college. The Junior school was full, but Ashcroft directed us to Beaudesert Park prep school, which was also a feeder school, who were able to take both boys that autumn term, Robert aged ten and Martin aged eight.

At age 18 one was liable for two years' National Service in the armed forces. It was possible to obtain a deferral and go up to university first, but most people preferred to get National Service over with on leaving school. However, as a 'colonial', I was only liable for National Service if I remained in Britain to work; this provision strongly reinforced my existing desire to work in Africa after Oxford, so I applied for deferral in order to take up my place at Oriel in October 1952.

On finally leaving Cheltenham at Easter 1952, there were six months before the start of the Oxford term. I went back to Kericho to stay with my parents and to pick up the threads of family life again. Jenny was still in her final year at Westonbirt and stayed in England that summer, before coming back to Kericho and then also going to Oxford in the following year to Miss Sprule's Secretarial College. Pa was travelling a lot on business, but also showing symptoms of his heart condition with acute angina, for which he received no treatment. I learned to drive and to play bridge. I got to know the young assistant managers on the tea estates. I helped my mother compete in the flower show and went fishing with her. I enlarged her appreciation of classical music and chose a record collection for her. We went up to Uganda on a business trip by car, and had a fishing holiday on the streams running off Mount Kenya: Nyeri, Embu, Meru and Nanyuki. On the road between Embu and Meru we were surrounded by a crowd of Kikuyu waving banana leaves and chanting in a sinister way: a premonition of the forthcoming Mau Mau rebellion. Ma was inclined to be sympathetic to my political views and the household became firm supporters of Michael Blundell's United Kenya Party and multi-racial politics, which was as radical as one could be in Kenya at that time.

With my botany degree at Oxford in prospect, it was arranged that I could be a volunteer at the new Tea Research Institute in Kericho and I would go there most days, where I most remember the extended coffee and tea breaks in Director Tom Eden's office and the reminiscences of research at Rothamstead and in Ceylon. I studied the 'weeds' of the tea estates, but also worked on building up the collection of *arachnidae* for the Coryndon Museum (as it was then called) in Nairobi. Pa had procured an interview for me with Dr Leakey when I offered to do some collecting for the museum before going up to Oxford. We considered dragonflies and beetles and eventually settled on spiders. They had to be captured by persuading the creatures to run into a test tube and then pickled in alcohol before describing them. This entailed a microscopic examination of their sexual organs and chelicerae. I duly passed over a collection of some 60 species to the museum. Six years later when I was in the Kenya Treasury, part of my portfolio was responsibility for the Coryndon Museum where Leakey was still its Director, and I recall somewhat fractious meetings over his reluctance to work to a budget.

Joining College Council

My connections with Cheltenham resumed some 25 years later when I became a member of its council and went on to serve on it for 15 years. This seems the appropriate place to record some recollections of this later involvement with the school.

Sir Ronald Prain was already president of council while I was a boy at college and was still in post in 1977 when he invited me to lunch at Whites. He had been responsible for my first job on leaving Oxford at Mufulira Copper Mines, as narrated in chapter 4, and he always regretted that he did not have an opportunity to persuade me to stay with Roan Selection Trust, which he chaired. More recently, we had met at dinner meetings of the Africa Private Enterprise Group, where I represented Standard Chartered on becoming a general manager. The other person at the lunch was Sir Alan Greenwood, a director of British Aerospace, who was shortly to take over from Prain. The purpose of the meeting was to persuade me to join the college council, which I was very happy to do. At the time, I was the only parent member of council which gave me an access to attitudes and issues within the school, as briefed by Robert and Martin. Council was drawn largely from OCs and when I joined its members included the Queen's private secretary, Sir Philip Moore, Sir Burke Trend, secretary to the Cabinet, and a former minister, Sir Frederick Corfield.

The headmaster, David Ashcroft, was almost at the end of his time, and had originally paved the way for Robert and Martin. He was not a strong leader, but was a civilised and nice man. He was infamous for having allowed Lindsay Anderson (an OC) to make his notorious public school film, *If*, on college premises, which had damaged recruitment for years, as well as relations with OCs. A new headmaster, Richard Morgan, was appointed in 1979. He had been a successful housemaster at Radley. He was not academic at all, but had strong leadership qualities and soon made his mark on the common room and on parents. I was appointed to chair the finance committee and when attending the termly council meeting often stayed at college house, so got to know Richard well.

The big issue when I arrived was that council was on the point of selling Cheltondale to the hospital authority, as the last piece of land to be given up along College Road, in order to provide much needed funds for modernisation. Politically, it was very helpful to have an Owenite on council at the time and endorsing the decision to sell. Robert left college before the house was closed down, but Martin was part of the rump of boys that was moved to run-off accommodation for his last two years, which he did not enjoy. I organised a 'wake' of former Owenites at the house before it was finally demolished and met again some former house mates.

College had a dismal relationship with its old boys, stretching back to Eliot-Smith's day. The Old Cheltonian Society was a strong body, but it had often been at issue with the school, usually over tradition-related issues. There was a fiasco funding appeal not long after I joined council so that when it needed development funds council had resorted to selling off parts of its estate, and four significant disposals had already taken place. With the sale of Cheltondale that process had reached its limit. I came to the view that college accounts must generate a surplus that could be devoted to improvements. This meant raising fees, especially for day boys. Morgan endorsed this, but it was controversial and therefore implementation was gradual. He was keen to accelerate matters by borrowing from the bank, where I was the foot-dragger to begin with, but it became an integral part of funding. Later, the school was able greatly to increase its numbers, with beneficial financial consequences.

Public schools were treated as charities by the Inland Revenue, although they did not come directly under the Charities Commission and their governance was distinctive. The headmaster was responsible for the academic life of the school and council members could seek information but not get involved. Morgan was quite territorial about this, although it was something of a joke between us that I had an inside track via Robert and Martin. The issue of accountability arose with the results on pupil numbers and academic results, of course, and bids for improvements. Here the bursar was a key figure and, if he played his cards right, a key adviser to the headmaster. It was something of a peculiarity that public school bursars were rarely finance professionals. When I joined council the bursar was a former naval captain and his successor was an air commodore. This made sense in terms of managing the facilities, catering and support staff but could be problematic when dealing with parents and fees, and even more so when it came to financial strategy and the business model of the school. As a consequence, I found that chairing the finance committee was quite demanding as well as absorbing.

One of the peculiarities of the educational scene in Cheltenham was the relationship with Cheltenham Ladies College, or rather the usual absence of one. Over the years there had been several attempts at collaboration, but they did not last. When I was at college there was a phase of joint music-making and I recall singing in a combined choir in a concert at CLC, but the venture came to an end with the discovery of a flirtation. However, in confirmation year I attended a weekend retreat with the Bishop of Gloucester with both college boys and CLC girls. I became friendly with one of the girls when we got to Oxford, and for many years afterwards. Robert attended joint art classes for a while and Morgan made another effort, before deciding to admit girls. But the truth was that CLC regarded themselves as being in a superior academic league and were not really engaged. Thus, even the common-sense alignment of term dates, to attract parents with both sons and daughters, was not achievable.

I was appointed president of council in 1988 and I have retained my Speech Day addresses for this and the following four years. In that year I reflected on my experience of the finance committee –

'What then is this education business? A large school operates from fixed plant whose capacity is difficult to adjust in the short term; in particular it is hard to increase pupil throughput once a certain optimum has been reached, without incurring very large capital costs. It is a labour-intensive business where more than 60 percent of total expenditure goes on wages and salaries. It is very competitive and not particularly profitable. In Cheltenham's case we are talking about an old-established business, which has the advantage of a well-known brand name, although customer loyalty as measured by repeat orders through the generations is somewhat disappointing (about 8 percent of college are sons of OCs at present). We operate from old plant, which means high maintenance costs, yet the period charm is no doubt a selling point. In recent years there has been growing evidence of improving quality of output – as measured by academic results, but also by strong demand for places, Cheltenham makes a useful contribution to invisible exports, but would not win a Queen's Award because it consciously limits its overseas intake.

'What all this boils down to is that Cheltenham College has to operate as an efficient educational service business if it is to equip itself to provide good education, in reasonably attractive surroundings, which compares favourably with the competition. It means that current revenues must make a significant contribution to the never-ending process of refurbishment and improvement.'

Richard Morgan retired in 1989 after twelve years as headmaster, and on reaching 50. This had been agreed at the time of his original appointment, so that he would have the opportunity of one more headmastership. However, it was not entirely straightforward, since Richard would have liked to stay longer and there was not an immediate major vacancy. I decided that the original deal must be adhered to, which led to some strain between us. He left to chair a newish educational trust, but not long afterwards he was appointed headmaster of Radley in succession to the famous Denis Silk and was a great success there.

During Richard's time at college there was an important change in the composition of the student body: the number of boy boarders fell as a result of the closure of Cheltondale, but day boy numbers increased by a third, necessitating a second day boy house. He persuaded council to admit girls to the sixth form in 1981 and there were 54 by the time he left and a girls' house. Overall numbers were up 13 percent at 559. Academic standards had been raised significantly and the curriculum broadened with a special emphasis on technology and computing, and there was a work placement industrial link scheme. The common room had been transformed and three quarters of the teaching staff were now Morgan appointments. There had been a large programme of improvements ranging from a new science complex to a new tuck shop, and funded mostly from cash flow. In an inflationary age boarding fees had been raised nearly fourfold. I concluded my Speech Day address that year by addressing him directly –

'Richard: I think everyone here is conscious that in you College has had one of its more outstanding headmasters, that in the Morgan Years College has been enhanced in reputation as a public school that delivers on educational attainment, but also one that provides a broader experience of education in cultural, sporting and social terms at a high standard. You are propelling the school towards 1991 and its 150th anniversary in immensely good heart, and for all this I convey our warmest thanks.'

Finding a successor to Richard Morgan was no easy task. We were in the fortunate position that his achievements were widely known and there was a large field of applicants. Given the varied demands of the job, I took the view that we should draw up our shortlist from individuals who were already appointed headmasters, so that there was a track record to assess. Furthermore, I decided to spend a day with each of the candidates in his own habitat, before the final interview. This led to one memorable experience where the candidate had invited me to inspect a new computer facility that was being developed in a large barn. We climbed a temporary stair to the mezzanine addition and I was invited to admire the view from a window. Unbeknown to him, the floor in front of the window was only plaster board and as I stepped forward I descended twelve feet onto the stone floor below. A circle of faces peered down at me as I pulled myself together and I heard the candidate say, 'I think he is all right; he fell just like a monkey.' Some ten years later, I had to have a little toe cut off that had become severely arthritic as a result of the fall.

At the final interviews Peter Wilkes from Ryde School, Isle of Wight was the unanimous choice and he joined college in the autumn term 1990, in the run-up to the 150th anniversary celebrations in the following year. The advent of a new headmaster provided an opportunity to re-state the school's aims which Wilkes seized: to increase the proportion of girls, enlarge the bursary programme, and broaden the curriculum to include the International Baccalaureate.

Cheltenham College had been founded in 1841 as the first of several new public schools, including Wellington, Haileybury, and Clifton, and it had a particular orientation to the military with its 14 VCs and to service in the Empire.

Planning for the 150th had already commenced three years earlier in 1988, starting with a special Remembrance Day service in autumn 1990 and reaching a high point at Speech Day the following May, which was held in the Town Hall due to the large numbers attending. There was an anniversary ball at college that evening, where 1 had a table with several contemporaries. 1 had an extensive correspondence with past and present secretaries at Buckingham Palace over a possible visit by the Queen. As Princess Elizabeth, one of her early official engagements had been a visit to college in 1949, when 1 was a prefect. After much to and fro, a date for a return visit was found in November 1991 which splendidly rounded off the year of celebration. There was a special chapel service, a tour of the school and a banquet lunch in hall. Sitting next to the Queen was a great honour and, as others have observed, Her Majesty was an observant, even witty, conversationalist.

1 retired from council after the celebrations so that the implementation of Wilkes's plans for college were no longer my direct concern. It was a sadness to learn that Peter fell out badly with council over academic strategy and had to leave, and it made me wonder whether this could have been averted if 1 was still involved – perhaps not. But it did bring home the crucial importance in a school of the character of its head and that person's ability to combine leadership of the common room, the confidence of the governing body, and the achievement of key results.

Some eight years later, and with grandchildren James and Olivia now at college, 1 was drawn into its affairs once more by agreeing to serve on a fundraising campaign board. By this time, college had set up a proper development office, had got on top of alumnus data and was organising regular events to keep OCs interested and in touch with the school. There were several notable successes with OCs who had prospered, and there was an altogether healthier relationship with them. 1 became a regular donor and was particularly associated with the restoration of the set of pre-Raphaelite lunettes in the chapel.

3. OXFORD 1952

I arrived at Oriel on an autumn day in October 1952 with a bike, a suitcase and a trunk of books — to the horror of my scout, who trundled all this over to my assigned rooms on the ground floor of the third quad. I was much disappointed to discover that I would have to share the accommodation with another undergraduate. We each had a bedroom, but a communal sitting room. He was a somewhat hearty and philistine individual who had come up to read Geography. As it turned out he was hardly ever in the rooms, except to sleep, so the sharing was not too painful. Undergraduates who wished to stay out late, carousing after the gates were locked at night, had various routes back into college; unfortunately one of them was my bedroom window until it was eventually discovered by the authorities and the loose bar was re-cemented.

The Provost gave a sherry party reception for the new intake. Sir George Clark was a distinguished historian of Stuart England and many of us stood an inch taller as he addressed us as 'Gentlemen', which turned out to be the customary mode of official address: the notice board was peppered with notes 'Gentlemen are reminded that ...' The burden of Clark's short address was to challenge us to stretch ourselves academically while up at Oxford, despite the many distractions of undergraduate life: we had all our lives to enjoy ourselves, but only one chance to get a good first degree that could profoundly affect our future prospects. I resolved to follow this advice. Many years later as the Director of the School of Oriental and African Studies when I spoke to the new student intake, I remembered the effect of G N Clark's words and paraphrased them for my own remarks.

New undergraduates were subjected to much solicitation to join university societies — the Oxford Union, the evangelical Christian Association and other religious groups, Scottish Dancing, faculty clubs, college sports activities and much else. There were several Old Cheltonians at Oriel, including two Owenites, which was comforting. Most freshmen had just completed their National Service, but a medical student from Rugby was like me, and Patrick Sellors and I became firm friends. He was eventually my best man, and I a godfather to his firstborn. Patrick was the son of a distinguished heart surgeon and he himself became a front-rank eye specialist and surgeon to the Queen and was knighted. Medical students had to spend long hours in the labs and dissecting room if they were serious, and Patrick and I fell into a committed work routine: lectures in the mornings, he in the labs and me in the libraries in the afternoons, and more reading most evenings. A movie on Saturdays. Oriel was a leading rowing college, but we both resolved not to get involved with this distraction so missed out on much of its social life.

I was delighted to discover that there was an East Africa Association at Oxford and promptly joined it. The core membership gathered in undergraduates with connections with that part of Africa, as well as members of the Colonial Service spending a sabbatical year at Oxford on the Devonshire Course. The trio running the society at the time was led by Hector Hawkins, who had served in the King's African Rifles for his National Service and had a settler uncle. He became a professional economist and, many years later, I was able to induce him to join me at Standard Chartered as its chief economist. David Le Breton also had a settler uncle. After Oxford he joined the Colonial Service and then the diplomatic service and, in retirement did a great job running the Overseas Service Pensioners Association, where we have kept in touch. Then there was a lively district officer, Oliver Knowles, on the Devonshire Course, and subsequently a colleague of mine in the Kenya Treasury.

Every society was required by the Proctors to have a member of the university academic staff as its Senior Member. For the East Africa Association it was Margery Perham, senior fellow of Nuffield College, Reader in Colonial Administration and the country's leading academic authority on colonial issues, active both as a government advisor and contributor to *The Times*. She had a special interest in Kenya's intractable problems and saw more sides to the controversies than most people, perhaps because her sister had lived out there. The Mau Mau rebellion had broken out that autumn so was much on the agenda at the society's meetings. In my second year I became its chairman and soon found that the glamour of Oxford could lure almost anyone in public life to come to address our meetings: leading businessmen, colonial exiles and aspiring nationalist leaders. It was a great crash course in contemporary affairs and in parliamentary lobbying — the Fabian Society, the Bow Group, the Movement for Colonial Freedom, the Joint East & Central Africa Council.

During this first term at Oxford — and while diligently working for the science prelims as well as starting on botany — I became aware of a unique Oxford degree that fired my imagination: an honours degree in Philosophy, Politics and Economics, or Modern Greats as it was called. It seemed to encapsulate everything that I found intellectually exciting. After weeks of ferment, I went to see the Dean of Oriel, Christopher Seton-Watson, and asked if I could switch courses from Botany to PPE. Changing schools was not unprecedented, but it was difficult. However, Seton-Watson was supportive and the switch was accomplished. The consequential challenge was that I would have to take the Social Science Prelims in one term from scratch, and this entailed extensive reading of English political history from 1688 — all new to me, plus a set book in French: de Tocqueville on the French Revolution. All went well, and I started on PPE properly in the summer term.

Seton-Watson was my tutor in politics and he quite soon encouraged me to set my sights on gaining a first. The Oriel economics tutor, Eric Hargreaves, was a former classicist who had worked in Whitehall during the war and had 'taken up' economics via an interest in Roman public finance. He was a nice, civilized man who suffered from piles and therefore sat on a rubber tyre in his armchair and bounced about like a cork when he was amused. He was a sceptical Keynesian and not much interested in micro-economics. So not a great deal of stimulus here, and this was compounded by my being paired for tutorials with a lazy and disinterested freshman until I was able to engineer a change to pair with Bryan Nicholson. He had a distinguished business career, including chairmanship of the CBI, and was also a prominent Oriel alumnus. For philosophy I was farmed out to a Magdalene graduate student, who was a good teacher, and this part of the syllabus changed my whole intellectual outlook for ever: I was fascinated by the Oxford school of linguistic philosophy and the scepticism that went with it; I really engaged with moral philosophy and all vestiges of religious belief were banished. Each term I came up early to stay in digs to prepare for the college exams on the first day.

The PPE syllabus provided for taking a special subject in one of the three disciplines and I decided to choose one from the politics list: the Political Institutions of the Commonwealth. This gave me as tutor one of its leading constitutional experts, Freddie Madden from Nuffield College. It also brought me into contact with another Nuffield don, Kenneth Robinson, who held a readership in comparative colonial administration and was an expert on French Africa. He had been tempted back to Oxford from the Colonial Office by Margery Perham. He ran a graduate seminar at All Souls with Professor Kenneth Wheare on federalism, to which I was invited. The independence of India and the London declaration of 1949, which recognised the Queen as Head of the Commonwealth, initiated a profound change in the politics and dynamics of the Commonwealth. It was accelerated by the contemporaneous unravelling of the colonial empires of the West. This was an exciting time to be studying constitutional change and Oxford was very much involved in providing expertise to governments, as well as providing an influential forum for leading politicians and civil servants to air their views. Commonwealth and colonial issues featured prominently in British politics in the 1950s, with passionate argument over the pace of democratic reform, the protection of minorities, the response to violence and terrorism, and their influence on Britain's relationship to the UN, to Europe and the USA.

What of ordinary undergraduate life? Patrick and I decided to take up snuff (from Frieburg and Treyer) and to wear bow ties as a matter of course. We bought fancy waistcoats — mine was mustard cloth and Patrick's a maroon and black silk taffeta. We sipped dry sherry, scorning the beery rowing crowd. We learned to punt the Oxford way from the rear. Girls were of minimal interest. Patrick fancied himself as a potential couturier and designed extravagant fashions, but I never remember him going out with a girl. I thought I might be keen on Sally, whom I had met at a religious retreat at Cheltenham where she was at the Ladies College. I took her out from St Hilda's, daringly sharing half a bottle of wine over a meal. I was invited to stay by her parents for a Christmas dance and took her to one in London. Just when I concluded that I rather liked her, she announced her engagement to her cousin Simon who had come up to Worcester. We met up again as married couples in Kenya, where he had a job with Oxford University Press, and were friendly for a number of years after we were both back in England.

One of the more interesting undergraduates who attended the East Africa Association was Sarah Nyendwoha, the first Ugandan woman undergraduate at Oxford. She was reading history and was a year ahead of me, as well as being much more mature. Her shrewd sense of humour was a delight. Sarah came from the Bunyoro kingdom in western Uganda. It was the time of the crisis between Kabaka Mutesa of Buganda and the liberal governor Sir Andrew Cohen, and Sarah was a sought-after interpreter of events. My parents rented a house in Oxford during their leave in the summer of 1953 and I invited Sarah round several times. Much later I learned that my mother was apprehensive that I would marry Sarah. She went back to Uganda to teach and married a Tanzanian art teacher at Makerere, Sam Ntiro, who became Tanzania's first High Commissioner in London. Their marriage did not last and Sarah became a distinguished women's leader in Uganda until she had to take refuge in Kenya for several years during Idi Amin's reign of terror. We met again in our seventies for a wonderful evening of reminiscences in Kampala. I joined a group of her contemporaries in order to remit a modest pension to Sarah for the rest of her life.

I had regular reading holidays with Patrick at their family cottage in the Chilterns, where we catered for ourselves, played some golf and put the world to rights. One summer I took myself to stay at The Trout at Lechlade for a fortnight to read on my own. I took a canoe up towards the source of the Thames and fantasized over the innkeeper's daughter. In my second year I had rooms to myself at last. As with my shack at Cheltenham, I personalized them: I fitted new curtains, and bought a Renoir print and a Paul Klee to add to the Hokusai. I gave lunch parties. At that time Oriel men had to go out into digs for their third year. Patrick and I found sparse rooms on the corner of Wellington Square for the autumn of 1954. We then had a stroke of luck: Margery Perham offered me the vacant flat at the top of her house in Bardwell Road. She lived there with her widowed sister, Ethel Rayne, who had been married to a soldier-colonial administrator in Somaliland which was the setting of her autobiographical novel, *Major Danes' Garden.*

Undergraduates were not permitted to live in flats at that time but, on petitioning the Oriel Dean (Seton-Watson), he gave special dispensation on account of Margery Perham's formidable reputation, confident that we would not incur the displeasure of the Proctors for disorderly living. The flat was straightforwardly furnished but for one enormous picture that had been given to Margery by Madame Rocco in Kenya: a nubile Masai belle dominated the sitting room wall and gave us a *succès de scandal.* We had become very keen on cooking and derived great enjoyment — and some esteem — from the recipes of early Elizabeth David and *Plat du Jour*, as well as learning the basics from the *Penguin Cookery Book.* I introduced Patrick to classical music and he introduced me to jazz. We were pretty serious students on the whole, working hard for our finals. Whenever concentration flagged, we had only to look across the garden to see Churchill's economic adviser, Sir Donald Macdougall, and also fellow of Nuffield, never-endingly working at his desk, pipe in mouth; we were also well aware of the late hours kept by Margery Perham below us as she worked away at her monumental life of Lord Lugard.

There was an essay society in college — the Oriel Colloquy — that met to listen to a paper and discuss it over mulled wine. I had been introduced to the novels of Virginia Woolf by a South African undergraduate with literary pretensions, Michael Power, and my encounters with Keynes of the Memoir Club soon led to a fascination with the Bloomsbury Group which has persisted over the years, notwithstanding modern debunking of its pretensions and the revelations of the private lives of its members. The notion of free-flowing conversation on literature, politics, high minded gossip, and a liberal critique of society, was immensely appealing to me. I was encouraged to read a paper to the Colloquy on the Bloomsbury Group. Some years later I recycled its wine-spattered text to a literary evening in Nairobi at the home of Sue and Thomas Chitty, the novelists. At Cheltenham my budding interest in Oriental art had led me to attend a dance recital by Ram Gopal, who did so much to communicate the Indian classical dance tradition to western audiences. I was entranced by the subtleties of Indian classical dancing and the

Margery Perham by John Rothenstein. Oxford, 1954

expressive power of eyes, fingers and gestures, as well as by the musical tradition that went with it. At Oxford, Ravi Shankar came to play at the Hollywell Music Room and I was hooked. One consequence was to kill off completely my previous enjoyment of the western classical ballet tradition, which now seemed to me completely arid by comparison.

Michael Power also introduced me to a remarkable network for students from the 'old' Commonwealth that was organized by the Victoria League for Commonwealth Friendship and the redoubtable Margaret Macdonald of Sleat. A circle of country house owners agreed to invite Oxbridge undergraduates to stay for a few days and to entertain them. I was paired off with a New Zealander from Merton at Christmastime 1953 for a three-centre tour of the shires. We started off at a large country house near Hereford, and were shown to our rooms by the butler before going down to drawing room tea. When we went to change for dinner my evening shoes had disappeared so I rang for the butler who impassively led me over to the unnoticed shoe cupboard. Our next stop was at a 19th century gothic castle in Cheshire. There was bridge after dinner, gargantuan breakfasts and pheasant shooting ('Don't shoot until they fly, and don't shoot a fox'). There was reminiscence of a grand birthday party where tiaras were worn; Artur Rubenstein had been invited and was asked if he would play some Chopin waltzes for dancing. Finally, we took the train down to Devon to stay in a crumbling mansion with a lonely old widow and her Danish au pair, whom we escorted to a Christmas dance at the golf club. Not so much surreal, as a time warp experience.

Living upstairs from Margery meant that there were frequent invitations to tea by her sister, or to meet an interesting colonial visitor, and I became increasingly absorbed with the exciting world of the politics of decolonization. I soon met her research secretary, Eleanor Glyn-Jones — a history graduate and daughter of a judge, who had successfully applied for a Nuffield Research Studentship to do a B. Litt on an aspect of the slave trade in East Africa. I was much smitten and Eleanor invited me quite often down to Nuffield. I took her to the Worcester Commem Ball and she invited me to stay with her parents. The 1950s were the heyday of Nuffield's influence on African studies, under Margery's leadership. Special funding had been attracted from the Rockefeller Foundation, several fellows and research students had research interests in the area, and all the great figures connected with contemporary African affairs came to Nuffield sooner or later. It was a heady atmosphere. Eleanor encouraged me to apply for one of the two-year research studentships after taking schools, and so did Margery. But shouldn't I be starting on a career?

I had been to the Oxford careers board and enquired about jobs in Africa for graduate trainees, and two prospects were indicated. John Holt was a Liverpool based shipping and trading company dealing with Nigeria and West Africa; it had a policy of hiring Oxbridge graduates and turning them into businessmen. I went for interview on the complicated proposition that I might first choose to do a higher degree if I was successful with Nuffield, and was also liable for National Service if first employed in the UK. Surprisingly I was offered a job on graduation, or to come and see them again in two years' time. I also applied to the United Africa Company, a subsidiary of Unilever, where there was a formidable group interview process, and which had the same outcome. Oxford graduates really had a choice in the 1950s. The Nuffield application was much harder. I had to propose a research topic and felt it should have an economic flavour. After much consultation — I went to see Peter Bauer at LSE, who had written on the Malaysian rubber industry for his own PhD, Herbert Frankel who had the chair of colonial economics at Oxford and had written on the South African maize industry and on its railways system, and talked about a tea study with my father — I proposed an economic history of the development of the East African tea industry, with an assurance of cooperation from the tea companies, and Frankel agreed to be my supervisor. The interview was before the combined Nuffield fellowship and was an intimidating experience, but I was by then sure of the support of Margery Perham, Kenneth Robinson, Freddie Madden, and Frankel. I was duly elected to a studentship in the spring of 1955 and before taking schools that summer.

I sat schools in June and wrote interesting enough papers for me to be summoned for a viva — with Isaiah Berlin as chairman of the examiners that year. He probed an answer I had written in the philosophy paper on distinctions between retributive and reformative justice and the occasion still comes back to me after all those years. I was awarded 'a good second', which was certainly fair, even though I had worked hard for a first.

Looking back, it is clear that I never entered fully into undergraduate life at Oriel, partly by not being interested in rowing which dominated the social life of the college, partly because I had to work so hard after switching from science to humanities, and partly because my interests became so absorbed in colonial affairs — the East Africa Association, living at Bardwell Road in my third year, and the lure of Nuffield. Having won the studentship, I felt that my real Oxford experience was just starting.

However, the Oriel connection was not lost. An Oriel contemporary, Peter Collet, took on a role to develop fundraising at the college and I started making regular financial contributions in the 1980s. I was then drawn into the fundraising circle, although none of my target names bore fruit. One consequence was that I became a founder member of the Raleigh Society in 2009, which comprises Oriel alumni who have made a reasonably generous financial contribution to the college.

In retirement, I was delighted to be elected an honorary fellow of Oriel in 2012, which I think was probably triggered by an Oxford assignment that brought me to the notice of the provost, the distinguished economist, Sir Derek Morris. Whilst still at Standard Chartered, I was asked to be an assessor for a funding application to the Economic and Social Science Research Council. It was the largest bid it had yet received: for £1 million to set up a new research centre in Oxford, The Centre for the Study of African Economies, which was the brainchild of Paul Collier, who had been a lecturer at Oriel. The bid was successful and I was subsequently invited to join its advisory council, and then to become its chairman for 14 years. Collier's aim was to establish a research agenda on African economies that also addressed leading issues in economic theory and policy, using novel data sets and advanced techniques. He set out to bring on a group of economists who would go on to appointed posts in the Economics Department and at colleges, with the result that Oxford became a renowned centre of economic expertise on Africa. It was a stimulating experience to play some part in facilitating these developments, and when I retired from my role the honorary fellowship was awarded soon after.

More recently, Oriel became embroiled in a 'Rhodes Must Go' campaign that burgeoned nationally into an anti-slavery and Black Lives Matter movement. Cecil Rhodes had been an undergraduate at Oriel and was a generous benefactor to Oxford, with the Rhodes scholarships and also to his old college, with a new building in his name facing onto the High Street and complete with a statue on its façade. The anti-Rhodes campaign had started in South Africa and had led to the removal of his statue from Cape Town University. It then moved to Oxford, led ironically by a black Rhodes scholar, demanding the removal of Oriel's statue. The new provost was an ex-permanent secretary from Whitehall and she sought a bureaucratic accommodation, acknowledging that the statue might have to go. This provoked uproar from alumni and I was one of those who wrote to the provost.

As an honorary fellow, I attended one of the meetings convened by the college. By then the fellows were minded to keep the statue, but to take steps to describe the historical context and to do more for black and ethnic minority members of the university. My note of the meeting observed, 'The discussion was somewhat dominated by serious young women with American accents who agonized about their personal feelings of being, as it were, contaminated by Rhodes.' A retired fellow wondered what the college would do about its piratical benefactor Sir Walter Raleigh and on the difficulty of getting undergraduates to understand the mind-set of the Spaniards in America. I observed that Oriel should not just 'contextualise' Rhodes, but should consider developing an accessible narrative on all its major benefactors. The unhappy outcome for the provost was that her appointment was not renewed for the customary second term. In my view, the basic mistake made by Moira Wallace was to think that this was a situation that was susceptible to constructive dialogue, instead of confronting the campaign with a firm articulation of historical context, including recognition of Rhodes' very real achievements.

In 2020 the Black Lives Matter campaign brought Rhodes to prominence once again, and a number of universities caved in over statues and named buildings on account of perceived links with slavery. The new provost, Neil Mendoza, was more politically astute in setting up a commission to advise the college, after the fellows had voted to remove the statue. I wrote to the commission hoping that it would not succumb to pressure and repeating the proposal that Oriel should sponsor an annual lecture on its benefactors. The commission reported after six months, recommending removal of the statue, and this was formally accepted by the college, but with the decisive caveat that procedural and financial complications and difficulties made its implementation undoable. However, the wider debate rumbles on and we have been reminded of earlier iconoclastic episodes, especially in England after the break with Rome. The essential ethical challenge remains of whether it is justifiable to impose a viewpoint on society to the extent of physically attacking symbols that offend its proponents. In the 17th century the flashpoint was religion; today it is slavery and colonialism.

I went to Nuffield in the autumn of 1955 and Margery Perham was only too happy for me to stay on at Bardwell Road. Patrick Sellors left to go on to the Middlesex Hospital and one of the new Nuffield intake came to share the flat — a Cambridge historian, David Adams, who was researching Roosevelt's New Deal. David was much more a man of the world than me, romantically good looking and attractive to women, with a talent for inducing sympathy for his current woes — whatever they were. He had already held a Harkness fellowship in America and was heading towards an academic career. We got on surprisingly well together. But my hopes of seeing more of Eleanor once I got to Nuffield were dashed as she had fallen under the spell of a charismatic Methodist minister who was doing a D.Phil at Nuffield, as well as finishing her own B.Litt, and was not seen at college in her final year. However, our paths were to cross again in Central Africa a couple of years later. During that summer vacation Margery had invited me to stay at her cottage on the Downs and the Governor General of Nigeria, Sir James Robertson, came to lunch. Amidst all the talk on Nigerian politics, there was some talk as to whether I might be appointed one of his ADCs, but a more exciting opportunity emerged.

The Report of the East Africa Royal Commission 1953-55 was published in June that year. It had been triggered by a dispatch from the Governor of Kenya, Sir Philip Mitchell, expressing concern over the pressure of population on limited natural resources under traditional African subsistence agriculture, and the Royal Commission was asked to examine how economic development might be stimulated in the region. The intellectual backbone of the Report was provided by Herbert Frankel of Nuffield, who had already been an adviser to Mitchell in 1946 and was currently a trenchant critic of the notorious development folly in Tanganyika known as the Groundnut Scheme. The thrust of the Report was rather against the dominant fashion in development economics in England of state-led capital investment, as expressed by left-inclining luminaries such as Arthur Lewis, Thomas Balogh and Nicholas Kaldor, with their emphasis on state mobilisation of resources and admiration for Indian economic planning. Instead, the Royal Commission report focussed on the liberating effect of market forces, the need to dismantle protective barriers to efficient land use, and the promotion of an open economy, urbanisation and mobility. It was an explosive doctrine in relation to the Kenya White Highlands and tribal land reservations, as well as to the protective paternalism of much colonial policy.

A notable member of the Royal Commission was Arthur Gaitskell, brother of the Labour Party minister, but in his own right the recently retired managing director of the Gezira cotton scheme in Sudan that was widely admired as a model of development enterprise and of fruitful partnership between private investors, the state and the peasant cultivators. He had just been elected to a Research Fellowship at Nuffield in order to write a book on the lessons of the Gezira scheme. Nuffield hosted a conference on the Royal Commission's Report shortly before the start of the Michaelmas term and everyone of note connected with East Africa was there. Margery arranged that I should be a helper and thus able to attend all the sessions. But there was also an ulterior motive: Gaitskell needed a research assistant and I was looked over for this role. We got on well and a deal was done in that the College agreed I should postpone the start of my own research for a year in order to work for Gaitskell. Thus, my Nuffield studentship started with my diving into the history of the Anglo-Egyptian Sudan, the Nile Waters Agreements, and the intricacies of irrigated cotton production.

The Gezira cotton scheme was rightly famed as an exceptional case study in development. It was fortunate in having as its historian a man who had not merely spent his working life there, but who had spent years reflecting on its special features and its problems, who had been instrumental in moulding its mature phase, and who was passionately keen to promulgate its lessons to a post-war world intent on hastening the pace of economic progress in poor countries. As Gaitskell was at pains to point out, the special features of the Gezira scheme did not spring from a single master plan or governing concept; instead, they were the product of historical circumstance and pragmatic response to experience, but suffused withal by some overarching principles and the impact of powerful personalities. It made for a compelling story.

Sudan in 1898 after the battle of Omdurman and the defeat of the mahdists was a unique imperial possession, albeit co-ruled with Egypt, which itself was effectively under British control. A conquered people and yet not a colony, but where a paternalistic government firmly asserted the paramountcy of native interests and the importance of winning the confidence of its new subjects. This meant, crucially, the recognition and registration of land ownership rights and a deep reluctance to alienate land to foreigners. The outcome was that the Gezira was not developed as a giant plantation in the ownership of either the state or of private capital. Nevertheless, external capital was essential to the development and management of a giant irrigation scheme. The solution that was evolved over a decade of debate and experimentation was a tripartite partnership between the Sudan government, a private investor and manager and Sudanese tenant farmers. The government borrowed on the London market under Treasury guarantee to build the great Sennar Dam on the Blue Nile and the main irrigation canals, and it took powers to rent the land in the Gezira from its traditional owners. The Sudan Plantations Syndicate was responsible for the management of the scheme under a time limited agreement — subject to break clauses and renewals, and for minor capital works, cotton ginneries and working capital. The farmers were selected by management (with landowners only having the right to one farm) and were responsible for the cultivation of the cotton cash crop and grain and fodder crops. The profits of the whole operation were divided three ways: 35% to the government, 25% to the company and 40% to the tenant farmers.

Gaitskell had a clear idea of the architecture of the book, but there was much detailed research to be done. I quickly realised that if I was to play a significant part in the project, I would need to be able to provide him with well-drafted, typewritten text. I taught myself to touch-type on my Olivetti portable 21st birthday present from my parents, and was thereby able to become intimately involved in the evolution of the book. This typewriting skill became an important asset at intervals in my later career — at budget time in the Kenya Treasury, and on several occasions at Standard Chartered. Sudan had only been independent for a few months when I went out to Khartoum in the autumn to research in the archives of the Ministry of Finance that Gaitskell's influence had opened to us. I stayed at the Grand Hotel — in an annex houseboat on the Nile

—and walked to the ministry each morning under the neem trees along the river bank. Gaitskell came out for a visit and we moved to a higher social plane, meeting the leading ministers and being invited to dine with the new British Ambassador, Sir Edwin Chapman Andrews. Dress was Red Sea rig: white trousers, black silk cummerbund, white shirt and black tie. 1 had bought a yard of cummerbund in Oxford, but failed to wind it tightly enough. Standing in the garden under the stars with a drink in hand, 1 was suddenly aware that the wretched thing was about to descend to my ankles and 1 had to retreat behind a shrub to rewind.

While in Khartoum 1 somehow befriended a radical young Sudanese journalist, Ahmed Tigani, and received from him an intensive induction into Sudanese politics and the heady influence of Egyptian and pan-Arab nationalism. One of my letters back to Nuffield recounts a memorable day:

'1 met Tigani about 10.45 outside the cinema Bramble, named after a famous patriarchal DC of Omdurman. We straight way set off for the market, and visited first the street of goldsmiths and silversmiths. We were poor customers — entering many shops, having all the wares displayed, but buying nothing. In one 1 came across the chap who sold me Isabel's necklace. He had a large picture of Azhari hung up and turned out to be a most political merchant. We visited the grain market, watched leather workers, and then entered the bustle of the vegetable market — mounds of chillies, spinach, mint, cucumbers, rice, capsicum, salt, limes, caraway seeds. Met a young Gordon College boy earning some money at a small stall and had a chat with him. Next was the market of women. They were all widows and sold the hand made caps which every turbaned Sudanese wears. Had an hilarious time trying on dozens of the things to find one that would fit, but Tigani would not let me buy one as they were asking about 10 shillings for it. A crowd gathered to watch the spectacle. We eventually extricated ourselves and plunged into a rather frightening maze of dark passages where leather tanning is done. Pretty powerful smells. Fruit seed is the tanning agent. Quite glad of a companion. Another maze of passages was an 'industrial area', where ivory and ebony work goes on. Spent a fascinating ten minutes in a shop watching various stages of work from raw tusk to polished elephant. One worker told me that it took ten years to become expert.

'Out into the blazing sunshine once more and wending our way through donkeys, bicycles, women with baskets on their heads, idlers, to the shop of a poet-merchant — a real life Hassan. We sat in his shop and drank Pepsi-Cola and had a long hilarious conversation about the vices and virtues of the British. He writes poems for a famous Arab woman singer, and he was careful to tell me that the BBC has some of his records. Two charming small children sat comfortably each on a pile of enamel basins and every now and then reached out to touch me. The poet told me how much he liked the British as friends but not as rulers and Arthur Gaitskell was a great man. We parted swearing life-long friendship.

'Pepsi-Cola has won an astonishing victory: everywhere one sees the incongruous sight of old wizened Arabs swigging away at their Pepsi. Wherever we went Tigani was greeted — he is evidently a well known and respected figure, despite his youth. I wormed out of him that he speaks often at political meetings, which accounts for part of it. We had another Pepsi with a friend who is a bed maker in the street of bed makers, and a new string bed was brought out for us to sit on and we passed the time of day pleasantly. We stopped frequently for short chats: with a café owner, an engineering student at Gordon College, an Egyptian shopkeeper (who had come back to win back some of the money he had paid out in bribes, I was told), a young man who could not get into the civil service but would not take anything else — yet, and so on. We walked through the red-light district — deserted now, and fetched up at a café where we met an Umma MP who called out that we made an odd pair walking round, one so black and the other so white (I was wearing white shorts and stocking too). I replied that Black and White was a famous whiskey and a much admired mixture. Hearty laughter and we sat down for a while and I had to eat a sweet jelly. Was glad to notice that the companion of the MP was an NUP man and great friends. Talked light hearted politics. The reason that Azhari hadn't a chance in West Sudan — where everyone is a great horseman — is that he cannot ride and so cuts no ice.

'At last we set off for Tigani's home — quite a long walk in the blazing heat — and arrived at 2.15. Actually, it was his uncle's house as his father is dead. Uncle a very pleasant man. Sat for a while, this time with fizzy orange, popularly called Freedom, because the factory was established during the independence period. A modest household and no pretensions. Washed from a tap in the garden and then sat down to lunch (on the floor). Fingers much in use. Very starchy. A large flat loaf each and an object like a large flannel also made of pastry. One broke this up into a plate and poured over it a spinach mixture and a soup and rice and ate with a spoon. Or alternatively dipped hunks of bread into the liquid. Meat in one's fingers. Melons and water melon followed. Had a long and interesting talk afterwards with Tigani and his brother Audulla over coffee. It was flavoured with a spice called *habahan* (mystica) and some was brought in — a kind of gum that gives off incense when burned.

'We had a long talk about the civil service and I was very impressed that Audulla was so concerned about the departures to the diplomatic service, the shortage of men with experience, and concern that standards might fall. Discussion turned to Egypt. Apparently Tigani received £60 a month during the honeymoon period between NUP and Egypt — 'Those were the days!' Although one may deplore the bribery, it is nevertheless impressive that these chaps were able to forgo it when Egypt had served her purpose. Audulla said that the man in the street still 'remembered' Egyptian rule in the 19th century and had no intention of letting it be repeated. Talked of the youth of the top men in the civil service: no chance of promotion for the juniors for ten years or so in the normal course of events.

'Afterwards visited the Mahdi's tomb and had permission to enter. Most impressive. Mystica incense filled the air, gorgeous silk brocade curtains with silver thread, crystal chandeliers. I signed the book.'

Gaitskell was impressed by my experiences. Margery Perham's research assistant, Isabel, ran into him at the annual meeting of the Africa Bureau and she wrote 'He said you were the best possible ambassador Britain could have and that you had penetrated the 'life' of the place in a way he had never succeeded in doing. Your future is made!' I wrote an optimistic appraisal of the first year of self-government in Sudan, and drawing some lessons for Kenya, which was published in the *Kenya Weekly News* at the end of August, following a meeting with the editor — Mervyn Hill — arranged by my father.

There was a second research visit in 1956, this time to the Gezira itself, along with Gaitskell. His Sudanese successor, Mekki Abbas (who had studied with Margery Perham) was our host. The routine was to get up at 6am and go to the office for a couple of hours and then back to breakfast, then work through till 2pm, followed by lunch and siesta. Maybe another hour in the office between 5 and 6pm. I worked diligently through the Gezira Scheme files to unravel the complex arrangements of a major irrigation scheme and its interplay with the tenants' associations and their concerns over the price of cotton, stage payments, debt, welfare. At the weekend we drove to the Sennar Dam on the Blue Nile for a picnic lunch, as Gaitskell was determined that I should see the great dam at the source of the scheme. A letter to Margery Perham captures the atmosphere of the day.

'There is a sort of island just below the dam where many years ago the resident engineer started a garden, and the idea was taken up enthusiastically. The place was filled with flowering shrubs and trees and made very lovely. We breakfasted there sitting beside the swimming pool, now deserted and empty. The spot was still beautiful, though wild now. The children's swing hung listlessly, and the parallel bars stood nearby as a perch for birds. A donkey grazed on the tennis court. The atmosphere was redolent of the people who had been there before. It seemed to be a setting for a Chekov play, I remarked, and Gaitskell immediately recalled a day when he brought Asquith's beautiful granddaughter down for a picnic. After bathing, he had lain on the grass while she read a Chekov story out loud to him. The place does not appeal to the Sudanese. The summer house is falling down; woodpeckers are making nests in the swing supports; and the pool is filling with leaves. Perhaps one day an archaeologist — investigating the monuments of the British Heyday — will take measurements of the swimming pool and, while having his picnic, listen to the crimson shrike warbling enchantingly in the jacaranda tree, as we did. And they.'

This letter had an interesting after-life. Years later, following Margery's death, a conference was held at Rhodes House, Oxford for the purpose of briefing her designated biographer.[2] A number of former academic colleagues gave papers on different aspects of her career, and one of them talked about her tremendous correspondence over many decades with colonial administrators in Africa, which were part of the papers deposited with the Bodleian. She was the matriarch of the Colonial Service and many men poured out their thoughts, if not their hearts, to her. Extracts from several such letters were read from her papers, including my letter from the Gezira. After I myself went back to Africa, I used to write to her regularly from Zambia and Kenya.

The Gezira book was licked into shape on the basis that I drafted chapters along the lines Arthur and I had discussed, and then he redrafted to his satisfaction. We had great debates as a result, not only on the Sudan, but on all contemporary colonial problems. Arthur was a director of the Commonwealth Development Corporation, a frequent mission expert for the World Bank, and of course also had a hotline to the Labour Party's colonial policy formation. He had been hugely influenced by the force of nationalism in the Middle East and in emergent Africa, and believed it could be harnessed constructively by the West in a 'partnership' relationship. We radical graduate students thought this was wishful thinking and that the nationalist movements would not compromise in their pursuit of untrammelled independence. Ghana was about to be independent, the Nigerians were thumping at the door, and then there was the controversial Central African Federation. There the African nationalist movements were blocked by a white settler government that gave a very different connotation to partnership (the accepted image was of rider and horse) to what Gaitskell envisaged.

Another research assistant saw the book finalised and through the press, and it was finally published in 1959.[3] It contained a handsome tribute: 'Michael McWilliam, my young research assistant at Nuffield College, was a quite invaluable help. His personal interest in the theme of the story, and his capacity to synthesise the issues, made a stimulating

2 This project failed to mature, but a not very penetrating biography by a Canadian historian appeared in 2012: *Into Africa: The Imperial Life of Margery Perham*, Brad Faught. I B Tauris
3 *Gezira: A Story of Development in the Sudan*, Arthur Gaitskell. Faber & Faber, 1959

contribution to the authorship.' Gaitskell remained a good friend and our paths crossed again a few years later.

My other – intense – correspondence at this time was with Isabel Ferguson, with whom I had fallen head over heels in love after taking her to the Pembroke Summer Dance. Fortunately, these letters will not have been archived. She had just graduated from Somerville — a bonny girl from Liverpool with a great sense of humour. It was a first love affair. I wrote wonderful letters from Khartoum and the separation only intensified my feelings towards her, weaving fantasies during those hot afternoon siestas. But the separation had the opposite effect on her. Passion cooled, and when I returned to Oxford three months' later we could not recapture the spirit of June. Isabel was a brave girl. Walking home one night after the theatre, she told me —sweetly — that it was all over. And in due course we became just good friends.

I flew down to Kenya after the Gezira visit in order to initiate my tea industry project, since my plan was to accomplish a B.Litt. thesis within the span of my two-year studentship, so there was just a year to complete the fieldwork and write it up. The critical step was to secure the formal backing of the Tea Board of Kenya so that the tea company members would allow me access to their records and to the time of their executives, and also to open the doors to government departments. The chairman was Sir Colin Campbell — head of James Finlay in East Africa, and subsequently chairman of the parent group in Glasgow. The other key personality was the Minister for Commerce & Industry, Sir Arthur Hope-Jones. I made a presentation to the Tea Board in Kericho and support was pledged, including a local research budget for travel and accommodation. My uncle Alan was secretary of the Tea Board at that time and was very helpful over subsequent arrangements. The Tea Board made a stipulation that if they were later to determine that publication of my thesis was inimical to the interests of the industry, access to it by outside parties could be prohibited. This sensitivity was due to the recent formation of trade unions in the agricultural sector and fears that aspects of the history of the tea industry could be used to embarrass management — on such topics as land alienation, and child labour. Nuffield accepted this restriction as a formality, but in the event my thesis was indeed 'banned' for 20 years, to the distress of diligent researchers in the Bodleian Library, who occasionally wrote to me.

In 1955 Nuffield still felt new, if not raw. The college was not yet residential, although being built on that basis, and my study was the prospective bedroom of a future suite of rooms, and hence just a work station. It meant that more time was spent in the Junior Common Room, and this perhaps improved our social life. Certainly, my time at Nuffield was much more fun than at Oriel. Two Nigerian students taught us High Life dancing and many of us had flats where we enjoyed showing off our culinary skills. The college appeared to have a bit of a chip on its shoulder vis à vis old Oxford and tried to assume the patina of tradition. 'The following tradition will commence on Monday' is apocryphal, but conjures up the flavour. My fellow research students were virtually all destined for careers in academia. Contemporary politics was a dominant interest, and especially the issues of end of empire. In the Suez crisis the common room staged a great seminar in which the protagonists were Max Beloff (pro) and Margery Perham (anti), and for years I kept copies of their scripts.

While still working for Gaitskell on the Gezira book, I read into such literature as was available on the tea industry and related topics and then went out to East Africa for four months in December 1956 to undertake field research. This comprised such material as the tea companies were prepared to make available to me, supplemented by personal interviews, records of the various statutory bodies and tea growers' associations, and government archives — mainly in departments of agriculture. The aim was to write an account of the development of the tea estate sector in East Africa, which was fast becoming a principal export earner for the region, especially in Kenya. The sponsorship of the Kenya Tea Board, and by extension its sister bodies in Uganda and Tanganyika, gave me privileged access to material that will probably never be seen again by researchers, given subsequent political developments. From this standpoint the banning of access to my thesis was a pity.

I started off in Kericho with the records of the Kenya Tea Growers Association (where my father had been its secretary for many years), those of the Tea Board and sundry papers from Brooke Bond. In the new year I flew to Uganda and made contact with economists at Makerere University, including Cyril Erlich who had studied the Uganda cotton industry and whose main interest was in music, and Walter Elkan who became a lifelong friend. I also met up again with Sarah Nyendwoha who had now married the art lecturer Sam Ntiro. I benefited from introductions to the government's economic adviser Walter Newlyn who enabled me to see more files than would otherwise have been allowed when I went to Entebbe to access official archives. Staying at the Lake Victoria Hotel I was able to start drafting parts of the thesis while enjoying the view over the lake. The Uganda Company arranged an estates tour that took me to the new development area in western Uganda, where lunch was disrupted by the news that elephants had got into the tea nursery and we dashed off with guns to no avail. Near Fort Portal I stayed with the Old Etonian bachelor tea planter Captain Naylor at his home on the site of one of Lugard's forts, Fort Waverley, and played rather drunken billiards after dinner.

I then flew down to Dar-es-Salaam to pick up the Tanganyika story, staying at the Palm Beach Hotel and writing up my notes sitting on the shoreline between swims. Then by car to Tanga and up the old German road to Amani in the Usambara Mountains, where botanical zinc labels on the trees lining the zig zag road were still visible. And finally back to Nairobi for a prolonged stint of archival research staying at the New Stanley hotel. After visiting the new African smallholder scheme on the slopes of Mount Kenya, my driver managed to overturn the car during a rain storm on the way back to Nairobi, but we clambered out undamaged. In Oxford I had got to know the rising political star Tom Mboya, who was enjoying a trade union sponsored stay at Ruskin College. He was now back in Nairobi and we arranged to meet up in the very different atmosphere there. We caused a bit of a stir when he came to have a drink with me at the hotel as Kenyans and whites did not then socialize in public although there was no formal colour bar. I also went to hear him address a political meeting in a poor district in the city as Tom was already emerging as a leading political figure. Tragically, he was assassinated when a minister in the early independence years.

My thesis opened with an analytical description of tea plantation cultivation and manufacture and its economic characteristics under East African conditions, showing that it was a highly profitable industry. The initial waiting period for the tea bushes to mature and associated factory investment had dictated a largely plantation sector, although the initial trials had been undertaken by individual pioneer settlers. It was an interesting exercise trying to assemble the history of these early beginnings, not least because my father was one of the first Brooke Bond estate assistants in Kericho in 1927, and my future step-father, Hugh Thomas, was one of the first James Finlay assistants and he had collected some of the early stories.

There followed four studies on different aspects of the tea industry. The chapter on labour reviewed a famous 1930s controversy over child labour, which was still prevalent at the time of my study. One was reminded of Victorian tales of chimney sweeps and of boys in the coal mines as one encountered the self-serving narratives of the value of earning one's living from an early age, of contact with 'civilisation' and the importance of 'small, nimble fingers' for tea plucking. I went on to survey issues of labour supply and labour force stability, which again had been major issues in Kenya's early colonial days. It was this chapter that made the tea barons nervous over the thought of the material falling into the hands of 'political agitators'.

The chapter on the international tea restriction scheme of the 1930s and 1940s provided a fascinating glimpse into the way that India (with support from the India Office) sought to prevent the emergence of a competing tea industry in Africa, and of the doughty fight put up by the colonial governors to allow development to take place. There was an interesting historical irony in that at the end of the 18th century China had similarly sought to prevent the establishment of the Indian tea industry by banning the export of seed. Companies like Brooke Bond and James Finlay were on both sides of the argument. As major producers in India and Ceylon they were in favour of international restriction, but as new investors in Kenya they wanted leeway to establish viable units there.

The tea restriction scheme sought to control new planting as well as imposing export quotas, and this in turn created a strong incentive to encourage domestic tea consumption. It resulted in cut-throat competition until Brooke Bond was able to establish price leadership. More interestingly, it led to the creation of a marketing cartel led by Brooke Bond. My father was the main deviser of this 'Pool' scheme and was responsible for administering it for many years. Not only did I have full access to the records, but also the opportunity of daily conversations over several weeks to unravel the politics of the scheme. On the outbreak of war in 1939 my father was appointed Food Controller for East Africa and the regime of price controls that lasted well after the war. Implicit in the thesis text on the workings of the Pool in the post-war period was a tribute to my father's diplomatic skills in securing pragmatic solutions to the frequent disputes that arose over the allocation of quotas when individual producers or even territorial interests diverged from the common purpose. One long term social consequence of the great efforts made to stimulate local tea consumption was that Kenya became a tea drinking society, with significant public health benefits resulting from boiling water to make tea and the preference for a milky, sweet concoction.

The final section of the thesis was concerned with the very recent introduction of smallholder tea cultivation by African farmers. This caused great anxiety to the established industry in Kenya because the example of smallholder tea in Ceylon had not been satisfactory, and policy evolved very cautiously in departments of agriculture in order to allay fears. By 1957 the first factory for African grown tea near Nyeri was about to open, and the government had embraced ambitious plans for expansion. My narrative failed to discern the significance of these developments and I was too influenced by industry scepticism. I should have been more alert to this because Gaitskell was a director of the Commonwealth Development Corporation and the CDC was about to make a major commitment to the smallholder sector

Frankel, although my official supervisor, took no interest in the progress of my thesis, and never sought to read my work or advise me. But I received help from an unexpected source. Ursula Hicks — wife of Professor John Hicks who was also a fellow of Nuffield — was much involved in studying the public finances of emerging colonies, and especially of federal structures. She and her husband came out to Kenya on a study visit while I was there in the summer of 1956 and my parents entertained them at home in Kericho. Ursula was a water colourist and I recall taking them to a local beauty spot with a view of the Nandi hills for a painting session. Ursula set up her easel and the Drummond Professor of Economics stood by holding a jar of water to wash her paint brushes. Back in Oxford, Ursula decided to step into the supervisory vacuum and read drafts of my thesis and made helpful suggestions. When my examiners were appointed, I was rather alarmed to discover that they comprised John Hicks and a young development economist, Arthur Hazelwood. However, the viva in All Souls went well and a B.Litt. was awarded, entitling me to an embroidered gown with a pale blue hood, trimmed with fake ermine. The garment came into its own thirty-three years later at ceremonies at the School of Oriental and African Studies.

It has posed a challenge in retirement as to whether I could turn my thesis into a readable book and eventually I took it up with two extended research visits to Kenya in 2003 and 2004 in order to bring the story up to date, but also to narrow the focus to Kenya. In the fifty years since writing my thesis Kenya had become the world's largest exporter of tea, ahead of India, China and Sri Lanka, as a result of an extraordinary expansion of its tea industry. The smallholder sector about which I had been so lukewarm in my thesis now comprised some 500,000 farmers each with an acre or more of tea, as a result of a remarkable partnership with the Commonwealth Development Corporation and the World Bank and the huge enthusiasm of farmers in the high altitude zones; they now had a cash crop and had been taught and successfully embedded high standards of cultivation. Side by side with these developments the estate sector had also greatly expanded and political controversy had been avoided because members of the new Kenya elite – headed by President Moi himself – had invested heavily in tea and their own estates were often managed by the big tea companies. The third major transformation had been a revolution in tea cultivation and manufacture, as a result of applying modern science to a very traditional industry, such that productivity and quality had been transformed. My friend John Nottingham had retired in Kenya from the Colonial Service with a Kenya wife and family and was now himself a tea farmer. In his company I was able to spend several days visiting smallholder farms where he knew the owners.

This was a tale worth telling and I got down to writing a book after another pause of ten years. Publication was initially a problem because the academic presses found the focus too narrow and wanted me to set the book in a context of post-colonial discourse, which I was unwilling to undertake. I decided therefore to self-publish with the help of an excellent editorial advisory firm and with Ingram Spark, who distribute through booksellers and Amazon. At that point a former colleague from SOAS, David Anderson, now professor of African History at Warwick, came to hear of my project and did me two great favours. He put my footnote references into academic format and then, as an adviser to the Bodleian, arranged that my archive notes and papers be taken into their Africa collections. *Simba Chai* was published in 2020 and was dedicated to my father.[4]

---

4 *Simba Chai: The Kenya Tea Industry*. Michael McWilliam. Ingram, 2020

BACK TO AFRICA

4. MUFULIRA COPPER MINES 1957

At the beginning of May 1956, while still in the early stages of my research assignment with Gaitskell on his Gezira book, I had decided that I needed to address my post-Nuffield career after the studentship ended in the summer of 1957. I had come to the conclusion that I was not really cut out for an academic career in comparison with the bright minds around me, but also that I did not really fancy taking up the deferred options of a management trainee with the United Africa Company or John Holt. Instead, I was attracted by the notion of working in the new Central Africa Federation and of making a contribution to this new state by joining one of the great Northern Rhodesian copper companies. Sir Ronald Prain was chairman of Roan Selection Trust, but also President of Cheltenham College Council, a friend of the Johnstons at Cheltondale (where his son was), and someone who I had already invited to Oxford to address the East Africa Association. Prain had quite a reputation in Britain as a reformist business leader on African advancement against the colour bar on the Copperbel. I wrote to him to enquire about the possibility of a job with RST, and the letter included the passage –

'I should like to do African personnel work. It seems to me that this aspect of industrial development is almost of more importance in Africa today than actual production, and I have followed with growing interest the activities of RST in this field.

I should be happy to cut short my stay at Nuffield to play some part in this work.'

In short, at that point I seem to have been prepared to ditch my tea thesis in order to get going. Arthur Gaitskell and Harry Johnston agreed to be my personal referees. After some delay I was made an offer of appointment as an African Personnel Officer by Mufulira Copper Mines. By this time I had been to Kenya and made my pitch to the Kenya Tea Board for financial support for my B.Litt thesis and so, in accepting the offer, I also made a request to defer starting until April the following year. Happily, Mufulira were quite content to wait, and in fact a further deferral was agreed to after the Warden of Nuffield wrote and asked that I should complete the academic year. It did not occur to me that this ready acquiescence might indicate that there was little interest in my arrival. However, it meant that throughout my second year at Nuffield I was in the unusual position of having a firm job to go to on the Northern Rhodesian Copperbelt – somewhat to the wonderment of my contemporaries.

The Copperbelt in 1957

I arrived in Northern Rhodesia at the end of July 1957, at a time when Central African affairs had been much in the news in Britain. The Central African Federation had only been launched in 1953 – with high hopes from its protagonists, especially for the perceived economic benefits of linking the three countries under a federal government. But there was also much controversy because of African opposition in Nyasaland and Northern Rhodesia to the racial policies of Southern Rhodesia and the well-founded fear that it would be the dominant partner. In Britain there was concern in liberal circles and especially in the Labour Party (in opposition), but by no means confined there. I had been a supporter of the federal project, but shared many of the concerns about the prospects for political participation by Africans and about the baleful effects of racial discrimination and the influence of Southern Rhodesian politics. RST under Prain's chairmanship was regarded as more liberal than the other great copper company, Anglo-American, as it was in the vanguard of pressing for African job advancement on the Copperbelt into 'white' job categories. My arrival coincided with the ending of a prolonged white mineworkers' strike on this issue that had shut down the industry, at a time of falling copper prices and related miners' bonuses.

I was highly politicised on colonial affairs after my two years at Nuffield and was keen to come to grips with the realities at Mufulira. I kept a detailed diary throughout my time there and used it as the basis for long dispatches back to Nuffield to Margery Perham and to Isabel, her research assistant, knowing that they would also be read by Gaitskell and others (and indeed ending up in her official papers). I kept copies of the main letters. This activity was soon supplemented by journalism – for the Capricorn Society newsletter, *Equinox*, where summaries were often repeated in the daily press, and the *Central African Examiner* in Salisbury, which was modelled on *The Economist,* including the practice of anonymous articles which suited me well. I became its Copperbelt correspondent. I have therefore an unusually detailed record of this period: my commentary on public events; my increasingly active political life; my efforts to demonstrate that it was possible to cross the race barrier and have meaningful contact with Africans; as well as an emotional roller-coaster with Eleanor Glyn-Jones, who had moved from Nuffield to a teaching post at the leading white school for girls in Salisbury.

All this was only possible because I did not have a real job to do. I had been parachuted into Mufulira by the RST head office (and it was well known that I was, in some sense, a protégé of Prain), but there was absolutely no idea of what to do with a graduate management trainee who was not an engineer and who wanted to specialise in African personnel: no plan had been made and clearly no guidance had been provided from above. Perhaps the hope was that I would be airlifted out again after a suitable interval.

The African Personnel Department (there was a separate one for the white miners) recruited and paid the workforce, administered the African mine township, provided welfare services, and was responsible for the company's industrial relations with the African Mineworkers' Union and the Mines African Staff Association, into which Africans in 'advanced' jobs had been placed. There were 44 Europeans working in the department, which had traditionally been the repository of long service mine employees of no marked ability. The head of the department, Twigg, had been at Mufulira for over 30 years – a courteous, very traditional and authoritarian South African, with no understanding or sympathy for the 'modern' African. His deputy, Torrance, was a relatively new arrival out of the colonial administration's Labour Department – ambitious, but also antipathetic to the aspirations and political stirrings within the African workforce; yet this was part of the mining group where Prain was trying to speed the pace of African advancement. There was one interesting person in the department, Dennis Lehman, a graduate of Wits University. Restlessly energetic, he was what one would term an authoritarian liberal, believing firmly that Africans should be compelled to follow the norms of European society as they moved from their traditional ways of life. He and his wife Eileen took me up and were hospitable and friendly, notwithstanding furious political arguments and disapproval of my political activities.

I read all the departmental files, which gave me a good grounding in the industrial relations scene. Otherwise, I did odd tasks when a spare person was needed – on the pay line, interviewing families who wished to qualify for improved housing, touring the townships, and I started Bemba language lessons. After being there a couple of months I wrote a paper proposing that Mufulira should adopt a strategy to divest itself from the administration and ownership of the African mine township, and detailed some of the steps leading towards economic rents and encouragement of home ownership and a stabilised labour force. Torrance said that the objective would be approved by RST, but that it was not possible to do anything about it for fear that the African National Congress would capture the town council. He handed the paper back to me i.e. the end of the matter, as well as of my hope of having something interesting to do. For significant stretches of the working day I had nothing to do.

After six months I was assigned to work underground on the early morning shift from 5.30am to 1.30pm. The lift cages were in three tiers, with some 50 bodies crammed into each compartment, and then away at an alarming speed into the bowels of the earth to the 1500 ft level, disembarking into a wide tunnel, well lighted with whitewashed walls. My diary noted –

'It was much hotter than I expected, and I was soon pouring with sweat due to the thick woollen vest I had been issued. And then the real business began, clambering down these frightening ladderways. The handrail was little comfort at an angle of 50 degrees, and I kept fearing that my gumboots would slip on the iron rungs. And then we clambered into the tunnel ends where the men were drilling. In one of them I had to do a Gary Cooper act and finish the last bit on a rope to where the men were drilling a raise at the top of a big stope, which plunged away into the darkness. In the dust the shadowy figures looked like Cyclops. They were chained to the wall as a safety device. The sound of several drills working together in a confined space is monstrous, like being shut in a room with an aeroplane. Any sense of direction was quickly lost and I plunged around like an aimless mole. Some passages had refreshing blasts of air blowing down them, others were still and hot. We came up again just before twelve. What a relief it was to see white light and to smell fresh air.'

The job consisted of patrolling the workings as a sort of race relations policeman. The idea was that this would be an emollient influence in a setting where the mine captains were white, tough South Africans and the chaps with the drills and shovels were black migrant workers from all over central Africa. If there was an incident, say from mishandling equipment, or someone being 'cheeky' or losing his temper, one held a hearing after the end of the shift at the mine head, with a potential for disciplinary action. Fortunately, I never had to deal with such an event so passed the mornings on patrol. One was up for a late lunch, with the rest of the day one's own.

The European township was laid out on hierarchical lines, with bachelor accommodation nearest to the mine, the mess and club house and ever improving family housing further away, with top management near the golf course. There was a housing shortage and I found myself allocated to a one bedroom cottage – number DE1 – that I had to share with a young Africaner who worked on night shift in the concentrator. Puttergil had already appropriated the closed verandah as his space so I had the bedroom, with the wash basin and shared wardrobe, and there was a loo and shower at the back. Pretty basic really. I was told that I could not expect to get a cottage to myself inside two years. After ten days I bought a four-year-old Morris Minor to give myself some mobility, and it lived under the mango tree outside the cottage. We had a room boy who did our laundry as well. When laundry was hung up to dry there was a risk of *putze* flies laying their eggs on the material and if the garment was not ironed thoroughly the hatched maggots would burrow into one's skin and create a nasty boil. This only happened to me once.

Living in a company town was a curious experience: it was a kind of feudal society where one was in a status relationship with everyone there, and which was presided over by the Mufulira Mine Manager, Frank Buch. One way of breaking out of the structure to some extent was to join societies. Within a week I was enrolled as a member of the Music Society, and soon had bought myself another clarinet and joined the small orchestra (my old one sold to Isabel when I left Oxford). My diary again –

> 'Life is full of rehearsals at the moment (*Water Music*, *March Militaire*, *Valse Triste* etc) and it should be funnier than an Alec Guinness film, what with a first violinist who has to get slightly tiddly before she can face an audience, and a conductor who is so busy keeping time with himself that he has no attention for anyone else.'

I have a concert programme from March 1958: orchestra, piano solos and songs and I had two solo slots for clarinet and piano –

> 'I am rehearsing busily for a sort of Victorian Musical evening. The stage of the Little Theatre is to be furnished like a drawing room; the performers will loll around elegantly and then while arranging a vase of flowers one will suddenly whip out a violin, or burst into song while adjusting her hair in the looking glass, or will discover a flute in the aspidistra. My contribution is part of a Brahms clarinet sonata and Bach's air for the G string. No audience is expected, and we shall have to lay on applause with a loud speaker to keep up our morale.'

I failed to record the actual event.

One evening a ballet was mounted at the swimming pool, where there was raked seating along one side of the pool and a performance space on the other. Deirdre, with whom I shared an office, had trained as a ballet dancer in South Africa and she ran dance classes at the Mufulira school. The evening was to show off the children's achievements, interspersed with songs and piano solos, but finishing up with *Danse Arabe* (Tchaikowsky), in which I was prevailed upon to lead a troupe of dancing girls – young men dressed in chiffon pantaloons, bras, yashmaks.

It was agreed, but not rehearsed, that on the night instead of exiting into the wings I would lead the troupe over the footlights and into the pool. Unhappily in my case the impact of the water separated me from my costume and, as the lights went up, Binti McWilliamaida was to be seen treading water and trying to put on his pantaloons before crawling out of the pool.

I also joined an amateur dramatics group. My first assignment was as prompt during a performance of *Ring Round the Moon*. But a more serious thespian experience was actually witnessed by my parents. They flew into the Copperbelt in mid-November in the Brooke Bond plane during a Central Africa tour and came over to Mufulira to see an evening of one act plays, including one in which I played Romeo in a village Romeo and Juliet farce.

Getting Real

After I had been at Mufulira for about three weeks I was having supper in the mess one evening and reading my airmail *Economist* when a freckled, fair-haired man put his tray down opposite mine –

'We must be the only two people at Mufulira who take *The Economist*. What brings you here?'

Dennis Acheson turned out to be an Oxford contemporary from Brasenose, a Rhodes scholar, who was now working as a metallurgist on the mine and would eventually become chief executive of RST. His father was a doctor at Ndola. It turned out that Dennis was an active member of the Capricorn Africa Society that was endeavouring to promote a vision of multi-racial democracy in central Africa as an alternative to continued white hegemony on the one hand and African nationalism on the other. We soon became firm friends and fellow political activists. Visits to his parents' home were a welcome breath of civilisation. One began to meet a few other kindred spirits. The mine published a monthly magazine and its editor, Dick Hall – Oxford and the *Daily Mail* – was a wonderful iconoclastic spirit to have around. Sadly, he left before the end of the year to edit the main newspaper in Lusaka, *The Northern News*. The district officer at Mufulira, John Wilson, and his exotic wife Dawn, also provided good company although he was unsympathetic to my political leanings. The district commissioner, Stokes, was much more in tune.

I had been met off the plane at Ndola by a member of the African Personnel Department, Ben Gisaka, and on the drive to Mufulira I was able to have my first conversation about Federation, the African National Congress, the mineworkers' union, and respond in turn to questions about British politics and Mau Mau. Doubtless this conversation was relayed, and my determination to open up a dialogue on current affairs was rewarded by soon getting to know a number of Africans working in the department. There appeared to be nowhere to meet but at the office, since Africans were not admitted to the mine's social club and the same applied to the town's café, so a pattern evolved of after-hours chats and – better still – Sunday morning meetings, since it was an established perk that one could go to the office on Sunday mornings and earn 'overtime'. In this way I quickly learned about African scepticism over job advancement into 'white' jobs, the resentment of office staff at being barred from the mineworkers' union and forced to join the Staff Association, that race relations on the Copperbelt were worse for educated Africans than in Southern Rhodesia, and that the Capricorn Africa Society was disliked because it had supported Federation and was seen to have betrayed Africans to racist policies from the south.

My letters to Oxford described and analysed the political scene, but I also tried to crystalise my thinking for a more public audience by writing for the *Equinox* newsletter of the Capricorn Society (where the pieces were reproduced in the *Northern News*) and for the *Central African Examiner* – both without attributable bylines.

'Partnership With Whom?' (*Equinox*, September 1957) analysed Welensky's strategy of incorporating African voters under stiff franchise qualifications that ensured they would be outweighed by white voters for many years to come, so as to make the proposals acceptable to the current European electorate, and ensuring that the nationalist Congress movements would never be elected. The article questioned the notion that only 'moderate' Africans should participate in politics in multi-racial societies and concluded 'It is more preferable to have sparks in the debating chamber than explosions in the countryside.'

'Social Advancement' (*Examiner*, October 1957) drew attention to the disparity between the copper companies' efforts to open up job opportunities for more educated Africans on the one hand, and the continued social segregation in the mining communities, and reflected my conversations – 'It takes very little enquiry to discover how acutely this ostracism is felt, or how quick is the response to any sincere approach.' I went on to argue that the mining companies should take the initiative by creating multi-racial club facilities and sport. 'For at present those few Europeans who are interested in meeting Africans on equal terms are on the defensive in a hostile environment.'

I wrote a more reflective piece for a South African journal that was published a year later.[5] It argued that the controlling European oligarchy in the Federation was fundamentally unwilling to concede power to Africans in the foreseeable future, and that the franchise schemes were devices to this end. White liberals were wrongly devoting their efforts to moderating these schemes rather than focussing their efforts on coming to terms with African nationalism. Only a policy of vigorous social and economic integration might have a chance of establishing a new African led elite in which Europeans might still have a role to play in public affairs.

The 'Social Advancement' piece had an interesting after-life. It impressed Frank Buch, the Mufulira Manager (not knowing that I was the author) and it led him to decide to invite four Africans to a reception for the Governor General, Lord Dalhousie, held on the premises of the Mufulira Mine Club in December (as he told Dick Hall later). This was the first time on the Copperbelt that Africans had been invited to a public social event on 'white' premises. A furious backlash was generated by outraged club members. Dick Hall gave the story to the press, where it generated headlines and a lively correspondence. I went to a noisy meeting at the club with three friends and we were barracked for our pains in speaking up. It was actually quite an alarming experience as we stood close together in a crowded bar with a crowd of hostile, tough looking miners. My long 'Oxford' haircut came in for derisive comment. There was front page news for days, since it was the first big race row since Federation involving colour prejudice by a group of Europeans. Dick Hall 'managed' the press with great skill. To cap it all, the Governor of Northern Rhodesia, Sir Arthur Benson, in his Christmas message made a sharp dig at the Mufulira racists who 'if they had been in the stable at Bethlehem on the first Christmas, would have had to have an

---

5 'The Central African Liberals', in *Africa South* Vol 3 No 1, October 1958, edited by Ronald Segal

indignation meeting afterwards. Because, you see the Three Wise Men were allowed in – and they were coloured men from the East'.

The objectors failed in their attempt to amend the club's constitution and the affair fizzled out. I wrote a reflective piece on the whole episode for the *Examiner* and attempted to draw a wider lesson by bringing in the formation of a new multi-racial club in Mufulira (by me!) and also recent outspoken sermons from the Methodist church. 'What appears to be happening is that public opinion is being slowly roused out of its apathy by the liberal advance guard. It is being brought home to ordinary people that they are faced with a fundamental choice affecting their social environment. One response leads the way of the Mufulira petitioners, the other to a gradual accommodation to a new pattern of living.'

Politics

The Capricorn Africa Society was founded by Col. David Stirling in the 1950s and was an idealistic attempt to form a multi-racial movement to reflect the plural societies of East and Central Africa. Branches had been formed in Kenya, Tanganyika, Nyasaland, Northern and Southern Rhodesia, and a great conference had taken place at Salima on the shores of Lake Nyasa in 1956. Dennis Acheson had been to Salima and there was a Capricorn branch in Mufulira, chaired by a British schoolteacher. The Capricorn Africa Society had been in favour of establishing the Central African Federation, but this severely compromised its standing with Africans in Northern Rhodesia and Nyasaland, as I was quickly made aware of when I began to develop contacts on the mine. In September 1957 the hot issue was whether Capricorn should sponsor a political party to challenge the ruling United Federal Party led by the formidable Roy Welensky in the forthcoming federal elections. David Stirling and the Southern Rhodesian element were all in favour, but the argument was more finely balanced in the north. After attending a Capricorn meeting in Luanshya I sent a dispatch back to Nuffield:

'Stirling has been encouraging the idea that Capricorn should form a political party, and these people were all very keen on it. I think it would be an unwise move... Capricorn has barely begun to hammer out concrete policies on local political problems. More serious however is that there seems to be a great illusion about Capricorn's appeal to Africans. It is thought that there is a mass of moderate opinion which would flock to the Capricorn banner but for the intimidation of Congress, and that if a party was launched it would form a great rallying point. It is a nice thought, but profoundly mistaken I feel.'

This did not stop me from spending a hectic weekend later in the month helping to produce an issue of *Equinox*, as part of an editorial group of four including Dennis Acheson. We worked till 2.30am drafting articles and then most of the next day preparing stencils, where my typing skills came in handy. Our editorial line was to challenge the Capricorn Africa Society's support for multiple votes and to argue instead for a broad common franchise. I had two articles, 'Partnership With Whom?', already mentioned, and a piece on the federal franchise arguing for a common roll that would enfranchise a substantial body of African voters who could be considered 'responsible' by virtue of their jobs. The press published extracts from *Equinox* for three days.

At the end of the month the Capricorn high command announced that a political party was to be formed. My scepticism had moderated by then, as I wrote to Nuffield –

'It is not at all easy to weigh up the arguments for and against such a development. I was frankly hostile to begin with, but now feel that given certain conditions, it could become an effective body. The key to the situation is, once again, a franchise for Northern Rhodesia, which will make or break its prospects. If there was a large enfranchisement of Africans on a common roll, so that they had a powerful say in an election, then the impulsion for Europeans to vote for liberal candidates would be much greater, since the parties would need African support to win... Here is the opportunity for the British Government to exert a decisive influence.'

In late October a meeting was convened in Lusaka to adopt a constitution for the new party. It was a memorable weekend, as my next letter to Nuffield recounted –

'The big excitement during the month has been the launching of the new multi-racial political party: the Constitution Party. Not an inspiring name, but the idea is that this party will strive to put into practice the ideals expressed in the Preamble to the Federal Constitution (unlike the Federal Party), and to work for

African aspirations by constitutional means (unlike the African Congress). I went down to Lusaka for the launching ceremony; it was a moving occasion. For a few hours it was as if a veil had been lifted and we had had a vision of a pattern of life that could come to pass in Central Africa. About 100 people of all races came from Southern and Northern Rhodesia – 250 miles from the Copperbelt and nearly as far from Salisbury. We met in the garden of Dr Scott's house, seated in a semi-circle under a tree in the cool of the evening. In the surrounding trees the birds sang an obligato to the speeches, and then later, when they were silent and hanging lights had been switched on, small bats skimmed noiselessly over our heads.'

First there were 'keynote' speeches from prominent individuals calling for the new party as the only way of gaining the initiative against the worsening trend of race relations and selfish white dominated legislation. It was very noticeable that not a word was said about Capricorn, and Stirling managed to keep himself in the background fairly successfully. The Party's constitution embodies the Capricorn precepts almost word for word. It was taken clause by clause; this was a fascinating experience largely due to Katilungu. He was unquestionably the outstanding figure there, having something important to suggest on nearly every clause, and a remarkable capacity for construing important points from the platitudes before us. This process took a couple of hours. We ended by appointing a large interim committee to get the party into motion – set up branches, raise funds, and discuss policies.

'Congress has been quick to move into the attack, demanding Chileshe's resignation from Leg Co as no longer representing African interests, and Katilungu's expulsion from the Congress executive.[6] Chileshe has answered back vigorously, while Katilungu has become chairman of the Copperbelt committee of the party, and in a joint letter today hits out at Congress. There can be no doubt that he has crossed his Rubicon now. According

6 Herbert Chileshe held a nominated seat for Africans in Legislative Council and Laurence Katilungu was the Secretary of the African Mineworkers' Union on the Copperbelt. Both had been prepared to enter into discussions with white liberals on broadening the franchise and both were apprehensive of the 'Africa for Africans' nationalism of the African National Congress and its leader Harry Nkumbula.

to my African assistant, his actions are being watched with bated breath by a considerable body of floating opinion on the mines, by men who would like to follow his lead, but are still scared to come out into the open.

'A large party of us were staying at a multi-racial hostel owned by the Government, and this was really the great part of the weekend. It sets a very high standard of comfort and service and is really the only place in the Federation where the races can live in equality (except for St Faith's Mission), for the Ridgeway Hotel is much too starchy. On Sunday I cleaned my teeth while Katilungu shaved at the next basin in the men's bathroom. So trivial really, and yet quite revolutionary out here, so that the incident is embalmed in my mind. The hostel is evidently used as a kind of club by the leading Africans in Lusaka and I met some delightful people during the day.

'The journey back to Mufulira was a rude contrast to the rest of the weekend. I was travelling in a Coloured's car along with three Africans. We broke down irreparably not far out of Lusaka, and had to abandon the car and hitch hike. It was dark by then, and not a car slowed for our motley gang. Fortunately, Katilungu's car came up behind with a friend of mine and some more Africans. I suggested that Jo and I were the only two with any chance of getting a lift, so everyone else (7 of them) had to pile into the car. Jo and I got home at 1am in three stages.'

A fortnight later I organised a small meeting in Mufulira of my circle of African contacts to discuss the new party and found that the euphoria at Lusaka was greeted with suspicion, as my diary noted —

'It was evident that there is no great enthusiasm for the new party, and that African opinion is so far quite unpersuaded that it has anything to offer them. Katilungu's membership has not carried much weight; it was interpreted partly as personal ambition and partly as a continuation of his feud with Congress.' (9 November)

However, the first public meeting of the party in Lusaka later in the month attracted an audience of 200.

The Mufulira branch of the Constitution Party was charged with producing a policy statement defining the party's attitude to Federation and we had a lively meeting to discuss Dennis Acheson's draft. I attended a similar meeting in Kitwe with Katilungu a week later on the franchise. There was an argument over whether the party was trying to win European support or African support and, taken to the vote, the latter view prevailed. At the end of December I was appointed to the executive committee of the party and also its Mufulira agent (Dennis was due to go abroad for a year on a company scholarship). Dennis and I expended much effort in trying to translate ideas about an African franchise based on income and education qualifications and match them to the realities of how many people would actually qualify under Federal Party proposals. We severely debunked the optimistic official estimates. (I wrote a detailed paper and sent it to Nuffield). At the same time, we engaged in lively debate with our African friends as to what might be acceptable to them.

The elephant in the room all this time was the African Congress in Northern Rhodesia, which was the principal vehicle of African political aspirations, but was passionately denounced by the Federal political establishment and by many in the colonial administration. At the end of November I wrote a reflective analysis of the situation for *The Examiner*, which was probably the best piece of political commentary that I wrote at this time. After setting the scene by reference to recent scare stories in the press and new emergency powers legislation –

'The fundamental point to grasp is that Congress is a mass organisation that claims, and receives, the tacit support of the vast majority of Africans in the areas in which it operates. Its organisation reflects this: loose knit, cellular, hydra headed. The strength of Congress is not based on a disciplined centralised hierarchy like that found in Communist parties, but lies in this mass allegiance which leaders can canalise for particular purposes. There is a figurehead, who on occasions has displayed charismatic qualities, but Mr Nkumbula's control over the movement is fitful. Congress is not just a society an African joins if he agrees with its aims, it is more like a citizenship he is born to. African opposition is regarded as a kind of treason and arouses similar emotions... The primary aim of Congress strategy is to weld the mass of the people behind the claim of the leaders for a rapid distribution of political power in favour of Africans. It is inherent in the situation that non-parliamentary techniques are used which may verge on violence, even though the leaders sincerely deplore it.'

After referring to other mass movements elsewhere in Africa, 'The imposition of Federation against the wishes of politically conscious Africans has been the major catalyst in the build up of the Northern Rhodesian African Congress, and has provided the touchstone for African fears of European domination and their own aspirations. Congress has tended to control such representative bodies as do exist, but they have been a completely inadequate outlet of political expression. Critics of Congress complain of the conflicting statements emanating from its leaders and the disparity between words and deeds. Such views impute a degree of coherence to Congress that has never existed.'

After giving some examples, 'West African experience suggests that the only way Mr Nkumbula could dominate Congress is to be in the vanguard of the political battle, and that moderation will not pay till Congress begins to be satisfied on some of its major objectives. The major focus of Congress politics in recent weeks has not been its anti-Europeanism, but the struggle that has been waged to become the exclusive organ of African opinion. Congress won the fight against the Capricorn Society hands down. On the Copperbelt it succeeded to the extent that mineworkers were as much Congressmen as unionists.'

I then reviewed the struggle for control of the African Mineworkers' Union: the intervention of the Government in deporting the politicised leadership in 1956, the subsequent efforts of Laurence Katilungu to sever any connection between the Union and Congress, and his provocative action in taking a prominent part in the formation of the Constitution Party. 'But it has become increasingly evident that he has failed to carry his union with him: faced with having to make a distinction between their allegiance to Congress and to Mr Katilungu, the majority of mineworkers see no reason to desert Congress. Mr Katilungu is now in a very isolated position... His action, instead of withdrawing the Union from politics, as he hoped, has made it the centre of a major struggle, which he is losing.'

Finally, I noted the pressure from European opinion for the Government to take further action against Congress. 'This would almost certainly be a mistake. That Government should arm itself to take effective and prompt action against disturbances of the peace is only sensible, but to carry this to the extent of attacking the body from which the disturbances mostly emanate would reflect a grave misreading of contemporary history. Every effort must be made to keep Congress leaders on law abiding lines, but its fundamental condition is unlikely to alter until the territorial franchise begins to bring it within the orbit of parliamentary procedure.'

My diary entry on 30 December read: 'A full column leader in the paper today on Congress that is almost an exact precis of my article in *The Examiner,* and it reflects a new line of thinking for the *Northern News.* Interesting.' And a day later, 'Frank Kibosha told me that it has gone down well with the local Congress boys.' Reading this piece sixty-five years later, one is struck by a sense of tragic inevitability. Northern Rhodesia was unprepared for early independence, yet was caught up in the irresistible tide of international pressure after the war to bring about a speedy end to colonial rule. African participation in the institutions of a modern state was minimal; the economically and racially dominant white community was socially unprepared to cede power; the conduct of the nationalist movement demanding the transfer of power was often alarming and there were valid apprehensions over the maintenance of law and order. Yet, Northern Rhodesia would become independent Zambia in 1960 with this mixed inheritance. My own career engaged again with the country some fifteen years later.

Kansuswa African Township was an independent township a few miles from Mufulira and not under the control of the mine. My friends arranged that we could meet there in its hall, thus not offending mine protocol, and drink warm Castle beer. My diary noted an interesting meeting at the end of January 1957 on the franchise and its implications –

'The Africans argued... that adult suffrage was really the only acceptable standard, but that if a selective franchise had to be accepted then literacy (standard IV) was the maximum they could agree to, and without any income tests. Looked at from the point of view of what constitutes a responsible voter, which is the same approach ostensibly adopted by the Federal Party, their argument was irresistible. They poured skilful scorn on the whole concept of linking political maturity with high income and educational standards. And in particular emphasised that if there is a powerful leader about, people will vote for him – or be afraid to oppose him – whatever their schooling and wealth.

'I tried to change the perspective of the discussion by suggesting that we look at the problem from the point of view of how long a transition period we want before Africans are in a voting majority. If one can make a decision on this question, then franchise fiddling has some meaning, and one can get away from these metaphysical discussions about 'civilised standards'. I am convinced this is the only way to tackle the problem realistically. But this is no panacea for success, as there is still a wide gap between the time period envisaged by Europeans and the much shorter one demanded by Africans.

'I feel increasingly doubtful whether the gap can be bridged amicably, and in particular whether the Constitution Party can bridge it. If it adopts a time period that has any relation to European politics it will fail to gain African allegiance and vice versa. Perhaps all it can do is to try and hustle European opinion and moderate Congress. An unenviable task. If one had to choose, I would rather the C.P. became an African party – a moderate wing of Congress with a trickle of European membership, than merely a poor cousin of the Federal Party.'

In February 1958 Dennis and I had a long meeting with the management board of Kansuswa Township to explore the scope for cooperation between CP and Congress, to work together on issues both organisations oppose in the present situation, and on the aims they had in common. 'They gradually warmed to the discussion... They did not find it odd that Congress and the CP could work together, which shows that the situation is still fluid and the opportunity is still open to us to forge a partnership between the two.' (7 Feb)

A full Convention of the CP was held over the weekend of 15 February, attended by about 50 delegates from Southern and Northern Rhodesia. Its purpose was to approve a set of policy statements and to elect officers. My letter to Nuffield sums up the experience –

'The Convention turned out to be a considerable personal success for me. I received the first applause of the day for my speech seconding the franchise policy. I had written the draft economic policy and, after introducing it, received a real ovation. The Chairman announced that the party had found its future Chancellor of the Exchequer. Then, because Colin (Morris) was ill, it fell to me to produce a motion on relations with Congress – the most important debate of the Convention. I wrote the speech in bed late on Saturday night. By offering a more mildly worded resolution in the middle of the debate, I was able to secure a unanimous vote in favour of cooperating with organisations with similar aims and instructing the party leaders to start discussions. The speech was reproduced at length in the press of the Federation (by 'Mr Mike McWilliam of Mufulira, one of the party's left-wingers') and, as I learned afterwards, has gone down well with Africans.'

In the following weeks we had two main preoccupations, of which the first was the Governor's new franchise for Northern Rhodesia (he had leaked his proposals to us before flying to London). We were concerned that he had seriously overestimated the number of Africans who would qualify for the vote, on the basis of the paper I have already referred to. For example, we worked out that only 10 Africans would qualify for the General Roll at Mufulira, against the official estimate of 40. We pressed for a commission to establish more authoritative figures. However, our main energies were directed to establishing a closer relationship with the Congress leadership. In this we were greatly helped from a surprising source – the Mufulira Special Branch officer, Bob Hunter, who was especially helpful in letting us know the whereabouts of Congress leaders. He had an intelligent interest in the African political scene and was on friendly terms with Dick Hall, Dennis and myself, as well as with leading Africans, and often had shrewd advice to offer. After the CP Convention I noted 'Bob Hunter came in this morning to find out what went on and had lots of good advice about spreading the word.'

My diary records five meetings in the following weeks. After two quite successful ones in Kansuswa we had our first encounter with Harry Nkumbula in Ndola. It was a somewhat difficult session and I noted 'He wasn't very enamoured of the idea that Congress members should be encouraged to join the CP as well... It will be something of a miracle if Congress continues to tolerate the CP' (23 March). We then experienced two boycotted occasions in Kansuswa followng an extraordinary event on 3 April. Having heard that Nkumbula was in Kansuswa, Dennis and I went out there in the afternoon, only to find a full scale police raid in progress with house to house searches, allegedly looking for stolen bicycles. Nkumbula and Co were flushed out and were not amused. Nevertheless, we arranged to call back at 9pm that evening and left a bottle of gin as an earnest. On returning –

'A Mozart programme was on the wireless as we arrived, and looking through the window, I saw Harry dancing a minuet with the pretty woman who had won the competition at the Mufulira New Year's Dance which I had judged.'

We entered the hall and were warmly greeted and soon settled down to talk, armed with Castle beers. My report to Margery Perham went on –

'I found Harry positively anxious to do business. Since we had met in Ndola the Congress leaders had realised that the Governor's proposals offered a real opportunity to Africans. Moreover they had been strongly influenced by an article in the paper by the Dominion Party chairman which argued, rather fancifully, that the Constitution Party would win the elections, and damned the White Paper accordingly. But to these Congressmen it meant that they at last saw advantages in some kind of liaison with us. We agreed to run a joint campaign to get Africans onto the voters' rolls, whatever the franchise. He said the Congress would support our candidates for the Ordinary seats if we supported the Congress candidates for the Special seats. This was pretty breathtaking.

'I then went on to discuss with Harry the general relationship between the two parties, and the terms of the statement I proposed to make at the public meeting on the following evening. The line we agreed on was that I should make no attempt to conceal the differences between us, rather the contrary, but then go on to say that through informal discussions I had found that the two parties had independently come to similar conclusions on certain important matters. You may be interested in the text of the statement I made. We finally left at midnight, exhausted but rather pleased with ourselves.'

Bob Hunter came in the next morning to hear about the meeting with Harry Nkumbula. He was furious about the police raid, of which he had had no knowledge. My diary noted, 'He was absolutely astonished at our achievement in getting Harry to talk practical politics with the CP, and said we had got further with him than any Europeans had yet done.' I had obtained a licence to hold a public meeting in Mufulira Town Hall that evening. There was an audience of about 50, half African and half European, and I was able to report on the understanding reached with Nkumbula.

As a counterpoint to the high politics of the CP, I was seizing any opportunity available to meet Africans on social terms. This wasn't easy on the Copperbelt since the colour bar ruled in all public venues. At Mufulira the Free Church minister ran a European-African Friendship Club which I started attending soon after arrival. Despite the Sunday school atmosphere, it provided a point of social contact. At Christmas he had a party –

'Dennis and I were dreading the occasion, but it turned out to be highly enjoyable, especially a vocal group who sang some delightful Copperbelt songs to guitar accompaniment: "Kiss Me" about women who go the beerhall and exchange drinks for a kiss; another about the man who comes to the village in a car at weekends and greatly impresses his girlfriend, but the car belongs to his employer, Costains.' I saw in the New Year judging a dancing competition in the Welfare Hall, as already mentioned. 'The events comprised the Best Dressed Woman, Jive and two divisions of ballroom dancing. Prizes included a cockerel, an enormous Muscovy duck, and a white billy goat which, like myself, was almost asphyxiated by the atmosphere, and then protested loudly when roused.' I had a dance with the competition winner who was subsequently dancing with Harry Nkumbula.

More seriously, within a few weeks of arrival I confided to my diary the ambition to set up a Current Affairs Association. The Welfare Office gave permission to use the Scout Hall, but counselled that it would be wise to call the venture a multi-racial club. On 21 November an inaugural meeting was held with 20 Africans present and it set up a steering committee. The first proper meeting took place in December, with myself as Secretary of the 50 Club, which was duly noted in the newspaper. Similar clubs were established around this time in two other mining towns. The problem at Mufulira was that there were only three white members. Even Dennis refused to join because he felt that it would compromise his worktime relationship with his clerks. 'I have been trying to convince him that one of the biggest things a multi-racial club can do in a company dominated place like Mufulira would be to demonstrate to Europeans and Africans that a social relationship can be cultivated as a complement to the Bwana relationship.' Driving one of the members back to Kansuswa Township after a social evening in January, Festus turned to me 'People are asking, Mr McWilliam, how you have become so famous in such a short time.' It is a sad commentary on the novelty of finding a European who can establish relations with Africans on a basis of equality and – perhaps this is the crux of it – have a similar political outlook.'

After a social event at Kansuswa where I danced a lot, trying to perfect the African rhumba, I learned subsequently that I had been given a nickname which translated to the same one I had had as a small boy at Kaptagat prep school – Jelly Bum.

My letters to Nuffield 'from the front' commenting on political events in Central Africa enabled Margery Perham to sustain sceptical concern at the way the new Federation was evolving, with supporting detail. She decided to pay a visit to Central Africa in February 1958 and to make a special trip to the Copperbelt. She went first to Lusaka to see the Governor, but her plane landed at Ndola en route so I made arrangements through Isabel to be there. 'We dived into a corner and chatted madly for ten minutes... I suggested she try to sabotage the official programme laid down for her at Mufulira on Thursday, so that I could take her to meet a few people who will not be 'official' spokesmen'. (My father was on the same plane on a business visit, and we were able to have dinner together that evening and talk about my ideas for getting out of the Copperbelt as soon as possible, which he supported). When Margery arrived at Mufulira, I was allocated ten minutes on the visit programme, but I then had a bright idea. The DC was a friend of mine and he agreed that I could drive Margery back to Ndola in my car, so we were able to have a proper conversation after all.

'We talked round and round the theme of whether there was any hope of avoiding walking the same melancholy path as Kenya with its increasingly uncompromising African nationalism.

It seemed that the only way to avoid it was for a very strong re-assertion of imperial authority, which would start by giving the Europeans a big jolt and firmly directing the country towards a free society. But even this is problematical, and very difficult politically because of Federation.'

Arriving at the house of the Provincial Commissoner, we met the Under Secretary of State, William Gorrell-Barnes on the doorstep (I had last seen him at a Nuffield seminar). Margery had the temerity to ask if I could stay for the official reception, and I had an enjoyable evening – right out of my station.

Eleanor

My Oxford chapter records that the idea of going for a studentship at Nuffield came from meeting Eleanor Glyn-Jones in 1954, having just commenced a studentship herself after being Margery Perham's research secretary. As my Copperbelt diary later recalled,

'If it had not been for my infatuation, I should never have been able to persevere with the Nuffield idea – convincing my parents, myself and Nuffield of my academic bona fides. I spent a weekend at Dyke House (her home) that Easter. But all the time I was uncertain whether she loved me, so much so that I dared not ask her. I knew that I had won her respect intellectually, which was quite an achievement, but for the rest I was at arms length. I took her to the Wadham Commem Ball, but my dreams of the romantic outcome came to dust.'

It turned out that Eleanor had fallen for someone who was already at Nuffield – Colin Morris, a Methodist minister with a charismatic personality, and she hardly appeared in College during my first year. I then fell for Isabel, as I have narrated. All these romantic disappointments were poured out to Morny Johnston, my housemaster's wife, on visits to Cheltondale in conversations around the drawing room fire or sipping a pink gin before dinner in the nursery.

There then occurred a rather amazing set of coincidences as Central Africa exerted a magnetic attraction on all three of us. On leaving Nuffield Colin Morris was appointed to a ministry at the Copperbelt town of Chingola, while Eleanor had actually secured a teaching appointment at the leading European girls' school in Southern Rhodesia – Chisipiti School in Salisbury. In early 1957 I went to Uganda to collect material for my tea thesis and while there received a letter from Eleanor to say that she was on her way out to the Copperbelt to marry Colin Morris and proposed stopping off in Kampala to see me. Not only that, but when she arrived I learned that the marriage would probably not come off, and that she was expecting Colin would break the engagement. I was staying at Makerere University with friends, and Eleanor and I spent a wonderful weekend out of time, talking, swimming, talking, visiting and still talking. God knows what effect it had on her, but all my old passion was reawakened.

And indeed, the engagement with Colin was broken off and he married another. In June Eleanor wrote to suggest that before starting my job at Mufulira in July I should fly first to Salisbury for a few days. This proved to be impracticable, so she then proposed to visit Mufulira in the school holidays in September for a week. 'I wonder how the next few days will go. In February when she stopped off in Kampala for the weekend on her way out to marry Colin Morris, it was just a crazy daydream to imagine that it might not come off. Now Colin is married to someone else! ... She knows that I was in love with her when I came to Nuffield, because I wrote and told her so when she told me about Colin.'

Arrangements for Eleanor to stay with a family fell through at the last moment so I had to book her into the somewhat Wild West Mufulira Hotel, run by a French manageress. 'I do hope she is a good girl,' she commented anxiously. But Eleanor spoke French to her and won her over immediately. The week passed in a torrent of political talk and activity and suppressed flirtation.

On the first morning, Eleanor took my car and drove to Chingola to make peace with Colin Morris, and later in the week he came over to Mufulira to have a drink with us. All very civilised. One of Eleanor's pupils was the daughter of the Mufulira General Manager, Frank Buch, who was at the apex of the social pyramid and I was much too junior to have met him yet. Eleanor phoned his wife and she and I were invited to family tea in the big mansion. General chat, cricket with father and son on the lawn, which exposed my inability to bowl, and his wife picked a gardenia for each of us on departing. At least Buch could now put a face to the troublesome left-winger in the African Personnel Department.

I tried hard to find a Congress leader for Eleanor to meet and eventually landed Albert Chiremba. 'None of the other Congressmen would come and compromise themselves, which is an interesting reflection on relations here. We met in my office as the only place available.' Later in the week I also got hold of the leading Capricorn African member, Jo Silwizya. My diary recorded the conversations in some detail, as well as the comment 'I only hope that Ross's CID does not find out about the meeting.'

I guess that he did, because on Saturday morning I was summoned to the presence of the Head and Deputy Head of the Department –

'Mr McWilliam, it has been reported to me that you have been meeting Africans in the office after hours and having political discussions.'

'Yes, Mr Twigg.'

'This is quite irregular and must stop.'

'There did not seem to be anywhere else to meet informally and to talk about current affairs.'

'Company premises are not to be used for holding political discussions and you should remember that you are an officer of the company.'

Given the prevailing culture this was perhaps a fair cop, and it showed rather pointedly that fraternisation across the race barrier was viewed with great suspicion. It did not seem to have occurred to me that I was perhaps putting my job at risk.

Through Eleanor's Salisbury contacts we were invited to Luanshya for dinner (and eventually to stay overnight) with Dr Fisher, the most prominent liberal on the Copperbelt, who had just resigned from chairmanship of the Federal Party in Northern Rhodesia. They had assembled quite a gathering of Capricorn types to meet Eleanor, including three Indians, and there was much talk of David Stirling's plans to launch a political party. Eleanor and I were very sceptical at this stage, as I have already noted. We left at dawn so that I could get to the office in time.

In that magical week, we would meet at lunch time at the mine swimming pool for a sandwich and a swim. My Oxford books arrived and Eleanor helped me unpack them and arrange them in the bookcase I had commissioned. I took her to dinner at a new French restaurant in Kitwe one evening. 'An enchanting evening and a splendid dinner: Petit Poussin peri peri; chocolate mousse, cheese and brandy. A bottle of Chateau Latour. A cigar. Wonderful to know that such a place exists on the Copperbelt. I scarcely dare express the thought, but I feel that Eleanor may come to love me.'

Another of Eleanor's pupils was the daughter of the General Manager of Kansanshi Mine, up on the Congo border, and we were invited for the weekend. On Saturday after lunch we set off 150 miles to Kansanshi over a stony road in my old Morris Minor. 'With 50 miles to go the radiator hose burst open. We bound it up with polythene bags and a bootlace, begged some water from an African homestead, and every time we came to a stream we stopped to fill up the radiator which boiled madly. Then one of the cylinders went too and we did not arrive till six o'clock.' It turned out that there was a misunderstanding over our arrival and we were not expected till Monday, not to mention that Eleanor's friend turned out to be male. Mrs MacFarlane took the situation in her stride, notwithstanding having three daughters home for the holidays plus a guest. Eleanor was taken in by a neighbour and I was imposed on the DC. We went to a dance at the club till 2 am. Nearly all the single women in Kansanshi were in our party, which made it the object of much attention. After dancing with one daughter –

'Thanks Denise, you sure made me sweat,' said one burly miner.

On Sunday morning we visited the old surface workings, where the ore body had been mined on several occasions since the 19th century. Meanwhile, a mechanic had restored my car to working order and we drove back to Mufulira in the afternoon, just in time for a farewell dinner party I had arranged with Madame at the Mufilira Hotel. Then up at 4.30 next morning to drive Eleanor to the airport.

My reflections on the visit and all those conversations reads sadly: 'We really did cover just about everything. The exception was our own relationship. I could not make up my mind to broach the subject. To talk about it would have meant defining it, and perhaps neither of us know where we stand at the moment. We have both got a lot to do on our own before we could think of getting married, and in any case the very idea has scarcely germinated. I may not have gauged Eleanor correctly, but I think that perhaps because of her own powerful character, she will only give herself to someone much stronger than herself. Colin was. I am not sure yet whether I am. She respects me intellectually and for what I have achieved, but I don't think I have sufficient weight of personality yet.

Despite her independence, Eleanor has quite an old fashioned outlook about the place of women in marriage.' Clearly, we had not got beyond being good mates, albeit with significant mutual attraction.

We exchanged letters during the autumn discussing the political situation, and then she went back to England for Christmas. 'A wonderful letter from Eleanor – a long intimate conversation, written curled up on her bed at Aldermaston; and for the first time she signs herself 'with love'. To complete the intoxication the pages exhaled that lovely scent she uses. The power of smelling is one of the most evocative of the senses; its special glory is the uniqueness of its associations.' She made plans to stop off on the Copperbelt for a few days on the way back to Salisbury – 'it is so hard to keep one's imagination in step with the slow pace of reality. Already in my mind we are lovers… It is four months since she visited me and now she is coming again. I wonder if at last reality can become more like the dream.'

Nine days later: 'Eleanor's plane was due at 6.40pm and so, with a 50 Club meeting at 8pm, I decided to take a picnic snack in the car which we could eat on the way back – sandwiches and peaches. Bathed and shaved and whizzed off at five. On the way I picked a bouquet of Rhodesian flowers: gladioli, gloriosa lilies, a royal blue trumpet, and a pale blue campion-like plant, and day-dreamed about our reunion, trying to guess what we might talk about and whether I should kiss her. The Viscount glided in noiselessly as it was getting dark and I waved as it taxied past. Soon the passengers were walking across the tarmac in the twilight in a straggling group. I waved again and then, unbelievably, I realised Eleanor was not among them. But of course she was just gathering up her bits and pieces on the plane. Two more women walked down the gangway, but they were only air hostesses. The door was shut. Bloody hell.'

It took some days for explanatory letters to arrive, during which time I imagined the worst. But the reality was prosaic: coming up from the country, a freak snowstorm had made Eleanor miss the plane and she had to wait a day for another flight. Phone messages did not get through. We continued to correspond. I planned a holiday with her in May, but this was overtaken by my precipitate departure from Mufulira in April. We never did meet again and correspondence petered out as I entered a new world – and relationship – in Kenya. I learned piecemeal over the years that Eleanor married a lawyer in Salisbury and that they had a family; that they moved to England to Exeter University after UDI; that she died from cancer in her fifties. There is left just the memory of an Oxford infatuation that blossomed magically at Mufulira and then was dissipated by separation and the distractions of busy lives a thousand miles apart.

At the beginning of November the Kansanshi Mine flooded and Anglo-American decided to abandon their attempt to resuscitate the mine. In late December Dick Hall, Dennis Acheson and I made a weekend trip to the ghost town, staying at the Solwezi guest house, and my diary provides a melancholy footnote to my romance with Eleanor –

'Gardens were beginning to become overgrown with a riot of flowers – the Macfarlane's one still looking lovely. The rest of the Copperbelt swarms with children, here there was only silence and clues to the past: a baby's chair on its side, a listless swing. Up at the mine the silence was even more penetrating. All those moving parts now still, and no dust. We peered down the main shaft and saw the rippled surface of the water barely 30 feet below us. Some machinery had been dismembered and moved elsewhere; more was in mothballs. An air of incongruous untidiness was given by pieces of abandoned equipment lying about in the open: two large tyres, part of a crusher, even a car. The gashes of the old Arab workings up on the slope above us seemed to make the hill smile quietly to itself at this, the fourth attempt to win its treasures; while scattered on the surface lay pieces of chalcopyrite, bornite, chalcolite and copper oxides to tempt man yet again. We took a beer into the deserted club, threw a desultory dart, read the notices.

'This morning Dick interviewed the mine secretary, and we learned some details of the last sad weeks. How bluff, hearty Macfarlane left a broken-hearted man. How the power plant failed on Christmas night and has not been restarted in order to save the shareholders' money. How the water failed this morning. By the end of January there will only be a caretaker and 25 Africans to preside over £1.5 million of investment written off.'

Breaking Out

It had taken only a few weeks in the African Personnel Department to realise that I was in a nonsense job; the problem was what to do about the predicament. By taking an intense interest in politics, writing about the situation to Nuffield and for the press, and joining in mine social activities through music and shows, I had attempted to extract some value from the experience of being in Mufulira. But there were still long days to fill:

'I am occupied on clerical duties that could be performed as well by my African clerk. I am doubtful whether many of them are even necessary.'

I tried to be philosophical about it –

'As a sort of rearguard action to defend my old personality I still wear bow ties and manage to keep my hair fairly civilized, despite the assaults of the club barber. The most difficult change is to settle into office routine: it is so incredibly tedious, with long spells of sheer idleness, that one wants to scream; and yet dimly in the distance one can see that it leads up to something interesting and important. So much in business seems to depend on an extensive experience of routines that are in themselves trivial, but it is hard not to fossilise before the opportunity arises.'

An old family friend, Meredith Hyde-Clarke, who had been Chief Native Commissioner in Kenya, and whose daughters went to Kaptagat School with me, was appointed to the Horneman Commission to investigate the industrial unrest on the Copperbelt. I managed to be his chauffeur one day to drive him over from Kitwe to visit the Mufulira management and our conversation confirmed my worst fears about my job.

'Surely you are not intending to stay here?'

'I thought I should give the job a chance for a year or two, and that I might be well placed if there was a shake-up.'

'You are far too good for this kind of job.'

My diary noted: 'He is very critical of the whole personnel management set-up. In fact, he says, the companies don't really know what the word means, and he has been very unimpressed with the calibre of the people he has met.' It was all very unsettling.

Shortly afterwards, my airmail *Economist* arrived and it carried an advertisement for a post of economist/statistician in the Kenya Treasury. I decided there and then to apply for the job and to ask Arthur Gaitskell and Professor Hicks to be my referees, with Margery Perham and Harry Johnston as personal ones (which they all agreed to do). 'I must not get too excited about the idea, though I can't help my pulse racing whenever I think of it. The possibility of a <u>real</u> job, where I would have to use my intelligence on important work has the effect of wine on a starving man. If at all, the Copperbelt is a place to come to when you can command some influence and really have a chance to tackle the many fascinating problems here; it is a wretched place to begin a career: no training, no scope, only long term prospects.... I am at another climacteric, like the ones when I decided to change from Botany to PPE in my first term at Oxford; and the decision to try for a studentship at Nuffield. I have been lucky so far, is it too much to expect it to hold again?'

As luck would have it, Prain visited Cheltenham the week before my letter arrived breaking the news to the Johnstons of my intended departure, and he had made a great point of telling them that he was very pleased with the reports he had had of me. Morny wrote, 'He explained to us in some detail why he could not, for your own good, contact you personally yet, but quite clearly there ain't much you do he doesn't know about and, up to when he was with us anyway, approved, but did also sympathise. He clearly had great hopes for you.' This made me feel bad for, after all, I had only been on the Copperbelt for four months. But the reality was that I did not have a meaningful job, and no one in authority had indicated either that this was a necessary apprenticeship, or that there was any career plan underlying it. Years later, after I got to know Ronnie Prain quite well, and after he recruited me to serve on the Cheltenham College Council, he would occasionally muse about might-have-beens. But given the subsequent nationalisation of the Copperbelt by President Kaunda, and the disappearance of RST as a mining house, there probably never would have been a great career path for me in Central Africa.

Meanwhile, my contributions to *The Examiner* as its Copperbelt correspondent suddenly led to my name being put forward to take over as Assistant Editor when Clyde Sanger left in January to join *Drum* magazine. Rather irresponsibly, I asked to be considered for the post, and the matter dragged on for a couple of months while the irresolute Editor dithered and eventually did nothing. Behind the scenes (I learned from Eleanor), RST – who subsidised the journal – was increasingly unhappy at its mounting losses, and it was closed down in the following year. It was a lucky escape.

I heard nothing about the Kenya Treasury job for weeks on end and, I suppose, must have lost heart somewhat. I was therefore in receptive mode when early in February 1958 I received a letter from Professor David Walker at Makerere, which started –

> 'I wrote to Ursula Hicks recently asking if she had any good economists she could recommend for a lectureship here at Makerere and she has strongly commended you to me and, moreover, has hinted that you might welcome a return to university life. I hope this is so.'

Although I had renounced an academic career on leaving Nuffield, this approach was flattering and I was now determined to escape.

I was able to talk to Margery Perham about the letter a few days later at Ndola airport, and she was much in favour of my going to Makerere (she was a member of the Inter-University Council for Higher Education Overseas, which oversaw the colonial universities), and I immediately wrote to David Walker. I explained that I had applied for the Kenya post, that John Hicks had written to me expressing some doubt about the set-up in Kenya (and urging me to keep my eye open for other opportunities), and that I was proposing to withdraw – with the approval of Margery Perham – and commit to Makerere. A few days later I had dinner with Professor Aidan Southall, who was head of the research institute at Makerere and was visiting Northern Rhodesia: he knew of the approach to me, had discussed it with Margery, and would do all he could to expedite matters.

The job seemed to be in the bag. I was on one month's notice at the mine. I decided to go to see my boss, Torrance, in mid-March to say that I intended to resign in May or June to go to Makerere, to which he responded that he thought I had made the correct decision. Matters then became rather complicated and fraught. First, I wrote to London to withdraw from the Kenya Treasury job, citing that I had heard that several of the Economic Research Division staff had resigned, and that I intended going to Makerere instead. Second, I received a raspberry from Margery for assuming that I had the Makerere job before the Inter-University Council had met. It suddenly seemed possible that I would end up with no job – having resigned from Mufulira, withdrawn from Kenya and failed to get appointed to Makerere. Third, I received a cable from Nairobi calling me to interview in April. I replied explaining the Makerere prospect and the concern over the resignations, and ending that I would still like to come for interview to understand the situation. This produced a robust response: by all means come for interview, but at your own expense, which would only be reimbursed in the event of being offered and accepting the job. My bluff was called in trying to keep two balls in the air at once, and I came to the decision that on balance I would prefer the Kenya Treasury to Makerere. I then applied for special leave to fly up to Nairobi.

Then came the bombshell. On Monday 7 April Mufulira turned down my request for special leave, but adding that if I still wanted to go to Nairobi I could take my discharge that weekend. I did. Clearly my continued presence in Mufulira had become an embarrassment to the mine. I did not have time to write up my diary until it was all over, but the narrative went as follows –

'The succeeding days were something of a nightmare, as there was not only the business of packing myself up, selling the car and paying income tax at Ndola, but also the problems of winding up my affairs with the 50 Club and the Constitution Party.

'50 Club Committee met on Tuesday to arrange programmes for the rest of the month and to make plans for the future. Unhappily there is a strong likelihood that the Club will collapse after I have left, because although there are several Europeans who would attend now and then, there is none keen enough to keep the thing alive.

'In Kitwe on Thursday to attend the executive meeting of their Club and to consider the memorandum I wrote. Had expected some difficulty, but opposition had melted and they accepted it as a plan of action.

'A talk with Stokes (the DC) on the White Paper and what had been happening in the CP. It is amusing how sympathetic the Provincial Administration is to us... and anxious that we should succeed. Stokes asked me to write him a memorandum on the White Paper. I didn't have time before leaving but will send something down to him.

'Over at Ndola paying tax, I called on John Adamson at his school. Harry Nkumbula had been to see him a bit upset about the statement I issued after our previous meeting. Apparently he had received a number of hostile telegrams from Lusaka, and was evidently trying to wriggle out. No doubt his position is a bit shaky, but he has no excuse for withdrawing since I discussed the points in detail with him in front of the Western Province Executive, not to mention all the others. However, I gave a copy of the full statement to John to pass on to Harry.

'A farewell meeting at the 50 Club on Wednesday, when Harry Makulu came to talk about his West African travels. My sadness at leaving Mufulira was entirely on the African side. I had made far more African than European friends and their despondency at my departure was very bad for my vanity. Unfortunately, it is all too true that I had 'got off the White platform' as Gaitskell puts it, more effectively than anyone else in Mufulira, and having seen this happen once there will be quite a bit of disillusionment. Stokes was quite concerned about this, as there was inevitably a certain amount of feeling that I was leaving them in the lurch.

'It was even sadder at Kansuswa. I went to have tea with John Taylor on Friday afternoon, and Francis and Festus came in later. I have a very special feeling for that town and the people in it – and they for me, since I was the first European to have mixed freely there and broken the stereotype of a Congress-ridden den of violence.

'I was holding a farewell party myself that evening in the Lehman's house for 30 people, beginning at 8. We had switched to beer at Kansuswa and I had difficulty in getting away so arrived half an hour late for my own party, sans supper. However I was in a rare mood of great elation, and the party was one of the best I remember, going with a terrific bang until after two, when all the drink ran out: 9 dozen beers, 2 whisky, 2 gin and a sherry! It was nice to have finished on that note.'

Twenty-five years later in the 1980s I visited Zambia, as it had become, in my capacity as group managing director of Standard Chartered for a meeting with President Kaunda to discuss the future of the Copperbelt. The nationalised mines were in poor shape. The chairman of Zambia

Consolidated Copper Mines was Francis Kaunda (no relation) and he had been a director of our local subsidiary bank. He arranged to fly me up to Mufulira in the company jet for a sentimental day's visit. It took ages to relocate my cottage, but eventually the image fitted, with the mango tree by the door. But now it was a mineworker's family house and there were several small children playing around. Due to the prevalence of migrant labour on the Copperbelt, the mines kept detailed records of all former employees against possible future applications for employment, which resulted in my discharge record being called up when I visited the mine offices. It recorded that I had resigned after eight months to go to East Africa and the form posed a question: would the mine re-engage the employee if he applied again to work there? The answer: No – McWilliam was unsuited to mining work. I was handed a copy as a memento.

5. KENYA TREASURY 1958

My parents knew that I was flying up to Nairobi from Lusaka on 15 April 1958 for an interview to join the Economic Research Division (ERD) of the Kenya Treasury, but in the rush of winding up my affairs at Mufulira I had not found time to tell them that my Copperbelt job had actually been terminated. They looked rather astonished when they saw me emerge from immigration loaded with tennis and squash rackets, clarinet, miner's helmet and other clutter. My interview next morning turned out to be pushing at an open door.[7] The Permanent Secretary was called out to another meeting, so the interview was with Geoffrey Ellerton, a former DC who had served in Kericho, and Cyril Martin who held the dual roles of head of the East Africa Statistical Department and Economic Adviser to the Kenya Minister of Finance, Ernest Vasey.[8]

My diary noted that Martin made a determined pitch: 'He explained that the ERD was not for people interested in pure research, as it was

---

7 This chapter draws on a contemporary diary and some surviving letters. My letters to Margery Perham are with the Perham papers in the Bodleian Library at Oxford.

8 Ellerton was a key figure in the transfer of power as secretary of the Council of Ministers; subsequently – as Sir Geoffrey – he had a distinguished business career in shipping and in the City, and he retired not far from our country home in the Cotswolds, where we resumed contact. C J Martin had worked as a statistician in the Cabinet Office under Lord Cherwell and made much of this connection. He was very ambitious and political and not liked by his staff, although I always got on with him. After independence he moved to the World Bank in Washington.

essentially a fairly high speed advisory body integrated into the Treasury. This pleased me a lot – I explained that if I wanted to do pure research I would go to Makerere, but was much more interested in financial administration and I asked if there were any vacancies in the Treasury proper. Ellerton said none at the moment, but I could always transfer later... (Martin) said the ERD had been a creation of Vasey's and as far as he could judge was the best of its kind in Africa.' He went to some lengths to account for the departure of the three members of the department as being unsuited to the work.[9] Martin 'emphasised strongly that to be a success in the ERD demanded good mixing and brain picking qualities; a capacity to switch quickly; and not minding that one's work was anonymous'. I drank all this in eagerly, and I was informed that I might be able to start at the beginning of May and so be involved in Budget work before Martin went on six months' home leave in June. However, there was then a prolonged delay, accompanied by some remarkable developments, which made my eventual appointment something of a cause célèbre, not to say a miracle.

The Treasury post was a secretary of state appointment and therefore had to be approved by the Colonial Office. At the end of May I went to see John Butter, the Deputy Secretary, to ask what was happening and was told that 'certain questions' had been asked about me, which sounded ominous. Earlier in the month during a visit to Uganda I had talked about the job with several people, including Walter Elkan at Makerere and Walter Newlyn, the government's economic adviser. 'They have all given a rather frightening picture of Martin and the ERD. To summarise: Martin is an extremely difficult person to work for, being jealous and possessive.' And with regard to his dual roles: 'In particular, his Kenya functions are subsidiary, but he objects to the ERD being used by anyone but himself.' All this very much corroborated Professor John Hicks's comments from Oxford. Nevertheless, both Walters advised me to go to the Treasury and see how things worked out.

There was then an unexpected complication. I received a much-delayed letter from Professor David Walker (head of the Makerere economics department) from England to say that the Inter-University Council had appointed me to an economics lectureship at Makerere at their April meeting (although this was unknown in Kampala when I was

---

9 They all went on to academic posts in Britain.

there in May). Given the problems my Treasury appointment seemed to be encountering, I wondered whether I should not opt for Makerere after all. I went to see John Butter again, which prompted him to send off another cable to the Colonial Office. I took the opportunity of asking whether my political past in Northern Rhodesia was an obstacle, 'remarking that I had no intention of concealing it or being ashamed of it, and that if there was any question of my entering the Treasury under any sort of cloud, with a dubious past, it would be better for me to reconsider the whole position. Butter was unwilling to discuss the subject, but he acknowledged that 'there was a question' of my political activities. For the rest he said that I was virtually certain to get the job and asked me to stay my hand for a few days more.' This now reads rather pompously, but perhaps it shows that I was conscious of my provocative conduct in the colonial context and was both proud of it and tempted to bluster. On 12 June I was summoned to the Treasury and told that the job was mine. 'Butter talked very nicely about my political activities – I was quite allowed to have friends amongst politicians of any race – in fact it would be a good thing. But I would have to be careful about what I said and what I revealed in the way of information.'[10]

A week later I received a letter from Walter Elkan to say that a major row had broken out between Makerere and the Uganda Government, who had objected to my appointment on seeing my security file and were proposing to declare me a prohibited immigrant. This exemplified the sensitivity of the colonial administration to a perceived threat of outside 'interference' when it was grappling with the fall-out from having deposed the Kabaka of Buganda, as well as explaining why I had never received an official letter of my lectureship appointment following the one from David Walker. The only thing restraining the university was a concern not to prejudice my new position in the Kenya Treasury. It was an extraordinary action by a government headed by the most liberal governor in the colonial empire, Sir Andrew Cohen. I brooded over the events of the past year, wondering what was so sinister about my behaviour: meetings

---

10 John Butter was in the ICS and involved in the horrors of partition at India's independence. He transferred to the Colonial Service in Kenya and was clerk to legislative council before moving to the Treasury, where I much admired his resourcefulness as Kenya grappled with the financial problems of impending independence. John and Joyce became friends and years later I saw them again in Abu Dhabi on a Standard Chartered visit where John was now the much valued financial adviser to the government.

with Congress members and with Harry Nkumbula? Publicly advocating that Congress should be brought within the parliamentary system? 'But I give up: there is clearly no hope of arguing with this secret inquisition, no means of challenging its verdict. Some bloody official has concluded that I am a Commie, or whatever the bogey is, and there is no one to gainsay him. It is a terrible commentary on British colonial administration.' Actually, a trivial explanation might be near the truth: the Constitution Party in Northern Rhodesia would be CP for short, and the Special Branch notes of our meetings, which were probably transmitted to Uganda as between colonial administrations, might well have used this shorthand and in Uganda this might have been read as Communist Party and reinforced the government's paranoia.

In the light of these events, it was all the more remarkable that the Kenya Treasury had taken me on. Margery wrote to say that she had sent a personal note to Vasey when the delay occurred. In July I met the Vaseys at a dinner party and he told me that after receiving Margery's letter he had read the file and failed to see anything startling. However, he did not mention to me that he had been to see the Governor, Sir Evelyn Baring, to get the matter settled, which he later told Arthur Gaitskell – with a message to be conveyed to me, 'that I shouldn't risk my career by playing George and the Dragon on Kenya politics, as I was doing in Rhodesia i.e. not to get publicly involved, and to bide my time and to keep to personal contacts. And that if I felt like exploding, I should come and see him personally, not as a minister, and let off steam.' This was a good illustration of Vasey's wise and liberal character.

How lucky I was at this stage of my life to have had influential mentors like Margery Perham and Ernest Vasey who could save me from the consequences of my enthusiastic engagement with the politics of independence in Africa. I have often wondered how I would have got on had the economics lectureship at Makerere gone ahead, with a career in academia, which Margery would have liked for me. The truth is that I wasn't a good economist and my maths was weak, and I don't think I would have made an intellectual mark. Yet, the academic world was intriguing and when I eventually came to run SOAS, it was an absorbing role. However, I might not have achieved such an appointment by going to Makerere. Meantime, joining the Kenya Treasury proved hugely interesting, and it also led me to Ruth.

With Ruth in 1958. Engaged, 1959

My father had arranged for me to rent for six months an empty guest house in the garden of a Brooke Bond house. These were quite a feature of Nairobi, since house owners with large plots were permitted to build a guest cottage for rent, which greatly helped to solve the housing problem for single people. I bought linen and crockery and cooked on a Baby Belling stove and was soon entertaining there with my Oxford recipes.

The Political Scene in 1958

Notwithstanding Ghana's attainment of independence in 1957 and the increasing tensions over the Central Africa Federation, Britain was still committed to a multi-racial strategy in Kenya as the Mau Mau Emergency drew to a close. This violent rebellion in 1952 by the Kikuyu people was put down through the intervention of the British army and with the imprisonment of its perceived leader Jomo Kenyatta, along with thousands of captured fighters. Subsequent research has shown that the rebellion had complex origins within Kikuyu society and its experience of colonialism, and that it had turned into something of a civil war. Nevertheless, the ending of colonial rule was clearly a dominant objective and all this provided a somewhat bizarre backcloth to Britain's policy of gradual constitutional reform.

Lennox-Boyd had succeeded Lyttleton as Colonial Secretary in 1957, following the first elections for Africans to join Legislative Council under a qualified franchise. Tom Mboya, fresh from a year in Oxford, had a trade union power base and was elected to the Nairobi seat. He quickly welded the eight African elected members into a formidable opposition group that demanded further constitutional change. Lennox-Boyd came out to Nairobi in October 1957 to finalise the next phase of reforms: increasing the number of African elected members to 14 and the number of African ministers to two. He also introduced a category of Specially Elected members, using LegCo as an electoral college, which was intended to demonstrate multi-racial backing for these members. Mboya persuaded his colleagues to boycott the elections for Specially Elected members (as being a distraction from further African advancement) and to refuse ministerial office, pending acceptance of further constitutional reforms, but he accepted the additional African seats for the elections held in March 1958.

This was the scene upon my return to Kenya in April 1958, and within days there was a major drama. Vasey was the originator of the concept for Specially Elected members and himself stood as a candidate, vacating his all-white Nairobi constituency. However, he was not liked by the conservative element in European politics for his liberal views (or by most of the elected members); meanwhile his natural supporters among the African elected members had decided to boycott this election. A number of the nominated official members of LegCo sided with the settlers, with the consequence that Vasey failed to get elected. He thereupon announced his withdrawal from Kenya politics, although the Governor persuaded him to stay on as Minister of Finance until he had seen through the 1958 budget.[11] There was much settler hostility towards Mboya and the African elected members, and indeed they were unwisely put on trial at this time for defamation which only enhanced their standing amongst Africans. Many government officials shared this hostility towards the African elected members, which I described in a long letter to Margery Perham, and continued –

'I feel very unpersuaded that the conduct of recent events has advanced the cause of multi-racialism in Kenya, or done anything but degrade the claims of European leadership here. If Tom has been unrealistic in his drive for 'undiluted democracy', surely all this passionate hostility is the worst way of dealing with him. Lennox-Boyd has rightly said that he cannot foresee the date when HMG will relinquish responsibility for Kenya, but it is tragic that he has felt unable to add more than an inane dispatch at the beginning of May, which defined the 'broad objectives' of policy in Kenya as: a prosperous country within the Commonwealth; the promotion of racial harmony and free opportunities; and the securing of individual rights of private property. If only he had made some attempt to allay African fears about the future pattern of society in a way that would show that the Rhodesian oligarchy was not going to be reproduced here, then the Africans might be induced to think seriously about the minorities problem. If only he had had the courage to say these multi-racial constitutions are but interim devices... But one could go on all night in this vein.'

---

11 I went to listen to the budget speech and a couple of nights later went to the local theatre where Vasey was playing the lead role in a Sacha Guitry farce, *N'ecoutez pas Mesdames*. Julius Nyerere, prime minister of Tanganyika, invited Vasey to be his finance minister under the new constitution, joining at the end of the year.

My experience in Northern Rhodesia had disabused me of any notion that entrenched rights for white settlers had a future. I was in the unusual position of knowing two of the African elected members personally from my Oxford days: Tom Mboya from his year at Ruskin College in 1955, and Jeremiah Nyaga from my undergraduate days when he was doing an education diploma and came to meetings of the East Africa Society. I had also met up with Tom on his return to Nairobi when working on my tea thesis and daringly had him to drinks at the New Stanley Hotel. Following a chance meeting with Jeremiah in late May, he invited me to lunch at LegCo. The group expanded to include Mboya, and three other elected members, Kiano, Mate and Ngala. It emerged during lunch that Jeremiah and Julius Kiano wanted to go to Kisumu the following day to attend a welcome home rally for Oginga Odinga, the charismatic leader emerging in western Kenya, but their transport arrangements had become problematical. I offered to drive them there, which was readily accepted. This was a great opportunity to get up to date and to gain some insight into the role of the African elected members, and I relayed details back to Margery.

Kiano and Nyaga had first hand experience of what was going wrong with the government's flagship land reform programme; in a word – corruption. The British administrative officers were in the hands of committees composed of interested parties, served by corruptible clerks, and there was an ineffective appeals process. This was tragic since the ambitious plans for raising rural incomes rested on granting land title to farmers where customary-use fragments of land had been consolidated into a single property. As constituency members of LegCo they were eloquent on police harassment. Africans were obliged to carry passes when moving out of their district, but the reality was that large numbers failed to do so and were vulnerable to frequent police raids. Again, Kikuyu found living in other parts of the country could be forcibly repatriated and dumped without any means of livelihood. I was greatly impressed by the time and effort devoted by Kiano and Nyaga to these personal stories, and conscious of how little this was understood by the whites.

While in Kisumu both Nyaga and Kiano were determined to purchase bead hats and cloaks. I teased them, but they were quite clear about the symbolism of a distinctive political dress that the elected members should wear, as a kind of badge of office. Interestingly, the bead hats, which were already being worn by Odinga and Mboya, were customarily only worn by Luo elders. I stayed at the Kisumu Hotel and the others at Odinga's hotel, but we had dinner together at mine and were joined by Mboya's and Odinga's agents.

Next morning I was collected for a political breakfast at Odinga's hotel. We were served a hearty 'English' breakfast and there was a jolly atmosphere. Odinga was benevolence itself and treated me like a Dutch uncle:

'I remember your father in Kericho during the war. How is he keeping?'

I almost expected him to give me a tip with a caution not to spend it all on sweets. I judged it wise not to attend the political rally to welcome Odinga (but 4,000 others did). At lunch time Jeremiah and Julius appeared with their hats and cloaks and said that they wished to stay on for the evening dance, so I decided to return to Nairobi and to respectability.

Margery's reply to my dispatch illustrated the intimacy of our dialogue, as well as concern that I should behave more like a civil servant (although I was still awaiting formal appointment) –

I find myself in general agreement with what you say, though perhaps I have more sympathy than you – surprisingly – seem to have for the settlers. So long as HMG shows so little sign of asserting itself and taking control, so long as the settlers are forced by the laws of self-preservation to fight with all the weapons that come to hand. And similarly, as you say, the Africans must reply in kind.

Generally speaking I feel depressed about our Government. We seem to drift equally in Malta and Cyprus as in Central and East Africa. It is this old British tradition that if you leave things alone they will sort themselves out. It may have been true of the compromising British, but it does not apply to these irreconcilable situations where only strong leadership and rapid action can control the drift to open conflict. But what can the Colonial Secretary, breaking down under the vast range of his activities and feeling himself short of both power and of money, contribute in the way of strong policy?

As soon as I got your letter I wrote off to Mr Vasey about you reassuring him – I hope truly – that when appointed you would settle down into being a well-behaved civil servant. But seeing how you have behaved in Rhodesia and now in Kenya, I begin to doubt whether I am right and whether you would not be happier in the academic setting. Even in that you would have to show a little more discretion I think. I had never thought of you as a revolutionary, except perhaps in the Oxford atmosphere, and I am divided between admiration and consternation. Write again soon.'

Despite becoming increasingly critical of Tom Mboya's hard line nationalist stance, I sustained good personal relations with him. In July he proposed that we should have dinner together. I was unsure where to take him and Tom proposed The Equator Club – the premier night club in Nairobi when the settlers were in celebratory mood. We dined on lobster cocktail and poulet poincarre, and had an enjoyable evening, with Tom relishing the sidelong glances at our table from the dancers. He told me that he was determined to break the present ban on a colony-wide party by using a legal loophole: each district association would take the same name and adopt the same constitution and coordinate as closely as possible in every other way. Tom himself had just formally assumed the leadership of the People's Convention Party in Nairobi. He also told me that he had given up drink; since he did not smoke either, it was an impressive example of self-restraint. It was commonly believed that African politicians quickly went to pieces over drink. My diary noted – 'That only leaves women!!' as Tom was then unmarried.

A week later Arthur Gaitskell was in Nairobi in connection with the proposed involvement of the Commonwealth Development Corporation with African tea growing, and I laid on a supper party for him in my guest house.[12] I am rather amazed now to see that I catered for 13: Gaitskell, the Vaseys, Farquarson (general manager of East African Railways and an old friend of Arthur's from Sudan), Alan Rake, Tom Mboya, Julius Kiano, Jeremiah Nyaga, and four girls. No wonder that I had a culinary reputation in Nairobi. My diary noted – 'Arthur thoroughly enjoyed himself, turning from high politics to frivolous chat, and was delighted that this kind of gathering could take place… Tom was emphatic in his support of CDC going into African areas, and undertook that the African

---

12 Gaitskell was a director of CDC and was particularly interested in promoting smallholder schemes. I had been sceptical of their applicability to African tea growing in my thesis, and was to be proved spectacularly wrong by CDC's role in Kenya, as acknowledged in my history of the Kenya tea industry, *Simba Chai,* published in 2020.

elected members would use their influence to overcome local suspicions. He was equally insistent that African participation should be a feature from the start, and wanted African shareholders.' I gave a similar dinner party for Margery the following year, with Tom as principal guest and Cherry Gertzel from Makerere was also there.

I ceased to keep a diary by 1959, as I became increasingly involved in my job and life in Nairobi, and my correspondence with Margery also petered out. However, I had been undertaking an economic survey in Central Province for the Treasury in connection with a proposed expansion of the Karatina electricity station and wrote another letter to Margery, 'One of the most worrying things about the provincial administration is their hostility to the African elected members. I kept hearing such remarks as 'We'll finish land consolidation by February if Tom Mboya leaves us alone.' If they run into some problem of popular prejudice, the LegCo members are not regarded as potential allies in overcoming it, but as incipient agitators who must be kept away at all costs. It is particularly silly in Central Province where they have such a good team as Doc Kiano, Jeremiah Nyaga and Bernard Mate.'

I concluded the letter: 'I have been enjoying life here in Nairobi more than I ever dared hope – both the job and outside it. The only nagging doubt is about the after-effects of "the affair". It seems to be rather widely known about in the Administration, and it is not altogether comforting to find myself known as "that left-wing chap who got into trouble in Rhodesia"!'

Margery's reply reflected the feeling of helplessness about Kenya in liberal circles in Britain, and she added a further titbit about the Makerere affair:

'As usual, I find your letter most stimulating. I cannot help regretting that you have not gone in for some kind of writing job, academic or journalist, because you do seem to get below the surface of things.

I was particularly interested in what you had to say about the settler contribution to the country's economy and the results of land consolidation.

I must say that I frankly do not see what should be done in Kenya or in Central Africa. This 'multi-racialism' is a kind of hoax and I fully sympathise with the Africans in refusing to have white colonists built into the constitution in a dominant status. At the same time, though

I admit we have always been wrong before in these calculations, it does not seem that the Africans in Kenya or in Northern Rhodesia are ready to take over. Nyasaland is a different proposition as it is compact and will probably weld itself into unity by the force of its opposition to Federation. The problem remains 'how to fill the gap'? The UK could do it if it went in with both hands and made it clear that it was not going to hand over to settlers or to Africans for the time being, but that it was going to have a thorough-going and dramatic plan for African betterment as well as courage, and I don't see this Government standing out against settler pressure in Central Africa or doing anything but a weak compromise for the next few years in Kenya.

Tom's game of perpetually sending out fireworks is I suppose quite a good one from his point of view. I have no idea whether there is any hope of the Government rallying 'moderate' opinion in the reserves etc, but all recent history proves that this attempt never comes off...

About your own position, I do agree that you must have been very worrying(sic). I should have thought the fact that you had (been) taken on in your present job would have cleared you completely, if you are now behaving with reasonable discretion! I don't mind telling you that I wrote to the Governor of Uganda and told him what I thought about it, but of course one can get no satisfaction, as under the law no reasons can be given for such action.

Is it true you are living alone without a servant and cooking wonderful meals?[13]

Cherry

My parents went on six months' home leave in May 1958 and soon after my return from Mufulira. This gave me the pretext to go to Uganda for ten days while awaiting an answer about the Treasury job, making the journey in a Brooke Bond tea delivery lorry. I went to see my Makerere friends, especially the economist Walter Elkan who I had met while doing research on my tea thesis, and also fellow Nuffield student Cherry Gertzel, who was now teaching in the department of Extra-Mural Studies.

Walter was a *kindertransport* émigré from Hamburg. He served in the

---

13 Yes. I took the view that having managed a flat in Oxford for three years, I could do the same in Nairobi, and did so until I married.

King's African Rifles in India towards the end of the war, and then went to LSE. He had come to Makerere as an economist at the Institute of Social & Economic Research, which launched his interest in development economics. Later, on returning to England he went to Durham and then to a chair at Brunel and we became good friends, with a strongly shared love of music. Cherry had an Hungarian/Australian provenance and was a dynamic member of the group of Nuffield students with a research interest in Africa, and it was she who taught me to dance the Charleston. Her academic career specialised in African politics, with posts in Kenya, Zambia, Manchester and eventually back to Flinders University in Adelaide.

After a week of activities with Cherry around Kampala, including a couple of dances and a visit to the tombs of the Kabakas of Buganda that were guarded by perennial wives, we made a trip to Hoima in western Uganda to see my Oxford friend Sarah Nyendwoha, who was now teaching there. The emotional temperature between us began to rise and by day seven we were in each other's arms. However, there was a problem, as my diary records: 'It was apparent that Cherry was under some restraint – sometimes it was like bringing Pygmalion to life, and then – like Cinderella – the clock would strike midnight and it was all over. On our last night she started with eagerness and then became infinitely sad and it all came out: she feels that she must not fall in love unless there is a prospect of getting married too, and she believes herself too old for me (30 v.25), so we must just be 'very fond' friends. True, I suppose. I am very fond of Cherry, but I kept feeling that it should have been Eleanor in my arms... What a legacy of sexual frustration to get into perspective.' Indeed.

A few months later Cherry visited Nairobi and stayed with me in the guest house, which meant more emotional strain. By then I was already working in the Treasury and had begun to fall under Ruth's spell and I realised that I needed to find an amicable resolution to our relationship and Cherry could sense this. An opportunity presented itself soon after when I was invited to be best man at an up-country wedding in Nakuru of two journalists whom I had got to know in Northern Rhodesia and were now working in Kenya. I proposed a rendezvous with Cherry at the Kaptagat Arms near Eldoret, to which I would drive after the wedding, and Cherry drove all the way from Kampala. We walked around the polo ground and the dam that was so familiar from my school days there and we reached an understanding that we could remain good friends. We had next door bedrooms and spent part of the night in a farewell cuddle, before going our separate ways next day.

Back in England in the early sixties and by now married to Ruth, we were invited to a dinner party in Bloomsbury by Kenneth Robinson – now director of the Institute of Commonwealth Studies, and Cherry was a fellow guest, having returned to England to a lectureship at Manchester. It was clear that evening that Ruth did not welcome a resumption of my friendship so we did not stay in touch. About a dozen years later, Cherry was teaching at the University of Zambia and I went to see her during a bank visit. She had baked a cake in my honour and it was a bittersweet occasion. I was now a family man with two children and Cherry had remained unmarried. We talked Zambian politics, but underneath shared memories bubbled up and feelings of mutual regard nearly broke surface. We met for the last time some six years later at a memorial conference for Margery Perham in Oxford when a number of former colleagues and students read papers. Cherry had flown all the way from Australia, where she was now a professor at Flinders University; our conversation was superficial and it was clear that she did not really wish to engage, which saddened me. The very lack of rapport, despite all the reminders on that occasion of our happy time at Nuffield, suggested that emotions and thoughts of 'might have beens' were being repressed by Cherry. One part of me would have delighted to revive a friendship and re-kindle her old vivacity. But I also knew that this was neither practicable nor wise.

The Nairobi Scene

I had moved into my guest house at the end of May 1958 when my parents went on leave, even though my Treasury job had yet to be confirmed. I bought a new, apple green Morris Minor for £588, having left Mufulira with £700 in the bank, so I must have been in confident mood. The budget debate was in progress in LegCo and I went there to listen to it and there encountered a Cheltenham College and Oxford contemporary, Alan Rake, emerging from the press gallery. Alan had edited the undergraduate magazine, *Cherwell*, at Oxford and was now editor of the East Africa edition of *Drum* magazine – the successful picture magazine aimed at the African market and launched originally in South Africa by Anthony Sampson. Alan introduced me to Nairobi's radical set and to the United Kenya Club.

At that time the United Kenya Club was the only multi-racial venue in Nairobi. Its weekly luncheons and occasional parties enabled one to get to know an eclectic range of people, several of whom became good friends. Alan, of course, was sympathetic to the figures emerging on the African political scene as restrictions on political activity were reluctantly lifted by the authorities and the Mau Mau emergency drew to a close. As already noted, the government was endeavouring to promote multi-racial politics and was deeply apprehensive of the emerging African nationalism that was being articulated by Mboya and his colleagues. Alan had the personality and charm to get on well with these figures and, in due course, he published the first biography of Tom Mboya.[14]

John and Joan Karmali were Nairobi's leading mixed marriage, having met in England as fellow pharmacy students. Although the Ismaili community was more open to western society than the more traditional Hindu and Muslim groups, the Karmalis had a hard time gaining acceptance for their marriage within John's extended family. They were a modern couple and worked hard in the social border lands of Nairobi society and were generous hosts. It was at their home that one was likely to meet the new African elected members and those emerging in the professions, together with liberal minded Europeans from the business community, journalists, the ADCs and personal assistants from Government House. John Karmali had a pharmacy business and also held the Leica agency. He was a leading wildlife photographer, especially of birds. He and Joan had been the moving spirits in founding a multi-racial primary school, against considerable foot dragging from the education department.[15] As Kenya's destiny as an African state became more imminent from 1960, Nairobi began to attract aid agencies and anticipatory diplomatic representation from India, America, Germany and the British Council. This added greatly to the interest of social life and the Karmali's house was one of the places to enjoy the emerging cosmopolitan atmosphere.

---

14 *Tom Mboya: Young Man of New Africa*, Alan Rake, 1962. Doubleday, New York
15 *Hospital Hill 1949-1973 – A School in Kenya*. Joan Karmali. Square One Pubications, 2002

Another generous host was J M Desai, a Nairobi businessman who had made it his mission to provide material support to the African nationalists and to facilitate the visits of Labour Party anti-colonialists like Fenner Brockway and John Hatch. He also hosted bridge parties where one was likely to meet Ernest and Hannah Vasey – a Jewish refugee from Vienna, with attractive worldly wisdom. Years later, on a bank visit, Hannah took me shopping with her friend Molly Rubin, and then to the cinema to see a film, *Prudence and the Pill,* a comedy about the new contraceptive pill.

Alan Rake was a member of a study group that had been set up by a radical member of the Christian Council of Kenya, Andrew Hake, and not long down from Cambridge. Its aim was to think about the economic implications of a transfer of power to an African led government. This was still a somewhat heretical concept in 1958. I was quickly empanelled and enjoyed its lively meetings. A bright graduate from Makerere attended several of them: Mwai Kibaki, who would later become President of Kenya. Another civil servant , John Parnell, was a regular member as was James Foster, ex-policeman and now personnel manager of the national power company. He was a devout churchman, socially conservative and yet strongly in favour of African political advancement. James stayed on in Kenya after independence and became a Kenya citizen and remained a good friend.

The study group published it report, *The Economic Development of Kenya* in late 1959. By then I was well-embedded in the Treasury and my participation had to be distanced, so I formally resigned from the study group and the CCK wrote to me 'the Report has been altered in such a way that you bear no responsibility for it in its new form.' I have recently re-read the document in the SOAS archives, where I had been able to arrange for Andrew Hake's papers to be deposited. In the study group we had been much influenced by the potential for government-led comprehensive planning, with India as prime example, so the crucial recommendation was for the establishment of a Planning Commission to mobilise and direct national resources. However, the overall tone was very balanced and moderate and was clearly aimed at persuading the powers that be rather than producing a radical manifesto. In fact, quite a lot of the drafting flowed from my pen as I put in many hours on drafting the report, and some of the text is repeated in my letters to Oxford.

I collaborated with Andrew Hake in mounting an extra-mural course for Makerere at Kiambu, entitled 'Choices We Face'. It looked at issues of planning, taxation, inequality and welfare, although most sessions boiled down to a discussion of how to achieve independence for Kenya. A candid letter from Andrew to the head of the extra-mural department in the SOAS archives conceded that we did not attract much of an audience –

'I am sorry to say it was poorly attended. The numbers fluctuated between six and nine, and on the third evening a torrential downpour stopped play altogether! We therefore feel that this should not really count as a Makerere class, and we certainly don't wish to claim our fees, but we feel the experience has been worthwhile for ourselves.'

Kenya was a great incubator for future executives of Shell, and I soon encountered both Cheltenham and Oriel contemporaries there. More exciting was to discover in their public relations department an eccentric young baronet, Thomas Chitty, who – as Thomas Hinde – was making a name as one of the 'angry young men' novelists of the era. Tom and Susan eagerly joined our non-conformist set and gave it great sparkle. There were adventurous safari weekends: one to see a waterfall on the Aberdare Mountains where we camped in a shelter and the drinking water froze at night; another into the northern frontier district to visit a place that was mined for salt by women living in caves in a hollowed-out hill, where my petrol tank sprang a leak from the stony track and it was repaired by a passing African with a piece of soap.

Tom wrote two novels around his experiences in Kenya and then left Shell for a writer's life. In *A Place Like Home*, the social setting is expatriate society such as he experienced in Shell, and there are some good vignettes of memsahib and sundowner party conversation about servants and Africans which reminds one with a shock how people talked at that time without embarrassment. In his next novel, *The Cage*, the main character is drawn from Cherry Gertzel who becomes involved with a young nationalist (modelled on Tom Mboya).[16] Susan Chitty also wrote a Kenya novel. *White Huntress* is a light hearted and witty skit on Kenya society, written around the adventures of two girls in search of

---

16 *A Place Like Home,* Thomas Hinde, Hodder and Stoughton, 1962. *The Cage*, ditto, 1962

rich husbands.[17] I recognised several of the events and locations: a tennis party weekend; a visit to Makerere; the social set around the Governor, Sir Evelyn Baring; and especially the portrait of the district officer who wins the heart of one of the girls.

I first met John Nottingham at Nuffield when he was on a sabbatical after a stressful period in the early days of Mau Mau. He was now a district officer near Nyeri and I had made contact soon after joining the Treasury and spent many weekends at his house at Ruringu. John had an exceptional understanding of the social and political tensions within Kikuyu society that lay behind the overt anti-white, anti-government Mau Mau rebellion: the class warfare between land owners (loyalists) and the landless (terrorists); the land grabbing dimension of the land consolidation programme that was being driven at breakneck speed by the provincial administration; and the strain of re-absorbing released Mau Mau detainees back into civil society. He was fast learning Kikuyu and was held in extraordinary regard by the people in his administrative division. John was later to co-author one of the first books on Mau Mau, placing it in its social and political context.[18] However, he was viewed as an eccentric, or worse, by his fellow administrative officers. Needless to say, he was sympathetic to the aspirations of the newly elected African members of LegCo, and he worked closely with Kiano, Mate and Nyaga – unlike his fellow district officers. Through talking to John one gained an exceptional insight into the post-Mau Mau scene in Kikuyuland.

Visiting John at his sparse bachelor house at weekends, we would sit by a log fire in the evening, Black Label Scotch to hand, and brood on events. The simple official narrative on Mau Mau of an atavistic movement riddled with revolting oathing and manipulated by sinister political figures, was hard to reconcile with what John was telling me. It was tragic that the activities of the new generation of Kenya politicians that I was getting to know were so compromised by the Mau Mau legacy. From my work in the Treasury I was privy to the initiatives being taken – with special funding form London – to plan for a better future for the

---

17 *White Huntress*, Susan Chitty, Methuen, 1963
18 *The Myth of Mau Mau: Nationalism in Kenya*, Rosberg and Nottingham. London and New York, 1966. After he resigned from the Colonial Service, John became a publisher and married into a prominent Kikuyu family, sending his daughters to English public schools (and one went on to SOAS). Forty years later, we resumed contact and he was very helpful over my research on the Kenya tea industry.

people of Kenya, but also of the difficulty of winning popular support in the polarised climate of Kenya's politics. There was a vociferous faction trying to safeguard white privilege and to resist moves to share power with Kenyans, let alone to see them in political control. Britain as the colonial power was in an invidious position and its compromises and reforms were attacked from all sides. John found himself increasingly at odds with official policy and blotted his copybook by refusing a posting to take charge of the rehabilitation programme for Mau Mau detainees.[19]

It was through John Nottingham that I got to know a prominent former Mau Mau leader, J M Kariuki, who wrote a remarkable book on his experiences, with a foreword by Margery Perham.[20] He became a minister after independence, but was then the victim of a political murder. As a result of this connection, I was one of the first white civilians to meet Jomo Kenyatta after his release in 1961 at a triumphal party in Nairobi City Hall. I was duly presented to Kenyatta and so experienced that famous penetrating gaze. During the evening I invited Kariuki's girl friend to dance with me (John had previously labelled her as the Madame Pompadour of Nyeri). 'Let's go,' she said, and I found myself glued from shoulder to thigh as we glided past Kenyatta on his throne.

Starting Work

Come June 1958, and I presented myself to the East African Statistical Department in the new High Commission building and was given a desk in its Kenya division. The Director, C J Martin, had by then gone on home leave. There was no specifically Treasury work indicated for me, and one could understand John Hicks's cautionary word about the role of the Economic Research Division, especially as I was not physically located in the Treasury. Instead, there was work to done in preparing material for the Statistical Bulletin and getting to understand Kenya's economic data series. The one surviving member of the ERD, Fitz de Souza, who was an executive officer, was an invaluable guide. I was introduced to the

---

19 Another district officer, Terrence Gavaghan, was allotted this task. I got to know him well in retirement. He devised and implemented a controversial programme that 'processed' a large number of detainees back to civilian life. But there was a violent dimension that led to the Hola Camp incident (in which he was not involved), and he felt he was made something of a fall guy by Kenya critics. He published a memoir: *Of Lions and Dung Beetles*. Stockwell, 1999; and also a fictionalised account, *Corridors of Wire*, privately printed.
20 *Mau Mau Detainee*, J M Kariuki. OUP, 1963

other members of the department. They included Duncan Ndegwa, an economics graduate of St Andrews, who was destined for a distinguished career culminating in Governor of the Central Bank; he also became a wealthy businessman, as became typical in independent Kenya.

I also met that morning, dressed in a turquoise linen dress, Ruth Arnstein, who was responsible for completing the first balance of payments calculations for East Africa. She was strikingly beautiful, with a blond pageboy hairstyle and a brilliant smile. Her features had been enhanced (as I subsequently learned, by England's leading plastic surgeon, who had straightened her prominent Jewish nose). Ruth quickly cast a spell over me and I became ingenious in devising stratagems to meet up with her. She enjoyed playing tennis and was intrigued by my new contacts in the United Kenya Club and in politics.

My first assignment for the Treasury itself was to undertake an economic survey to assess whether economic development in Central Province warranted expanding a government-owned hydro-electric plant near Nyeri. It was in a priority area for increasing rural incomes with new cash crops with special funding from the British Treasury.[21] Unsurprisingly, I came out strongly in favour of the investment.

A more serious engagement followed when a senior Treasury colleague wanted to make more use of economic data in briefing the Finance Minister and enlisted my help. We evolved a pattern of quarterly briefings on the economic situation, marked Secret in red to increase their allure, which were distributed to the Governor and Council of Ministers under the Finance Minister's signature. It was a brilliant ploy to compel attention and I laboured enthusiastically to help make the document an interesting read. The work got me known in the Treasury and made me au fait with what was going on, such that I soon developed a strong desire to jump ship to become an Assistant Secretary there.

In 1959 the Colonial Office announced that it was prepared to consider late entry applications to the colonial administrative service through a special appointments board, and I decided to apply. When it visited Nairobi in January 1960, its chairman turned out to be Sir Arthur Benson, the liberal former governor of Northern Rhodesia, who had intervened in the race row at the Mufulira mine club that I have

---

21 *A Plan to intensify the development of African Agriculture in Kenya.* Government Printer, Nairobi, 1954

described. He would therefore have recognised me from the application form. He took an active part in my interview with the board, which went on for an hour and a half. I was accepted to transfer into Her Majesty's Overseas Civil Service, with the rank of assistant secretary, and this was implemented almost immediately. My initial schedule of responsibilities included the education vote, income tax policy and the public debt – all instantly absorbing as one was introduced to the rituals of inter-departmental correspondence and minute writing. The great thing about Treasury procedure was that one was encouraged to advance views on important topics without danger to the outside world, since they were sifted by senior officers before decisions were taken.

Ruth

An office romance was slow in taking off, not least because Ruth had been in Nairobi since April 1957 and already had a wide circle of friends and admirers and was having the time of her life – beautiful, brilliant and with a touch of the exotic from Jewish Vienna. She had rooms with another Viennese émigré, Inge Brown, now divorced and living with a teenage daughter and running a poultry business, Quality Eggs. Inge also had admirers and doubtless was somewhat jealous of Ruth's attractions. Some incident, never explained, led her to expel Ruth without warning one day. I had become enough of a swain for Ruth to turn to me for help in removing her belongings to the house of a colleague of ours until she could find a guest house. My increasing fascination with Ruth made it easier – as well as essential – to bring my relationship with Cherry Gertzel to an amicable conclusion. Cherry had already visited Nairobi after I had joined the Treasury and Ruth was aware that there was a history between us. Hence the Kaptagat assignation that I have already narrated.

By late 1958 my ingenuity in finding occasions to meet Ruth and to do things together had begun to bear fruit, and she became my recognised girlfriend and we kissed after outings. Ruth had been learning to ride a horse and she arranged to stay on a farm in Sotik (not far from Kericho) for a few days in November. I went home to see my parents for the weekend at the end of her visit and Ruth agreed to come and meet them on her way back and spend the night. I slept in a tent in the garden and Ruth had the guest cottage.

'A nice child, not terribly pretty but unusual – made me think of the face of Mona Lisa,' my mother wrote in her diary afterwards. My mother was evidently in some difficulty over making up her mind about my girlfriend and she devoted rather more space to what we ate for dinner.

We had to drive back to Nairobi in convoy in our own cars. Following this visit, Ruth accepted an invitation to come to Kericho for Christmas, along with Alan Rake. We drove up together in my car and Ruth mainly remembered the journey for the furious political argument between Alan and myself for most of the journey over the tactics of Tom Mboya and the African elected members.

Ruth was a sensation at the Christmas dance at the Tea Hotel, where she wore an off-the-shoulder, shocking pink petal dress. Alan caused a different sensation when sardines were played after a dinner party and he got into a cupboard with a young innocent who did not appreciate his advances. Another day we took fishing rods and a picnic to Elephant Pool on the Itare river and there are some evocative snaps of the outing.

Not long after this something went wrong with our relationship; perhaps I had taken too much for granted that Ruth was 'mine'. At any event, she was suddenly not available for dates and then to my horror I discovered that she was going out with someone in our tennis group and that I had been dropped. Miserable weeks ensued, made more humiliating by the expiry of my guest house lease so I was living at Muthaiga Club with my parents until a new guest house became available, and while they were waiting for a house in Nairobi after my father's departure from Brooke Bond. I rebuffed any tentative questions, asserting grumpily that Ruth was 'just an office friend'. She and I were still working in the same office building and only a few rooms apart, so our estrangement was grist to the office rumour mill. There was no confrontation and we just avoided each other.

One day towards the end of March Ruth asked me to call at her guest house after work and I drove there a prey to wild thoughts. She explained quite calmly that she had become pregnant by George Delf and that she was proposing to fly back to London to her parents to seek an abortion, but she needed help to achieve this and to deal with the office. I did not attempt to probe the situation, apart from taking in that the affair seemed to have ended. Instead, I sprang into action. I bought her an air ticket next day and took her to the airport, and then went to see C J Martin and spun him a story that Ruth's father had had a heart attack and she had taken the first available plane. A colleague and I packed up her belongings and he took them into store at his house.

George Delf went into denial, feeling no responsibility to help Ruth either emotionally or financially, so did not distinguish himself. But what about our relationship? I wrote long letters to Ruth that have not been saved, but I retained the five letters she wrote to me from London. She was there for almost exactly a month. Her first letter thanked me for the telegram that I had managed to send to her at Entebbe airport in Uganda on the way home: 'Everything seems so peaceful here after Kenya'. As to the pregnancy, 'No one here treats it as a tragedy, so I feel you would be wrong to do so too.' And she ended, 'Write soon and keep well.' All the letters ended 'Love, Ruth'.

Unsurprisingly, Ruth's feelings about George fluctuated sharply. At one moment not wanting to be too hostile, at another she was scathing over his irresponsibility for starting an affair when his real girlfriend was about to arrive in Nairobi. Ruth's mother took a very broadminded view and was not inclined to be censorious; she said she was reminded of the Heine poem in Schubert's *Dichterliebe* (*Ein Jungling liebt eine Madchen*), where a young man is jilted by his girl and then marries another on the rebound, which leads her to do likewise and the young man is heartbroken. I remained pretty hostile to George and went to see him to stump up some money. Ruth plunged frantically into the London scene of concerts, theatres, exhibitions and shops and found it hard to respond to my renewed declarations to her. The nearest to her state of mind came in mid-month, 'I hope you are not feeling too depressed are you? I can't tell you how wonderfully I think you have behaved over the last few weeks. I can't imagine at all what you feel about everything. If you think it would help at all to write about anything then please do. I have tried to write to you several 'letters of substance', but when I have covered five pages I find that most of what I said wasn't really true, so I tear it up again. Honestly I don't know what I feel about anybody or anything at the moment. Most of the time I don't think of any of it but just enjoy London! Terribly escapist I am afraid, but it's the only true statement I can make.'

Ruth had a nervous relapse a few days before she was due to fly back to Nairobi and her mother nearly stopped her departure. But Ruth was resolved to return, partly because she did not wish to risk forfeiting her entitlement to long leave at the end of the year. Her last letter concluded, 'I am looking forward to seeing you again, I hope everything will sort itself out somehow. With love, Ruth.' We never mentioned George Delf thereafter.

Ruth arrived back in Nairobi at the beginning of May 1959. I had booked her into a government hostel, Thika Road House, until new lodgings could be found. It was pretty austere and after a few days she moved into an hotel not far from my new guest house in Westlands, and from there to the annex of a substantial mansion. A whirlwind courtship ensued – but how and when to pop the question? Perhaps as a sign of problems to come, I found it hard to articulate my personal feelings and I was probably also made apprehensive by the personality that had been revealed in her affair. It became apparent that Ruth was waiting for a formal proposal and I was finding it hard to choose the occasion. At last, on the night before my 26th birthday, sitting in the car after returning from an outing, I asked Ruth to marry me and she accepted.

The following day we went round to my parents at lunchtime to announce our engagement. They gave a celebration dinner party soon afterwards and we chose records of Beethoven's *Archduke Trio* as their engagement present. Ruth said that her mother would pass on to her a lovely sapphire and diamond ring as the official engagement ring, so I bought a gold bracelet set with topaz stones from my exiguous resources. The ring arrived by post in time for Ruth's birthday on 11 July, when our engagement was announced officially. We had an office celebration and Ruth's landlady hosted a super cocktail party at the weekend.

We were, I suppose, quite a glamorous couple in our circle and we were much felicitated over the next few months before Ruth's home leave fell due in December. We saw a lot of my parents because, in order to save up for the wedding, I gave up my guest house and went to stay with them. Our plan was to marry in London in March 1960 before the end of Ruth's long leave, when I would take local leave and fly to England. A substantial complication then arose, triggered by Ernest Vasey. He was due to take up the post of Finance Minister in Tanganyika in early 1960 and raided the Kenya Treasury for talent. A senior colleague had agreed to go, and then Vasey approached me in November to join his economic planning team, which was very flattering. I was desperate to get out of the moribund Economic Research Division, but could not be confident

With Suzi and Fritz in Vienna. Wedding, 1960

at that point that I would be successful with the Secretary of State's appointments board when it came out to Nairobi in the new year. Ruth and I agreed that Tanganyika appeared to be the more reliable exit, but was Vasey in a position to deliver?

Uncertainty over the possible appointment paralysed our wedding planning and Ruth's letters from London began to get a bit desperate. Eventually we decided that I would fly to England on 1st February on seven weeks' local leave and get married on 5th March and that we would have a touring honeymoon on the Continent. I would then fly back to Nairobi and Ruth would come out by sea with the car and our wedding presents. In London I stayed with a Viennese friend of Ruth's parents until the wedding at St John's, Hampstead. My parents were unable to come to England for the occasion and my only relative there was Aunt Gladys. Patrick Sellors was my best man and on the evening before the wedding we dined out in Charlotte Street and I gave him my collection of bow ties. On the continent we drove to the Riviera in wintery conditions in our new Simca and got stuck in snow in the Maritime Alps behind Nice and had to be rescued by a tractor. Our destination was Santa Margherita on the Ligurian coast, before turning back to France and Paris. There, I had the humiliating experience of asking a waiter for some water and being told the time in response.

I had written a rather tough letter to Vasey explaining that although my preference was to go to Tanganyika, I was concerned about the procedure and actual availability of the post and that if I was offered the Kenya Treasury post by the appointments board in January I would accept it. I met Vasey at the United Kenya Club and he told me that I could consider the job as definite and that there would be a job for Ruth as well. However, by the time I flew to London on 1st February there had been no further news whereas the appointment to the Overseas Civil Service had come through. While in London I had the temerity to seek an interview at the Colonial Office to ask about my future and was firmly put in my place: it was not for me – a junior official – to try to arrange my own career path, which would be decided by higher authority. In the event, nothing transpired about Tanganyika; meantime I had purchased a tropical suit, thereafter known as my Dar-es-Salaam suit. I remained on good terms with Vasey over the years when, in retirement, he became special adviser to an Indian business group, the Chandarias, as they built up a substantial international group on the basis of their original Mombasa plant making aluminium hollow ware. I encountered them again both at Standard Chartered and at the Commonwealth Development Corporation.

One of my unrealised ambitions has been to write a memoir of Vasey, especially his role as Kenya's finance minister in the 1950s. I brought back to England a substantial dossier of Treasury material, which I eventually deposited with the Bodleian. I also encouraged Joan Karmali to write a more personal memoir and she did quite a bit of work before giving up and handing over the material to me. In turn, I placed this in the SOAS library and only recently discovered that the papers had been transferred to the Bodleian's colonial records as well. Meantime I have drawn attention to Vasey's importance in my chapter for the Oxford History of East Africa and also in an essay contributed to Margery Perham's festschrift (see below). I wrote *The Times* obituary.

St Michael's Road

Ruth's journey back to Kenya by sea was prolonged by the continued closure of the Suez Canal following the Suez Crisis and coming round the Cape took a month. I went down to Mombasa by train to meet the Union Castle liner and watched it steam into Kilindini harbour from the golf course. After some hours we were on the slow night train back to Nairobi to stay at Muthaiga Club for a while until our kit arrived and our new home was ready. Ruth had had a great adventure on the way out when, at Durban, she had disembarked to spend the day with relatives from Vienna. Following some row between the ship's captain and the port authorities the liner left before the advertised time, and without Ruth on board. Fortunately, the first officer noticed her arrival at the quayside and stopped the ship until a pilot's launch could bring Ruth alongside. She was then expected to clutch a rope ladder in the open sea and clamber on board. On declining such a feat, an able-bodied seaman was mobilised to carry her. There was then a great issue as to whether she should be surcharged for the delay, which divided the ship, and she also featured in many an East African snap album as the passengers crowded to watch the episode.

I had found somewhere to live while Ruth was on leave. Our first home was a ground floor flat (one of four) in a newish building designed by a local architect who lived above us, and set in a large plot. With my parents' help we recruited Mulamu to cook and clean for us. St Michael's Road in Westlands was close enough to the centre of town for us to return home for lunch each day; alternatively, we could go to the weekly lunch at the United Kenya Club, or to Muthaiga Club for an occasional treat if there was an overseas visitor to entertain. There was a lot of evening socialising, but weekend activities were the high points, even with Saturday morning office hours, with visits to friends in the colonial administration and adventurous picnic outings. Life in Nairobi was highly enjoyable. We had a cosmopolitan circle of friends and a lively social life, with no family responsibilities as yet. Both Ruth's job and mine in the civil service carried considerable responsibilities and were intensely interesting. The uncertainties caused by the announcement in 1960 of self-government with independence to follow in 1963 was also a stimulus to make the most of the present.

The Rupture with Brooke Bond

Brooke Bond at that time was very much a family-run business and there were several Brookes in the firm. My father had been something of a protégé of Gerald Brooke the chairman in the 1930s, but he had now been succeeded by his son John Brooke, who was not a strong personality and whose hobby was collecting fungi. Gerald Brooke's brother was in charge of the printing factory in Reading and his son, Oliver, now worked in Kericho. In the post-war period a forceful personality, Tom Rutter, and himself the son of a Brooke Bond director, emerged as the power in the firm and became deputy chairman. His brusque methods struck terror in Kericho and he was ruthless in weeding out low performers. At some point he must have determined that father was not delivering what he expected as head of the East Africa marketing function and had become an obstacle to his plans. His solution was brutal.

My mother started keeping a diary in 1958 and five volumes up to 1962 have survived various house clearances. They are a kind of commonplace book, with a continuous record of the weather, of menus and dinner party guests, of every fishing trip – her great recreation, and they mostly capture the surface detail of life. She did not use them to communicate her thoughts and feelings, except very occasionally, or to explain 'for the record' what was happening to them, or what other people said. Yet during these five years Pa had his career terminated, Jenny and I had somewhat complicated courtships before getting married, my parents moved to Nairobi to a new life and made plans to retire to Gloucestershire instead of to the Kenya coast, as originally intended. Tantalisingly, there is only very circumstantial evidence to go on and one eternally regrets the missed opportunities in later years to unravel their history. Margaret had a remarkable capacity not to dwell on the past and to live for the present, which rather discouraged much curiosity.

At the beginning of 1958 Rutter and his wife spent nearly three months based in Kericho and there was much mutual socialising, with no hint in the diary of any difficulties, except once towards the end of their stay when Ann Rutter snubbed Margaret. One notes also that Rutter made a visit to Rhodesia with two executives and excluded Pa. My parents left for home leave in England on 7 May and commenced a happy leave in a rented cottage near Minchinhampton, collecting a full complement of wild orchids from favourite sites they had discovered over the years. Pa paid his obligatory visit to head office on arrival, 'where he had a wonderful day, everybody friendly and no atmosphere or adverse criticism'. They were invited to spend a night at the chairman's home at the end of the month. This was evidently something of a relief, for Margaret commented a bit later of Pa having been 're-instated at the London office.'

On 27 June a letter arrived from John Brooke asking questions about company labour having been used to maintain their large Kericho garden (itself a company property) and going on to disinvite them both from a company dinner in early July. Margaret noted, '(this) may have serious repercussions. Feel a mountain is being made of it deliberately... Now this will put Dougal right back where he was before.' It seems therefore that there had been some earlier upset. On 3 July there was a further letter from John Brooke terminating Pa's employment, without any further explanation. It took more than eight weeks for the severance terms to be clarified: Pa was deemed to have resigned and was to receive six months' salary from the end of his leave. There was to be no pension, only the payout of a modest provident fund which would not yield anything like a satisfactory income. They were to vacate the Kericho house at the end of the year and pay their own removal expenses and no return passage to England was offered. No announcement was made to Brooke Bond staff in Kericho, the news just crept out. My parents had no property of their own and almost no savings, as they had been living up to their income (and educating Jenny and me in England). Pa was coming up to 54, and in the normal way would have had one more tour before retirement. Their assumption up to that time was that they would retire in Kenya.

'Devastated' is an over-used word these days, but it correctly describes my parents' state of mind and this comes through in the diary, despite Margaret's aversion to introspection. In these months she notes quite often that she had been unable to sleep. Pa did not have a face to face meeting with either Rutter or Brooke and did not attempt to fight the decision, fearing that it would only worsen the severance terms and his prospects for further employment. He was already suffering quite marked chest pains at this time, which the company doctor persisted in asserting were not heart related (although he was to die of a heart attack eleven years later). One cannot help speculating whether his health condition had begun to affect his work adversely, as he had become much quieter and was inclined to be moody. In June 1958 I had just begun my new job in the Treasury and wrote urging a more aggressive stance, which at least helped to boost their morale. Jenny was working in the Brooke Bond head office in Kericho and found the situation quite difficult. She dropped out of social life for a while and this seems to have precipitated her relationship with John Black, a former Kaptagat schoolmate who had recently joined James Finlay on one of their estates. Under company rules he was not allowed to get married on his first four year tour.

Pa's inclination was to retire forthwith to England and they began to build castles in the air over buying a house in Frampton Mansell where brother Jim lived. However, their financial situation eventually made him realise that he needed to continue working in Kenya for a while longer in order to build up some savings, and his two brothers strongly urged this. Pa was not a great networker in the Kenya business world, but he had a reputation in government circles from his wartime job as Food Controller and then as a member of the Tea Board. He received two encouraging letters from ministers (Michael Blundell and Arthur Hope-Jones), which somewhat allayed his anxieties over the future and they returned to Kericho at the end of October. Pa was introduced to the head of Mitchell Cotts, a long established agency and merchanting business in East Africa and the Middle East, and a job was confirmed to start in February to develop overseas markets for agricultural exports. Everyone was very nice to my parents, but with no official explanation of his defenestration, there were some embarrassments. There were just two months, including Christmas, to pack up and bring to a close their twenty-seven years in Kericho, and all their married life to date.

Margaret wrote a remarkable three page letter to John Brooke – a moving retrospect of their time in Kericho and what had happened to them. She describes their homecoming from leave: 'everything spic and span and smelling slightly of polish. Wide smiles from our boys, and news of their families... We relaxed at last and gazed down the garden, a riot of colour. This garden that has caused such heartbreak.' She recalled the early days: 'Twenty-seven years ago we lived at Cheboswa in a little two-roomed house with a tin roof. What excitement when we were told we were having a new house built of concrete blocks. Several times a week we walked three miles over there to see how the house was progressing and while the house grew the garden was born.' The garden became well known and part of the life of Kericho: 'We received letters from strangers saying they had heard about our garden and could they come and see it.... Armfuls of flowers were given away frequently for happy and sad occasions, bouquets for brides... a wreath for the Company every year for Remembrance Day. Flowers for the church.' Then to the nub of it: 'For years and years the garden has been more than our staff of four could manage, especially as Dougal is away so often, at least once every month. For years and years any Factory labour that was idle was sent over to help with tidying up, always leaves to be swept and paths brushed and the boundaries kept neat and tidy... Everyone has known about the Factory labour being used on the precincts of this bungalow, you knew too.' And then to England on leave in May and John Brooke's two letters. 'Be gone! Two more months and out you go. No personal interview, just the report of a junior in the firm, sent to London. This report about a man who has been thirty-two years in the firm and a Director for over half of them. Thirty-two years of true and loyal service'... 'I can't help thinking the reason for Dougal's dismissal is not the real one, but the only one you could find.' In conclusion, 'It is all very difficult to understand. I would like to think one day, however far away, we shall meet again and you will tell us both simply and honestly, just what exactly and where we went wrong, because I am in this too.' Her letter was never responded to.

Settling into Nairobi was not all that easy for my parents. The new job with Mitchell Cotts was slow to develop and there seem to have been quite long periods when Pa did not have anything to do and he became quite frustrated. Luckily, he was still a government appointed member of the Tea Board and he enjoyed attending the quarterly meetings back in Kericho, although Margaret did not always go with him. Remarkably, Pa appears not to have harboured resentment over his dismissal from Brooke Bond, and he remained on good terms with his former colleagues. Owich and Adienge, their two long-standing servants, transferred to Nairobi, which was a great boon to Margaret, but she became easily depressed and was susceptible to heavy colds that were hard to shake off. It was fortunate that their house was within walking distance of the Arboretum, where they went most evenings. A favourite weekend outing was to take a picnic to the Mua hills at Machakos. Kericho friends came to stay and there were frequent visits to the cinema and the Donavan Maule repertory theatre. Ruth and I saw them for tea or lunch pretty much on a weekly basis. Margaret worried over Jenny's future until her engagement to John was announced in November 1959, and then worried about the venue for the wedding until it was eventually arranged to hold it in Kericho, with the reception in our old home and garden.

Compared with the intense social life they had been used to in Kericho, Nairobi had its vacant patches, and one has the impression that they were fundamentally unsettled. Margaret had lost the will to be a corporate wife and did not wish to engage with the Nairobi business community. A rare outburst in September 1959 revealed her feelings, when a Mitchell Cotts director was due to stay for a week and then Pa mentioned that his wife would be accompanying him. Margaret put her foot down and refused: 'Dougal thinks I am most unreasonable and uncooperative – I ought to be able to take these things in my stride. I'm willing to admit I'm at fault, but I KNOW I can't take it. Maybe something to do with having a bellyful of that sort of thing for years past with B.B.s – duty dinners and visits. I loathe them. For God's sake! Can't we live the lives we want to at our age? I sometimes wish Dougal had never taken on the job and we were living in our little cottage in England. There, I have said it now and mean it. When we went through those awful months at home last year, though they were grim enough at first, Dougal and I grew closer together spiritually than we have been for years, and we were very happy in each other's company. Now this job is taking him away from me again and I will have to wait until he is sixty before we can do things together. When he left me this morning he kissed me and said – sorry about this – I will find a way out – it was so sweet of him – I wept. I feel old and tired and unsociable, which to be quite fair isn't a natural thing for me. I want to be allowed to live quietly in our very own home – to have time to do things I want to do in the house and to have the children there with their friends, and enjoy their company and perhaps one day I may become the person I used to be.'

Assistant Secretary, Treasury

My new job at the Treasury got under way in March 1960, on returning from the wedding. It was completely engrossing as to the files, but it also carried prestige in our social circle and it came with some engaging external roles.

Education was on my schedule and I found myself a governor of the two leading settler girls' schools. The Kenya High School, or heifer boma to the irrelevant, was under the redoubtable leadership of Miss Stott for some fifteen years. Ruth and I were duly invited to Speech Day (hats and gloves), evoking memories of our own school occasions. Ruth promised not to giggle providing they did not sing 'Jerusalem' at the end. From my seat on the platform I spied the music teacher tiptoeing towards the piano and, indeed, '*And did those feet in ancient time*' soon rang out in this Kenya hall. The event at Limuru Girls' School had a different flavour, as the preferred school for up-country parents where the girls could keep ponies. There was a nativity play and the wise men arrived at a canter through the wattle plantation; shepherds sleepily watched their flocks in a clearing until awakened by angels in white nightdresses standing up in the bracken, singing their carol and clutching arum lilies, one of which was held by the music mistress, who beat strict time.

That winter the headmistress, Veronica Owen, was faced by a parental revolt. Following the announcement earlier in the year of self-government under an African prime minister, she decided to make plans to admit African girls to the school. Rumours swept the Highlands that this would lead to the moral degradation of their daughters, and someone had the bright idea to circulate juicy passages from Malinowski's *The Sexual Life of Savages*, under whom Jomo Kenyatta had studied briefly at LSE. A parents' meeting was convened in Nairobi and the school governors were bidden to attend. Most of them ignored the summons but, as Treasury representative, I felt bound to go and became the focus of fierce attack. I saved my bacon with a line of argument that as a Kenya settler's son I could understand the fears, but that (speaking for the government) the school would ensure that proper standards were maintained at the school. Veronica and I became good friends.

The preparations for independence in all three East African colonies placed strains on the working of the East Africa High Commission and the customs union, since both Uganda and Tanganyika felt that Kenya was gaining disproportionate advantage from the arrangements. Not only were all the main inter-territorial institutions based in Nairobi, but Kenya was clearly evolving as the business and manufacturing centre for the region and this evoked jealousy. A commission was established under the chairmanship of Sir Jeremy Raisman, former finance member of the Viceroy's council in India. I was made the point man for Kenya to prepare and coordinate our submissions to the commission; it was a fascinating task.[22]

The 1960 Lancaster House conference, which accelerated Kenya's independence timetable to 1963, resulted in a financial crisis in the country and was a major challenge to the Treasury. The flight of capital from the country destabilised its financial institutions and torpedoed the Treasury's assumptions for tax revenue and the financing of its development programme. A rescue operation had to be organised for the building societies, that was managed by the Commonwealth Development Corporation. A major economy exercise was mounted to reduce government expenditure and plans were made to break down the highly centralised colonial administration into a regional structure, in anticipation of political developments. Plans had also to be made to

---

22 The Raisman Report advised against breaking up the common market and the common services and concentrated its proposals on measures that would improve their operation, together with recommendations that would offset the uneven distribution of benefits. At the institutional level it proposed the replacement of the High Commissioner by the chief ministers of each country, sitting as the Heads of a re-named East Africa Common Services Organisation. Financially, it proposed that a fixed percentage of customs and income tax revenues be placed in a Distributable Pool, half of which would finance the common services and half would be divided equally between the three governments. The result would be to make Kenya pay for a larger proportion of common services and to bring about a fiscal transfer to its neighbours. These proposals were accepted and implemented.

transform the Colonial Service into a domestic African administration and to phase out its large expatriate element. These developments both sharpened the ambitions of the emerging Kenyan leaders, as well as feeding the apprehensions of the about to be displaced settlers and the political atmosphere was tense.

In such a high profile colony as Kenya, with its many social and political connections to Britain, the London press took a keen interest. *The Guardian* established a resident correspondent, Clyde Sanger, who had been editor of the *Central African Examiner* which I had written for while at Mufulira, and we now became close friends. I also got to know the Africa correspondent of the *Financial Times*, Robert Oakeshott, who became a regular visitor. We evolved a somewhat underhand arrangement whereby Ruth became the designated 'our correspondent' stringer, with the name of Ruth Pickering (her mother's maiden name was Suzi Pick). The outcome was that the FT carried rather well-informed pieces on the Kenya economic scene for a couple of years.

While I was busily involved in the Treasury, Ruth had also become a Kenya civil servant under the rules of that time. She had been compelled to resign from the Colonial Service on marrying a fellow officer, but she was permitted to join the Kenya government service as a locally engaged officer (and thus without the expatriate pay allowance). The head of Establishments was sympathetic to our situation and invited us round to his house a couple of times to discuss the possibilities, where we were plied with powerful vermouth cocktails. The upshot was that Ruth was appointed to the Ministry of Commerce and Industry and was soon promoted to Assistant Secretary to the same rank as me and we derived some amusement from engaging in official interdepartmental correspondence from time to time. However, the ministry's permanent secretary was a temperamental figure and six months later Ruth had a major row with him, with the finale in public going down the main staircase in the Secretariat. She was quickly transferred to the Ministry of Agriculture and was a great success there. When it became apparent that the White Highlands would have to be opened up rapidly to African farmers, Ruth was assigned to work on the path-breaking application to the World Bank to finance these innovative settlement schemes.

By the summer of 1961, with our first home leave beckoning in September, we began thinking seriously about our future prospects in Kenya. I had been much influenced by discussions with a Treasury colleague and he and I had drawn up lists of British companies that might be interested in our talents and experience. Meanwhile, Ruth was coming to feel that Africa was not the place to start a family. But for these influences, I would have been inclined to stay for the fascination of the preparations for transition to independence, and in the knowledge (and perhaps delusion) that I was well placed for an interesting role thereafter as a friend of Tom Mboya and other political leaders.[23] By September the outline of the Colonial Service redundancy scheme was emerging: long-service officers would have an incentive to stay until dispensed with, whereas young officers had every reason to start a new career. We knew that we should be in the early exit group and our going-on-leave farewells were tinged with sadness as we set off for Italy, Vienna and London.

We knew that we would not be returning if I succeeded in landing a job during my leave. Only a few months earlier we had seriously contemplated buying a house in Nairobi and settling down there; now we were leaving my homeland and our exciting life in Nairobi for an uncertain future. Would my work experience in Africa count for anything in England? We had no capital, nor anywhere to live there apart from staying with Ruth's parents in their modest flat. Would we ever feel at home in England?

It was sad too to be leaving my parents. We saw them for tea, or lunch, or supper at least once a week, and we knew that it made a great difference to their lives to be in touch in this way since they still felt themselves newcomers in Nairobi and were not happily settled there. Offsetting this was the joy that Jenny was so happily transformed since her marriage, and Margaret was thrilled to be invited to go up to Kericho to help make curtains and covers for their new home, and then to be invited to stay for Christmas at the end of 1961. My parents went on home leave in the summer that year and clinched a deal to buy a plot of land on the edge of Oakridge village with a marvellous view. But they had a sharp disappointment on visiting the planning officer who told them there was no hope of obtaining permission to build a house there.[24] They would really have liked to retire to Gloucestershire at that time,

---

23 This was not entirely fantasy: a year after I had returned to England, Tom Mboya sent me an invitation to his wedding.
24 Planning permission to build a house was eventually granted.

but knew that they could not afford to do so for several more years.

They returned to Nairobi unsettled by our imminent departure and by uncertainty over their own future; in particular whether Pa was to be invited to succeed brother Alan as Secretary of the Tea Board at the end of 1962. Alan was thoroughly ungracious about this, although he owed his own position there entirely to my father, and kept suggesting that he might be asked to stay longer, or that there were doubts about offering the position to Pa. Relationships therefore were a bit strained, even though they saw a lot of each other socially. The truth was that Alan was very self-centred, and could be moody as well, and he was not good at the little gestures that Margaret would have appreciated. There was also a health issue. Driving up to Kericho at Christmas '61 Margaret wrote in her diary –

> 'Out of the blue Dougal started talking about his health and told me quite matter-of-factly that he was quite sure he wouldn't live to a ripe old age; that he had Thrombosis! He wondered whether he would stand the English climate. He upset me terribly and I cried my eyes out.'

It was typical of Pa that he was clearly making no serious attempt to understand his medical condition and how it should be treated. Margaret was no better, and the subject was banished from further discussion.

Writing About Kenya

The East African Economic Review had been published since 1954 as the journal of the Economics Club of Kenya and its sister body in Uganda, rather than being an offshoot of Makerere or the Royal College in Nairobi. It was effectively run from the East Africa Statistical Department. The Economics Club of Kenya embraced economists and others working in government service, leading bankers and businessmen, including political figures like Ernest Vasey. We met about half a dozen times a year at the Norfolk Hotel and the society had the prestige and connections to capture while I was there: Eugene Black, President of the World Bank, J.B.Loynes from the Bank of England and Professor Max Gluckman, the distinguished social anthropologist at Manchester.

Ruth and I were naturally keen members of the Economics Club and I became a contributor to the *Review* for several years. The only paper that I read to a meeting of the Club was within a few weeks of being appointed to the Treasury in 1958. 'Is There a Case for an East Africa Central Bank?' was an attempt to apply the analysis of a recent book by Newlyn and Rowan to the contemporary scene.[25] Walter Newlyn was now the economic adviser to the Uganda government and in 1952 had concluded that it was premature to move from currency board to central bank. My paper re-assessed the arguments and concluded that the time for a central bank was now ripe, but with a significant rider: that the hesitation in taking this step 'lies not in financial backwardness but in the politics of East African cooperation.' I received letters from Newlyn and from John Butter agreeing with this assessment. Of course, all three countries set up central banks of their own soon after gaining independence.

My next article for the *Review* was on the Kenya tea industry, based on my B.Litt thesis and with the benefit of more recent data.[26] The analysis of the economics of the plantation sector was rather better than in my thesis and had benefitted from sitting in the statistical department where I had access to two agricultural censuses. Tea growing by African smallholders was by then well under way and I was able to include a discussion of this important development. The article was re-published by the Kenya Tea Board and was widely ready in the industry. Half a century later, I eventually published a full history of the Kenya tea industry, by which time Kenya had become the largest exporter of tea to world markets and more than half a million small farmers grew tea as a main source of income.[27]

In light of my later career, it seems prescient that I wrote several articles on financial topics, in addition to the one on central banking. To some extent this flowed from my responsibilities at the Treasury, where I managed the bond issues of the government and I was also responsible for administering an experiment with savings bonds, which was the subject of my next article.[28] Launched in September 1959, the savings bonds offered tax free appreciation over a seven year period, with a guarantee of the original capital investment. Following the

25 *Money and Banking in British Colonial Africa*, W.T. Newlyn and D.C. Rowan. My paper was published in the *Review* in January 1969
26 'The Kenya Tea Industry', *East African Economics Review*, 1959.
27 *Simba Chai – The Kenya Tea Industry*, Michael McWilliam. Ingram, 2020
28 'A Savings Experiment in Kenya', *East African Economics Review*, December 1961

Lancaster House conference in early 1960 and the announcement by the British government of an accelerated pathway to Kenya's independence, there was a crisis of confidence and flight of capital from the country. All savings institutions suffered withdrawals and the building societies were rescued by the Commonwealth Development Corporation, so this savings experiment became a footnote to a much larger problem. I also wrote a study of the banking sector which was completed after I had left Nairobi.[29] It documented the quite impressive maturing of the colonial banking system in Kenya, but also pointed up a number of policy issues concerning the allocation of credit and the development of the money market. The crucial role of the banks in pumping funds into the country from London during the 1960 confidence crisis was highlighted.

In the run-up to independence there were several reports on Kenya from international agencies and I wrote critical reviews of two of these documents. The UN Economic Commission for Africa (ECA) published an ambitious study of East African trade in 1962, which reflected a number of a priori views without much knowledge of contemporary realities in the region.[30] The British government arranged for the World Bank to undertake economic survey missions to the African colonies as they approached independence and such a mission was organised for Kenya at the end of 1961.[31] The mission lacked available informed expertise, and did not engage significantly with the Kenya government in probing issues, but nevertheless assembled much useful information. I concluded that it was an opportunity missed.

I left Kenya in September 1961 with a substantial collection of documents and publications with a view, at the time, of writing a book. Over the following couple of years, and with an undemanding job at Samuel Montagu, I devoted much effort to marshalling my thoughts on what had been happening to the Kenya economy and I had some opportunities to communicate them. Shortly after returning to London, I was contacted by Arthur Gaitskell who had been approached by a

---

29 'Banking in Kenya 1950-1960', East African Economics Review, June 1962
30 ECA Economic Bulletin, Voll II, No 1. 'East African Trade', East African Economics Review, December 1962
31 The Economic Development of Kenya, IBRD. John Hopkins and OUP, 1963. 'Notes on The Economic Development of Kenya', East African Economics Review, June 1963. 'The World Bank and the Transfer of Power in Kenya', Journal of Commonwealth Political Studies, May 1964.

leading member of the nationalist party, KANU, to give advice on the new government's economic plans. Joseph Murumbi had been a prominent exile nationalist and was well connected to bodies like the Fabian Society. I had invited him to Oxford to address our East African Association, so we were acquainted. Gaiskell wanted my help in participating in the assignment and I was invited to a meeting at the Paddington Hotel with Murumbi, Gaitskell, an agricultural economist, Klaus Phillips, and the Ariel Foundation who were financing the project. Ariel was a slightly mysterious body funded by big business interests in Africa and with an office at Shell's headquarters. My up to date knowledge was of considerable interest and in the following weeks I produced a substantial 20,000 word document.

There was a wider context to the project, as became apparent from one of Gaitskell's letters, 'What with the Congo and Rhodesia situation, the uncertainties in Kenya make me very concerned about Africa and one feels that the situation needs a real conjoint effort from the Western world.' He went to talk to the Colonial Office and was strongly encouraged to take on the assignment, as there were apprehensions that Kanu might turn to Russia or China for help. All this was very exciting, just as I was about to start at Samuel Montagu. However, my own role was ambiguous. I wrote to Gaitskell explaining that I wanted to be placed on the same footing as the economist Phillips – as a retained consultant from Samuel Montagu, with the fee going to the bank (and incidentally demonstrating to my new employer that my colonial experience had demonstrable value). He agreed, but the Ariel Foundation demurred: they had not bargained for me when retaining Gaitskell, and in any event were apprehensive that my Colonial Service background might be off-putting to Kanu. But they were prepared to pay me something in respect of my initial paper. This turned into a somewhat embarrassing haggle, with the eventual receipt of 75 guineas.

Meantime the Gaitskell mission had been announced in the Kenya press and I received a letter from Donald Baron in the Treasury, who knew of my connection with him, asking to be put in touch which I was happy to do. In writing to Baron, I drew attention to the politics of the project –

'(Gaitskell) was made aware from unusual sources in both London and Nairobi that the 'authorities' were very much in favour of him doing this job, and he had put off other commitments as a result and is now very keen to make a success of the assignment. The weak link, as you will be aware is Murumbi and the divided state of Kanu. (My reading is that this is very much a personal gimmick of Murumbi's, but I may be wrong). There is a risk therefore that the whole operation may misfire, but I think Gaitskell feels that it is a risk that must be taken. I think (and I may be putting a gloss on our conversation now) that Gaitskell sees his task as (a) helping Kanu come to terms with the realities of their economic inheritance, and (b) trying to devise policies, especially on the development front, that they can sell to the electorate and to the outside world as well.

'To round off the tale as far as I am concerned, I thought at one time that I might play a fairly active role, as it seemed to me a unique chance to try to get Kanu to face a few economic realities, and I believed I could contribute something of value. Hence my energy in writing a paper![32] I do not think the Ariel people bargained for me however, when they retained Gaitskell, and I am rather expecting to drop out of the picture now.'

In April, Gaitskell showed me a copy of his report and I exchanged comments with him. By now the weakness of Murumbi's position was apparent and Gaitskell himself was becoming pessimistic, 'Actually, I don't at all know whether to go any further with the Kenya exercise or not. It is a little difficult to know if they still want me or if I can be of any value to them.'

Unfortunately, I failed to retain a copy of my original paper, but I decided to use the material for an article for Chatham House's journal, *The World Today*.[33] In it I analysed the serious public finance crisis that Kenya faced in the run-up to independence: the effects of the collapse of confidence in an economy dominated by non-African enterprise, leading to the flight of capital and the undermining of government revenues from taxation and reduced borrowing capability; the implications of suddenly having to retrench a relatively sophisticated, centralised and development-oriented administrative machine; the likely problems of

---

32 I sent a copy to Baron.
33 *Economic Problems During the Transfer of Power in Kenya*, Royal Institute of International Affairs, April 1962

disappointed expectations. It was a thoroughly gloomy piece. Gaitskell wrote appreciatively and I was told that the article was being taken seriously in the Colonial Office.

This article was followed a year later by a more extensively researched piece for the leading American journal, *Economic Development and Cultural Change.*[34] The public finance problems were restated, with a conclusion that Kenya would go into independence having to rely on foreign aid to balance its budget. There was a detailed analysis of the unpreparedness of the civil service for independence and the attendant rapid Africanisation of its members. The final section developed the argument that Kenya's lack of preparation for an African led government had been fostered by the myths of multi-racialism since the war, coupled with a belief that the importance of the dominant role of non-Africans would continue to be accepted. The sudden realisation that there was going to be a process of rapid substitution of black for white farmers in the Highlands and in the civil service was a profound shock and it was threatening to destabilise the economy.

Both these articles were published before the details of Kenya's independence settlement with Britain were known. In the event it contained very generous arrangements by the British government for transitional support and for the funding of land purchase in the Highlands. I would like to think that my public airing of the issues played some part in reaching this outcome.

Kenneth Robinson, now Director of the Institute of Commonwealth Studies in London, organised a *festschrift* to be presented to Margery Perham on her official retirement and he invited me to contribute a chapter based on a seminar paper that I had read at the institute. In it I discussed the influential role that the settler members of Legislative Council played in the early post-war period, and concluded –

> 'Finally, one may note the settlers' tendency to encourage strong government intervention in economic matters, whether it be to regulate agricultural production, control marketing, determine industrial location, or organise the labour supply. Kenya became a highly controlled economy in the post-war period and much was expected of the government in its economic performance.

---

34 *Economic Viability and the Race Factor in Kenya,* Vol XII No 1, October 1963

It produced over the years an outstanding government machine and a habit of intervention in economic matters.'[35]

Sir Evelyn Baring was Governor of Kenya during the Mau Mau Emergency and himself took a strong interest in economic policy. On retirement, he was appointed chairman of the Commonwealth Development Corporation, which played a pivotal role in the successful development of tea growing by African farmers. Baring was one of the pro-consuls whose oral testimony was wanted for the Oxford colonial records project promoted by Margery Perham, which is now deposited with the Bodleian Library. She undertook the formal interview with him on the political aspects of his governorship and I had the privilege of interviewing him in 1971 on his economic record. I have retained my 'issues' note on which the conversation was based, although I have yet to go back to Oxford to inspect the transcript.

Margery Perham was a joint editor of the Oxford *History of East Africa* and she invited me to contribute a chapter on post-war developments in the economy of Kenya to volume 3. The book had a dire publishing history, with changes of editors and recalcitrant contributors and it did not finally appear until 1976.[36] Writing this chapter meant that I was able to round out the story of independence and, more importantly, to reflect on the whole post-war period and to develop several themes. One was the dynamic effect of European agriculture in Kenya and the country's emergence as an economic hub. Another, was the stimulus given to the colonial administration by the settlers to raise its game well beyond the standard in other African colonies. A third was to highlight the crucial partnership of Governor Baring and finance minister Vasey in maximising economic opportunities, notwithstanding the burden of the Mau Mau emergency. When I arrived at the School of Oriental and African Studies in 1989, I was flattered to discover that my chapter was on the required reading list for the students of one of the masters degrees.

---

35 'Economic Policy and the Kenya Settlers 1945-48', in *Essays in Imperial Government*, Basil Blackwell, 1963
36 'The Managed Economy: Agricultural Change, Development, and Finance in Kenya', in *History of East Africa,* volume 3. Oxford, 1976

THE CITY

6. SAMUEL MONTAGU 1962

In July 1961, before we went on home leave, the Kenya Government published the terms of a limited retirement scheme for expatriate officers in the Colonial Service – limited because officers could apply to retire but the decision rested with government, since it needed to ensure an orderly rundown of the service. As already noted, Ruth and I had already decided that I must take the opportunity to look for a new career while on leave and, if successful, I would resign anyway. I had drawn up a list of possible target employers and wrote to them before departure. My nine letters yielded three invitations to interview, from Ford Motor Company, Guest Keen & Nettlefolds, and British Transport Commission. Additionally, through Arthur Gaitskell I was called to interview by the Commonwealth Development Corporation, and a family friend of the Arnsteins was able to arrange for me to be interviewed at the merchant bank at which he worked, Samuel Montagu.

GKN had no vacancy, but the ex-Colonial Service personnel manager was very helpful with suggestions. I did not pursue British Transport beyond the first stage. At Ford, after a long day of interviews I was offered a post in its well-regarded finance department, subject to confirmation. At CDC I was interviewed by the formidable general manager who made it clear that I was being seen because of Arthur Gaitskell and that he did not think too much of civil servants, but offered a management trainee post.

At Samuel Montagu I was seen by two partners; they shook their heads and said that I was too old at 28 for starting in the City and there was no current vacancy in the bank. However, I then received a letter asking me to come in again, when I was received by David Montagu who said that the chairman, Louis Franck, was by chance in the office that afternoon and would like to have a look at me. As my letter home recorded –

'I was led into a luxurious, green panelled room with old masters on the walls and a few minutes later a tall dynamic man walked in and took me to pieces in about seven minutes of quick-fire questioning, mostly about family and I felt a bit like a horse having its teeth and fetlocks examined. A few days later I was summoned by another partner, Louis Eisinger who gave me the toughest interview I have had – tough because I gradually realised that he was going to offer me a job at the end of it providing I did not make a blob. When the offer came I clinched on the spot –

> 'Taking this job in preference to Ford is of course a risk, but the opportunity is immense if I can make the grade, and I think I can. The risk is that there is no settled routine or administration to the job; it depends on brainpower and developing a strong commercial sense. It was emphasised to me that there are practically no regular posts in a merchant bank – such an institution goes in for what its members are capable of handling. They have created a new post for me and given me much more salary than a beginner's salary. In other words, they are backing a judgement that I will be able to make a contribution to the banking business of the firm when I have found my feet – which I am expected to do within a definable period. I feel it is a unique chance for a breakthrough.'

This was not a bad description of how Samuel Montagu saw itself in the 1960s as it sought opportunities to evolve out of its traditional foreign exchange and bullion trading business under the dynamic leadership of a Belgian, Louis Franck. Thanks to Julius Weinberg I had landed a job in one of the inner circle of accepting house merchant banks. Montagu was home to a number of Jewish refugees from central Europe, and the bank had been notable in helping such refugees, and Weinberg was the most able of them. He had been with a private bank in Vienna and was now head of the foreign exchange and sterling money market departments, with outstanding success. Montagu was one of the first banks to trade the new euro-dollar market that had resulted from US exchange controls, and he was immensely hard working. Every evening he took home the bank's position to St John's Wood and traded from home until New York closed. He and Irene had no children, were close friends of the Arnsteins, and very fond of Ruth. Julius knew that Louis Franck owed him a favour and it was my good fortune to be the beneficiary of this.

It had been a bit diminishing to discover in all these interviews that no one seemed to be impressed by what I had been doing in the Kenya Treasury and that the best offer owed much to a family connection of Ruth's. Clearly it was going to be quite a challenge to establish oneself back in England.

During the autumn of 1961 we were active in picking up our English contacts again and this included several visits to Oxford. On one of them we met up with John Hicks, my thesis examiner, and Ursula – both of whom had been so helpful over career advice while I was in Africa. Ursula told us about a new project she had for a book on the public finances of federations in the Commonwealth, and she asked if Ruth would be interested in being her research assistant, if funding could be obtained. This came to pass, with the result that Ruth and I could both look forward to 1962 with new jobs. It was somewhat amusing that my job was thanks to Ruth's family and Ruth's job arose from my Oxford connections.

Starting at Montagu

On the first working day of 1962 I made my way to Old Broad Street in the City, with bowler hat, umbrella and Opa's great Viennese overcoat adapted for me. There was heavy snow and many did not get to work that day, including my new boss Michael Richards for whom I was to be personal assistant. He was down with flu, so I did not really start for a week. I was warned on all sides that Richards would not be an easy man to please. A blunt Yorkshireman and a successful City solicitor who had been legal adviser to Sigmund Warburg in his early days, Richards had acquired control of a small issuing house, Hart Son & Co, and had also established an industrial holding company, named Wood Hall

Trust after his home, that took stakes in promising companies with a view to flotation or full ownership. He had been courted by Montagu, who wanted to break into the arena of new issues and mergers, and had only recently sold Hart Son to Montagu in exchange for a stake in the merchant bank and a leading partnership role. However, the chemistry was not working very well, as Richards was essentially a loner, and this had given rise to the bright idea that I should be attached to him as his personal assistant, and thereby help to integrate Richards' contacts and expertise into the bank. It was a tall order. I had met Richards once in the weeks before starting work and we had had a pleasant enough conversation. A story went round that a reason for my recruitment was that my B.Litt degree from Oxford was thought to be a legal qualification, and hence my suitability for being attached to Michael Richards.

Samuel Montagu had one in-house corporate finance expert in Andre Luboff, who had been recruited a few years previously by Louis Franck to sort out his own tangled financial affairs. Luboff was of Russian émigré extraction – his father had fled after the Revolution, allegedly in a barrel; he was a Cambridge economist and had a brilliant mind and was very hard working, with exacting standards. Fortunately, we hit it off and I learnt an enormous amount from him as a proper corporate finance function was gradually established over the next several years under his leadership. I kept a diary during these first nine months which recorded a mixture of information and impressions about the bank, earnest notes on financing techniques, commentaries on transactions, and accounts of my attempts to get interesting work to do.

Although it was a respected Accepting House (its bills accepted for discount by the Bank of England), Samuel Montagu was not top-drawer City in the sense of its leading partners being scions of the English financial establishment. Its origins were a Jewish pawnbroker from Manchester a hundred years ago, and its specialisation had been foreign exchange and bullion dealing. Of the founding families, Moses Samuel's son had become the first Lord Swaythling, but his son was more famous as a cattle breeder and had no interest in the City; however, David Montagu, in the next generation and now in his thirties, was the rising star partner. The very orthodox Franklins had been a dominant influence for a long time but had now withdrawn from active participation, following Louis Franck's arrival. What had transformed the firm was the restless energy of Louis Franck, son of a Belgian central banker who had come in like a whirlwind on the bullion side shortly before the war. He had been with the British army in West Africa (and collected a CBE) – in some role with the Free French, I believe, and became chairman after the war. He was one of the big personalities in the City at this time and was very cosmopolitan in his network of contacts. According to Luboff, he had made an enormous amount of money and David Kynaston quotes him as saying that he was now able to live on the interest on his capital. The Partners Room was reconfigured. On the international-ist side there was Louis Eisinger – a Hungarian with sharp commercial insight; Horace Halperin who operated from the Paris office; John Nash – Australian educated from an influential Hungarian family (Nagy); Rudi Bleichroeder from the Berlin banking dynasty; Paul Jeanty (nephew) who operated from the Zurich banking subsidiary. Linking into British respectability were David Keswick from Jardine Matheson (his brother was on the Court of the Bank of England); Everard Hambro of that ilk, who specialised in the Middle East bullion market which he knew from war service; John Hansard – ex-Shell South America; Peter Beale – recently retired chief cashier at the Bank of England; and then there were David Montagu and Michael Richards.

Of all these eleven names only Bleichroeder (equities trading) and Richards had what one might call straightforward line responsibility for departmental activity in the bank, although David Montagu had made himself a specialist in gilts and the discount market. On a day to day basis Samuel Montagu was run by its experienced managers. However, unlike the non-executive directors of the clearing banks, the Montagu partners involved themselves in particular pieces of business that interested them, took charge of transactions, brought in new business connections, took a close interest in markets and trading (both for the bank and very much also on personal account). It was all great fun in a dilettante way. The old style partners' room had double desks and open phone conversations. Only Richards and Blei spent their working days away from this room.

As David Kynaston narrates so engagingly in his history of the City,[37] the 1960s was a period when the old carapace of City conservatism was cracking under the challenge of new personalities and market opportunities, with Sigmund Warburg and Kenneth Keith as key figures

37 David Kynaston, *The City of London Vol IV*, Chatto & Windus, 2001

– not to mention the impact of rogues like Harley Drayton and Robert Maxwell. Both Louis Franck and David Montagu scented opportunity and the bank took a number of initiatives that had considerable potential, but it was the bank's misfortune that these two able individualists lacked the qualities needed to build institutional capacity, nor were they able to make room for someone who could do this for the bank. Montagu's great strengths were in the expertise and initiatives of its trading activities – in bullion, foreign exchange, euro-currency and sterling deposits, and equities. To expand beyond a prosperous niche player required increasing amounts of capital, which was beyond the capacity of a private bank and these activities increasingly became the province of giant banks over the next decades. The opportunity for Montagu was to be an innovator, adviser and arranger and, indeed, it made London's first foreign currency loan (to the Kingdom of Belgium), had a role in the first euro-currency loans and innovated in investment management. However, the capability to develop these initiatives was lacking and other merchant banks were more successful in developing industrial connections and advisory teams to raise capital for industry and advise on acquisitions. In short, Montagu struggled to evolve beyond an entrepreneurial private bank.

Montagu had a number of *stagieres,* as Louis Franck liked to call us: young men recruited through connections with the partners. The concept was that one would sink or swim through one's own efforts to acquire relevant skills and to demonstrate value to the firm. The bank laid on occasional departmental seminars, which I found valuable, but otherwise there was little in the way of formal training and – unsurprisingly – there was a high attrition rate. Several bright chartered accountants were gradually recruited and marshalled under Andre Luboff, the most notable being Richard Stein with whom I became close friends. He eventually left to become finance director of Reckitt and Colman. Many years later, I was able to recruit him to become finance director of Standard Chartered. Every now and then Louis Franck or John Nash or David Montagu would throw a dinner party for the *stagieres* – mainly I suspect for the host to show off, rather than attempting to discover anything much about us. But perhaps it set us an aspirational standard. I find I have retained a number of irreverent limericks from those apprentice days:

Louis Franck
Runs the bank.
When asked should he lend money to So and So
Shouts, 'NO!'

Paul Jeanty
Said to his Aunty
'My only hope is the bank
Of uncle Franck'

David Samuel Montagu
Thinks he knows a thing or two
But those to whom he acts as financial adviser
Are none the wiser

Evy Hambro
Is a sham pro
He thinks he can produce a merger without flaws
By going shooting on the moors

John Nash
Will join a Board in a flash
Provided the share price is certain to double
And it's no trouble

Around the end of February I was invited to lunch with the Directors by Eisinger and recorded the experience –

'There was sherry beforehand in the Partners' Room, where I met for the first time John Nash and old Sydney Franklin, who is gaga and sits at a little table in the corner. A delicious meal for eight with Hambro presiding in the Directors' Dining Room – panelling from a French chateau and a Dutch Still Life at either end of the room. First, *oeufs Florentine* and the white wine started flowing. It was followed by a large fish which I, as the guest of honour, had to attack first. More wine. Plates then cleared to leave our silver table mats with the Samuel Montagu monogram in the middle, and rare cheeses were served with port. Conversation was genial, non-stop, and much about travel. Nash was recently back from Hong Kong. Hambro was off to the Persian Gulf on Sunday and Richards to Australia later in the year. Franck had just phoned in from Zurich and Montagu had cabled from Jakarta. Busy bees.'

Finding a Role

I tried hard to make myself useful to Michael Richards, as his personal assistant. He was always very pleasant to me and occasionally took me out to lunch. It was more difficult to become involved in actual transactions, although I was allowed to read all his correspondence and papers. Peter Marlow, the Personnel Manager, went to a lot of trouble to help me – perhaps because he himself had had a hard start in life. He was a *Kindertransport* Jew who had been rescued by the Rothschild family. Working first on the Rothschild estate, he had trained as an accountant. We became social friends after I left the bank and kept in regular dining contact until his death.

Thanks to Marlow I spent a few weeks in the investment and stock dealing departments until Richards had something more for me to do.

'Montagu are the only large merchant bank which goes in for stock dealing (i.e. speculation) in a big way. The department has about £500 000 to play with and seems to make 4 percent gross on it. Over and above this there is the normal clients business. We also do a substantial arbitrage business in stock with the Continent and America.'

And then in April, 'I decided to 'have it out' with Richards over getting some work from him. Quite a frank conversation from which a new tactic has been evolved, which has been surprisingly successful so far. I go into his office first thing in the morning and sit there until he throws me out with some work or takes me to a meeting. Delightfully simple! Let's hope the breakthrough has started.'

I became involved in a Stock Exchange flotation, perhaps partly influenced by the fact that it was a family business owned by relations of Ruth's father. The Stern brothers, family from Vienna, owned a timber import business and also a manufacturing company making garden sheds. I worked on the prospectus, made site visits, and then was dogsbody as the flotation got under way. Richards spent a lot of his time running Wood Hall Trust, and it was interesting to look over his shoulder on the day to day issues. However, I was still not fully employed and he was happy to give me up to David Montagu, who had decided that he now wanted a personal assistant as he went about demonstrating that he too could win fee earning transactions for the bank. The most interesting transaction with him was another flotation – this time of a South Wales drapery business that had been started by the Rivlin brothers' father, himself a Russian Jewish tinker who first tramped the valleys with a large valise. I visited all the stores and again worked on the prospectus. Another transaction was a successful hostile takeover bid by a well-known Kenya Indian family, the Madhvanis, of a sterling tea company in South India. I mainly recall having to organise the celebratory lunch in one of the Gilbert & Sullivan rooms at the Savoy, and the anxious consideration of a suitable vegetarian menu.

In May 1962 I was made secretary of a committee that had been formed with the aim of livening up the domestic business of the bank and Richards and Montagu were its driving forces. An onslaught was to be made on the provinces to acquire new clients, especially among the smaller expanding firms. There was even mention of regional offices at a later stage. Richards was emphatic that this must be done through personal contact, drinking and eating etc. I diarised, 'Clearly some gentlemanly polish is going to be rubbed off some of our elegant types in the process. It nice to know that ideas are stirring behind the old world façade.' Of course Montagu was not first in this field and other merchant banks had representative offices or branches in cities like Liverpool and Leeds. I researched prospects for a visit by David Montagu to Glasgow, where he discovered a Jewish lawyer, Alex Stone, who had banking ambitions and had established the British Bank of Commerce there. Montagu bought a stake in this enterprise to some fanfare, to be the spearhead of its provincial strategy. However, the connection never thrived.

Under Luboff's guidance I undertook a major study of the Malaysian tin industry – then very fragmented – for a Singapore client who contemplated consolidating the sector. It involved a substantial section on commodity price prospects and statistical scenarios that were beyond my mathematical capability. However, through Ruth (now at LSE) I was able to commission a young economist, Meghnad Desai, to do a piece of econometric analysis for the report. Many years later, as Director of SOAS, we met again, now as a professor at LSE and I followed his political career under New Labour, as Lord Desai, with occasional further encounters.

During this first year at Samuel Montagu I felt under pressure to come up with ideas for new business and sketched out several possibilities. Of these diary thoughts, only the colonial connection was taken up by the bank. I made contact with Sir Ernest Vasey, who had paved the way to my joining the Kenya Treasury and was now the Tanzania finance minister, and arranged for him to come to see David Montagu. Proposals were made for acceptance credits and gilt secured lending. The bank was supportive of my contacts and allowed me to undertake two overseas visits, with somewhat tenuous business potential. My academic writing on Kenya and my participation in seminars at the Institute of Commonwealth Studies led to me being invited to attend the inaugural meeting of the International Congress of Africanists in Accra in December 1962 as a member of the British delegation, representing business interest in Africa. Montagu not only allowed me to attend and paid my expenses, but devised a business development agenda around the visit.

I stopped off first in Sierra Leone, having discovered while in the Investment Department that Montagu managed the investments of the Sierra Leone marketing board. The town was redolent of Graham Greene and *The Heart of The Matter*. On checking in to the hotel the comely receptionist watched me signing the register and beamed:

'Oh, Mr Williams, there are lots of people with your name in my part of town.' And one had a vision of lonely forebears visiting Freetown and seeking business, like me. I went to see the marketing board and also the Bank of England man who was setting up a central bank. He and I got on well and a proposal was floated for Montagu to offer a revolving acceptance credit to finance produce exports. The matter was progressed after my return until I suddenly received a personal summons from the legendary Hilton Clarke, Principal of the Discount Office at the Bank of England, who exercised a prefectorial oversight of the discount market. I had committed the crime of trying to pinch business from the British Bank of West Africa; this was not cricket and I was sent away with a flea in my ear. However, the episode burnished my reputation at Montagu, who strongly disapproved that Hilton Clarke should have jumped on me, rather than 'having a word' higher up the chain.

I arrived in Accra several days before the conference and, thanks to Peter Leslie, a rising Barclays DCO executive whom I had first met in Kenya, I had been invited to stay with their General Manager in Accra, Julian Wathen. It was an encounter that was to have several consequences for my career. With Wathen's influence and energy I was able to meet several ministers, leading business figures, and have lunch with the British High Commissioner. My Montagu agenda was to market their bullion dealing, custody and lending services and I was able to meet the feared Governor of the Central Bank, Amoaka Atta, and had quite a friendly interview, but without tangible result.

The intensive discussions with Wathen about the country's development ambitions led me to formulate a daring proposition: that Montagu and Barclays should collaborate to promote investment in Ghana. We were able to take some initial positive soundings and then I took the idea back to London. Michael Richards was somewhat bemused at my written-up proposal, but agreed to back me by setting up a meeting with the Barclays general management. There, we encountered some scepticism and a barely concealed view that Wathen had had another of his brainstorms and must be led back onto safe ground. Nevertheless there was clearance to develop the proposals. But the Montagu directors themselves had second thoughts about the project and the commitments it might entail for them. In February 1963 I wrote to Wathen explaining that they had decided not to pursue the matter further.

As to the Congress of Africanists, I found the proceedings fairly tedious and parochially academic. By good fortune, my good friend Alan Rake (Cheltenham and Kenya) was now editor of *Drum* magazine in Accra and, after two days of conference proceedings, I absconded to stay with Alan and Jenny for the rest of my stay. This led to an adventure at the weekend,

'On Sunday we drove 95 miles down the coast to the charmingly named port of Elmina, where there are two fine old forts. We decided to have a bathe before lunch and it was gorgeous to loll in warm sea again. We thought all our things were well in sight, but while we were sunning ourselves dry someone crawled up and stole Alan's trousers, watch and car keys and my trousers plus all my camera kit. It was a nasty blow. The rest of the day was a bit of a nightmare. Jenny and I hitch-hiked back to Accra (in swimming clothes), while Alan guarded the car, to fetch spare keys. A friend then drove us all the way back again. Finally, a long session at the police station.'

The second visit was to India and my first encounter with the country that had been such a crucial part of Britain's imperial story. The visible poverty was startling, as was the friendliness and intellectual range of our hosts. The cultural legacy in Delhi ranging from the Red Fort to Lutyens to an evening of Indian dance was entrancing. I had been invited to be the City representative of a Chatham House delegation to India, comprising its Director, Kenneth Younger, Sir Edward Boyle for the Conservatives, Shirley Williams for Labour and Professor Dennis Austin from Manchester University, for meetings with the India Council for International Affairs in Delhi. This was a consequence of being drawn into Chatham House's orbit as a result of my involvement with Kenya issues and the article for *The World Today* in April 1962. Montagu agreed to the expedition and paid my expenses, adding on a business visit to Bombay and then to Nairobi.

The discussions in Delhi were a great education for me, although I doubt that I made much contribution to the policy dialogue on Anglo-Indian relations. Afterwards I flew down to Bombay to meet with Montagu's Indian bullion counterparts, Premchand Roychand, for a stimulating couple of days to learn about the silver business. The insatiable demand for silver jewellery for weddings had given rise to a large smuggling business from Dubai to Bombay. Premchand was the leading silver trading house. I then flew to Nairobi. There I talked my way round the bazaar with much help from J M Desai, who I had got to know in our Kenya days, to try (without success) to foster interest in Montagu's bullion and India connections. It was of course marvellous to be able to stay with my parents for a few days.

EED

This increased visibility in the bank resulted in my being employed by other directors from time to time when they thought they had landed a deal: a study on firms in the Potteries for Eisinger; and also for Evy Hambro, who felt he should get into this exciting new game of mergers and new issues, but combined with gastronomy and I recall a business breakfast at Quaglino and a working lunch at his country house. And then a more significant role came my way at last when Samuel Montagu and Midland Bank joined a continental consortium of banks to found a venture capital institution whose English name was Enterprise for European Development (EED). It was modelled on a famous American company, American Research & Development, founded by a charismatic Frenchman, General Doriot. The European clone was under the direction of Arnaud de Vitry and a prestigious group of shareholders was assembled. The office was in Paris, but much of the opportunity was thought to be in Britain. Montagu was designated as the UK arm of the firm to investigate and put up proposals to the EED management board and this was to be my role.

As it happened, Samuel Montagu had quite a history of private equity investment in promising business enterprises. There was a nursery subsidiary, appropriately named Capulet Trust, to hold such investments and this was Eisinger's principal occupation. There were several other 'special situation' investments held in other subsidiaries, including the Bland Welch Lloyds brokerage. According to Luboff, the directors tended to keep the juiciest propositions for themselves rather than for the bank. Wood Hall Trust was another example of a holding company investing in promising businesses in which Montagu had a direct stake. Thus, there was a culture of opportunistic investment into which the EED participation fitted. I plunged into this new role with enthusiasm – to the extent that de Vitry made a determined effort to get me to leave Montagu to join EED in Paris. My interest in novelty and in the ambitions of entrepreneurs made me a sympathetic interlocutor when investigating leads, but I was not necessarily a penetrating examiner and was often not ruthless in terminating unsuitable proposals. However, there was little time pressure and I had the enjoyment of exploring a number of intriguing propositions that came to nothing. In particular, much effort was expended on a new photocopying technique in a field that Xerox came to dominate. Another was a concept for a miniature helicopter – the Grasshopper.

EED eventually made two significant investments in the UK which I worked on. One was a pharmaceutical company that commercialised new drugs that had been developed independently of the majors – often with a herbal origin. It eventually ran into severe intellectual property problems. The other, and much more significant, investment was to back a young Cambridge mathematical wizard, Ian Baron, for one of the early super-computers. The problem was that the project had an insatiable appetite for capital and eventually EED had to pass the baton to deeper pocketed investors. I talked a lot with the National Research & Development Corporation which had been set up with public funding to foster the commercialisation of new inventions, and it became increasingly apparent to me that banks were constitutionally unsuited to taking the primary stage risk in commercialising new technology. This was more likely to take place within large industrial groups, or else with the backing of a business angel. Banks wanted to see a track record – and the prospect of selling on – to trigger their enthusiasm, which was what was happening with the other Montagu investments. Writing fifty years after these events, it is appropriate to note that the name of Samuel Montagu today is associated with the private equity arm of its now parent banking group, HSBC.

Somewhere To Live

My starting salary at Samuel Montagu was £1,250, to which we added £533 from Ruth's job for Ursula Hicks in Oxford. We had come back to England with savings of £1,400 and then the Treasury agreed to release me under the early retirement scheme as I was already on leave, for which I received £1,160 by way of pension commutation and redundancy, coupled with a friendly message –

> 'Mac (the Minister of Finance) has asked me to say that if there are any suitable posts of office messenger in your Banking House, he would be interested.'

Thus, we had something in excess of a year's income in reserve and thought we might buy a house. In this we were quickly disabused: the building society told us that we were not even eligible for a mortgage since we did not have a track record of regular saving with them. Even flat hunting proved difficult at that time and Ruth's parents generously proposed that we live with them at Swiss Cottage until the problem was resolved. This entailed making up a bed for me on the sofa in the sitting room every evening, as there was only a single bed in the spare room. Even more generously, they took themselves off to Switzerland for 6 months during 1962 to Locarno, partly to test whether they would prefer to live there.

Ruth became pregnant early in 1962 and Robert was born in September. Ruth's parents were back in Boydell Court by then, so accommodation with a baby was quite a squeeze. However, we had found a solution to our housing problem in the summer: Ruth had an introduction to the manager of the Duchy of Cornwall estate in Kennington, where cottages were being modernised as they fell vacant and then let to suitable middle class tenants. We passed the vetting interview and were promised the next conversion in the autumn. The timetable slipped and we eventually moved into 45 Courtenay Street in deep snow in February 1963, with our five-month-old son.

Our new home was a two-bedroom terrace house, with a front room that became our study. There was a paved yard and a flower bed behind it – perhaps 30 feet away. A dressing table and a lovingly painted child's chest of drawers is still part of my household itinerary, as is a stone lion that was retrieved from a building site in St John's Wood one weekend, which has been transferred to each of our subsequent homes and now guards the front door at Yew Tree Farm. Shopping was in the Lambeth Walk, where there was a laundrette. Pram pushing took us to Kennington Park past the Beefeater Gin distillery, or to Lambeth Bridge and a view of the riverscape, as old snaps testify. The neighbourhood was nourished by the aroma from the Marmite factory. The neighbours in Courtenay Street were mostly traditional South Londoners, except in the converted properties. Next door was Tim Taylor, a barrister with the Public Prosecutor's Office, and Biddy. Their son Matthew was born at the same time as our second son Martin in November 1964; he developed a great musical talent and reappears in our story.

While we were settling into Kennington, my parents also sorted out their future. It had been a stressful experience because the Kenya Tea Board was slow in coming to a decision over appointing a successor to uncle Alan as its Secretary on the one hand, while Mitchell Cotts was also slow to make up its mind about the future of its cashew nut processing business, so kept Pa dangling on a string. However, Alan retired at the end of 1962 and Pa succeeded to the post and my parents moved to the Tea Board house and were able to sell their own house. Meanwhile, discouraged by the planning officer's disapproval of new building in Oakridge Lynch, they purchased a bungalow there and were able to stay in it when they went on leave in September 1962. Indeed, with Robert just born, we drove up to Oakridge on several weekends to see them and show him off. Planning permission was eventually granted to build a new house and their final leave in 1966 was dominated by the completion of Stream. My parents finally left Kenya in 1967, forty years after Pa had first arrived there, to retire to their beloved Cotswolds. It has been nice to read in Margaret's diary that in 1962 there had been a reconciliation with the Brooke family and, more striking, with the Rutters, so there was a proper closure on the Brooke Bond saga.

Having achieved a home of our own at last, we also needed a nanny for Robert so that Ruth could develop her own career. After the research assignment with Ursula Hicks she was appointed to run the research division of the Economics Department at LSE. By good fortune, a family friend of the Arnsteins had trained as a Montessori nanny in Vienna and was now looking after her mother. Lore Haas agreed to come to look after Robert during the day, although this entailed an arduous journey from Swiss Cottage, which she kept up for three years. In the summer of 1963 we were able to take our summer holiday at Oakridge, along with Lore. The next year my parents came on leave so we had our holiday with them, as we did in the succeeding two years. We got to know all the Cotswold picnic spots on our daily expeditions. Robert had been given Austrian *lederhosen* by his grandparents and very much looked the country lad. Martin was born in November 1964 and soon began to appear as well in the holiday snaps. We led a frugal existence at this time, very much dominated by bringing up a young family in combination with getting launched on new careers.

Finding An Exit

Interesting as the work could be, it gradually became apparent to me that I was not going to be marked out for rapid progress at Samuel Montagu. This was rubbed into me when Richard Stein was promoted to manager status in 1965 and I was not, and I began to think about career alternatives. David Montagu expressed the view that because I was not a chartered accountant (like Stein) I was not qualified to be a full member of the Corporate Finance Department, regardless of other considerations. Instead, I was offered the role of personal assistant to the director who now had responsibility for the department, as well as other duties. He was an acknowledged authority on 'working' the complex exchange control regulations of that time for international companies. I was quite cut up by this development and still have the notes in which I tried to work out what to do. Publicly, I accepted the new role, but the episode made me alert to career alternatives.

I had actually been approached by Pa's stockbroker before this, with an invitation to join his firm, but I knew this was not for me. And then there had been the EED approach. The Inchcape Group was an old established trading company with operations from Kenya through India to Hong Kong and, as other firms of its kind were doing, it began to transform an internal finance unit into a merchant bank – Grey Dawes. An advertisement appeared for a general manager to develop this merchant banking business and I applied. My C.V. looked good and to my delight and then growing consternation I progressed through the interview stages and was offered the job. By then I realised that I had interviewed too successfully, and that I would not be able to deliver on their expectations. Fortunately, I had the wit to withdraw.

I was now sensitised to opportunity, coupled with the feeling that the experience at Samuel Montagu could be turned to good account. In May 1966 I was approached by the Ministry of Overseas Development (where my Oxford friend Hector Hawkins was already one of their economic advisers) with a proposal that I should apply for the post of economic adviser on East Africa, on a two-year appointment. I decided to explore the matter on the assumption that Montagu would second me, and I was duly offered the post. However, on putting the proposition to Montagu's I was 'met with a completely negative response: Africa is not considered to be an area of significant interest for the bank and no value was seen in one of their business development executives going to the ODM on secondment for two years.'

I then had the bright idea of approaching Julian Wathen at Barclays DCO, who by now had returned to head office as general manager responsible for staff and, being him, all sorts of initiatives for enlivening this still traditional bank. My enquiry was whether Barclays DCO would be interested in a proleptic recruitment, following my stint in Whitehall as an economic adviser. Wathen called me in for an afternoon of interviews, starting with his chairman Sir Frederick Seebolm, and a serious effort was made to persuade me to jump ship and to join a fast management stream that my friend Peter Leslie was already on. It would entail an initial appointment to one of the regional head offices – most probably Lagos – as an assistant to the local director. I had the temerity to write back that this proposal was not sufficiently interesting, and I proceeded to outline a preferred, imaginary job in head office to undertake financial and economic appraisals of new developments in the bank's operations. Wathen shrewdly responded that my proposal was for a specialist role that would be a dead end, whereas he was indicating a path that could lead to the top reaches of the bank.

'I still think that Barclays Bank DCO has got something to offer to M D McWilliam, and of course I am sure of the contra to that!'

He went on to suggest another meeting in due course to consider the matter further and I now became aware of the domestic implications of the Barclays proposal. It was clear that to progress up their management ladder one would have to accumulate considerable experience in their overseas network, starting with Nigeria. (Peter Leslie's route to the head of the bank took him along the way to Sudan, Kenya, Congo, Algeria and the Bahamas). This was not at all appealing to Ruth. She had by now been made administrator of the Economics Department at LSE and had established a particularly close rapport with Professor Ely Devons, the head of the department – of which more later. There was no prospect of Ruth getting a job in Nigeria under the increasingly restrictive regulations affecting expatriates, added to which the thought of taking two children under five to that country was daunting. I prevaricated therefore.

Coincident with this exploration, I began to be courted by The Standard Bank. This conservative institution was undergoing a transformation engineered by a new chairman, Sir Cyril Hawker, and deputy chairman, Cyril Hamilton, both implanted by the Bank of England with a very public agenda to bring about renewal and consolidation amongst the British overseas banks. Standard had its major business in South Africa (and until very recently had been called the Standard Bank of South Africa), and it also had an important presence in Central and East Africa. In the previous year there had been two significant developments under Hawker's leadership: Standard had acquired the British Bank of West Africa, whose geography ran along the coast from Gambia to Cameroon; even more significant, Chase Manhattan Bank had become a major shareholder alongside three long standing clearing bank shareholders, and with a resident director – Chuck Fiero – sitting in the bank in London. Sir Cyril had also imported an economic adviser from the IMF to build up an economics department, and I began to meet Helen Thompson at Chatham House meetings. She reported to Fiero on her discovery of this Oxonian, ex-Kenya Treasury, merchant banker and she soon found herself in an emissary role, which duly led to my meeting Fiero himself.

Fiero had been recommending that Standard should set up a market research department with strategic capacity, and he now saw me as the person to lead it. This would be a head office post. My imagination was quickly fired and I took the decision first to close off negotiations with ODM, and second to go with Standard rather than Barclays. That summer, while on holiday at Oakridge, I took the plunge to resign from Samuel Montagu and join Standard Bank as Principal of a new Market Research Department, with a useful £500 increase in take home pay. I remained on good terms with Julian Wathen and, indeed, he remained influential in my life for many years. It was he who brought me onto the governing bodies of the Royal African Society, the Overseas Development Institute, and the School of Oriental and African Studies. He always chided me as 'the one who got away', but I doubt if I would have had the same opportunities as came my way at Standard Chartered. And Barclays would never have worked for us as a family.

7. STANDARD CHARTERED BANK 1966

Moving from Samuel Montagu to Standard Bank was also to move between two contrasting City cultures. Montagu had the mystique of a family controlled accepting house with a reputation in the rarefied worlds of bullion dealing, trading in foreign exchange and the new euro-dollars. Its staff were cosmopolitan and clever and it had the glamour of recent initiatives to broaden its activities to new issues and corporate advice. Standard was a very traditional member of the British overseas banks – London headquartered institutions with conventional branch banking networks mainly in the areas of British imperial expansion. The London staff managed the head office administration while the City branch handled the counterpart transactions of the overseas branches – confirming letters of credit, discounting bills of exchange, deploying sterling in the discount market. The overseas staff had careers abroad and only a handful of men ever came back to senior positions in head office. The general managers were not directors of the bank and only attended board meetings to present and report. A high proportion of staff lived in south London suburbs and tramped across London Bridge every morning. It was a shock to discover that the bank still worked on Saturday mornings.

I was allocated an initial team of four: a bank clerk who was familiar with the bank's procedures, a recently recruited graduate working in

Commercial Services, and two specially recruited graduates from South Africa and LSE. The latter generated an immediate social problem: between his recruitment on graduating and his arrival in the autumn Richard Clare had grown a luxurious beard. However, beards were not permitted under staff rules. Clare stood his ground and I eventually brokered a compromise that he would have his beard trimmed to a smart profile. As at Montagu, I arrived at work wearing a bowler hat and with a rolled umbrella to find that only the City manager did likewise. With the rank of Principal, I was eligible to lunch in the Senior Dining Room along with other department heads, and was the object of much curiosity, coming from a merchant bank and with Oxford qualifications. There was also a general canteen, a senior ladies' lunch room, one for the City manager, another for the general managers and, finally, the Chairman's dining room.

As already noted, I had been recruited from Samuel Montagu in September 1966 at the instigation of Fiero to set up a new department of Market Research with a Chase-driven agenda. What was Chase hoping to achieve? The grand strategy was probably to bring Standard progressively into the orbit of Chase, and probably to acquire the bank eventually. In the short term, however, Chase wanted to interact with Standard's corporate customer base and to stimulate Standard to adopt modern marketing methods to capture new business and to have strategic objectives. Standard's management was deeply traditional: 'touting for business' was a pejorative phrase; customers came to the bank of their own volition because of its reputation; price competition was all but eliminated by formal inter-bank agreements; there was a firm tradition that commercial banks did not 'poach' staff from each other. In these circumstances it was unsurprising that change was being driven from the board of directors over the heads, so to speak, of the general managers. They were now to be undermined from within, with my new department as a key instrument in the process. It is easy to see now that this approach had serious weaknesses, but the conventions of the time precluded more robust management reorganisation. Furthermore, the personalities to deliver a different approach were not readily identifiable in these circumstances. This perhaps explains why the individuals who are remembered as bringing about decisive changes in the overseas banks are the bank chairmen and not their chief general managers: Sir George

Bolton at Bank of London & South America, Lord Aldington at National & Grindlays, and it is right to include Sir Cyril Hawker in this group.

In its first years Market Research had two broad strands to its work: garnering a deeper understanding of the competitive marketplace and deepening our knowledge of the bank's customers and their financial requirements. On the latter, a range of studies was undertaken tabulating and analysing the African interests of British companies and the extent to which they were customers; and studying the financing needs of sectors such as South African wool exports or Ghana hardwoods. Of course, the implication of such work was to seek new business, but cold calling, or touting for business, was considered ungentlemanly by nearly everyone. A much preferred technique was the heavy City lunch, with much talk of sport and a gentle allusion to trading conditions with an indication that 'it would be nice to do more together'.

Understanding better the competitive marketplace was more exciting because there was an implied agenda of potential corporate action behind these studies. In the late 1960s the potential of the euro-dollar market was not widely understood and the associated loan techniques were still being evolved. Much effort was devoted to interpreting Bank of England statistics. The Bank of London and South America had established a name as euro deposit gatherer and lender and Standard was determined to follow suit. George Preston was recruited as a director in 1969 after heading the Bank of England's foreign exchange department with a mandate to develop an international division at Standard. Already, as a shareholder in the consortium bank, Midland and International Banks that was set up in 1964, Standard had been able to second several staff to learn about the new lending techniques. However, my most important work for Fiero was a series of papers on each of Standard's competitors in the overseas banking world to tease out their distinctive features. I was made well aware that Hawker wanted to bring about more consolidation in the sector, but was not privy beyond that.

Leaving aside an element of empire building there was a persuasive rationale for banking consolidation, leaving aside operational considerations. Between 1957 and 1965 British colonial Africa had been turned into independent states without bank nationalisation, except in Tanzania, but there were threats of this happening in Zambia and Ghana. A secessionist civil war had broken out in Nigeria, while the collapse of the Central Africa Federation had been followed by Rhodesia's unilateral declaration of independence and the country was subjected to sanctions. The Africa risk factor had increased markedly. New currencies were not formally linked to sterling so that the seasonal funding of African commodity exports such as cocoa, groundnuts and palm oil acquired a new risk dimension. This was a major consideration in leading the Bank of West Africa to welcome its merger with Standard in 1965. The massive funding of Kenya branches from London in 1960 during the confidence crisis that year was a portent of the strains that could arise. The widespread incorporation of branches into separately capitalised banks created problems of their own by locking up capital in multiple jurisdictions; in particular a disproportionate share of Standard's capital became locked up in its South African subsidiary.

As for the Chartered Bank, it had lost its branches in Libya, Iraq and Aden in the Middle East, and further east in Burma, Vietnam and China, while its subsidiary bank in India had been nationalised. In the twenty years after the war, the future of foreign banking in emergent Africa and in Asia was by no means assured in the face of widespread economic nationalism and state led development. All this added up to a persuasive case for diversifying geographical risk. But it could also be coupled with a business development argument for better servicing international businesses with operations in these countries. These considerations were a far cry from the optimistic world of imminent political independence that I had left behind in Kenya and been so supportive of. The emerging realities were now more sobering, where single minded nationalism had been fractured by the rivalry of strongmen and competing ideologies added to the difficulties of government. There was now an additional factor: how could Standard navigate its relationship with apartheid South Africa and yet remain a welcome investor in the rest of Africa?

Induction Tours

Early in 1967 I was sent on a tour of the bank's main businesses in Africa: Nigeria, Ghana, South Africa and Kenya (Rhodesia was out of bounds because of UDI). Macleod, the chief manager in Nigeria had not welcomed Standard's acquisition of Bank of West Africa and I was made to feel this. He did not deign to see me and I was put into a grotty downtown hotel in Lagos until rescued by more friendly staff and moved to the Ikoyi hotel where overseas visitors were normally accommodated. The bank's traditional business had been focussed on crop finance of groundnuts and palm oil and on financing imports under letters of credit, and it was hesitant to engage with the new secondary industries that were springing up, but Peter Nice, the marketing manager, was determined that I should be aware of the potential and I spent some fascinating days in his company visiting textile mills and other new industrial undertakings in different parts of the country, including sight of the great groundnut pyramids in Kano – sadly long since vanished. In Ghana my surviving recollection is of dining with Lebanese customers and eating home-made hummus for the first time, and also a dinner with Jonny Johnston, the charismatic chief manager who I was later to have a lot to do with in Nigeria.

Arriving in South Africa I was sent to Cape Town, Port Elizabeth and Durban before reaching the head office in Johannesburg, and it was not difficult to discern that Standard was a major South African bank which was beginning to fret under the ownership and corporate headquarters of distant London. There was a powerful South African chief general manager, Bill Passmore, who was somewhat under a cloud in London at the time for a large lending commitment that had gone sour on diamond mining in South West Africa. Unlike in Nigeria, he took the trouble to talk to me about the bank. However, my key encounter was with the bank's chief economist, Conrad Strauss, who was already marked out for greater things. We became good friends as he rose rapidly through the ranks to the top of the bank, but unlike me he was given a strong grounding in hands-on management. The government of South Africa was implementing both its apartheid policies and asserting Africaaner hegemony and Standard was engaged in a struggle to preserve its banking leadership role against the government-favoured Volksbank. It was a situation in which staff from London – from the chairman down to lowly me – were under challenge to show that we understood and stood behind our South African colleagues as they manoeuvred to adjust to the regime.

Kenya was managed by another strong-willed personality who ran his fiefdom almost independently of London, especially as Standard's chief executive in London at the time had no overseas banking experience and had reached the top from the bank Secretary's department. Norman Smith did not deign to meet me either, but I had several enjoyable days in my former Kenya stamping ground. My tour had brought home the powerful franchise that Standard had in Africa, with self-confident local management that rather despised London head office and its pettifogging controls.

My banking education was further enhanced the following year when Fiero arranged for me to have three weeks with Chase in New York. Here I was given an intensive exposure to the way that Chase went about marketing its services, which included sitting in on several sessions of its graduate training programme and culminating with an audience with David Rockefeller himself, who talked openly about the prospect of a closer association with Standard. New York is an exciting, even frightening, city as I learned to navigate the steamy subway. Looking for a meal one evening I was picked up by a man who revealed lascivious intentions and I had some difficulty in extracting myself. In contrast to the gleaming skyscraper of Chase Manhattan Plaza, Standard had a crowded office on Wall Street under the thumb of an amiable control freak, who nevertheless arranged a theatre outing. I also managed to visit a couple who were friends of the Arnsteins and had to answer a million questions in their flat on Central Avenue which was filled with memorabilia from Vienna.

Back in London I was promoted to Manager in early 1969 with enlarged responsibilities in charge of a Business Development Division. We did feasibility studies for new branches in the UK and I recall cold calling engineering companies in Sheffield and walking round Covent Garden fruit market trying to engage importers of South African oranges in our trade finance services. The bank had never engaged in anything as rash as budgeting its revenue, expenditure and profits for the year ahead and there were strong views that this would be tempting providence, or worse. At Fiero's prompting I undertook a financial analysis, territory by territory, as a prelude to persuading an initially reluctant management that it would actually be useful to look forward, and I ran the budgeting project for the first two or three years before it was absorbed into the finance department. The notion of managing the balance sheet and targeting profits was still rather novel and Chase's pressure was critical to developing increased financial self-awareness.

Merger talks between Standard and the Chartered Bank of India, China and Australia were announced early in 1969, although not consummated until right at the end of it. Fiero was then re-assigned to New York with a consequence that I was rather adopted by the new director from the Bank of England, George Preston, and effectively became his sherpa on a series of investment initiatives over the next several years.

Implementing the Merger

Settling the terms of the merger of Standard and Chartered banks took up most of 1969, due to the difficulties posed by the Chase and NatWest shareholdings, as Duncan Campbell-Smith explains in his history of the bank.[38] A holding company, Standard & Chartered Banking Group, had been formed; this was a fudge since it left the two operating banks largely independent, with none of the vital integration issues addressed or resolved; indeed the merger lacked the support of Chartered's senior management. Even the integration of Bank of West Africa with Standard had been a drawn-out affair, where the two chief general managers at the time were scarcely on speaking terms although in neighbouring offices when I arrived in 1966, and of course they had separate luncheon rooms. History was now repeated. The deal had been done at board level, where management was not represented in either bank at the time, yet making the merger work depended upon executive action.

A merger steering committee was formed, headed by Standard's vice chairman, Cyril Hamilton and also included George Preston and Ray Reed (Standard's chief general manager). His opposite number refused to be involved and Chartered was represented by his heir apparent, Ronnie Lane. I was appointed secretary of this committee and was tasked with formulating and monitoring proposals for making the merger a reality. In short, this was very much a diplomatic exercise without a tight timetable and it took three years to integrate the head office administrations of the two banks. It also took three years for Standard Chartered to evolve a group logo, which appeared for the first time on the 1973 annual report. Consultants had been appointed to design one, but my department also played with ideas. Nobody liked the consultants' proposals so we

---

38 *Crossing Continents – A History of Standard Chartered Bank*. Duncan Campbell-Smith. Allen Lane, 2021

proffered the logo developed by Selwyn Pokroy and a designer friend: the intertwined S and C. It was received with acclamation and has survived all the subsequent upheavals in the bank.

In 1971 I had been elevated to the rank of Assistant General Manager, Corporate Planning and hence was eligible to lunch with the general managers. The Institute of Bankers took note and invited me to create a case study for their prestigious Cambridge Seminar in 1971 on Marketing of Bank Services. We worked diligently in the department to produce a detailed scenario of a German bank turning its London office into a branch to take advantage of the liberalisation being encouraged by the Bank of England under its Competition and Credit Control paper. A fellow member of the seminar was a rising Bank of England executive, Rodney Galpin, and we went punting together. He was my nemesis in 1988.

I had become conscious of a growing mismatch between the bank's ambitions to expand outside its traditional areas into fresh territory and new markets and its continuing reliance on a very limited talent base to manage these initiatives. Towards the end of 1972 I addressed a memorandum to general management to express my concerns and to make some proposals. 'Almost without exception, Standard's policy has been not to recruit trained staff on any level for these new areas of activity, and indeed to rely wholly on evolving appropriate skills through operating experience in the markets concerned.' I noted that the bank had recruited no graduates in 1971 and that two of the three recruited in the current year had applied through personal connections. Meanwhile, 13 staff with an average of 11 years' experience each had left for other City institutions but there had been no matching inflow of experience. I proposed that the bank should expand its London-based 'promising officer' group to include staff serving abroad and also by competitive recruitment, with the aim of developing a cadre of mobile international bankers, but also to recognise that there were special skill areas outside the traditional hierarchy e.g. in trading and IT. The personnel departments of the two banks were separate units and I recommended that they be amalgamated 'as a matter of urgency'. The paper caused a stir, but progress was slow in opening the bank to a wider talent base. The merchant bank proved to be a source of talent for the wider group, but we did not recruit directly into general management until 1985. The personnel divisions of the two banks were only amalgamated in 1971.

I became deeply involved in one particular project: to integrate the two branches of Standard and Chartered in Hamburg under Standard's German manager, Werner Neumann. This was fiercely resisted by Chartered's influential Scottish manager, Neil Macmillan, who had established a powerful fiefdom over many years and I had to step delicately. The project was linked with a proposition that I might be appointed as general manager for Europe and to this end I spent the winter of 1972 having German coaching lessons, followed by a fortnight's residence in Hamburg, accompanied by Ruth, who was of course bi-lingual. Chartered had a stake in a private bank in Hamburg, Conrad Heinrich Donner, and joint ventures with it in Holland and Switzerland. I became good friends with the senior partner, Jochum Peters, and a much later outcome was another joint venture with Donner in Central America.

Ruth and I hired bicycles, where one could pick up and leave them at different stations, and we also got to know well Werner Neumann and Ingrid. As a young soldier in Berlin at the end of the war, Werner was advised to surrender to the Americans rather than to the Russians with the consequence that he became an interpreter in the Hamburg prisoner of war camp, from which he was hired by Standard when it re-opened its Hamburg branch. After a working visit to South Africa, where Werner was much admired, a practice developed of sending promising young managers to Hamburg during their overseas training. I was there one year when the group arrived. On their first evening the men were taken to the notorious Reeperbahn. First, we spent an hour or so at a traditional beer hall, drinking and singing; then the group was taken on a tour of the establishments and – by arrangement – entering one of them to witness a show. The young men from Puritan South Africa were deeply shocked and, hopefully, inoculated against returning there. Macmillan was eventually appointed general manager for Europe in 1975.

Sherpa to Preston

My first interesting project with Preston was a project to circumvent the Bank of England's quantitative limits on the banks' sterling lending. Malta was a member of the sterling area so that a bank located there could lend to UK borrowers without limit. Samuel Montagu proposed that a bank be established in Malta to undertake such business and the shareholders were to be Midland Bank, Standard Bank and the National Bank of Malta, with Standard responsible for the management of the enterprise. I had the job of setting up the bank and finding a manager from within our overseas staff. Malta International Banking Corporation was duly launched at the end of 1969 and for several years there were enjoyable visits to Malta for board meetings, but it is ironic in retrospect that a former Bank of England executive should have taken a leading part in circumventing the Old Lady's rule. It did no harm to my prospects to spend time with Hamilton and Preston in this way.

I supported Preston on two more, somewhat *outre*, ventures: a finance company in Geneva – Établissement Financiere de Placements – and a Spanish leasing company, Liga Financiere, and both entailed enjoyable sorties with Preston to board meetings in Geneva and Madrid. Nearer home, I persuaded the bank to invest in a newly established computer leasing company that had been set up by two brothers on graduating from Imperial College, and then in a securities company that specialised in arbitrage of South African shares with dual quotations that was a good customer of City branch. A while later it was discovered that the books of Dominion Securities were in a mess, with hints of fraud, and the bank was involved in much effort to sort matters out and eventually closed the business.

Preston had two larger ambitions for diversification: bullion dealing and merchant banking. On the latter, he felt that Standard should have its own merchant bank to provide advice to corporate customers and to engage in the liberalising City markets, and that this could be achieved from scratch rather than purchasing an existing institution. To this end a joint venture was established with Tozer Kemsley & Millbourn, called Tozer Standard Chartered, but this did not work well and by 1977 the merchant bank was a wholly owned subsidiary – Standard Chartered Merchant Bank, into which Standard's development corporation was folded. Between them, Chartered and Standard had several merchant banking investments overseas. In the East there was a joint venture with Arbuthnot Latham in the Gulf and in Malaysia and Singapore, and in Hong Kong a joint venture with Schroders that was fast becoming a notable new issue house under the leadership of Wyn Bischoff. In South Africa there was a thrusting wholly owned merchant bank, and Standard had a joint venture with Arbuthnot in Kenya. I enthusiastically promoted the notion of a network of group merchant banks and the Malaysian and Singapore entities became wholly owned.

The big prize and challenge was thought to be a merchant bank in Nigeria. The idea was to establish a joint venture with Chase, but there was ambivalence in New York and it became increasingly apparent that Chase's main interest was to promote euro-dollar lending business. Meanwhile the Nigerian authorities were difficult and greedy. Chase decided to go it alone and at that point we became aware that Schroders were interested in the country so we joined forces on a complicated proposition to set up a merchant bank with the Western Region government. It did not help that our Nigerian chief executive, Sam Asabia, took against Schroders and the project ended in tears.

There was an unexpected outcome in that the man leading for Schroders expressed a strong desire to come over to Standard Chartered. Ansell Egerton was duly recruited to head the merchant bank and to develop the group network. This proved to be a disastrous appointment in that, once ensconced, Egerton provided no leadership and seemed mostly concerned to have a good time at corporate expense. Peter Graham decided that Egerton must go and one morning in 1976 he was summoned and dismissed. Graham then turned to me and announced that I was to take the chief executive role at Standard Chartered Merchant Bank on top of my other responsibilities as a regional general manager until a replacement was found. For the *stagiere* who was not going to make it at Samuel Montagu this was quite an uplift, but Graham was evidently testing my capacities. This took over a year to accomplish. It so happened that the bank had been charged by the Bank of England with supervising the winding down of the merchant bank subsidiary of old established Chartered Bank customers, Wallace Brothers. This was undertaken by one of its executives, Robin Baillie, with great skill. It became obvious to me that he would be the right person to head our merchant banking interests, which he did with great success and subsequently joined the board of Standard Chartered.

Mocatta & Goldsmid

Preston had a strong conviction that there was an opportunity for Standard Chartered in the bullion market. At that time the London market was conducted by relatively modestly capitalised merchant banks and bullion dealers, whereas the other main market in Switzerland was conducted by the major banks there who had the capacity both to trade on a larger scale and to do attractive bullion lending business. He feared that London's traditional important role would migrate to Switzerland unless larger banks became involved and it seemed a 'natural' that a British overseas bank like ours should acquire one of the bullion dealers. Achieving this objective turned out to be quite a challenge. To begin with he set his sights on Sharps Pixley (owned by Kleinwort Benson), but it was not for sale. He then failed to persuade the Bank of England to allow Standard Chartered to set up its own bullion dealing operation and become an additional member of the gold and silver fixings. Finally, he turned to Johnson Matthey, the industrial refining company whose silver dealing business had also been granted a banking licence. The board of Johnson Matthey seemed amenable to a deal and I was put in to investigate the business, encountering half-hearted cooperation from management. A more serious obstacle was that the chairman, Lord Robens, was attached to the idea of owning a bank and when Preston thought a deal had been agreed Robens suddenly pulled out. Preston was furious and the Bank of England was not amused. As a coda, Johnson Matthey Bankers subsequently got into serious financial difficulties and the Bank of England enforced a rescue operation in which we became heavily involved.

Meantime, another bullion opportunity presented itself. Hambros Bank owned Mocatta & Goldsmid, in some ways the doyen of the market. However, Hambros had lent heavily to a Norwegian shipping company that was now in difficulties as a result of the oil crisis. At the prompting of the Bank of England, Jock Mocatta called on Preston in early 1973 to tell him that Hambros were having to dispose of its subsidiary and enquiring whether Standard Chartered could be interested in replacing them. What might have been a straightforward transaction turned into a complex negotiation as a result of an agreement and joint venture between Mocatta & Goldsmid and a then mysterious New York figure, Dr Henry Jarecki, which included pre-emption rights to him in the event of Mocatta & Goldsmid being sold. Preston became exasperated at the situation, with the result that I became an intermediary in intense negotiations over several weeks. Jarecki was in a position where he

Elephant blessing. Garland welcome. Ship launch. SS Ocean Prosper. Jarecki on right of Mocatta Financiere

was able to broker a deal whereby he acquired Mocatta for a nominal consideration and on-sold it to Standard Chartered at its market value. The outcome was that Jarecki became a 45 percent shareholder in Mocatta & Goldsmid and Standard Chartered became a 30 percent shareholder in Jarecki's US business, Mocatta Metals. Preston became chairman of Mocatta & Goldsmid. [39]

Over the years Henry Jarecki and I became good friends, especially over the silver crisis in 1979 and following events and he was a candid and valued adviser. Jarecki's emergence as an innovator and forceful presence in the bullion market was itself a remarkable story. He came from a wealthy German Jewish family in Silesia with shipping and coal mining interests. Fleeing Hitler in 1938 the family reached New York as penniless refugees. Henry's father was a doctor and Henry followed him, becoming a psychiatrist at Yale and a pioneer in the treatment of mental illnesses with drugs. An innate flair for business surfaced in the 1960s when Henry worked out that there was money to be made from US silver certificates which, at the time, comprised a quarter of the currency in circulation. By purchasing the certificates for slightly more than their face value and tendering them to the Treasury for their silver bullion content and selling it, he could make a return of 3 percent or better after all costs. The US Treasury eventually called time, as it was running out of silver bullion, but not before Jarecki had organised a substantial business operation. This led him to make contact with Mocatta & Goldsmid in London in his search for hedging protection and extra funding. With the price of silver trending upwards, Jarecki spotted a further opportunity with the US silver coinage, where the bullion content had become worth more that the coins' face value. Another substantial operation was launched to buy coins from the public, which Mocatta supported and participated in a joint venture company, Mocatta Metals, and entered into the governing agreement already referred to.

George Pullen's Deals

As already noted, both banks had fostered strong personalities in some of their overseas operations who dug themselves into their bailiwicks for

---

39 Jarecki has published a fascinating account of his progressive involvement in bullion dealing to become a leading innovator and force in the market: *An Alchemist's Way*, Dr Henry Jarecki. Falconwood Press, 2021

long tenures. Such was the case in Singapore, Tokyo, Seoul, Hamburg, and San Francisco where Norman Eckersley was in charge of Chartered Bank of London. He had succeeded in aligning his remuneration with that of American bankers and networked brilliantly. For some while he had been urging George Pullen to take advantage of an opportunity to make an acquisition in California and in early 1973 a prospect was lined up. Liberty National Bank had been started by the Denebeim brothers, with an emphasis on mortgage finance, and now had a small network of branches. Pullen was intrigued and, somewhat to everyone's surprise, he proposed that I be sent to San Francisco to evaluate a deal. I was installed in a suite in the Fairmont Hotel on Knob Hill and forbidden to show my face while I pored over the accounts for several days and had long meetings with the Denebeims. I was taken to see some of the bank's branches, learned much about banking in California and formed a favourable opinion of the deal. In communication with London I fronted the negotiations to conclusion. It was a heady experience.

Pullen was responsible for another acquisition transaction in early 1974 involving the Chartered Bank's trade investment in the Wales- based hire purchase company, Hodge Group, which also held a banking licence. The secondary banking crisis that year threatened the funding of the business and there appeared to be a compelling logic to bring the whole entity into Standard Chartered in order to protect its funding, since this would also enhance the group's UK earnings; moreover, both Standard and Chartered had developed successful hire purchase subsidiaries overseas. Sir Julian Hodge was a difficult personality and I was tasked with winning him and his senior staff to the takeover on visits to Cardiff and also with liaising with Schroders, our financial advisers, over its terms. The deal was consummated as market conditions deteriorated and Standard Chartered was much criticised by financial commentators for overpaying on the deal. More seriously, Sir Julian objected strongly to renaming his creation as Chartered Trust and he became a thorn in our side for years afterwards. The notion of forging a worldwide hire purchase network proved to be a chimera.

Time to mention Sir John Major. One day the City Office manager called on me to say that one of his lowly clerks was a prominent Conservative councillor in Lambeth and was responsible for a larger budget than he had: would I be prepared to take Major into my

Corporate Development area, where he would have more opportunity? This was duly effected. Major had already had an interesting experience in the bank when he was one of the volunteers to go out to Nigeria for six months to help deal with the financing of the groundnut crop after the Igbo clerks had fled, following a sectarian massacre in Kano. He had been involved in a motor accident and was in hospital for many months, supported by the bank. We soon learned of Major's ambitions to enter Parliament. He campaigned unsuccessfully for St Pancras North in the two elections of 1974, supported by colleagues, after which he succeeded in being adopted for the safe seat of Huntingdon for the next election, which was not until 1979. At the prompting of a colleague, I wrote a memo to Lord Barber suggesting that it would be in the bank's interest to have an MP with direct knowledge of the City and that instead of requiring a successful candidate to resign on being elected, as was currently the City practice, we should enable the person to keep his job and adjust the workload to suit the House of Commons. This was accepted and when Major was elected in 1979 he continued to have a job in the bank until he became a Parliamentary Private Secretary in 1981 and was on the government payroll. Barber took a benevolent interest in his career and no doubt provided valuable counselling for the young MP, who demonstrated a marked ability to master a complex brief.

Nigeria

Early in 1974 I was promoted to full general manager and moved into an executive role in relation to the bank's overseas network, with responsibility for Nigeria, Zambia and Malawi in mid-year, and to take on India at the end of the year upon the retirement of Jimmy Russell. The transition was anything but easy. I inherited a management crisis in Nigeria. Bank of West Africa's star manager, Charles Harding, had succeeded Macleod and found himself being micro-managed from London by a Standard Bank person who had no management experience on the ground, let alone in West Africa. He resigned in a huff and had then been replaced by a Standard man from East Africa, Ron Piercy. On account of his lack of experience of West Africa a controversial decision had been taken to transfer the mercurial Irishman from Ghana, Johnny Johnson, as executive deputy chairman. The two men did not get on. Over the next three years Nigeria proved to be a taxing responsibility.

It was a time of post-Biafra war, oil boom, military coups and aggressive nationalism. I visited the country eight times in three years and have retained my tour reports.

I made an inaugural visit to Lagos in February 1974 before formally taking over as general manager in July. A visiting general manager would expect to stay with the chief executive and the bank residence had been built accordingly. However, Piercy had another message to convey and I was booked into the Ikoyi hotel and left to find my own lunch on the morning of my arrival. I was presented with a new management chart that had been promulgated a few days earlier without informing London. Piercy was an experienced banker, but his management style was to centralise communications onto himself and to be jealous of his prerogatives. He was reluctant to seek support or advice from head office and he had no sense of the importance of communicating and getting to know the board of Nigerian directors and making use of their influence. He was desk bound and saw no merit in getting round the country and visiting corporate customers, or networking in Lagos. At bottom he did not like Nigeria or Nigerians. Johnson was the polar opposite. He was not a good manager or banker, but he was an inspired networker with all the advantages of Irish blarney and he got on well with Nigerians. With a Nigerian chairman living in far-away Zaria except when he had to come to Lagos, Johnson effectively became the face of the bank and did this with panache.

The ending of the secessionist war in Biafra enabled the great oil discoveries in the Niger delta to be aggressively exploited and a massive economic boom was under way. One consequence was an edgy nationalism coupled with growing corruption of the public services. There was much money to be made, but probity was at a premium. Foreign owned businesses not only had to incorporate separate companies with a significant Nigerian shareholding, but were expected to bring Nigerians into senior management as work permits for expatriates were progressively toughened. By the time that I came on the scene Johnson had had a great idea: that we should entice the deputy governor of the central bank, Sam Asabia, to come over to Standard Bank Nigeria as its chief executive designate. I was taken to meet Asabia and fell for the plot. Standard would be the first large company to appoint a Nigerian as its chief executive. The plan was that Asabia would step into Johnson's shoes as vice chairman and chief executive when Johnson retired 18 months hence in October 1975. Asabia was keen to make the move and the appointment was announced that autumn to great acclaim, except for the British High Commissioner, Sir Martin Le Quesne, who gave me a severe dressing down for selling the pass too soon. Ron Piercy was also not amused.

Asabia came to London for an introduction visit and I spent much time with him. He was a Christian Yoruba and had married a Scottish schoolteacher. I made the mistake of taking them to a rather explicit production of *Pericles*. It was soon apparent that they were both quite prickly over status, which was a warning. Piercy's reaction was to build barricades rather than to build bridges, so the relationship was perhaps doomed from the start. It was notable at the board meetings that I attended that Piercy was reluctant to speak or give a lead. In retrospect, the Asabia appointment was misconceived in seeing him as a replacement for Johnson, whose position had been created very much *ad personam*. As Le Quesne correctly observed, the move to appoint a Nigerian chief executive was premature, and when it did become necessary it would have been better to make the appointee managing director and chief executive straight away, and then to have retained an expatriate chief operating officer for a while. The original Piercy appointment was also a mistake and should have been someone with experience and feel for Nigeria at that unsettled time, and someone who would respond to the challenge of supporting a Nigerian successor.

Leaving aside these personality dramas, there were serious operational issues to be addressed in Nigeria as the bank grappled with the changed economic circumstances for which the military government and the civil service was quite unprepared. Somewhat counterintuitively, the government was indecisive in managing the economy except for nationalistic measures such as the decree requiring foreign companies to take in Nigerian shareholders. There was only a modest industrial sector with all sorts of supply gaps, especially in relation to construction, with the consequence that the oil bonanza gave rise to a huge import boom and much resulting congestion at Lagos port. It became not uncommon for 50 ships to be standing off Apapa docks waiting to unload. This in turn led to smuggling and other short cuts.

Perhaps the worst aspect was that the central bank continued to operate as if foreign exchange was a scarce commodity that needed meticulous controls. Imports were usually shipped under letters of credit established by local banks and the central bank insisted that foreign exchange would only be released upon the presentation of full import documentation. Mistakes and oversights in the issuing branches and in London where credits were confirmed, and in the central bank itself, led to a huge backlog of delayed payments. Every one of my visit reports had a section on these problems and on steps to improve document processing. Of course, the bank in London could release payments to exporters pending receipt of funds from Nigeria, but this entailed an exchange risk now that there was a separate currency that was not tied to sterling, and the exchange risk had to be carefully monitored and controlled. These difficulties revealed inefficiencies and lack of training in the Nigerian branches, but also the overcentralised administration of the old Bank of West Africa, which had a long tradition of nannying controls and reluctant delegation.

One of Johnson's strong points was the close rapport that he cultivated with our Nigerian directors and key government officials. Chief Henry Fajemirokun was the leading personality on our Nigerian board and Johnson made sure that I got to know him well. He was a big man in every sense and one of his conceits was that he only drank champagne, which had to be produced in Clements Lane whatever time of day he called. On more than one occasion meetings at his palatial residence helped to resolve problems in the bank. But there was a distaff side in that Chief Henry's own import agency business was perpetually on the verge of over-trading and breaching its loan facility arrangements, which did not endear him to Piercy. We tried to keep matters in order through close liaison with his expatriate general manager, but Chief Henry expected special treatment in recognition of his board role. This was a small example of a wider problem that dogged the bank in most countries: managing the relationship with an entrepreneurial and influential and valuable customer who stretched the bounds of banking prudence. It needed much experience and finesse to keep the balance, and not everyone managed to do this.

I made a point of trying to visit branches and customers in different parts of Nigeria, which was some relief from the personality clashes in Lagos, and one experienced the vibrant energy of this extraordinary country. In 1975 I visited the eastern branches that had been caught up in the Biafran war, driving from Port Harcourt to Onitsha. The bank had

had a remarkable experience in the war in that a Nigerian member of its staff, Coker, took charge of them and maintained meticulous records in exercise books, and was able to hand over an essentially 'clean' bank when it was all over. The great Onitsha market was already thriving again and its dynamism was memorable. It was commonly said at the time that an alternative currency had been established during the war in terms of tins of the Danish dairy product Peak Milk (the tin had a picture of Cameroon mountain), and that almost any product could be purchased in terms of so many tins of Peak. The other great market was in Kano. I still wear an embroidered green waistcoat of the sort worn by men over their white robes when going out. I collected several pieces of wood carving and bronze casts over the years, including a rather impressive figure from the Plateau area that required an export licence from the national museum (courtesy of chief Henry).

My visit to Jos coincided with a weekend race meeting. The clerk of the course came up to the bank manager in some perturbation to say that one of the race judges had failed to show up and would the general manager from London be prepared to stand in? I was led to a tin hut on stilts by the finishing line where our task was to hang the tin number plate of the first three horses on the outside wall, and then to duck out of sight in case the crown disapproved of our verdict. The last race was the so-called Tribesmen's Race when men in medieval chain mail, with helmets and swords, lined up and after much shouting and wheeling about, were off. For this race the judges had to stand by the finishing post to identity the winners.

Mallam Ahmadu Coomassie, the Nigerian chairman, lived in Zaria in the far north of the country. He was a tall dignified man who had originally been a schoolmaster before moving into public administration. In the 1930s he had made the Mecca pilgrimage overland. It was decided to invite him to England in 1975 and Ruth and I were tasked with looking after him. He said he would like to attend a Shakespeare performance at Stratford upon Avon, and we were able to book for *Henry IV Part 2*, staying at the Hilton. Coomassie was something of a sensation in the tourist audience since it soon became apparent that he knew the play better than anyone else and in the comedy scenes everyone took their cue from him. Back in the hotel we had a Shakespearian moment when Coomassie asked the desk clerk for the direction of east so that he could say his prayers. It was pointed out, but the doorman promptly contradicted his colleague with another direction and was in turn contradicted by someone by the lift. One year, Coomassie invited me to Zaria for the Eid Festival. As guests of the Emir we were seated in his stand as the local headmen came to pay homage. Attired in chain mail and fully armed, the procedure was for a group of them to gallop towards the grandstand shouting praises and then at the last possible moment to rein in their horses in a cloud of dust – a thrilling spectacle.

There was a final visit to Nigeria as general manager in September 1976 for a board meeting, but also in connection with the government's decision announced in June on a tight timetable that foreign banks had to reduce their shareholding to 40 percent by selling shares to the government. Asabia's connections and influence were valuable in the opening discussions and Standard Chartered was the only bank that tabled a detailed legal agreement. The document was not accepted by the government negotiators, but it meant that we had more precise points to argue than the other banks. The finale on 30 September was somewhat typical of Nigeria: the government was determined that all 14 agreements would be signed that day. We had secured an 8am meeting with the negotiator, which took place with interrupting phone calls and other banks waiting their turn impatiently outside the door. I decided to exploit the situation by taking the line that the only way the government could obtain a signed agreement from us that day was to concede the six principal issues we had raised. Two hours passed before a compromise was finally achieved. Eventually, at 3pm everyone assembled in the minister's ante-chamber –

'All chairs were taken (and held onto) by members of the press and television while we waited for about three quarters of an hour. The Minister then summoned us and read out a homily which included a strong reassurance about non-interference (but also a galling reference so far as we were concerned, regretting that no bank had been prepared to re-invest its share disposal proceeds). There was then a great flurry of agreements being signed in triplicate and large trays of champagne were produced. Sam Asabia proposed a toast to the Minister and to the bankers of Lagos.'[40]

40 *Lagos Negotiations – Final Meeting.* Memorandum for Executive Committee, October 1976

A sad but not unexpected outcome of the new deal where, inter alia, it had been provided that the bank's executive committee would be led by the vice chairman and chief executive, was that Piercy announced that he was unable to accept the situation personally, and requested early retirement. It was accepted.

Zambia

Being allocated responsibility for the bank's operations in Zambia was personally gratifying in that it brought back memories of my time on the Copperbelt in 1957, and it also meant that I was familiar with the country's history. Zambia had become independent in 1964, on the break-up of the Central Africa Federation. Under the Presidency of Kenneth Kaunda and under the influence of a group of radical British advisers, the government had embarked upon a programme of nation-alisation, starting with the mines of the Copperbelt controlled by Anglo-American and Roan Selection Trust. On two occasions there was a risk that the banks would be nationalised, which had been averted, but foreign ownership was viewed with suspicion. At independence the country had a very poor endowment of educated countrymen and the situation was not helped by the prevalence of South African racial attitudes amongst too many whites. Standard Bank Zambia had 21 branches in the country in 1974 and of the 256 staff in supervisory grades, 112 were still expatriates; additionally, the bank still employed 25 white secretaries. It was disappointing that a British owned bank had made so little headway in adapting to the new circumstances of independence.

An important development before my arrival was an initiative by Sir Cyril Hawker in London to recruit a Zambian diplomat, Elias Chipimo, with the intention that he be appointed chairman upon the retirement of a distinguished white farmer who had taken out Zambian citizenship. Chipimo was ostensibly being trained as a banker, with the rank of deputy chairman and a portfolio of executive responsibilities. He was distinctive in being one of a small group of leading Zambians that opposed Kaunda's nationalising agenda and was strongly in favour of private enterprise and an open economy, yet he retained good connections with ministers. Less happy, was that Chipimo showed little aptitude for business management, albeit was charming withal. The scene was set for another version of my Nigerian experience.

On my first visit in 1974 I concluded that the bank should exploit the currently favourable climate and arrange for a local share issue on the new Lusaka stock exchange with the main purpose of securing a panel of local investors supportive of an independent bank. This was agreed to and a flotation took place the following year with 10 percent of the bank's capital held by private investors.

The managing director, Des Bloxam, was an energetic and able banker and in the four years since his transfer from Kenya he had established a leading reputation in the Lusaka business community and good relationships with officials by the time I arrived on the scene. Standard was recognised as the leading business bank. However, it had a weakness on the retail side and a limited deposit base, largely on account of the predominantly expatriate management who had little interest in expanding the Zambian customer base. My efforts to galvanise a more enterprising approach fell on stony ground.

During 1974 the copper companies suffered an acute cash flow squeeze on account of bottlenecks at their export ports in Tanzania and Angola, coming on top of a need to maintain larger supply stocks for the mines. Standard was banker to the Anglo-American connection on the Copperbelt and so quickly felt the pressure on liquidity as funds were withdrawn. By October the advances/deposit ratio had reached 93 percent. Bloxam exercised great ingenuity in arranging short term borrowings from less affected banks and the central bank and running off the portfolio of Treasury bills, all without causing comment. There was a need for external support which the Bank of Zambia was initially reluctant to concede, but a substantial facility against copper stocks was eventually arranged by Standard.

The financial situation deteriorated further with a foreign exchange crisis following a collapse of copper prices. The IMF became engaged and we kept in close touch with its Africa division. This led to an innovative transaction in late 1975 when Standard Chartered agreed to lend $30 million to the Bank of Zambia in anticipation of it agreeing a facility with the IMF. This was only possible on account of the relationships Bloxam had established in Lusaka, the support that I was able to mobilise in London and the deft handling at both ends of the mercurial Governor, Bitwell Kuwani. On one of his London visits he had us in fits of laughter over lunch about a shopping expedition in the West End to buy a pair of dancing shoes, with the necessary demonstration. More seriously, the episode was a good example of the classic banking adage of knowing well and having confidence in a customer at a personal level. There were several more transactions with the Bank of Zambia, as well as some declines.

Zambia attracted closer attention at board level in London than it might otherwise have merited because Standard's deputy chairman, Sir Robert Taylor, had been financial secretary in the colonial government of Northern Rhodesia and he naturally retained a close interest in the affairs of the bank. Additionally, there had been the somewhat impulsive initiative by Sir Cyril Hawker in hiring Chipimo. Bloxam's one blind spot was a failure to handle well this premature appointment. It was evident that Chipimo had no talent for detailed management and, with hindsight, he should have been deployed more systematically on public relations with government and in helping the branches expand their local customer base. As it was, I spent much effort in finding ways to remove points of abrasion between the two. In early 1977, when Chipimo had at last been appointed chairman, a point had been reached where the Zambian board formed the view that Bloxam would have to be reassigned. Sir Robert and I flew out to Lusaka and spent several days 'knocking heads together' as the saying goes, redrafting their respective roles more carefully and making clear that it was not part of a chairman's job to take part in the day to day running of the bank. However, in my note of the visit I concluded that a new managing director should be found within a year. Bloxam was actually within two years of retirement and he decided to go early rather than have another posting.

Apart from these issues, two other events remain with me from my visits to Zambia. The first was a Sunday picnic with Des and Shirley Bloxam on the banks of the Kafue river – a barbecue with liberal helpings of Castle beer on a hot day. After lunch they had a siesta and I decided to walk along the river bank and do some bird spotting. Suddenly there was an explosive noise and an enormous crocodile rushed in front of me and belly flopped into the river. Fortunately, it had taken fright rather than turning aggressive.

As noted earlier, the boss of Nchanga Copper Mines, who sat on our Zambian board, arranged for me to fly up to the Copperbelt in the corporate jet and to visit Mufulira Copper Mine, where I had worked in

1957 – some of the time underground at the 1500 ft level. Appropriately kitted out, I was taken down the mine in the terrifyingly fast lift to visit a working area again. Afterwards a little joke was played out. Because most mine workers – Africans and Europeans – were target workers who might return for another tour, detailed personnel records were retained by the mine in case a person reapplied, with comments on suitability for re-employment. My record from 17 years ago was produced:

'Prepared to Re-engage: No'

'McWilliam stated he was leaving because of insufficient work. Head of Department stated he is unsuitable for re-engagement for African Personnel Department.'

Chief Personnel Officer: 'This man had intelligence and ability of a very high standard which was not made use of in APD. In my opinion he would be suitable for any administrative position calling for these attributes.'

India

India held a special place in the collective mind of the Chartered Bank. It was the country where the first overseas branch was opened, in Calcutta in 1853. With the loss of its Far East branches during the Second World War, India sustained the bank for the duration. It was to India the post-war intake of covenanted officers for the overseas service were generally sent on their first posting – all bachelors and housed in so-called chummeries. By the mid-1970s the picture was very different: India was a giant suffocating under state socialism, whereas the Far East was vibrant and prospering. Old habits died hard and the great branches in Calcutta and Bombay were often reserved as a last posting for a senior expatriate who had little incentive to rock the boat. The general manager that I was replacing had himself been a conservative India chief manager and was in the habit of making an annual state visit, while the chairman, George Pullen, who had been an advisor to the Viceroy during the war, also enjoyed high profile visits.

My appointment was the first senior 'cross pollination' posting as between Standard and Chartered, and must have been the source of some apprehension. Perhaps on this account, it was decided that my inaugural visit to India should coincide with James Russell's farewell tour. It followed that wives should accompany us and Ruth was advised to bring hat and gloves for Calcutta and for the President's reception on Independence Day. This was held at Lutyens' great complex in Delhi, where of course we had privilege seats for the great parade. The ensuing reception was held in the rose garden of the palace. There was a slight breeze blowing and a puff of wind suddenly removed Ruth's wide-brimmed hat and deposited it in the middle of a rose bed. At this point a tall soldier in gorgeous uniform stepped forward and with his lance scooped up the hat and presented it to Ruth. She had no social problems during the rest of our stay as the incident had been picked up with glee by the gossip columns.

Chartered had suffered a severe setback in 1969 when its subsidiary bank, Allahabad Bank, was nationalised along with all other domestically incorporated banks. This left Chartered with branches in only seven cities and with no ability to enlarge its network. Although profitable and able to remit its after-tax profits to London, the bank was severely constrained from any growth due to its tiny deposit base. This was exacerbated by London's reluctance to incur foreign exchange exposure to India by remitting capital, or to allow other than very modest exposure on trade finance. Little had been done to find ways of alleviating the resource problem and I noted a number of possibilities in my report, but prefacing my comments –

> 'The posture of Chartered in India is not impressive, except in so far as it still reflects the glories of an earlier period. The bank appears to be on the defensive, the staff somewhat demoralised, several of the branches run down in appearance. Altogether there is a lack of vitality and confidence in the future. It was particularly surprising to face enquiries on Chartered's future intentions in India from within and without the bank... .The immediate priority is the establishment among staff and customers of a sense of confidence that Chartered sees a future in India and has serious objectives there.'[41]

Despite his title, the chief manager was not responsible for all the branches in India, which dealt directly with London on many issues including lending. This divide and rule policy meant that the managers had never been brought together for a meeting. The chief manager was

---

41 *Visit to India*, January 1975

based in Calcutta – the traditional seat of imperial power, except that the government had long since moved to Delhi, while Bombay had emerged as the main business and financial centre. My visit coincided with the arrival of Neville Green to take over the Calcutta branch and the chief manager role, with his previous service being mainly in the Middle East. Green was an able, energetic and ambitious banker and we had a burgeoning relationship over the following years culminating in a general manager role in London. Green quickly came to the conclusion that the headquarters of the bank should be moved to Bombay and during the year I was able to secure a reversal of Russell's decision shortly before he retired to maintain the status quo.

Green had a major challenge in modernising the bank, which still maintained hand written ledgers on account of union opposition, and I gave him full backing. Peter Graham had decided to hold the first Standard Chartered strategy conference in London in the autumn of 1975, shortly before his assumption of the role of group managing director, and Green and I decided that we would hold a similar event for India the following spring. The event was held over a weekend at a resort in Goa and all the managers were brought together for the first time (with their wives). An indication of its novelty was that the British High Commissioner, Sir Michael Walker, flew down from Delhi to address the gathering, and the Governor of the Reserve Bank also accepted (although on the day he was represented by the Deputy Governor). The event gave Green a strong mandate to implement his modernisation plans, and provided a welcome signal that Chartered Bank had woken up in India.

I had been an admirer of Indian culture since my school days, attending performances by the classical dancer Ram Gopal in Cheltenham and getting interested in classical music at Oxford by hearing Ravi Shankar and others. Now visiting Madras, I was overwhelmed by the bronze sculpture of the Chola period in the museum there. Our manager was a devout Hindu and through Anantha Krishnan's influence I paid a special visit to the temple at Kanchipuram, which was known for its Chola sculptures. Seeing them was another matter. I had to undergo a sort of purification before being admitted to the inner sanctum, where I was then presented with a bowl of holy water to drink, which presented a dilemma for a western gut. I decided to bow low and then to pour the holy water over my head (and suit). Sighs of approval all round and I was then shown their collection, where against expectation all the figures were dressed. On the way out I was taken to the temple elephant to be blessed. This involved the animal curling up its trunk and then placing the tip on my head and expelling a long draught of hay-scented stomach odours.

The bank's handsome 1920s branch in Bombay contained latticed stonework to let in some fresh air to the main banking hall. Unfortunately, the town pigeons had taken advantage of the openings and roosted at the top of the Grecian columns in the hall and, inevitably, their droppings fell on the clerks below. Peter Pickering, the manager, at last obtained approval to install air conditioning and this meant sealing the filigree ventilation screens. What about the pigeons? He instructed his two expatriate assistants to meet him at 5am on the day work was to start for a pigeon shoot. Word somehow got out and, on arrival, they found a band of enthusiastic pigeon spotters to assist in the great shoot.

Well after my time the bank's earnings in India developed strongly, especially after it was able to purchase its principal rival, National & Grindlays Bank, from its then Australian owners. Standard Chartered has even had an Indian chief executive for a while. India may never rival China for opportunity, but its important place in the group has been re-established.

The Gulf

The end of 1976 saw the retirement of another of Chartered's traditional bankers. Tiny Finlayson was responsible for the branches in the Gulf, where he had spent much of his career before the advent of great oil wealth, and where Bahrein was the largest business. Peter Graham decided to accelerate an announcement that I was to be the next senior general manager from April 1977 so that I could take immediate responsibility for the Gulf, and also prepare the ground for a new general manager portfolio embracing the Gulf and the Indian sub-continent. My diary noted that the move 'caused rather a stir since it meant by-passing several senior colleagues.' They were all older than me and change was in the air. My own portfolio was now to comprise Tropical Africa, Middle East and Indian sub-continent, North America, merchant banks and Mocatta.

The bank had lost its branches in Iraq and Aden through revolutionary nationalisations, and it was now confined to the Gulf with Bahrein as the controlling branch where we were bankers to the ruling family. After visiting all the branches in Muscat, Sharjah, Dubai, Abu Dhabi, Qatar and Bahrein my verdict was clear: 'The importance of Bahrein and the centralisation of authority there has not been beneficial to the rest of our business... It is impossible to avoid the evidence of mediocre premises, very small market share of deposits and lending, the much greater prominence of the British Bank of the Middle East, the past record of poor staffing.'[42] In effect, Chartered had failed to recognise and engage with the explosion of wealth taking place along the Gulf following the oil discoveries there. My remedy was to abolish the role of chief manager for the Gulf held by Bahrein and to have the individual country branches report directly to the general manager in London.

During my tour I encountered two reminders of my days in Kenya. Muscat was the only branch in the Gulf where women clerks were to be seen at their desks. The explanation was that their parents were Omani Arabs expelled from Zanzibar after independence and revolution, but where colonial schools had been open to both sexes and many spoke English. The branch was happy to employ these educated women. In Abu Dhabi I met up with Sir John Butter, the director of finance there, who had recruited me to the Kenya Treasury in 1958 and fostered my early career. He and Joyce had a house on the creek and we had a pleasant lunch together. I also acquired an antique Persian rug in unusual circumstances: the branch manager told me that a junior from the Foreign Office had over-extended himself by buying Persian carpets and now needed to sell several in order to get straight with the bank. The upshot was the purchase of a 1930s Bokhara rug.

1975 Strategy Conference

Peter Graham was due to take over as managing director in early 1976 and he had resolved to hit the ground running, as they say. He decided to convene a group strategy conference in the autumn of 1975, with attendance from senior managers from all round the group, and a huge effort was mounted by Corporate Development to organise papers and presentations for the event, which was held at the Park Lane Hotel. The conference was intended to symbolise – and dramatize – the emergence

42 *Tour of Gulf Branches,* November 1977

of an integrated banking group. There were ambitious objectives, not only in the traditional strongholds in Asia and Africa, but also in Britain, Europe and North America. On the table were the recent acquisitions of Mocatta & Goldsmid, Hodge Group, Liberty National and the development of merchant banking and eurocurrency lending. However, as Duncan Campbell-Smith's history recounts, Graham had a much more ambitious agenda in mind of major banking acquisitions in Britain and America, with an aim that these two mature economies would account for half of group earnings. The first of these forays was a bungled attempt in 1976 to acquire Bank of California through a public offer, without first gaining the support of its controlling shareholder. With hindsight, this headstrong initiative marked the start of a decade of corporate turmoil during which time I twice frustrated a disposition by Graham to sell Standard Chartered after other initiatives had failed to deliver his vision.

Notwithstanding the failure of the Bank of California bid, Graham remained resolved to expand the bank's presence in North America and attention turned to branch development. Following a strategy meeting in the summer of 1977 I went to New York and Canada in September and my report reflected the spirit of the time, with its opening passage:

> 'For Standard Chartered North America represents a new frontier almost as potent in its significance as the new horizons were to the frontiersmen of an earlier age: a great continental market still open to foreign banking, a currency which now dominates world trade and capital movements, and above all an opportunity to develop an additional counterbalance to the hazards of African banking.'[43]

The challenge was that the actual profit contribution from North America at the time was only some 4 percent of the group total. The immediate agenda therefore was to press on vigorously with new branches and keeping an eye open for possible acquisitions. This proved to be a slow -moving caravan since the well-entrenched and much-liked chief manager in New York was within two years of retirement and had little appetite for changing the status quo. However, Graham's luck changed in 1979 when he was successful in purchasing Union Bank in California. This promised

---

43 *Visit to United States and Canada,* September 1977

to satisfy one of his key objectives: at a stroke a quarter of group assets were now in North America. We will return to this scene.

The Silver Crisis

The Mocatta investment in 1973 had been well timed in that the bullion markets were active and good profits were earned in the ensuing years. Mocatta & Goldsmid in London was a traditional bullion dealer and member of the gold and silver fixings that traced their origins back to the 17th century. Its counterparties were central banks and bullion speculators, mostly of long standing. The scene at Mocatta Metals in New York was utterly different. Henry Jarecki was the pioneer in the development of computerised trading and option trading. Sophisticated programmers and mathematicians developed trading systems that were underpinned by complex algorithms and designed for screen-based volume trading. At the same time Jarecki developed business relationships with mining companies and industrial users and taught them to use his systems. He developed a large silver lending business. In all this he was paranoid about risk mitigation; he had a fundamental credo that bullion dealing was about exploiting market imperfections through arbitrage, and was not about predicting the future price of silver or gold.

Standard Chartered was never entirely comfortable with the fractured shareholding structure, and it became a strategic objective that one day the bank should buy out Jarecki's stake. It entailed the heroic assumption that it could manage the businesses without him and completely overlooked the sophistication of what was going on in New York and our crucial dependence on Jarecki himself. Early in 1978 I went to Moscow with him on a mission to persuade the Russian central bank to use Mocatta as the distributor for an issue of Russian gold coins at the time of the forthcoming 1980 Olympic Games. It was a somewhat surreal experience, commencing with the arrival at our hotel –

'Do you think we will be spied on Henry?'

'They are probably too inefficient, but if we find that our rooms are one above the other on separate floors, instead of next door, then we should be alert.'

My room was 458 and Henry's 558.

At our welcome dinner in a leading restaurant, Jarecki handed over the large box of Havana cigars that we had bought at Heathrow.

Consternation from our hosts, who quickly placed the gift under the table. Going back to the hotel Henry opined that our event must have been under observation and that it would have been assumed that we were attempting to bribe the central bank.

Our mission was unsuccessful but the trip provided an opportunity to appraise Jarecki of the bank's strategic aims with regard to Mocatta. He was very shocked and was only partly mollified on learning that the policy had been driven by experiences Chartered had suffered in the East. He became much happier after attending Standard Chartered's annual meeting later in the year upon hearing Lord Barber explain to a sceptical shareholder that the justification for purchasing Union Bank on a price earnings ratio of 20 was that it was 'a strategic decision'. He immediately drew my attention to the phrase at luncheon afterwards.

Meanwhile, the real bullion world was becoming dangerous in 1978. The Hunt brothers in Texas had started to squeeze the silver market by causing a shortage of physical silver and its price was rising dramatically. The episode has been well told by Stephen Fay in his book *Beyond Greed*[44] and authoritatively so by Jarecki in his memoirs. At that time Mocatta Metals owned some 40 million ounces of silver that had been leased out to industrial users and had naturally hedged its position on the Comex exchange. But this gave rise to a problem in that the exchange required cash margin to be deposited with it in support of futures contracts, so that as the silver price rose Mocatta Metals needed ever larger lines of bank credit to draw on to provide these cash deposits with the exchange. The situation was further complicated by a specific transaction with the Hunts, whereby Mocatta Metals had lent the brothers $50 million that was secured by 10 million ounces of silver deposited with it, but now worth getting on for $200 million. The Hunts became restive over Mocatta Metals' credit worthiness, as did some banks. Jarecki had deliberately not arranged a large line of credit with Standard Chartered in order not to complicate the relationship, but the American lending banks began asking where did we stand with regard to our New York investment? One tense morning when we were discussing the situation, Graham turned to me and said that I had better get over to New York forthwith and visit the banks there to reassure them that Standard Chartered stood behind Mocatta.

---

44 *Beyond Greed*, Stephen Fay. The Viking Press, 1982

I rushed home to gather the proverbial toothbrush, left a note for Ruth as I had been unable to get her on the phone, and managed to catch the daily Concorde from Heathrow. Flying faster than the speed of sound I arrived in New York at 9am their time that same morning. On my way to the World Trade Centre I took a call from London in the limo and authorised a guarantee of $50 million for Mocatta from the car. Arriving at their offices I found the Hunt brothers ensconced in the board room, Texan boots on the table and drinking coke from a can. I was wearing a pin-striped suit and was carrying a rolled umbrella, which epitomised the clash of cultures. The New York banks were duly mollified and Jarecki was subsequently able to put through a transaction whereby he delivered 10 million ounces of silver to the Hunts and cancelled the related forward position, thus getting back some $200 million of margin cash with which he could repay his banks. It was a stressful few days while Mocatta was still under pressure and it was made worse by a cold phone call back home to Ruth, who clearly had not appreciated my sudden departure.

Union Bank

The acquisition of Union Bank in 1978 was formally completed in early 1979 and in May that year I flew to Los Angeles to examine how its operations would dovetail into the group network. Its international division, which included import financing, provided by far the largest component of the bank's profits. Union had a very extensive network of correspondent banks and had representatives in all the Latin American countries; it was not involved in medium term euro-dollar lending, nor had it developed a professional foreign exchange trading capability. It was therefore relatively straightforward to integrate Union's operations with Standard Chartered's bank and country risk systems and to designate it with a lead role in Latin America.

That year we decided to have our family holiday in America and to visit New York, Washington, Las Vegas and California. I was encouraged to make social contact with Union's executives while there and we were royally entertained and became aware of some of the tensions at the top of the bank. We then motored up to San Francisco, where we met Eckersley and the Denebeim brothers, with whom we went sailing in San Francisco Bay. We even went on an overnight camping trek with the sons of the bank's lawyers, sleeping in the open in bed rolls and during the night caribou grazed over the camp site.

A curious thing then happened in our relationship with Union Bank. Harry Volk, who had built up the bank and then sold it to Standard Chartered, announced that he would retire in a year's time and told Graham that there was no one suitable to succeed him in the executive team. Graham evidently took the view that there was no one in Standard Chartered either to lead the bank (although there was at least one credible candidate in David Millar who had just come to London after a very successful time in charge of Hong Kong), and instead engaged head hunters. In doing so, he somehow missed the opportunity to establish that the appointee owed his position and allegiance to London. A strong-minded American banker, Jim Harragin, was appointed whose ambition was to build a large regional bank in western America with Standard Chartered's balance sheet support. I attended his first strategy meeting in Palm Springs and saw Harragin put his stamp on the executive team. It is puzzling why Graham made the choice he did and my conclusion is that he had set his heart on achieving his strategic aim of a large wholly owned US bank subsidiary and the issue of exercising control over it could be left to another day. He evidently did not see that Standard's experience in South Africa gave a warning signal of how a successful bank subsidiary could slip the reins. With North America as part of my portfolio, I attended Union Bank board meetings and facilitated Harragin taking responsibility for Standard Chartered branches in the rest of the country (he quickly absorbed the Chartered Bank of London branches and dispensed with Eckersley's involvement). He then set his sights on out of state acquisitions.

South Africa

A notable omission from my portfolio when I became senior general manager in April 1977 was South Africa, and this was for a curious reason. Lord Barber had been contacted by the South African chairman and told that I was thought to be 'hostile' to South Africa due to my activities in the past and was therefore not welcome as a director of our South African subsidiary, as had been intended. It took a while to unravel the story. There was an arrangement whereby promising South African executives were sent to London to learn about the group and Corporate

Planning was one of the departments visited. It had been my practice to give them a pretty free run of my files and to discuss any issues of interest. I had forgotten that one of the files contained the papers of a World Council of Churches study group on South West Africa that I had attended in my early months at the bank and that a spokesman for the SWAPO freedom fighters had come to one of the sessions. The government of South Africa was fighting a losing war in the country that eventually became Namibia, where Standard was a leading institution. A young manager had read the file, was shocked, and evidently reported on his return that McWilliam was in dialogue with the enemy, or some such.

Explanations were given and accepted, but the incident revealed how sensitive South Africa had become to outside criticism, even in an ostensibly liberal business institution, and that one would have to be mindful who one was talking to. I was then able to make something of a state visit there in March 1981 having been appointed a director of the bank; accompanied by Ruth we visited the regional centres of Cape Town, Durban and Bloemfontein before reaching Johannesburg. We were at a bank reception in Bloemfontein as news came through of Mugabe's election victory in Rhodesia and there were many long faces in that very conservative community. In contrast, we had an evening with friends of Ruth's parents from Vienna who were active in the anti-apartheid movement and supportive of the nationalist movement. We went on to Salisbury a few days later, where the population were still celebrating with the distinctive elbow movements of Mugabe's cockerel election slogan.

Under the leadership of Conrad Strauss, the South African banking group was on a strong growth path, notwithstanding the problems created by apartheid. However, the board had rather fallen under the influence of one of its members, the dynamic business figure Donald Gordon and his Liberty Life insurance group, and to the extent that Standard had acquired a significant stake in his holding company and Liberty in turn was a major investor in Standard with an unsatisfied appetite. There were ambiguous signals from the South African government as to whether we should be reducing our shareholding, and this was exploited by the local chairman with pressure to reduce it in favour of local institutions, including Liberty.

South Africa was encountering increasing problems in its international trade, on account of apartheid, and the South African management began seeking credit lines from Swiss and other banks and it also concluded that it needed its own subsidiaries in Hong Kong and London, which put some strain on our relationship. Nevertheless, South Africa needed Standard Chartered's international backing: in addition to supporting our subsidiary we maintained a large line of credit for the Reserve Bank and offered training to its foreign exchange dealers. On one memorable occasion I had agreed to attend a special anniversary dinner at the Reserve Bank in Pretoria. When I got to Heathrow to board the flight I discovered that I had failed to bring my passport. A phone call to South Africa by BA resulted in my travelling without one and then being escorted off the plane by a government official and provided with a special pass for the duration of the visit.

Standard Chartered's annual meetings were a torrid affair on account of apartheid. For up to an hour Lord Barber would field questions and pressure that we should disinvest and he would argue that collaboration was preferable to disengagement and that the bank's leadership in South Africa was liberal and reformist within the system. I very much endorsed this stance. In support of this approach, we maintained good personal relations with the South African executive and I was invited to their strategy conferences and reciprocated. It was a balancing act, yet in investor terms the writing was on the wall as the South African connection was damaging to our share price and was a concern to the Bank of England.

Royal Bank of Scotland

In early 1981 Graham sought to complete his strategic plan to acquire a British domestic bank, by means of an agreed merger with Royal Bank of Scotland. The deal had the blessing of the Bank of England. He had an additional incentive to pursue the matter because he had become aware that Standard Chartered itself was a possible acquisition target and that the Bank of England would have no *a priori* objection to a suitable approach. To everyone's astonishment, and with the explicit disapproval of the Bank of England, Hong Kong & Shanghai bank put in a rival offer and a bidding war commenced. There was uproar in Scotland at the notion that their flagship bank should come under outside ownership and the government took the easy way out by referring the matter to the Monopolies & Mergers Commission. I had not been involved at all in the prior negotiations, but Graham decided that he and I should make a round of visits to major institutions in the City and in Scotland and to the Treasury to argue our case.

We then had the tedious process of the MMC hearings where we were led by a QC, and then came the verdict that neither bid should be allowed to proceed. It was a sad blow for Graham a year before his retirement, since it left a gaping hole in his strategy of balancing emerging markets with mature economies. The vehemence of the Scottish opposition to the transaction was a severe shock. Campbell-Smith is rightly critical in his bank history at the failure to anticipate this; as he points out, an alternative presentation of the deal as an acquisition of Standard Chartered by Royal Bank would very likely have overcome the political problem of Scottish nationalism. However, this overlooks the personalities: the leadership of Royal Bank at the time was weak, while Graham was the driving force of the proposed deal; moreover, he thought he could rely on a close personal link with the RBS board through its chairman, Sir Michael Herries.

As often happens, a failed corporate deal is liable to put the parties in play with investment banks, as they examine – and provoke – alternative scenarios. Early in 1982 we became aware that Lloyds Bank was contemplating a bid for Standard Chartered when Sir Jeremy Morse spoke to Lord Barber seeking an exploratory meeting with Graham and myself. We declined to engage and, to our relief, they backed off. The incident set in train feverish analysis of our situation and my memorandum of the implications went into some detail of what might happen after a successful takeover, and what defensive tactics were at our disposal. Instead of Standard Chartered acquiring a major UK profit centre in Royal Bank, we were now faced with likely dismemberment of the group in order to fit in with Lloyds Bank's corporate structure. Defensive measures that could boost our depressed share price were reviewed, but only one manoeuvre seemed to have the prospect of killing off a hostile bid. This related to Royal Bank once more. The proposition put to us by Lazards was that we should purchase Royal Bank's English banking subsidiary, Williams & Glynn, and thereby make ourselves unattractive to Lloyds. My analysis was very positive but, sadly, informal soundings revealed that Royal Bank was not prepared to contemplate a disposal. A hostile approach on our part was out of the question. We heard no more from Lloyds that year, but we had been warned.

Deputy Managing Director

I was appointed deputy managing director in August 1979 and held the post for nearly four years before succeeding Peter Graham. During this period we implemented the acquisition of Union Bank, then there was the Royal Bank bid and its extended aftermath. As the heir apparent, albeit with no promises, I was also exposed to other parts of the group and particular problem issues. I had stepped into Preston's shoes on his retirement with oversight of the group's so-called international operations – foreign exchange dealing and euro-currency lending, the merchant banking network and the shareholder relationships with South Africa, Nigeria, Union Bank and Jarecki.

Looking again at my tour reports of the period, perhaps the most significant visit was to Hong Kong in December 1980, the territory where Graham had made his reputation. I plucked up courage to put on record my view that we were significantly underestimating our potential opportunities in Hong Kong as it emerged as a major financial centre and gateway to China. This was because the business there was still being micro-managed from London on Chartered's traditional systems by people divorced from the dynamism of business life in the colony. I argued that we needed to treat Hong Kong as a major business in its own right and devolve authority to its management accordingly, since we had an outstanding manager in Bill Brown.

I had a sharp recollection of one of my first executive committee meetings a couple of years previously, taken by Graham, when Brown's proposed appointment to Hong Kong had been vetoed by the meeting on the grounds that his Japanese wife would make him unacceptable to our major Chinese customers. The person sent instead was a failure so Brown was appointed to Hong Kong after all where his ability was recognised by the Governor with his nomination to Legislative Council. Following my visit, the constraints on the bank's expansion were duly loosened, including re-establishing an active presence in mainland China, and also the creation of the first general manager post outside London, with Brown as the incumbent.

As a director of First Bank Nigeria representing our shareholder stake in the bank, as opposed my previous role as the London general manager grappling with operating issues, l had to make three visits to Nigeria in the first part of 1981. The problem with the board was that the new chairman had his own agenda to bring about a dominant government shareholding in the bank. The context was a forthcoming capital issue to comply with regulatory standards. The details are now arcane, but my reports recount disputatious board meetings at which l defended Standard Chartered's desire to maintain its shareholding. The significance of the episode, beyond the event, was probably that it reinforced my reputation for diplomatic handling of difficult situations, and hence my claims to the succession.

In early 1982, shortly after the Lloyds Bank episode mentioned above, l attended a strategy meeting in South Africa and was invited to address the gathering. My paper gives an indication of the way my views were evolving. l started with a frank admission of the seriousness of the Royal Bank setback: 15 months had been dominated by the bid and monopoly enquiry and Standard Chartered itself had become a takeover talking point. The bank had been left with a growing financial problem at group level in order to generate UK earnings sufficient to cover the cost of the dividend and the rising costs of the corporate headquarters, and additionally to add significantly to group reserves in order to finance capital expenditure on computerisation and to meet increasingly strict regulatory standards of the Bank of England and other regulatory authorities. l articulated a strong commitment to preserving the independence of Standard Chartered – and associated Graham with this sentiment.

Group Managing Director

In October 1982 the Standard Chartered board appointed me as the next group managing director to take effect seven months later on 1st June 1983, shortly before my 50th birthday. In the early months of the new year l made two significant visits in my designated capacity. The first was to America to California, New York and Washington. At Union Bank the main issue was the assumption by Union of management control of Standard Chartered's branches in the USA, where l endorsed a considerable simplification of the arrangements for managing New

York's banking operations, and intervened in a prickly dispute over the control of the service centre for processing the group's dollar transactions. In New York I visited eleven major banks, including the chairman of Citibank and of Chase in order to introduce myself, and also the New York Fed. I also attended a board meeting of Mocatta Metals which was having a prosperous year, and learned that Jarecki would be spending several months with Mocatta in London in the new year.

In Washington I visited the World Bank, IMF, IFC, Eximbank and what I described as 'a formidable viva voce examination with Governor Wallich of the Fed.' The most worthwhile meeting was with the Africa Department of IMF to review our central bank relationships. I had been able to recruit Dr Jonathan Frimpong-Ansah as an adviser after his retirement as Governor of the Bank of Ghana and then chairman of our bank there. With his able assistance we had made a particular effort to cultivate the central banks in Africa and this had already led to important transactions in Zambia, Zimbabwe and Ghana, and with others in prospect. The Ghana facility, where we had stipulated special conditions, was very much current at the time. As I noted: 'Standard Chartered's rather special role with a number of central banks is recognised and appreciated and the point is very much taken that continuing close consultation with the Fund will be to our mutual interest.'

My other visit was to the Far East to Indonesia, Singapore and Hong Kong. It was my first visit to Jakarta and the purpose was to gain a better understanding of the rather unusual nature of our business there. Jakarta was both exotic and chaotic and my report noted: 'It is a situation which places a premium on resourcefulness and adaptability; on knowing how the Indonesian business world operates without the bank becoming compromised by the prevailing corruption and ambiguous moral standards; it means that the bank must comply with the comprehensive banking regulations while at the same time looking for loopholes; that it will not purchase favours from the authorities but seek its objectives by persuasion and authority; that it will have as its principal commercial customers businessmen who invoice earnings overseas... In our manager Radford we have a man for the country.'[45]

In Singapore I met the head of the Monetary Authority and the chairman of the major property company with whom Chartered had

---

45 *Visit to Indonesia*, April 1983

a joint venture shipping company. I toured the new bank property under construction and admired the view from the 25th floor and then spent some time on the intricacies of how the merchant bank and commercial bank should complement their respective activities. In Hong Kong I stayed in the flat on the top floor of the bank and met a number of major customers, the Bank of China, the Financial Secretary and noted: 'Chartered is widely seen to have been uniquely prudent vis a vis the property boom... Bill Brown's outstanding personal position is everywhere in evidence.'[46]

Leading up to the June handover date, Lord Barber summoned me one morning and asked if I would accept the appointment of Peter Graham as deputy chairman with an office and secretary on his retirement as chief executive. I realised at once that this was already a done deal and, in effect, I was to be monitored by my predecessor. I had an inkling of what this would imply, particularly with regard to interference in management appointments and any reorganisation, but I also recognised that Graham's experience was an asset and that we had worked well together. A more confident ego might have led me to jib at the prospect of my predecessor breathing down my neck; instead, I told Lord Barber that I would welcome the appointment. The consequences proved fatal to my career five years later.

I started keeping a daily diary shortly before taking up the new role. This was a pre-meditated decision, influenced by the publication of Richard Crossman's diaries as a minister, to record what it was like to be the chief executive of a large bank at a time of revolutionary changes in the City. Its institutions were having to adapt to the break-up of cartel structures and the incursion of thrusting US and other banks as London evolved as the leading financial centre in Europe. David Kynaston has written arrestingly about this period in his history of the City of London,[47] but I had an inkling that no one at the time would be keeping a detailed insider story. The diaries were made available to Duncan Campbell-Smith for his history of the bank and the typed version has been deposited with the London Metropolitan Library along with the bank's archives.[48] For me, now, they help to correct fallible recollections.

---

46 *Visit to Hong Kong*, April 1983
47 *The City of London: Vol IV A Club No More*, David Kynaston. Chatto & Windus, 2001
48 *Crossing Continents-A History of Standard Chartered Bank*, Duncan Campbell-Smith. Allen Lane, 2021

Also, from a perspective of 40 years later, one may hazard some more general reflections on those turbulent times. Where I quote or refer to diary entries, I will indicate the date in a footnote.

Although Graham only moved to an office down the corridor, he was almost immediately appointed chairman of the Crown Agents. This agency had become a scandalous casualty of unwise financial operations in the London market and needed a major clean-up, which Graham delivered. This assignment had the beneficial effect for me of reducing his interactions with me. Lord Barber attended the bank on a daily basis and expected to be kept fully informed of events by the chief executive.

On 1st June I flew in from an Opec conference in Vienna and held a meeting of Executive Committee to outline a revised pattern of meetings and procedures. On the next day I made a formal address to the full general management of the bank. In it I developed two main themes; the first addressed the coherence of Standard Chartered Group as a business entity, and the second was about improving the effectiveness of its operations.

'If we are to be more than a stock exchange holding company with investments in a variety of banks and branches around the world we need to clarify to ourselves in what ways these various elements hang together; what ability they have to generate business for other parts of the Group and because they themselves are members of the Group; to what extent this leads to any enhancement of overall profitability; the extent to which a stronger sense of Group identity will assist in the market differentiation of Standard Chartered as compared with other banking groups and to what extent this brings beneficial results.'[49]

On business effectiveness I referred to a contemporary takeover battle and went on –

'I think that a ruthless outside owner of this bank who was unaffected by sentimental attachment would achieve a substantial release of under-employed capital, a release of manpower on unrewarding services, a reduction in costs and a consequential improvement in profit and cash flow. It should not need a bid

---

49 *Address to General Management,* June 1983

situation to call forth that kind of management review of our operations and of course we should never forget that we are not an invulnerable institution. I therefore intend to conduct such a wide-ranging review as if we were under the threat of outside predators.'

I ended with a reflection on how to sustain authority in a large institution without crushing initiative or blocking the airing of problems. It seems striking now that I chose to articulate the problem in relation to those who worked in the bank, rather than those who owned it – the shareholders. My concern, evidently, was to modify the bank's reputation for top-down governance by indicating ways in which I hoped to receive advice and information from within the community of the bank, with a robust executive committee and a willingness to listen to grass roots comments when travelling. This was on all fours with my concern to develop career openings throughout the extensive geography of the group – not just for the expatriate officer class but also for managers selected from country banking networks.

I am not sure that I saw the connection at the time, but my enthusiasm for devolution and 'self-government' as the country branch systems matured (especially in Hong Kong, Malaysia, India and Singapore) had a clear parallel with my support for colonial self-government in my Oxford days and subsequently. I was – I now think – pre-disposed in favour of delegation of authority to country banking heads. Paradoxically, Chartered's branch networks were better prepared for this than in Africa, but they still suffered from over-centralised control from London, as my tour reports illustrated. In Africa, by contrast, rapid decolonisation had resulted in the incorporation of separate banks but still with an over-reliance on expatriates due to under-trained local staff. Nevertheless, a philosophy of management was germinating that was against the fashion of the times, which saw maximising shareholder value as the primary aim of management. In contrast, I saw the bank as an institution working to long term horizons in which a person spent his working life acquiring deep knowledge of the societies in which it operated, and where the bank sought to play a constructive role in its many jurisdictions.

The follow-up was to set in motion a group-wide review of operations with a view to releasing capital from low performing and non-performing assets, pinpointing the businesses with the best growth potential and, conversely, those to be down-graded or closed. This was to be combined with a drive to improve efficiency and to cut costs, and linked with a computerisation consultancy. The general managers were challenged that they were accountable for the results of the territories that they were responsible for and would be reporting to Executive Committee on them during the year. Nothing dramatic came of all this. The general managers were defensive of their bailiwicks rather than ruthless. One can see now that a quite different process would have been required in order to make a significant financial impact. Equally, it is evident that the top management of the bank – starting with me – was not of that disposition. We were pragmatic gradualists and too much imbued with a sense of historic legacy, and perhaps also thought we had more time to bring along the desired changes than the outside world would allow.

On the group integration theme, I held a retreat at a country house in September with Harragin from Union Bank, de Villiers from South Africa, Brown from Hong Kong and Endacott from Singapore, plus my two deputies, Millar and Baillie, for the home team. Harragin was a bit prickly and jealous of his bailiwick, but de Villiers was very positive and perhaps reflected South Africa's need for international support. Brown was upbeat on Hong Kong's prospects and Endacott was complacent.

The year was rather dominated by South Africa and its investment in the Liberty Life insurance group, which itself had become a dominating shareholder in the bank through its chairman Donald Gordon. There were considerable reservations in the South African board as well as in London, while the water was muddied by uncertainty over the government's policy towards foreign ownership. In the end an investment was approved and the finance minister also clarified that Standard Chartered had until 1991 to come down to 50 percent ownership, contrary to the advice we had been receiving from within the bank. A tiresome tailpiece was that we had been mis-advised on the London Stock Exchange aspect of South Africa's investment in Liberty and were informed that it required the approval of London shareholders. We appealed twice and I eventually went before a full meeting of the Quotations Committee – and won!

The IMF meeting that autumn was dominated so far as we were concerned by Hong Kong's property crisis and its government's decision

Vienna Opera Ball. President Mugabe at bankers' dinner. Her Majesty opens new HQ. Queen Mother at the opera

to peg the currency against the US dollar, rather than to let it float (and depreciate). I was very sceptical of the wisdom of this decision, as was the Bank of England at the time, but was proved wrong by subsequent events.

Jarecki made two extended visits to London in order to integrate Mocatta & Goldsmid more closely with his operations in New York. I had several long conversations with him, particularly over implementing computerisation and how best to deal with the difficult personality of Stuart Tarrant, the chief financial officer recruited by Graham before his retirement, who refused to forge a close relationship with me.

Graham was still obsessed by the Royal Bank situation and wanted to build up a share stake through market purchases. This was cleared with Whitehall and the Bank of England was informed – without commenting. Schroders declined to take informal soundings of the Royal Bank's chairman. However, the manoeuvre was scotched on learning that Lloyds Bank had already purchased 15 percent of the target and then went on to increase its stake to 21 percent during the year. Meanwhile, I had been warned by a colleague that Graham would try to control people and events in the bank[50] and that he had his eye on becoming chairman, which I had already deduced.[51] A slightly sinister aspect was that he was very thick with a corporate consultant who was angling to play a role in the bank,[52] and eventually did in a rather extraordinary way.

1984

In the year before Big Bang there was an unusual amount of 'noise' in the City as stockbroking firms contemplated mergers or selling out to banks, large institutions eyed each other, and all manner of financial businesses contemplated their future. Standard Chartered was in the thick of this discourse, both as a potential suitor and as a bride, and even as an abduction, as a result of the unfinished business of how it might bulk up its UK operations. This can be seen now as an unfortunate distraction in so far as it got in the way of the more fundamental issues of reforming the way that the group was managed and of improving its financial results. The need for a solution, or at least a clear way forward for its UK

---

50 Diary, 29 April
51 Diary, 6 July
52 Diary, 20 May and 22 December

strategy inevitably entangled the two themes during the year. As far as City firms were concerned, talks were held with four stockbrokers before deciding not to be involved[53] and with several investment managers.[54] However, the other shareholders in the consortium bank, Midland & International Banks, were bought out in order to bulk up UK earnings. Several propositions were explored in retail banking without result.[55]

The possibility of large re-alignments in the banking sector was very much in the air, with the Bank of England monitoring the situation. One train of thought was a merger between Standard Chartered and Midland, where the chief executive was enthusiastic, or at least for us to purchase a portfolio of branches, or one of their subsidiaries.[56] But an insurmountable obstacle was Midland's disastrous ownership of Crocker Bank in California. Another trail led to Lloyds, where the Bank of England opined that it would be 'a good fit'.[57] Barber was friendly with their chairman, Sir Jeremy Morse, and I got to know Brian Pitman, their powerful chief executive. Both these fancies clashed with my core desire for independence. Yorkshire and Clydesdale banks were mentioned, without serious follow up.

And then there was the Royal Bank situation, which bubbled almost continuously between February and August. Graham kept coming back to the topic and Jarecki commented to me at one point that it reminded him of a married couple who hoped to resolve all their marital difficulties by having a baby. In all this there was one serious manoeuvre. Citibank had a new, able and energetic London chief who was determined to acquire a sizeable presence in the British domestic banking scene. Kent Price conceived the notion that Citi and Standard Chartered should jointly purchase the Williams & Glynn banking subsidiary of Royal Bank and a detailed proposition was worked up. I took it to a special board meeting in August, but the non-executive directors refused to sanction the approach and it lapsed.

This board refusal came on the heels of a more ambitious transaction that had also been turned down by the board: to purchase a sizeable US

53 Diary, 16 March, 27 July
54 Diary, 11 June, 25 July, 20 August
55 Woolwich and Cheltenham building societies (17 August, 6,7 December); instore banking with British Home Stores (23 February, 12,27 July); Thomas Cooke (26,27 June, 6,9 December)
56 Diary, 3 January, 23 and 27 February, 16 March, 22 May
57 Diary, 3 January, 27 and 29 February

bank – Continental Illinois – that was in the hands of the receivers. Again, much work had gone into refining a proposition in conjunction with Harragin at Union Bank. These two episodes damaged my standing with the board.[58] Barber and Graham had been kept fully informed as the proposals matured and – I had assumed – were supportive, but neither backed me when opposition surfaced on the day. The episode revealed both poor communication and lack of engagement (and confidence?) from the two individuals who should have been in a position to counsel and support me and it was an ominous sign for the future.

Our interim results in August received a bad press, notwithstanding good results at the trading level, and *The Guardian* wrote of a lack of confidence in the management (22 August). All these events made for a poor backcloth to the real business of the year: the review of operations and its consequences. Arthur Anderson was doing an important consultancy on computerisation and Booz Allen had been commissioned to advise on the structure of head office. To cap it, I held a group executive gathering in August at Leeds Castle which was attended by the chairmen of Union and South Africa and by Jarecki, as well as senior bank management.

The outstanding issue that had emerged from these reviews was the need to empower management in the main country banking units and to work out the appropriate balance of centralisation and decentralisation in organisational terms. Behind that lay the prickly question of matching key jobs to actual people. On the main issue the consultants and I were very much of the same mind, as was the Leeds gathering, and I was quite pleased in my end of year reflections on the number of organisational changes that it had been possible to introduce under the cloak of the consultants. Arising out of my conversations with Gareth Jones of Booz Allen, I increasingly articulated my thinking in 'federalist' terms (and he gave me a passage by Alexander Hamilton to frame and hang in my office). I was eventually able to formalise these thoughts in a keynote address to an international banking conference in Switzerland, organised by the PA Consulting group in September 1985 and published in the booklet of the conference proceedings. The address was a plea for international banks to ground their operations in the individual societies in which they had operations on federal lines, rather than the

---

58 Diary, 26 July

prevalent command and control structure from a global headquarters.[59]

The matching of people to jobs lay behind much of the discussion at Leeds Castle. Jarecki sent me some insightful notes after the meeting which pinpointed the sore spots and they remind me now of the details. Overseas the main problem areas were Singapore and Malaysia where there had been a failure to bring on local management and to engage with non-traditional local customers and our banks there were stagnating. In London there was a huge difficulty over the leadership of technical services and computerisation, which was under the control of a Standard lifer of somewhat flamboyant personality who was distrusted by South Africa, Union Bank, Arthur Anderson, and by Tarrant. The apparently obvious solution was to replace him and this I did not do, spending too much time looking for compromise solutions. There was also a problem at the merchant bank, where Baillie's reluctance to delegate had led to a situation where he could not see the wood for the trees and it was affecting his health.

The most awkward personality was Stuart Tarrant, the very able chief financial officer recruited by Graham and now finance director. He made a point of not being a team player and seemed to delight in making trouble, including for me with some directors. Jarecki's conclusion was that Tarrant needed further major responsibility against which he could be measured, and after much talk he did agree to take responsibility for computerisation. Apart from a weakness against 'cutting throats', there was missing from my own thinking a greater readiness to go outside the bank for the skills and experience that was lacking. There was not a closed door because we did recruit a number of individuals, but my underlying presumption was that we should be making the best we could of our dealt hand of career bankers and this undoubtedly slowed down the needed transformations. Finally, I did not take on Jarecki's concluding advice: 'Warn the Board that the bank will go through 18 months of difficulty and depressed profits while you reorganise, but assure them that it will come out trim and strong at the other end... Tell the Board what I am doing and let the Board tell me to stop if they don't like it, and that I would quit if they told me to stop.'

Throughout the year there was a worrying dialogue with the Bank of England over our balance sheet exposure to South Africa. Under the

59 *Banking in the 1980s – The Point of No Return.* September 1985

evolving rules of internationally agreed standards for assessing banking risks – the so-called Basle rules established under the auspices of the Bank for International Settlements – banks were held to be responsible for the risks of their subsidiaries. This affected the amount of capital they had to hold at parent company level which was monitored by their regulatory authority. Standard Bank in South Africa was a cuckoo in the nest to put it mildly and it was growing rapidly. The Bank of England was particularly concerned about its foreign exchange exposure – not only to Standard Chartered, but also its obligations to other banks overseas. We endeavoured to persuade it that the market accepted Standard in South Africa as a separate risk, but we were unsuccessful. An additional problem was that the Bank thought that the South Africa Reserve Bank did not exert sufficient authority over the foreign exposure of its domestic banks.

These concerns meant that the Bank regarded our capital ratios as inadequate and below those maintained by the clearing banks; whereas in their view our ratios should have been stronger than those of the clearers because of our business in emerging markets. The only clear-cut solution to this problem would have been to reduce our shareholding in South Africa from that of owning a subsidiary to that of having an investment in an associate bank, i.e. from owning over 50 percent to under 25 percent, when the rule would not have been applicable. This was the path we had followed in Nigeria. Barber was against such a step for South Africa, and so was the local board; the result was to put a strong spotlight on our financial figures and to keep us very much on the Bank's watch list.

The other recurring issue during the year was Hong Kong in the wake of the 1997 negotiations with China and its depressed market. It was unfortunate timing that the question of the renovation versus redevelopment of our Hong Kong main building was current, and with the example next door of the grandiose redevelopment of the headquarters of the Hong Kong & Shanghai bank, which had received international acclaim. Barber was suspicious that Brown was trying to keep up with the Jones's, but there were also divided counsels within the executive on the best course of action. Eventually it was decided to redevelop.

Events at Mocatta had started happily in the year, with the plans to celebrate Mocatta & Goldschmidt's 300th anniversary in some style. A history of the company was commissioned from Tim Green, my neighbour in Rosendale Road days, who had become a noted commentator on the gold market. A grand City dinner was planned and Henry Jarecki fell in with my idea to sponsor an opera at Covent Garden. I had wanted Richard Strauss's *Der Liebe Der Danae*, with its incident of Apollo seducing Diana disguised as a shower of gold, but the opera house jibbed and we settled for a new production of *Der Rosenkavalier* and its memorable betrothal scene of the presentation of the silver rose. The Queen Mother graciously consented to attend the opening night and it was altogether a splendid occasion.

There was a much less happy bullion experience later in the year. I was summoned to the Bank of England early on Sunday 30th September, along with the owners of other bullion market firms, to be informed by the Deputy Governor that Johnson Matthey Bankers was insolvent as a result of imprudent lending to commercial customers (not its bullion trading). The Bank had determined that the company must be rescued to preserve the reputation of the bullion market and that the participation of the other market members was required in order to make the rescue work. The Bank of Nova Scotia had been identified as a potential purchaser of Johnson Matthey. A solution was required that day and before the market opened on Monday morning.

The four of us – from Rothschild, Samuel Montagu, Kleinwort Benson and myself – were shut into a room and periodically fed and watered and kept away from the other parties involved. We decided to offer £5 million each by way of support and this was fed into the negotiations. Hours passed and at 6.30 we learned that the prospective deal with the Bank of Nova Scotia was falling apart and that the clearing banks were being difficult. By this time we had developed reservations about helping Bank of Nova Scotia into the bullion market. There was a long evening of parallel negotiations and at midnight we were summoned by the Governor of the Bank of England and asked to 'save' the deal by offering more generous support. As spokesman for our group I said that we had an alternative solution whereby the Bank of England itself should take control of Johnson Matthey Bankers and run it down. We were asked to withdraw and reconsider our position. Summoned back at 1 am we reiterated our proposal and, after a pause, he said he would accept it provided we increased our collective indemnity from £20 to £30 million. We agreed and left for home just before 2 am.

Fortunately, there were no adverse market reactions to the public announcement on Monday morning. I then phoned Henry Jarecki in New York who was furious. He felt that as a 35 percent shareholder he should have been fully consulted and, anyway, his strong view was that Johnson Matthey should not have been rescued but allowed to fail. Henry was quite right about the lack of consultation, but his view on the solution did not acknowledge the still just prevailing ethos of the City: that the old established members of its clubs should sort out their difficulties amongst themselves and present a united front to the world. We at Standard Chartered were already well aware of the crumbling ethos – that our century's old position as an overseas bank no longer ensured Bank of England protection against a hostile takeover. It was still in the future that the Bank would actually take a dramatic step to underpin our independence. At this time, when we were called to the colours over Johnson Matthey, I felt that we had to comply.

Henry was upset for quite a while. He managed to stir up trouble in Parliament over the rescue through a chance friendship with David Owen, the former Labour foreign secretary, who was briefed to ask probing questions to the embarrassment of the Chancellor, Nigel Lawson. Apart from the issue of rescuing a member of the gold market, which was the City's concern, the episode had revealed a notable weakness in the Bank of England's supervision of banks, in that Johnson Matthey Bankers had built up such a large and poor quality loan portfolio without its knowledge. This led to changes within the Bank and Rodney Galpin was appointed head of banking supervision. As a final irony, the Bank of England charged Standard Chartered with handling the liquidation of the Johnson Matthey bank. Graham was appointed its chairman, Preston joined the board, and a senior executive from our merchant bank moved over to implement the rundown.

These developments did not stand in the way of my joining a prestigious Mocatta occasion during the IMF meetings in Washington that autumn where Jarecki had managed to secure Henry Kissinger to give an address on gold, as the final part of the tercentenary celebrations.

1985

The year was notable for the maturing of a corporate plan for Standard Chartered for presentation to a group-wide strategy gathering early in the following year; for the resolution of our capital adequacy worries with the Bank of England; for what looked like a breakthrough in developing a stronger business presence in Europe; for ten overseas visits to different parts of our empire; and for continuing but unresolved searches for a larger presence in the UK. What was essentially a good year in operating terms was undermined by unfavourable external developments as I wrote in my dairy review of the year: 'All the political news seems to have been against us, plus our extensive exposure to exchange rates and we are very vulnerable to a predator [the share price was half of n.a.v.], apart from it being bad for Board morale.'[60]

The corporate plan occupied a huge amount of time, including a top-level meeting at Hever Castle in April with participation from Conrad Strauss and John Harrigan. There was also a general management gathering at Leeds Castle in September and a special board meeting in December. The document was written in the language of federalism: creating nationally significant and locally managed banks within our franchise, linked by binding sinews and mutually supportive strategies. The meeting at Hever Castle contributed the most insightful contributions, especially from Strauss and Harrigan, but also from the chairman of Schroders, Wynn Bischoff, one evening and from the banking partner of Booz Allen on another one. There were three astringent messages: move top management and costs out of London to key operating areas; ditch low prospect areas (at the time meaning South Asia, Europe and the Gulf); buy in top management skills to replace weak executives. The board meeting in December liked the strategy document, although there were some echoes of the points recorded above. Strauss copied to me a memo sent from one of his managers who had attended a course in London which contained the comment – 'Michael McWilliam is changing things, but probably too slowly.' It strikes me now as a not-inaccurate epitaph.

The capital adequacy problem was resolved by persuading South Africa to have a large rights issue to which Standard Chartered did not contribute, with the consequence that Stanbic moved from being

---

60 Diary, Review of 1985

a subsidiary to an associate investment in the group balance sheet and we were no longer having to support the growth of the South African bank with London capital. At the same time a new class of capital funds was 'invented' in the London market – perpetual capital floating rate notes, which were subscribed to by institutions other than shareholders and they boosted the capital base of the bank. We moved aggressively to issue both dollar and sterling denominated perpetual notes. These developments moved our capital ratios firmly into the Bank of England's safety zone and were fortunately timed in that the South African government declared a debt moratorium in August in response to a withdrawal of credit by, mainly, US banks. This drew attention to the fact that Standard Chartered was South Africa's largest bank creditor. Our supportive stance increased our influence with the Reserve Bank.

The political landscape in South Africa was changing rapidly as the following incident illustrates. I was a member of a dining club, The Africa Private Enterprise Group, that had been set up in the 1960s as a forum where the major British companies with investments in Africa could exchange views and receive confidential briefings from the Foreign Office (who were members) and others. The practice was that the companies took it in turns to host a dinner and a speaker, and Apeg (as it was called) was an extremely valuable network, especially in the years of aggressive nationalism. We had been tipped off that the leader of the South Africa African National Congress in exile, Oliver Tambo, would welcome an opportunity to talk to Apeg, and I offered to host the occasion. I was rather proud to be hosting such a bridge-building event between the international business community and the ANC, especially as it was the first function to be held in our magnificent new headquarters building in Bishopsgate.

Tambo was accompanied by Thabo Mbeki, the future President, and it was altogether a remarkable occasion in that while reiterating the ANC's advocacy of hard sanctions and the need for violent opposition to the apartheid government, Tambo largely disarmed us by his manner, his historical grasp and reasoning approach. Mbeki was also impressive on economic matters and I am sure that we all had a different view of the ANC by the end of the evening.

A few days later I was in Johannesburg for a board meeting and Lord Barber had just been made a member of the Eminent Persons

Group, appointed by the Commonwealth to talk to the South African government about reform. As I noted at the time –

> 'The political situation dominates all conversation. Stanbic directors and social contacts are all on the liberal end of the spectrum and therefore highly critical of the way the government is handling things. It is a distinctive feature of the South African scene that business leaders are so far in front of government in their thinking and readiness for radical reform. There was naturally great interest in our recent meetings with Chief Buthelezi and Oliver Tambo and not a word of criticism at having made such contacts.'[61]

At the Hever Castle meeting in April Conrad Strauss had strongly urged that we should do a merger deal with Midland Bank. This was not a new idea, as a year earlier there was an informal approach from Midland to the effect that they would be receptive to selling part of their network, or even more, since they were nervous about a hostile bid from Citibank. (11 January). Since then I had had friendly conversations with Midland's chief executive, Geoff Taylor, and our merchant bank advisers were positive. More serious discussions resumed in May based on a holding company structure for the two banks, and we got down to detailed discussions, including key appointments, and with both chairmen on side.

A curious feature of the discussions was that Citibank again wanted to be involved with us as a declared partner who would purchase various pieces of Midland, including a portfolio of branches. It was accepted that their American subsidiary Crocker Bank would have to be disposed of. This became the stumbling block as Midland wanted to resolve this problem first and there were complications with the US authorities. The whole issue suddenly went dead in the middle of July and the next public event was the announcement that Kit MacMahon, deputy governor of the Bank of England, was to be chairman and chief executive of Midland. We presumed that this development was the cause of the stoppage in our own talks. It is a nice speculation whether Hong Kong bank would have intervened again if we had got to the point of a merger deal with Midland, since they ultimately purchased the bank.

---

61 *Visit to South Africa*, November, 1985

There was another approach that came to nothing later in the year when th:chief executive of Abbey National building society invited me to lunch – 'In a very few minutes we were into the issue – whether it made sense for a merger to be thought about in 1987 when AN would convert to a plc. I was delighted to find that they have done a lot of work on the topic and that we saw things very much in the same way.'[62] Despite setting up working parties and going into a lot of detail, it emerged that the management of Abbey were not really on side and discussions fizzled out in December, without a formal conclusion. In reality, Birch had switched his attention in another direction.

I convened the first meeting of executives from all our banks in Tropical Africa in July. This group of banks were by far the most profitable in our portfolio, but they had shown very little growth in recent years. With the conspicuous exception of the bank in Zimbabwe, where the conference was being held, the local executive leadership was conservative and lacking in initiative. The conference was an attempt to inject some dynamism, but also to underline the concept of 'corporate good citizenship' that I had been evolving with our Africa adviser, Jonathan Frimpong-Ansah. In these countries Standard Chartered was one of the leading banks, if not the most prominent one, and there was a distinctive aspect of my federal thinking for Africa that our banks there were in a position to play a leadership role. Our weakness was that we had too few individuals with the capability to rise to the new opportunities. We were still painfully short of African managers and had only just begun to think of pan-African postings for them. There were still too many expatriates and few of them were enthusiasts for the new Africa.

The most significant development in our African banking had been a willingness in London to take on larger country risk exposure in trade finance and in the series of transactions we had undertaken in consultation with the IMF to smooth out foreign exchange shortages and enable key imports to continue. This was relationship banking of a high order, depending on establishing a rapport with central bank governors and finance ministers, as well as getting to know key officials in Washington. Here a new adviser I had taken on played a crucial role – Munir Benjenk, who had just retired as a regional adviser of the World Bank. A Sephardic Jewish refugee from the Turkish takeover of

---

62 Diary, 16 September

Smyrna, brought up in Vienna, multi-lingual, opera loving, Munir added a welcome dimension to our rather closed society. At the IMF meeting in Seoul that autumn I was able to hold some 30 meetings with country delegations and IMF officials, thanks to Munir's networking skills.

Our most successful Africa initiative was with Ghana. Following an earlier loan to the government in anticipation of its first IMF facility, we had a further approach in early 1984 when we learned that Libya had withdrawn from supplying oil on credit and the government turned to us for help. I noted: 'The position is unbankable according to normal criteria, but I don't feel we should leave it at that.'[63] Over the next eight weeks a proposal was refined to provide a loan of $120 million in anticipation of an IMF facility, and also to execute a gold swap of $70 million, and I eventually signed a loan agreement with Addo, the Governor. 'Something of a milestone, let's hope it does not become a millstone.'[64] When I visited Ghana in May 1985 my report noted –

'Standard Chartered occupies a unique position at the moment, since it is well known that we financed the government in advance of the first IMF facility, that we financed the oil import programme, that we have organised successive ECGD lines of credit and led the commercial co-financing in the Ashanti Goldfields project with the IFC, and these points were given further prominence during my visit.' However, I went on to note – 'SCB Ghana shows signs of neglect from years of management that has acquiesced in declining standards and also by Head Office; the two are obviously linked. Neither is an acceptable stance for the future and we have a singular opportunity to correct matters which we must now seize. We need to focus on the board, on management development, on accounting equipment and computerisation, on corporate and large personal customers.'[65]

This criticism was directed at past Bank of West Africa general managers, but it was also a call to arms to the current incumbent who was new to the West Coast.

We had also developed important banking relationships with Zambia, stemming from Des Bloxam's day. This now led to an intriguing might-have-been situation. We picked up a hint from Anglo-American's

63 Diary, 15 February
64 Diary, 8 May
65 *Visit to Ghana*, May 1985

resident director in Zambia, who sat on the bank board, that the government was having second thoughts about its nationalisation of the copper mines and that it might be receptive to a privatisation proposal. I worked up a scheme after talking to the chairman of the International Finance Corporation, and to IMF and the World Bank officials, and then received a message that President Kaunda would receive me in January.

Just before setting off the World Bank called and asked if Standard Chartered would give a large bridging loan to Zambia to purge $150 million of arrears owned to the IMF and so as to enable a new programme to be launched in conjunction with a generous World Bank aid programme. We agreed to do the loan and I went to meet the President at State House. I was received alone and Kaunda was well briefed and absolutely charming. There was much play with his characteristic large white handkerchief. He accepted my memorandum, but that was the last we heard of the matter. It was pure theatre.

Standard Chartered Merchant Bank assumed a better shape during the year. After a near-miss mistake, a good new chief executive was recruited from Hong Kong in Patrick MacDougall. He quickly resolved the investment management problem by recruiting an energetic duo from Lazard, who promptly set about establishing a credible unit. He also recruited – again from Lazard – an able project finance team led by David Gemmell, which provoked a protest by their chairman to Lord Barber. More significant was a rationalisation with International Division which assumed responsibility for all euro-currency lending, leaving capital markets with SCMB. International Division was expanding cautiously its professional trading activities in foreign exchange and now gilts, but as I noted at the time: 'We are being less ambitious than the clearers in the scope of our trading activities, but I hope will have a smoother build-up.'[66]

It was only gradually becoming apparent that the main significance of Big Bang was not so much the acquisition by banks of stockbroking firms – which was attracting all the publicity – but the development of trading capability in all manner of financial instruments: foreign exchange, deposit and interest rate swaps, debt securities and – yes – equities. From being a customer related activity, banks were now trading on their own account and discovering a vast new source of profit for themselves, and then their star traders. The bonus bonanza was born.

---

66 Diary

Our UK strategic problem remained unresolved at the end of the year. Apart from the discussions with Midland and with Abbey National, time was spent on Girobank and on the Wellbeck:inance subsidiary of Debenhams. As I noted in my review of the year – 'My problem is the market demand for performance and whether we will be left to work out our own salvation.' This was not an idle thought as we were well aware that there were several unorthodox potential predators nosing around the market at this time, who ran their slide rules over Standard Chartered. B.A.T. was looking to diversify beyond tobacco into financial services; British & Commonwealth was on the acquisition path; and then we became aware of the South East Asia business tycoon, Tan Sri Khoo Tek Phuat, who came to lunch one day, 'We entertained Khoo Tek Phuat, the great loner financier from Singapore, who has just bought a stake in Exco and might well mount a full bid. He is very interested in the UK financial sector and talked of buying into Midland and into Royal Bank. We were all wondering about his intentions regarding SCB.'[67]

I took the family for a fortnight's holiday in Kenya over Christmas: a Samburu lodge, Christmas Eve at Treetops, Christmas Day lakeside Naivasha, a camp site in the Mara and then down to the Coast. We played family bridge after the game viewing, but we guessed correctly that this would be the last family holiday with just the four of us and I regretted not doing this safari at a slightly younger age. Robert was pining after his girlfriend and I think they both enjoyed most the night life at the Coast.

Lloyds Bank Bid 1986

This was the year for launching the long gestated corporate plan. It was blessed by the board at the beginning of January before presentation to a group-wide conference of 100 delegates in early March in our new headquarters building. The meeting took place against the background of ominous rumours and manoeuvres which served to heighten the importance of achieving the goals in the plan. Looking over the document more than thirty years later, several things stand out. The mission statement is not only couched in federal language, but it is expressed in what has since become known as 'stakeholder' terms – 'serving the interests of customers, shareholders, depositors, employees and the community.' This was far from Milton Friedman's

---

67 Diary, 27 November

contemporary declaration that management's sole concern was profit maximisation for the benefit of shareholders. There was stress on improving financial outcomes to achieve a target return, but there was no mention of sustained profit growth as such. During the course of my opening address I made a declaration that assumed great significance in the coming weeks –

> 'I am totally committed to preserving the integrity of Standard Chartered – not because I think we are a valuable antique, but because I believe we have a valid business mission as Standard Chartered. The Corporate Plan is a crucial document in enabling us to make orderly plans to preserve our independence.'

The early weeks of the year were filled with preparations for Her Majesty the Queen's visit to open our new headquarters, but this was also interwoven with negotiations to implement the full consolidation of the Mocatta group by buying out Jarecki, save for a residual 5 percent in the US company. I was happy that Henry was able to attend the royal opening on 20 March. Barber had accepted my suggestion that we turn Crosby Square into an oriental pavilion with a magnificent *shamiana* canopy, where everyone was assembled for the ceremony. The event started on a tense note as the Queen's cavalcade arrived ten minutes late and it was apparent that she was not amused. The magnificent atrium of the building contained 35 foot magnolia grandiflora, a large teak elephant standing by a runnel, and a statue of one of the founders of the Chartered Bank (and founder of *The Economist*), James Wilson that had been retrieved from a piece of waste land in Calcutta by Neville Green. The event went well and I had the honour to show her round the building; as ever, Her Majesty was most effective and at ease when meeting groups of staff.

Meanwhile, I was much occupied with formulating a defence strategy in the face of a possible hostile bid and was strongly urged on by Goldman Sachs. They were beginning to make their mark on the London scene as corporate advisers with a distinctive focus at this time on handling only defence mandates. Bob Hamburger had been assigned to cultivate Standard Chartered and he quickly won my attention by his pro-active energy, which was rather in contrast to our established advisers, Schroders. One of his early proposals was that Standard Chartered should take itself private for about five years while we implemented our reforming corporate strategy. Since those times private equity firms have made a major business from this kind of transaction, but it was then rather novel, especially as applied to a bank –

> '(Goldman Sachs) are satisfied that it would be achievable without difficulty and would be well supported. The technique is to form a Newco, capitalised at say £1,000 million, to bid for SCB, but financed 30% equity and 70% debt. Nil equity remuneration but a refinancing or flotation after five years, having paid off much of the debt. The management would be put into 5-10% of the equity.'[68]

I was able to get Graham and Tarrant on side initially, but not Barber who 'is clearly suspicious of the whole thing and – one suspects – much more inclined to a white knight solution with Royal Bank or Lloyds.'[69] However, this led Barber to set up a defence committee of the board which met for the first time in February. 'A very despairing discussion. Barber was only concerned with the personal gain that might accrue to executives, Page and Tarrant formed an axis which said that the only future for SCB is to merge with a clearing bank and that we have no hope on our own. No-one else seemed disposed to argue.'[70] The next meeting was worse: 'Barber was openly hostile to the buy-out defence; I clashed with Barber and with Tarrant on the commitment to remain independent. Lord B left without speaking to me.' My concluding comment was 'The combination of Tarrant positively wanting to see us merged into a clearer, plus an elderly board with no spunk for a fight, is daunting and it is hard not to feel that our days of independence are numbered.'[71] The following day I cancelled a skiing holiday in Austria to concentrate on the threatening situation.

Come Friday 4 April, 'The lightning finally struck today from the unexpected – till the last minute – quarter of Lloyds Bank. Morse asked to come and see Lord Barber and I tried to stiffen him to say that a bid would be unwelcome, which is just what they wished to discuss, so they retreated. Barber and Graham went round to the Governor to repeat the message and were told that a merger might be 'no bad thing' with Lloyds.

---

68 Diary, 16 January
69 Diary, 25 January
70 Diary, 11 February
71 Diary, 14 February

A further message from (Lloyds) that they had decided they must make an announcement of their intentions. We succeeded in getting them to modify it, to make clear the initiative was entirely theirs. We then put out a cold sentence that the approach was a surprise and not welcome.'[72]

My diary provides a daily commentary on the course of the bid and its ultimate defeat on 11 July against all public and especially, media, expectation. We had successfully mobilised three major new investors and a posse of supporters to purchase shares, especially in the closing days, in a masterful operation masterminded by David Mayhew at Cazenove, as described further below. The arithmetic was fascinating. 20 percent of the share register was owned by small investors who stayed loyal. Of the rest, over 40 percent accepted Lloyds' offer and the rest sold their shares to our new investors. This meant that some £400 million was mobilised to defeat the bid. The outcome was that Lloyds only controlled 45 percent of the votes and their bid failed. The share register now comprised –

Old loyalists	20%
New supporters	35%
Unfriendly	45%

This was hardly a stable-looking outcome for the future, notwithstanding the euphoria of the moment at having won our freedom. I had received a marvellous letter from an executive in Deutsche Bank during the battle, quoting Pericles: *'Der Gerheimnis das Leben ist der Freiheit, und der Gerheimnis der Freiheit ist der Mut.' The secret of life is liberty and the secret of liberty is courage*, and I read this out to the press, standing in front of the bank. There were celebrations to follow and our director of information, John Pank, composed a Victory Ode (with some poetic licence):

When we were opened by the Queen
At Bishopsgate (a sylvan scene
With grandiflora polished bright
From preparations in the night)
There was a predator around
Who sniffed the air and pawed the ground
Then galloped to our brand new door
To make a bid on April 4
This was rejected firm and free

---

72 Diary, 4 April

'A hostile bid what's more' said we
And then and there our claims unfurled
Of Strength in Depth across the world.
Advisors? Well we had a few
Like Cazenove and Schroders too
But first in line in Rolls and Jag
We had our friends at Schroder Wagg.
Night after night they drafted clauses
Verbs and sentences – and pauses,
Documents galore wrote they
In white, in red, in blue and grey.
The USA showed there were cracks
In Lloyds attack; so Goldman Sachs
Were brought on board to keep ahead
Of juicy problems with the Fed.
Inexorably things progressed
On TV, radio and press.
The name of Standard Chartered grew
'Til almost everybody knew
We wished for independence, and
Fulfilment of strategic plans.
Then came an oriental coup
From Y.K.Pao from out the blue
Which left dear Lloyds a little fraught
At fighting Robert Homes a Court
Plus Donny Gordon, Tiny too
As well as old friend Tan Sri Khoo.
Lloyds tallied 45 per cent
Perhaps our win was heaven sent?
Or was it due to just one man
Who's will and ever steady hand
When all seemed fairly desultory
Propelled us all to victory?
The press presumed that Lloyds would win
And suck the Standard Chartered in,
But, fearless Michael won the day,
Our hearts, our thanks – and time to pay!

Group Managing Director. Defeat of Lloyds Bank

A peculiarity of the bid was the tactical mis-steps made by Lloyds, which conducted the affair through its in-house merchant bank, although Brian Pitman was also known to be much influenced by the successful takeover specialist Hanson. At the outset, when Lloyds announced its intention to bid, it seemed unready and nearly ran out of time. It then became apparent that Lloyds had not realised that it would be operating under US rules because of the previously announced sale of its Californian subsidiary, which had the effect of preventing Lloyds from purchasing more than 5 percent of our shares in the market, whereas under the London code it would have been able to buy up to 30 percent. Its American complications also put it out of phase with the Takeover Panel's timetable and it had to ask for extra time. As Christopher Fildes pointed out in *The Spectator* – 'As the barristers harshly say, a man who is his own lawyer has a mug for a client.'[73] Lloyds was also hard-nosed over its bid pricing and Standard Chartered shares remained above the offer price, even when the price was raised. Essentially, Lloyds disregarded our defence document which set out to prove that the sum of the parts (as demonstrated by key valuations prepared with our advisors) was worth more than their offer.

To the extent that the 'hidden value' argument had force, it was to the effect that Lloyds was trying to buy Standard Chartered on the cheap at 750p a share. I had considerable difficulty in securing authority from my Board to reject out of hand a revised offer from Lloyds below 900p, so was in the clear when it came back with only 825p. However, we knew that many institutions were sceptical of our defence and we needed a clinching back-up. One avenue was quickly disposed of. The day after the bid announcement the chairman of Credit Suisse flew to London for an exploratory meeting, but the follow-up raised problems and their interest faded. Later in the month we received an approach from the Australian bank, Westpac, and a team flew to London to explore a merger, but again talks fizzled out. There was a rumour that Midland were minded to intervene, but we quickly ascertained that they were not in a position to act.

Goldman then strongly urged that we must find new investors – so-called white knights, and one of their key specialists, John Thornton, flew into town. This became my primary task during the rest of the bid

---

73 Diary, 18 July

period, apart from work on the defence documents and the politics of the board. Khoo had already declared an interest, but it was hard work to clarify his intentions and pin him down. He began by contemplating a rival bid, and then wanted to involve his new stake in Exco, and he finally ended up with about 6 percent in the closing days. We had developed an important banking relationship with Robert Holmes à Court in connection with his ambition to acquire Broken Hill, and he became increasingly intrigued and engaged, eventually buying 5 percent in the closing days, subsequently increased to 9 percent.

The most dramatic intervention was from Y K Pao, the Hong Kong shipping tycoon who was a major customer of Hong Kong Shanghai Bank. Initial expressions of moral support to Bill Brown in Hong Kong were followed by increasing interest and phone calls to me, and he began buying shares at the end of June. I phoned Hong Kong one morning to ask if he could clarify his intentions –

'How much do you want me to buy?'

I took a deep breath: 'I would like you to be a 10 percent shareholder by the last day of the bid.'

'I will take the evening plane and meet me at Gatwick at 7 o'clock tomorrow morning.'

When I arrived the following morning I found that YK had already been for a swim in the hotel pool and was ready for action. We phoned David Mayhew to say that YK was prepared to take his stake to 10 percent and Cazenove started buying our shares and devasted the market by spending about £100 million in a few hours. Lloyds were furious and demanded an inquiry by The Stock Exchange, which was refused.

This was the clinching intervention, but it is worth recalling that there was also quite a posse of friends of the bank who bought shares to help defeat the bid. A group of Hong Kong customers was mobilised by David Wong (with whom I had been to Japan for his ship launching). Between them they bought over 1 percent. Jarecki and Tiny Rowland bought similar stakes. Numerous other discussions were held, the most time wasting being with Donald Gordon: a special vehicle had been set up with approval of the Reserve Bank as regards foreign exchange, but Gordon kept pursuing multiple objectives of his own and in the end this was a damp squib.

The bid defence was made much more difficult by divisions within our own camp, starting with my chairman, Lord Barber. Although he had been chancellor of the exchequer, Barber was not financially sophisticated, certainly as regards banking, and he made little contribution to the issues facing us. His talent was representational and diplomatic, where he could be highly effective. On the fundamental issue he did not have a strong belief in Standard Chartered remaining independent and he was not averse to the Lloyds approach. Almost certainly there had been some prior informal contact between him and Sir Jeremy Morse and there was the worrying incident on the first day when Barber was told by the Governor that he saw merit in the combination. Peter Graham wobbled on the issue more than once, and then there was Stuart Tarrant, finance director, who was openly in favour of Lloyds' bid. A more confident chairman could perhaps have dominated the situation; instead, Barber went along with my initial announcement that the approach was unwelcome and with my refusal to talk to Lloyds. In public thereafter Barber loyally supported the defence. Internally was another matter.

With Schroders supporting me, Barber was prevailed upon to resist a further request from Morse for a meeting. But on 15 June Tarrant went to see him with a memo opposing our rejection of the bid and the white knight strategy and announcing that he intended to vote for Lloyds.

A board meeting had been convened for next morning to review the bid defence document and, with adjournments, it lasted all day and nearly brought my career to a speedy close. It started calmly enough as we reviewed the papers. Barber then adjourned the meeting and had a closed session with the non-executive directors to tell them about the approach from Morse and about Tarrant's intervention. The resumed session was a skirmish between Tarrant and me until the lunch break when Barber had the outside directors to himself and lobbied hard for entering into immediate negotiations with Lloyds. Tarrant had left the building. When he returned, the afternoon was spent in an endeavour to get him back on board, without my involvement.

I was eventually summoned at five to be told by Barber that they were being blackmailed by Tarrant with a threat of revelations about legal impropriety in the bid defence and a demand to abandon it and to start immediate talks with Lloyds. He told me that he and Graham had decided to go along with this. No plausible evidence was produced and I said I could not agree and that I would make a public statement. Barber then reconvened the board meeting with Tarrant absent, made his case and called on me to respond. A vote was taken and I won 7 – 5, or 7 – 6 if Tarrant had been there. Morse was told immediately and so was Tarrant. I was left gobsmacked, as they say, that Graham had supported Barber, not to mention the others.

It emerged subsequently that Tarrant had contacted the Takeover Panel about the white knights defence and I had to respond to their questions. On the penultimate day of the bid, 10 July, Tarrant took the extraordinary step of going round to the Bank of England enlarging on his concerns to Galpin. These boiled down to an assertion that I had contravened the Companies Act by offering financial inducements to the white knights to purchase shares in Standard Chartered. All this manoeuvring was quite wearing. On the morning of Sunday 13th after Lloyd's bid had been defeated, I decided to phone Tarrant. I said that I understood he would now be resigning and this should be done as soon as possible. He concurred and he said he wished the separation to be amicable and that he intended to clear his desk by Monday lunchtime.

I had been thinking about a replacement and fastened onto Richard Stein, my colleague from Montagu days, who had gone on to an impressive career as finance director of Reckitt & Colman and then of British Oxygen. We had kept in touch socially over the years and I was aware that he was looking for a new challenge. Richard agreed to come to Standard Chartered, very much out of personal regard, and he did an outstanding job until retirement, albeit disliking the political tensions. On retirement he signed up as a mature university student and completed a PhD on Roman archaeology.

The Bank of England had followed the takeover battle closely and perhaps had some difficulty in striking the right balance. Stimulated by Tarrant's mischievous interventions, Galpin (now in charge of bank supervision) was particularly concerned about the role of the white knights. The Bank would have been aware of Barber's views, which probably accorded with its own, judging by the Governor's comment on the first day, as already noted. Officially the Bank was neutral, as when it refused to take sides when Lloyds sought its support over its US regulatory problems. Conversely, it opposed my application to the Office of Fair Trade seeking a referral on competition grounds. However, it could not resist some nannying as when the two chairmen were summoned round to the Governor who expressed concerns over a rough house developing during the bid battle. Luckily, Barber had been briefed by me and gave no comfort at all. Nevertheless, Galpin insisted on vetting our defence circular and demanded a number of drafting changes to tone it down.

It was a shock to discover later in July, after the failure of its bid, that Lloyds had not given up on their ambitions as they filed an application with the Fed (which became public knowledge) to increase their shareholding to 30 percent and with a view to going to 100 percent. They had not informed the Bank beforehand and Barber and Graham received a sympathetic hearing when they went round to the Governor to protest. However, the Bank decided a month later not to make a formal objection to the Fed and I noted petulantly, 'It seems incredible and I suppose the only conclusion to be drawn is that the bank supervision area is actually in favour of LB making a renewed attempt.' (18 August) We heard meanwhile that Khoo had been approached by Lloyds to sell his stake. This was all very unsettling, but in the event there was no action. More irritating was a hostile press fed by Tarrant with stories about the white knights and of my imminent replacement by Y K Pao's son.

The white knights were suspicious of each other. All three had been appointed to the board on 19 August and they found it hard to settle to our governance conventions. Y K Pao and his son were the most pushy, wanting both enhanced status and the right to delve into management issues. Khoo involved me in much manoeuvring to link with his other investment in Exco, and possibly more widely. And then in November there was an announcement from Brunei that the government had taken over the National Bank of Brunei, which was 70 percent owned by Khoo, as it was insolvent due to large loans to him. We forced him to resign from the board and in the expectation that he would sell his 6 percent stake. He did not and eventually his family made a large fortune from holding on to their investment. Holmes à Court was by far the most constructive shareholder, although we had been warned that he could be a 'restive' one. Also, we had a large loan exposure to his Bell Group and a difference of opinion with the Bank of England as to how this should be assessed.

The fallout of the bid battle extended to our board. On 28 July I received a phone call from Hong Kong to say that there was press speculation there that Barber would retire as chairman. This was prescient as the next morning he announced his retirement, without any arrangements in place for his successor. I formed the view that it would be difficult to undertake a proper search and that Graham should be appointed as soon as possible for three or four years and I went to put this to him. Given the difficulties I had experienced with Peter, this recommendation may appear surprising. But I was conscious that it would be very difficult to introduce a new figure of standing at that time; moreover, Graham was widely recognised as an experienced banker who had recently handled successfully two public assignments with the Crown Agents and the International Tin Council. A less worthy consideration was that I presumed to think that in three years' time – with our major issues sorted out – I myself could be a candidate. And this also was in the minds of some members of the board.

Graham's succession as chairman did not proceed entirely smoothly. After the September board meeting I became aware that there was opposition to Graham succeeding Lord Barber and the outside directors met together to review the situation. A couple of days later Sir Derek Mitchell (former Treasury permanent secretary) came to talk about the meeting when I enlarged upon the case for Graham to succeed Barber. He followed up with a letter, commenting first on my paper, 'I like the style and attack of 'The Post-Bid Agenda'... it is very important and it demonstrates your role as architect and builder of a revived SC.' He went on to support the Graham proposal for a short tenure while a successor was found: 'Over this period you might emerge as the obvious candidate.'[74] Then a few days later, Lord Pennock called for a long chat on strategy but leading up to a discussion on the succession. He asked for my views and I seemed to convince him that Graham was the only choice – though he wanted to have a two year limit. He then discussed the notion of my succeeding Graham, which he seemed to think logical, but felt there should be a rival external candidate in mind, who was still a banker.[75] Agreement was reached that Graham should succeed Barber after the 1987 AGM for a term of three years and this was formalised at the October board meeting.

The most visible post-bid action was an attack on central overhead costs. In company with a voluntary redundancy programme, 170 posts

74 Diary, 16 September
75 Diary, 19 September

were abolished and 300 staff took early retirement. There were seven departures from the general management cadre. There remained work to be done to streamline committees and to enforce more accountability of the general managers for their business areas, with performance standards and budget discipline. This still left me with two difficult personal issues. David Millar was far from stepping up to a role of chief operating officer and still had 18 months to go before normal retirement; he was something of a totem figure in the Chartered Bank and had succeeded Peter Graham in Hong Kong with great success, so there was no possibility of forcing his departure. My difficulty was with Graham who saw the need for change but was insistent on saving face. The eventual solution was to raise Millar's status and to arrange for business operations across the group to be divided between three senior general managers, and to bring forward his retirement to the end of 1987.

My other problem was with Robin Baillie after Stein arrived. He became increasingly difficult to deal with and then had a recurrence of stomach ulcers. Matters came to a head in December when I myself had been confined to home for several weeks with a mixture of mild pneumonia and secondary smallpox – doubtless also evidence of strain – 'Baillie phoned to say that he had written to Lord B requesting early retirement on grounds of ill-health w.e.f. the AGM. He made it plain that he attributes the situation entirely to me, which is disturbing and sad.'[76] The solution here was that I proposed to Barber that Baillie be retained as a non-executive director and in this capacity he did an outstanding special task in the following year in the complex arrangements for disentangling ourselves from South Africa, and we managed to remain friends.

I had a lengthy review of the post-bid situation with the Bank of England in October and was rather disturbed by the way that the discussion went: 'Upon reflection, I do not like the tone of the Bank of England meeting, since Quinn seemed to have a brief which argued that we have a doubtful future as an independent bank and wishing to 'prove' this by reference to: the balance of home and abroad business; the prominence of trading revenue as compared with lending ; excessive loan gearing; inadequate dividend cover; too low return on equity. All disputable in detail, but it is worrying that the Bank of England should

---

76 Diary, 11 December

have assembled such a charge sheet.'[77] This contributed to a gloomy end of year assessment of our situation –

> 'We are really in a very dangerous situation now: our share price is out of line with the sector and sustained only by takeover hopes; it now looks as if our results will be disappointing, which will lead to further external criticism; neither Pao nor Holmes à Court has offered anything much in the way of positive support or steadying commitment; soundings of other banks have so far led nowhere; the senior management is very unsettled; we are unable to recruit people of talent; there are some very tough problems to be solved in systems, budgeting, marketing and the will may not be there. This adds up to a depressing catalogue! I am seen both as the man who may have to go, but also as the person on whom any revival of our future depends. This can only be accomplished by a radical reshuffle of the top executive which itself will be controversial. Unless I can pull it off, there will be a strong pressure to go into the arms of another bank – if not Lloyds, then perhaps Midland if they played their cards with subtlety.'[78]

1987

The ostensible agenda for the year after the defeated Lloyds bid was to improve the operating results of the bank, enhance its capital adequacy ratios, and to implement management changes that would produce these outcomes. Strengthening the executive team was a euphemism for replacing a number of senior old-time bankers and here I encountered problems, as mentioned above. I could be – and was – criticized for not being tougher in weeding out more quickly senior figures who were not up to the demands of our new situation. There is force in this, although it perhaps does not sufficiently acknowledge the difficulties of achieving reform from within an organisation, as opposed to the greater freedom of action of a new broom from outside. This is surely a factor in the frequent appointment of consultants to 'do the dirty work'. Yet the changes actually achieved were not inconsiderable. 'Out of the 17 London general managers and executive directors in mid-1983 when I

77 Diary, 16 October
78 Diary, 20 December

took over, only 6 were still with the bank. 5 reached normal retirement and 6 resigned or retired early at my request in order to make way for more competent successors. Out of the team of executives numbering 21 at mid-year as many as 7 had been recruited directly into the bank at this senior level and 8 were promoted from within the service.' [79]

This mundane agenda of organisational reform, better budgeting and business development, was overlaid during the year by distracting and damaging external events and by an extraordinary disintegration of the Standard Chartered board and the collapse of Graham's authority.

To recall first the external events. In the early weeks of the year there occurred a persistent and vicious vendetta in the press against the bank and myself, led by a journalist on the *Evening Standard* and fed by Tarrant; it culminated in an irresponsible piece in the *FT* asserting that a deliberate bank-funded share support operation had been put into effect, which would have been illegal. The Bank of England panicked. I was on holiday in Austria at the time and received a call to learn from Graham that the Bank had persuaded him and Barber to 'request' an inquiry under the Banking Act, but also that a writ had been issued against the *FT*. The terms of reference of the inquiry went far beyond the alleged offences and, in effect, it became an investigation as to whether Standard Chartered was being managed by 'fit and proper' persons.

The short inquiry postulated to us by Galpin became a year-long inquisition with detailed questionnaires and lengthy interrogations. The Bank of England decided not to publish the Inspectors' report in light of the confidential information it contained and, instead, issued an announcement on 19 January 1988 that comprehensively demolished Tarrant's mischief making: there had been no concert party between the White Squires to gain control of Standard Chartered; there was no illegal financial assistance by the bank for share purchases; there was no breach of insider dealing. Leading counsel then advised that our libel case against the *FT* would prevail, but we decided to close down the action with a court settlement and put the whole unpleasant episode behind us.

The inquiry provided a poor backcloth to our relations with the Bank of England. It became evident that Galpin and his deputy Brian Quinn were increasingly persuaded that we were a troubled bank that could

---

79 *Managing Standard Chartered*, 12 October 1987

not sort out its problems. The technical issues revolved around loan provisioning and capital adequacy, but deeper concerns were fostered during the year by tell-tale meetings with some of our directors and by Graham himself. In October after a routine meeting at the Bank I was asked to leave with Graham remaining behind. He later told me that much of the discussion related to enquiry about our management and that Quinn had swallowed the line that the management was poor and the bank was 'drifting'. This was disturbing as I could not be confident that Graham would have been at all robust in rebuttal. It later emerged that the Bank was already listening sympathetically to other 'solutions', and I noted in my diary that it did not seem to see its role as helping us to resolve our problems, but rather to be an eager mid-wife to any respectable deal that came along, or even as a matchmaker.[80]

The event that perhaps best symbolised the board's loss of confidence in the bank's future – and in its chief executive – commenced on the eve of our AGM in May 1987 when Barber was to hand over the chairmanship to Graham. 'PAG had a riveting visit from McMahon yesterday while I was at ExCo. Midland was given a rough time by the BofE at their annual review and told to take action on their ratios. Result: McMahon came round to offer us Clydesdale Bank plus Northern at about net asset value of £300 million and pre-tax profits £50 million. It looks like the answer to a maiden's prayer'.[81] In the following weeks we worked furiously to evaluate the proposition, against pressure from McMahon for a quick decision. However, 'PAG is quite nervous and lacking his old, confident bounce.'[82] This was quite odd since the deal represented the fulfilment of his own strategy that had started with the Royal Bank; whereas, 'In my bones, I feel the deal must be right for us but it will be hard to make a credible justification in the time.'[83] I realised that we would have to dump South Africa if we went ahead. I finalised a proposal, which Graham and Fletcher supported – 'PAG and I then went round to see McMahon and he accepted our offer with alacrity and expressed himself confident of being able to take it through his board tomorrow... It all seems a little too good to be true.'[84]

---

80 Diary, 1 December
81 Diary, 7 May
82 Diary, 25 May
83 Diary, 26 May
84 Diary, 27 May

However, it was not to be. Y K Pao took strongly against the deal and Holmes a Court agreed with him. On the morning of the board meeting Y K Pao and Holmes à Court together went to Graham and informed him that they had decided jointly to veto the Clydesdale acquisition. I was called in to be told this and then we went into the meeting where the same announcement was made. I restated the case, but no one was prepared to stand up to the juggernaut with the result that the cornerstone of our corporate strategy for the past 10 years was torpedoed without a whimper or protest from the non-executives. During the rest of the meeting it was proposed and agreed that South Africa be sold, that we prevent a proposed acquisition by Union Bank and even be prepared to dispose of Union. I diarised sourly, 'A good day's work.'[85]

By chance I had arranged a gathering of the general managers that weekend and noted, 'After dinner, I gave GMs a full account of the issues of the past week and their implications – essentially that the management is on trial and that the actions of YKP and HaC should be seen as a proxy for the market doubts about the bank, in which we will not be able to raise capital or take major initiatives until we are seen to be doing a lot better. It is fortunate that the meeting took place at this time because of the chance to weld the team together and to convey a tough message.'[86]

The decision to dispose of our South Africa investment led to difficult negotiations with our South African board which had its own agenda as to who should buy the shares. The transaction also had political dimensions because of the large outflow of foreign exchange that would occur as we repatriated the capital. Baillie went to Johannesburg to represent our interest and handled matters with great skill. The final lap involved my agreeing to help the Governor of the Reserve Bank by agreeing to double the facility we had to $200 million. The bank that had been established nearly 130 years ago was at last to be fully owned by South African investors, but it was a sad ending for its founding parent and for the personal relationships that had been forged over the years. This disposal was not enough to satisfy the Bank of England and it became clear that we would have to sell Union Bank as well.

Whereas these events forged management into a stronger team, the opposite had occurred with the board of directors. Its cohesion had

---

85 Diary, 9 June
86 Diary, 12 June

been severely tested during the Lloyds takeover bid by Barber's desire to talk to Morse and his manoeuvres to this end. Graham proved to be unstable and Robinson from Schroders became unsettled. The launch of the inquiry under the Banking Act thoroughly discomposed him. I had to attend a special meeting of non-executive directors that he convened and managed to head off a demand for a separate board investigation. Robinson then went to see the Bank of England on his own to enlarge on his concerns. Sir Derek Mitchell called in one day and revealed there was discontent over Fletcher as deputy chairman and that there was concern about Graham as chairman – he was felt to lack purpose and clarity, to be wobbly and forgetful. I noted, 'We should have an interesting summer.'[87]

Pao wanted to form a triumvirate of Graham, Holmes à Court and himself to direct the bank, which was successfully resisted, but the outcome was a move to enhance the role of the chairman. I was able to control the drafting of the document and gradually to secure Graham's agreement to a text. However, Graham's own motives in this exercise remained unclear. He then decided to give an assignment to his consultant friend, Broadbent-Jones, to make proposals on strengthening the board. He talked his way round the directors (notably missing out two executive directors), and gave me a sobering account of a discontented body and I noted – 'There is clearly a large amount of distancing from a perceived 'failed' managing director, which will be hard to counter.'[88]

Broadbent-Jones then made a presentation to a board meeting in November. A bizarre two hours ensued. Broadbent-Jones had the notion to retail to the board in colourful language what he said were ten generally held views by the directors – mostly highly critical of the bank. No. 6 was that the managing director has lost the confidence of the board. When he had finished, the executive directors dissociated themselves from the observation and so did three of the other board members, which led him to say that he was really referring to Pao and Holmes à Court who were not present. It was rather obvious however that Graham and Fletcher (deputy chairman) were in the same camp and had not dissociated themselves. I was furious about the meeting and next morning I went to see Graham and went for him over the way it had been conducted; he was defensive and quite disconcerted when I

87 Diary, 1 June
88 Diary, 27 August

pointed out that he had conspicuously failed to stand by his managing director and would be assumed to go along with what Broadbent-Jones had said. He did not seem to have realised this.[89]

The blatant attempt by Broadbent-Jones to prepare the way for my replacement fizzled out for the moment. The more immediate consequence was a move, initiated by two directors (Robinson and Page), to form a chairman's policy committee to deal with the crisis. I attended a meeting in Graham's office which revealed the divisions in the board when the duo excluded deputy chairman Fletcher from the new committee in his presence, but added Pao and Holmes à Court. I noted in my diary that the group had effectively declared Graham incompetent, pushed aside the deputy chairman and formed a kind of regency.[90] My end of year assessment was thoroughly gloomy:

'We have therefore ended the year with a rudderless board, a pronounced lack of confidence in Graham and Fletcher, and divisions and uncertainty as to how the situation is to be resolved. There is rather little confidence in me and the executive, although the changes made progressively during the year and the 1988 budget presentations have improved our image with some. Pao and Woo (his son) seem almost totally hostile to the executive and use every chance to show this. Holmes à Court and Newman (his representative) were once in close alliance with Pao, but have moved apart and are now almost totally supportive – having wreaked much damage in the meantime. Finally, in this catalogue of woe, it has become apparent that Graham has failed to support his executive, has contributed to the denigration on key occasions, and has consequently lost our confidence as well. This picture of a divided and drifting board has been communicated to the Bank of England and to the market, by various parties, and has contributed to the dangers facing the bank – not least because the board has floundered on every important policy issue during the year.'[91]

The immediate cause of all this agitation was an extraordinary intervention by American Express, advised by David Scholey at Warburg.

---

89 Diary, 18 November
90 Diary, 18 December
91 Diary, Review of 1987

I returned from a brief visit to South Africa in November to an urgent meeting with Graham when he told me that he had received a visit from the chairman and chief executive of American Express Bank to propose that they make an agreed cash bid for Standard Chartered. The two banks would be integrated under the Standard Chartered name with Graham as chairman and then subsequently floated on the market with American Express retaining a 20 percent stake. Graham then went round to the Bank of England to discover that Galpin knew all about the proposal and was not opposed to it and, indeed, he proposed that he chair a meeting of the two sides. It emerged subsequently that Scholey and American Express had made a presentation to the Bank back in June and had received encouragement. This no doubt lay behind the hostile meeting with the Bank that I had noted on 1 December. I also learned that Graham had started conversations with American Express before I had left for South Africa without telling me.

It was not easy to control one's emotions in this situation, but I argued strongly that if we were to throw in the towel we should both look critically at the American Express proposal and also at possible alternatives. On the former, I was astonished to discover what little preparation had gone into their approach when we had the first working meeting – 'The two chaps from American Express arrived at 10 o'clock and we spent a farcical morning. It was clear at once that they had no detailed plans to place before us and were quite unprepared to sell themselves. They seemed to think that we would eagerly lay out the details of the bank's affairs upon the assumption that an 'in principle' decision to merger had already been taken.'[92] I reported to a reluctant Graham that it was a fiasco.

As regards alternatives, I first went to see Peter Leslie, now chief executive of Barclays International, and after two meetings he advised that Barclays could not contemplate a total offer but were prepared to consider (a) taking an immediate 15 percent stake; (b) jointly evaluating the larger step over a two/three year period; (c) and finally that the ball was in our court to say whether we wished to pursue matters. (4 December). There was no appetite to get down seriously to responding to this. I also went to see Brian Pitman at a safe house to bury the hatchet with Lloyds and to have a constructive discussion. The stumbling block was capital

92 Diary, 7 December

adequacy; he would have liked to respond, but could not see his way to raising the extra capital that would be needed in present conditions.[93] A third possibility then arose when Goldman Sachs reported that the chairman of Trustee Savings Bank had been thinking about an approach. However, the bank was suffering criticism for its purchase of Hill Samuel and it did not prove possible to progress matters in our time frame.

The tensions raised by these developments exacerbated my problems with the board and above all there was the growing lack of trust between Graham and myself. Newman (Homes à Court's man) became sympathetic and phoned to review the scene, noting the defeatist attitude of Graham and Fletcher, that Graham was a prisoner of the policy committee group who themselves were panicking and lobbying himself and Pao.[94] Speaking to Mitchell one day, he confirmed the lack of confidence in the executive and that Graham was denigrating me and saying that my opposition to American Express was to preserve my job, and also that Fletcher was promoting himself as alternative chairman.[95] The year was ending on a menacing note.

End Game. 1988

The satisfactory outcome of the Inquiry in January might have been expected to lead to an improved atmosphere in the board, but the tensions over the American Express approach and the difficulties in bringing the US disposals to fruition precluded a peaceful start to the year. I worked hard on an Amex paper demolishing the proposal for the January board meeting and had the satisfaction that both Holmes à Court and Pao had concluded that a deal was not in their interest so I was hopeful that there would be agreement to terminate the matter. However, without prior warning Graham announced at the board meeting that he was in disagreement with me and in favour of a deal and launched into a 14 point speech. Pennock demanded that the meeting continue without the executive directors, at which I insisted that the company secretary withdraw as well in order to make the gathering informal. In the afternoon Graham informed me that there was no majority for continuing with Amex, although he said he had obtained authority to request the chairman to produce another proposal.

---

93 Diary, 11 December
94 Diary, 14, 15 December
95 Diary, 16 December

I then had a furious row with him for not discussing his views with me beforehand and launching his attack in the way he did.[96] I then had the satisfaction that American Express decided not to return with a revised proposal and the appeasement party was defeated. Standard Chartered had been saved for the second time.

The Bank of England had been informed of the discussions with Barclays and their dead end. It was also told by Warburg's of a more exotic intervention by the Ford Motor Company, which had been giving serious consideration to a major diversification into financial services in the UK and to an approach to us. I received a visit and there were several exploratory meetings before the issue was overtaken by events closer to home.[97]

The Bank of England now decided to make a dramatic intervention of its own when the Governor addressed a formal letter to the Standard Chartered board at the beginning of February expressing its concerns about the condition of the bank and ending up – 'The Bank now requires the Board of Standard Chartered Bank to consider, as a matter of urgency, remedial measures to secure the interests of depositors. It is the Bank's wish that the Board should address the strengthening of management, the restoration of the group's capital adequacy and an increase in sovereign debt provisions to a level comparable to that of the English and Scottish clearing banks. The Board's proposals should be submitted to the Bank by the end of this month.'

I convened a meeting of executive directors to plan the response and we decided that the best form of defence was attack, with a series of comprehensive responses to the various allegations. We debated without conclusion what the Bank was really getting at: was this a prelude to a forced reorganisation of the board and management? Was the Bank a party to bringing about a forced merger with another institution, as seemed to be the case with American Express? Or was it just ministering an electric shock to stimulate improvement?[98]

A lengthy reply was agreed with the board, supporting a somewhat grovelling covering letter and, at my suggestion, a draft was sent to Galpin in advance which Graham and I reviewed with him. It was essentially

---

96 Diary, 14 January
97 Diary, 11 January
98 Diary, 5 February

acceptable, although he paused over the management section for a while to test board support.[99] I was not present the following day when the letter was formally approved by the board committee and signed. 'Sadly, it deleted the phrase stating board support for the management, with no attempt by Graham to lead.'[100] During the preparation of the reply to the Bank's letter Newman phoned before departing for Australia to say that there was a group of directors against me and the next few weeks would be dangerous. He also said that he had been asked about management at a meeting at the Bank and told them he felt the bank had been cleaned up and that to make a change at the top now would be disruptive.[101]

Three days later on Thursday morning, the lightning struck when I was summoned by Graham just after nine and found Fletcher with him. In strangled tones he informed me that on the insistence of the Bank of England, and with the concurrence of the non-executive directors, I was to be retired with immediate effect and handed me a press announcement to be issued that day, which would also say that Galpin would take over as executive chairman towards the end of the year.[102] There was no point in having a row and I did not seek to challenge the event, but it was immediately apparent that Graham in his usual way had not given any attention to the separation practicalities, so I declined to allow the press announcement to go forward until I had taken legal advice.

I immediately convened my executive team to explain what had happened; colleagues were suitably shocked but also quickly fatalistic and adaptive to the new situation. Robert and Martin were both working in the City and I asked them to meet me at lunchtime at a wine bar to break the news and I phoned Ruth at the School of Hygiene. Given the tense atmosphere in recent weeks, the only real surprise was in the timing. I could not help noting the irony of Pa's summary removal from Brooke Bond in a similar coup and at the same age and my feeling indignant at the time of losing the advantage of a prominent father just as I was starting at the Kenya Treasury. Did Robert and Martin feel the same?

On the formal aspect, I phoned an old Cheltenham contemporary who was now senior partner of Stephenson Harwood and he agreed to act for me, with much sound advice. By Friday evening I had had the

---

99 Diary, 25 February
100 Diary, 29 February
101 Diary, 17 February
102 Diary, 3 March

press announcement re-drafted, had secured an exchange of letters with the Deputy Governor that my departure had nothing to do with the Bank of England Inspectors' report, and had negotiated a severance memorandum on compensation, pension etc. I had emptied my filing cabinets and it remained to say farewell to a tearful secretary, Win, to have a glass of whiskey with my PA, Tony Jennings and to be driven home for the last time in the bank's Jaguar. There was a flood of letters in the following days and much press comment.

It is difficult to pinpoint when the Bank of England came to the conclusion that it should intervene directly in Standard Chartered, or assess the relative weight of several influencing events. But it is hard to avoid the conclusion that the Governor's letter of 3 February was a piece of theatre and that a decision had already been taken to remove me, and then Graham, and to impose Galpin as executive chairman on the US model. The detailed appendices accompanying our response letter should have led to second thoughts, but by then it was too late. Two factors probably brought the situation to a head. First, was the collapse of the approach by American Express which, as we have seen, had been waived on by the Bank. It knew, by then, that none of the clearing banks was in a position to take on Standard Chartered, and it cannot have been happy to learn of the interest of the Ford Motor Company.

The second consideration was that preparations were at an advanced stage for a rights issue to increase the capital of the bank, for which timing consent had been obtained, and where Cazenove and Schroders were geared up for a series of meetings with institutional investors, with myself. Had the issue gone ahead, it would have been difficult then to remove me. Behind this was the Bank's awareness of the demoralisation of the board and the lack of trust in Graham. One should recall, as well, that there was quite a tradition of Bank of England executives moving into commercial bank chairmanships: Sir Jeremy Morse to Lloyds, Chris McMahon to Midland, not to mention Sir Cyril Hawker and the colleagues he brought into Standard. Thus, the Galpin move had good precedents. There is one intriguing piece of evidence that Galpin thought his mission was still to marry Standard Chartered to another bank, from a lunch he had with Henry Jarecki in April –

'He told me about his fascinating lunch with Galpin on Monday – at the latter's request. It appears that Galpin sees his mission as to dispose of SC as a whole or in pieces, but has a morale problem of being reluctant to discuss the matter internally... Galpin's attitude explains a lot about the uncritical way in which the Bank seized on the approach by Amex last December.' [103]

Once in charge, Galpin implemented a significant narrowing of focus in the bank's activities, including the disposal of Mocatta and retrenchment in merchant banking and in Europe and he appeared increasingly pleased with improvements in results. His appointment effectively gave a public message that the Bank had thrown a protective cloak around Standard Chartered and there was no more talk of hostile bids.

There remains the puzzle of Peter Graham's conduct. We had worked well together when I was his deputy and he was chief executive and he must have proposed my elevation to succeed him. More ironic was my endorsement of his appointment as deputy chairman, instead of retiring from the bank; this prompted Henry Jarecki to comment later that it reminded him of Louis XVI signing the legislation to introduce the guillotine during the French Revolution and then being executed by one. I was astonished that Graham should not have been wholehearted in rejecting the Lloyds bid and I can only conclude that he had been talking to Tarrant and this led him to support Barber's desire for negotiations. Peter had seen himself as a successor to Barber yet, when this happened unexpectedly soon, he was unprepared for the role and proved incapable of handling a disunited board. Even more disappointing he became interfering and devious with me and was somehow not capable of seeing his role as one of guidance, let alone partnership, in overcoming our difficulties.

I waited a year before writing some reflections on these events and my assessment was still quite harsh – 'Graham was completely incapable of handling the white squires or the board as a whole, and he really only wanted to get back into the executive driving seat. He failed to support his chief executive – as Tony Barber did in public – and was incapable of developing a clear differentiating role.'[104] With a longer perspective, one is left with a feeling that we both lacked the capacity to master together those tumultuous events and fractious personalities.

---

103 Diary, 27 April
104 March 1989

Another friend wrote that my defenestration reminded him of the fate of Admiral Byng in the Napoleonic wars – court marshalled *'pour encourager les autres'*. The bank was indeed galvanised after my departure. The white knight problems also faded away with the neutralisation of Khoo and the deaths not long afterwards of both Pao and Holmes à Court. My abiding satisfaction therefore has been that I had saved Standard Chartered twice from being taken over so that it could go on to demonstrate its potential as an international bank with deep roots in the societies of Africa and Asia. At a personal level, however, the reflection is sadder. In my generation men joined Standard or Chartered in their twenties as a lifetime career and went on to develop great loyalty to their bank and to the colleagues they served with in different countries. In a real sense it became 'home' to them. Some notable individuals even managed to stay in the same location for long periods and form deep local attachments; one thinks of Tokyo, Seoul, Singapore, Nairobi, Hamburg, New York and San Francisco. It was this sense of belonging that made me so determined to preserve the independence of Standard Chartered. It was tough therefore to have one's career suddenly terminated. I had lost my boyhood home in Kenya and now had lost my career home in Standard Chartered.

The Legacy of Big Bang

The 26 years that I spent in the City, evolving from *stagiere* at Samuel Montagu to chief executive of Standard Chartered saw the end of an era on how financial business was conducted and the opening phases of a new one which came to be symbolised by Big Bang. It was the starting gun for the transformation of the whole financial sector and ushered in a period of innovation and competition of astonishing dimensions. I will conclude with some reflections on what happened to the ethos of the City as a consequence of the new ways of doing business and the very different people now involved.

The world that was swept away by Big Bang was by no means a perfect one. The regime of fixed commissions made for a comfortable living. Insider trading and the exploitation of the ignorant outsider was not unknown. The old boy network could provide a cover for bounders. Conservative caution could easily become hostility to innovation. As an example, I was given a job title with 'marketing' in 1969 – the first in a City bank – which horrified an older manager who expostulated: 'You don't mean to say that you will be touting for business?' The Old Lady kept a watchful eye, but relied on codes of conduct rather than regulation and the law, but its authority was already being challenged as we have seen with the Hong Kong Bank's intervention in our proposed merger with Royal Bank. The dismantling of barriers demarcating different categories of financial activity was undertaken both by the aggressive incursion of banks into previously disbarred arenas, as well as by traditional operators flexing their muscles with new activities. To achieve this required the hiring of people with different skills and different approaches to the conduct of business: more competitive and aggressive; numeracy trumping connections; an intense focus on transactions over other considerations. It was the culture that came with the 'new' men that came to dominate the City, which now became a magnet for able and ambitious individuals from varied backgrounds, with an appetite for risk and where those with trading skills commanded a premium.

Two aspects of this new environment were particularly significant. First, the emphasis on the skill and performance of an individual led to greatly increased mobility of successful ones, and the old convention that firms in the same line of business did not recruit from each other went by the board. For example, traditionally the clearing banks did not poach staff from each other, nor did Hong Kong Bank from Chartered. In any case banks began recruiting talent from the big consultancies, from industry, even from Whitehall. The model of a lifetime career with one institution was discarded in favour of managing one's own career and involving several employers. One of the consequences was a loss of loyalty to an institution and concern for its reputation, and there was much diminished collegiality and tolerance of sub-par performance. This was in marked contrast with a world in which a young banker grew up with fellow workers, often since leaving school, where they played in company sports teams, knew each other's families, worked together in different locations, adjusted to each other's foibles. All this bred a tolerance and camaraderie and identification with the company and great loyalty. It also set standards of conduct. The conservatism, reluctance to change, even plain inadequacy that the old culture often tolerated was a significant downside, but it is also sad that its positive aspects were being swept aside in the brave new world.

The second, and corrosive, aspect of this new world was the rapid spread of individually tailored remuneration packages, and especially of performance bonuses, as opposed to pay scale ladders and a rate for the job. Corrosive because it pitched the individual against colleagues and against the wider interests of the company. I was responsible for introducing the first wave of bonuses for senior management at Standard Chartered and I well recall the tensions that immediately came to the surface. And this was at a time when bonuses were calculated as a mere percentage of basic salary, rather than a multiple of it as subsequently became commonplace.

The growing prosperity of the City in the nineties and noughties, and the evident rent seeking that became evident, led on to the notion of bonuses for everyone and to the spectacle of employment costs soaking up a growing proportion of revenue, and above all to the phenomenon of the City rewarding itself way above the rest of society. The bonus culture and high rewards for those in management positions spread to ancillary professional services and then more widely in the business world, to the public services and even to academia.

The energising of the City as a result of deregulation, and in the context of light touch regulation, was phenomenal. This was also the era of the rarely questioned primacy of shareholders over other stakeholders, and also of an associated emphasis on short-term results as the measure of success. Astute managers learned to game the system in the interest of their bonuses and share options, even to the detriment of the longer-term health of their companies. The most harmful consequence for banks in particular was the opportunity for divergence between the interests of managers of these institutions and their customers. One instance was the development of proprietary trading – undertaking transactions purely for their profit potential and unrelated to customer needs. Banks built up large trading rooms in foreign exchange, debt instruments, equities, commodities, and even set up special purpose investment funds to hold such assets outside their official balance sheets. Over time, as we have since learned, it led to widespread illegality as well: the manipulation of benchmark interest rates and other scams. It was arguable of course that proprietary trading boosted shareholder returns and was on that account an appropriate activity. It is also the case that the abuses that have emerged were correctible, given tougher regulation eventually. But the more fundamental issue is the motivation of the participants: who were they working for?

It was not only in proprietary trading that managers developed an economic interest unrelated, or in opposition to, customer needs. A more sinister phenomenon was the pressure on staff to force feed financial products to customers, regardless of their appropriateness or real need, because they generated fees and bonuses. Several examples come to mind. Many governments were persuaded to take on sovereign debt in disregard of economic and fiscal prudence. This was perhaps the extreme example of irresponsible transaction banking where the deal makers collected fees and bonuses, while it was only years later that debt provisioning, shareholder losses and taxpayer involvement became necessary. Another was the sub-prime scandal in America, where households were persuaded into inappropriate and unrepayable mortgage debt, which however could be packaged into high yielding and sophisticated investment products to be sold to investors around the world on a large scale, and which became the trigger to the 2007/8 financial crisis. Nearer home there has been the scandal of banks forcing unsuitable products onto retail and small business customers: PFI loan insurance, interest rate swops, forced reorganisation of businesses. Once again, the rewards for the staff involved were collected well before problems emerged and only shareholders were eventually penalised.

Such examples illustrate how the changed culture of banking produced a situation in which personal reward was at the expense of bank customers, and then of shareholders, and eventually of taxpayers. At the highest level hubris was much in evidence before nemesis struck. Lloyds' bid for Standard Chartered was an early example, where having made a great success of concentrating on the domestic market, it was tempted to play on a wider stage. Sadly, the fever returned with the later folly of its HBOS acquisition. And then there was the megalomania of Royal Bank.

The abuses that have come into prominence over the past 20 years are correctible and have been addressed by tougher regulation by the Financial Conduct Authority and the Bank of England, including mandatory stress tests, enforcing capital buffers to absorb risk, ring fencing domestic retail and transaction banking from so-called investment banking. Such measures will reduce the risk of another financial crisis. But we are still left with the residual problem of the culture of those who manage these institutions. Essentially, the glamour and high rewards to individuals in financial services needs to be reduced. Income and wealth inequality as between the City and the rest of society is excessive and a fairer balance needs to be struck between the rewards to management versus shareholders and customers.

Here, on a closing note, something interesting is now taking place in many large banks. Whether driven by fear of regulation and fines, or by the experience of large losses incurred by imprudent policies, banks are engaging in elaborate programmes to change the behaviour and motivation of their staff. I have been able to learn something of one such endeavour where a bank has prominently distributed a corporate code of conduct to its staff. This elaborates three key values: honesty, prudence and responsibility, and three key behavioural standards: initiative accompanied by accountability, team and relationship building, linking corporate success to customer success. There has been a three-year programme to develop staff interpersonal skills and to think about work-life balance, including families and customers. It is a reflection on the times we live in that such an elaborate programme is necessary and one has to wish it all possible success. Such initiatives should make banks into safer institutions. However, one must also acknowledge that a genie was let out of the bottle in the 1980s that damaged the culture of banks and many other institutions. It is not yet clear where lies a new balance between capitalism and society.

ACADEMIA

8. SCHOOL OF ORIENTAL AND AFRICAN STUDIES 1989

My appointment as Director of the School of Oriental and African Studies (SOAS) was an extraordinary piece of good fortune. There was a tradition of City membership of the Governing Body and I had joined it in 1987 at the instigation of Julian Wathen, who was already a member. I was not altogether enthusiastic in view of my Standard Chartered commitments and had not yet been to a meeting by March 1988, although I had been to lunch with the retiring Director, Jeremy Cowan, and had met briefly Lord Maclehose, the chairman and former governor of Hong Kong. SOAS had advertised for Cowan's successor at the beginning of the year, with a closing date for applications in mid-March and, unbeknown to me, my name had been mooted and then set aside in view of events at the bank. On the weekend of my departure from Standard Chartered, Wathen and Maclehose had discussed the new situation and I received a call from the former asking if I would be interested in SOAS. If I was, there was no time to lose as I had barely a week to obtain the application form and submit a full C.V. etc, before the selection committee met to make an interview shortlist. Ruth and I had already decided that I would not seek another City role and would look elsewhere for a fresh challenge, given that I was not yet 55, and I threw my hat into the ring.

For academic credibility I was able to point to my Oxford B.Litt thesis on the East African Tea Industry, a chapter on the post-war Kenya economy in the *Oxford History of East Africa* and some articles. I could even say that I had passed a government exam in Swahili on joining the Colonial Service.

I was shortlisted and two referees were then required. I asked Lord Barber to cover my banking career and Professor Kenneth Robinson – fellow of Nuffield in my day and subsequently Director of the Institute of Commonwealth Studies at London University, vice chancellor of Hong Kong University and deputy chairman of the Royal Commonwealth Society. The selection interviews were not until 31st May, which gave me about ten weeks to find out about the job and understand the working of the university system. My friend Arnold Shipp from Samuel Montagu was already on the Governing Body and a member of the selection committee and he was prepared to vouchsafe that there were four candidates: two academics, a diplomat and me, but no internal candidate from SOAS. This suggested that, after two lengthy internal Director appointments, there was now a desire to look outside and that my challenge was to establish credibility to head a university institution. On Ruth's advice I decided that my strong suit would be mastery of current university issues, especially the complex funding of London University, as well as finding out as much as possible about the scene within SOAS.

First, we decided to have a three-week holiday in Kenya to get over the dramas of the preceding weeks at the bank and we stayed at The Nomad, a traditional hotel favoured by Kenya residents on the coast south of Mombasa. We had a timber cottage with a palm leaf thatched roof under coconut trees facing straight onto the beach. A retired Standard Bank manager we met in the bar on arrival lent us his car as he was about to go on leave and we were able to visit the Foster brothers down the coast and do a bit of exploring. It was a blissful setting and just what we needed.

I had brought out with me an armful of SOAS annual reports and other documents and we spent hours sitting in deckchairs analysing and discussing them. As Secretary of the School of Hygiene & Tropical Medicine, Ruth was quite an expert on the funding of London University and the politics of Senate House so my homework was thorough. On returning to London I was able to meet the recently retired SOAS Secretary, Ted O'Connor, whom Ruth knew well, and to spend a day with the retired historian of Africa, Professor Roland Oliver who I had known from Nuffield days and who had many sharp insights on the School. The interview on 31 May was before a panel of nine, headed by Lord Maclehose, and was tough, although I did have the opportunity to demonstrate my understanding of the university system. Afterwards, I walked over to Ruth's office at the School of Hygiene gloomy about the outcome. At 10pm that evening Maclehose phoned to say that I was their choice. The only interesting detail he was prepared to add was that I was the unanimous choice of the four internal academics on the selection committee.

This happy outcome meant that I had acquired a new career within three months of leaving Standard Chartered, even though the appointment would not be effective for another 18 months at the start of the academic year in October 1989. I had avoided second-best roles in the business world – the Ted Heath effect as I called it, of glowering at my successor from the sidelines – and now had a chance to achieve something noteworthy in a very different field. It was perhaps surprising that SOAS should have made such a non-traditional appointment and there seem to have been several ingredients to its decision. Although SOAS had suffered severe staff reductions when the university funding regime imposed cut-backs, many of the posts had been restored as a result of the Parker Report and the School had meaningful financial reserves. However, morale in the School was very low and there was a tangible demand for fresh leadership. My predecessor, Jeremy Cowan, had managed the economies skilfully, but he was seen to be remote and pompous and more concerned with his role at Senate House than at the School. There had, one learned, been widespread hopes of two internal candidates (Professors Yapp and Parkin), both of whom had declined to apply for the Directorship. Of the actual shortlist, nobody liked the idea of a diplomat ('grace and favour') and I guess that I had prepared myself much more thoroughly than the two external academic candidates.

Looking Back
London University was constructed on a very different basis to Oxford. The latter comprises a central degree-awarding institution with academic departments, research facilities, library and it appointed the academic staff. University students were recruited by financially independent colleges whose fellows mostly held university posts as well.

In short, Oxford was a unitary university. In contrast, London comprised a collection of institutions that appointed their own academic staff and recruited their own students, and were responsible for teaching their own degree programmes, and their own research and libraries. However, they all awarded the University of London degree and there was a central governance structure with mechanisms to maintain comparable standards. In short, it was a multi-campus federal structure. The University Grants Committee (UGC) allocated government funding to Senate House for distribution to the constituent colleges, and this had become the cause of significant tensions.

The School of Oriental Studies (as it then was) became a component of London University in 1916, after protracted birth pangs, and it followed an unusual pattern of development up until the 1960s. The School was conceived as a manifestation of imperial policy: that it was desirable – even necessary – that a country ruling and trading with such an extensive empire in Asia and Africa should have an academic institution that studied the languages and cultures of the individual countries and was able to pass on this knowledge to those responsible for government and business there. There was also a needling factor at work in that Germany and France already possessed academic institutions covering this same geography.

Following an impressive launch, it then emerged that the intended beneficiaries in Whitehall and the City were notably reluctant to come up with tangible support by way of finance or language acquisition and the School had to manage on very exiguous resources for many years. Its faculty comprised some notable language scholars who, however, showed little interest in the contemporary world or engagement with those involved; it was essentially a scholarly research institution. As a pale reflection of the original vision, the faculty coped with a modest annual intake of missionaries, administrators and businessmen who were exposed to Asian and African languages on short courses. It was a sore point with the School that the India Office stuck to its links with Oxbridge for its ICS probationers, while the Colonial Office was particularly opposed to academic language instruction in England and also preferred Oxbridge for its general course. The quality of the faculty ensured that the School was acceptable to London University, but it failed to develop a successful relationship with the outside world.

Wartime needs then led to two singular developments: the organisation of a crash programme to impart a degree of Japanese language competence for surveillance purposes in the war theatres, and also a role in the censorship of communications in Asian languages, but there was no tangible legacy.

Planning for the post-war world opened new vistas and the School was able to play an influential part in the setting up of the Scarborough Commission on the provision for Oriental, African, Slavonic and East European languages that reported in 1947.[105] Its members were all drawn from the public service and none from academia. The School of Oriental and African Studies (as it had now become) submitted a bid already prepared for the UGC for a dramatic increase in staff to 151, as compared with 42 in 1939, but at the Commission's instigation this was increased to 266 and duly endorsed. The report was accepted by government and became the basis for the expansion of the faculty in the following years. A singular feature of Scarborough was its explicit articulation of the need to establish 'strong departments' independent of student demand. This orientation was reinforced by the School's decision to implement the main staff expansion in the language departments. The lack of interest in the contemporary societies of Asia and Africa is striking. It significantly undermined the School's perceived mission to enable Britain to engage with and understand better these countries at such a time of change.

Thus, by the end of the 1950s SOAS was a rather odd institution with a large concentration of language scholarship that was patently unrelated either to student demand or to meeting the needs of government and business, as envisaged by Scarborough. When Cyril Philips became Director in 1957 there were only 22 undergraduates and out of a faculty of 148 no less than 101 were in the language departments. At this point things got better under its dynamic new Director. The delayed review of the Scarborough dispensation eventually took place in 1960, with Philips as an active instigator. He had already begun to re-orientate the School away from its classical past and towards the contemporary world with departments of geography, economics and politics. This was powerfully reinforced by the recommendations of a report instigated by the UGC

---

105 *Report of the Interdepartmental Commission of Enquiry on Oriental, Slavonic, East European and African Studies*: HMSO, 1947

led by Sir William Hayter from which SOAS received 10 new posts in social sciences as well as postgraduate funding.[106] Philips also gave impetus towards recruitment of undergraduates, with the appointment of an education officer and numerous courses for both teachers and sixth forms that gradually were reflected in increased numbers.

Philips was a visionary Director and an effective networker with US foundations and within the university. It led to his appointment as vice chancellor of London University, which was an unpaid post held concurrently with the SOAS directorship. It was to the School's overall advantage, especially the achievement of the new building to house the library and academic offices, which was later named after him. But this also distanced Philips from the faculty. Worse, he had to contend with a backlash from the language departments over their diminished status, and also with the unrest that took place in universities in the late 1960s on the part of both students and staff. At SOAS this exposed what had become a remote and autocratic administration. Philips's transforming directorship ended on an unhappy note in September 1976.[107]

These internal strains might have been expected to quieten down under the new Director, Jeremy Cowan, but for a drastic change in the external weather; its impact on the School formed a crucial background to my own appointment. Britain's economic difficulties, accompanied by high inflation, led to the termination of the benign regime of university funding and quinquennial settlements; instead, there followed years of cuts and delayed hand to mouth awards. If SOAS was to remain solvent this would require a drastic shrinkage of its faculty. The School was hit especially hard by the requirement that overseas students henceforth pay an economic fee, since more than a third of its students were from overseas compared with a national average of about 10%, and also by the policy shift to make university funding a function of undergraduate numbers. Its student-staff ratio was about 4 to 1 compared with 10 to 1 nationally. Cowan had the invidious task of managing this situation. Solvency was preserved without mass sacking by the fortuitous circumstance that a cohort of Scarborough era staff were nearing retirement and the UGC

---

106 *Report of the Sub-Committee on Oriental, Slavonic, East European and African Studies*: HMSO, 1961
107 Philips wrote a brief history, *The School of Oriental & African Studies*, that was published by the school in 1967 and then an autobiography, *Beyond The Ivory Tower*, Radcliffe Press, 1955, in which he expressed his frustrations.

had offered to finance an early retirement programme. Together with natural wastage, the faculty was reduced by some 50 posts to 150, with language departments bearing the brunt.

Cowan then set up a committee under Professor Yapp to map out a new academic model for SOAS that embodied the new funding regime based on student demand. This required a painful prioritisation of subjects and a recognition that some languages would have to be given up altogether and others receive much reduced attention. In all this Cowan showed great skill in teasing ad hoc financial relief from the university and the UGC on several occasions, as well as some new posts. His major achievement was to secure a new report on the special needs of the field covered by the School, and substantially to ventriloquise its content. First, an ex-ambassador on the Governing Body was appointed to undertake the report and then, when he gave up the commission, Sir Peter Parker was appointed. He was a prominent businessman, already on the Court of the university and himself one of the war time Japanese language trainees. He relied heavily on a member of the School's staff in drawing up the report.[108] The result was a resounding re-statement of the original case for Britain to have a strong competence in its universities in the languages and cultures of Asia and Africa. For SOAS the outcome was an award of 18 new posts.

Another initiative with great potential was the introduction of fee earning diploma courses for target markets. One was a matriculation course for Japanese students to enable them to attend London University and with a Japanese partner; another was on Asian art connoisseurship in conjunction with Sotheby's.

It was sad that Cowan's skill in steering SOAS successfully through these difficult times was not more appreciated within the School. He had become an unpopular figure and morale was low. I inherited a rather unhappy and divided institution.[109]

---

108 'Speaking for the Future': a review of the requirements of diplomacy and commerce for Asian and African languages and area studies. UGC, 1986
109 A centenary history of SOAS was published in 2016, The School of Oriental and African Studies – Imperial Training and the Expansion of Learning, Ian Brown. Cambridge, 2016. Earlier there had been an edited volume of essays published by the school, SOAS Since the Sixties. 2003. Both volumes review my period as director.

Towards Raisman

Knowing that I was living in London during the 18 months before succeeding him, Jeremy Cowan most generously took steps to get me more closely acquainted with the School. He had set up a working party on academic organisation to try to resolve the dilemma of whether area centres or discipline departments should be the basis for organising the faculty and he invited me to attend two open meetings in the winter of 1988, when the alternatives were vigorously debated and voted on. The unhelpful outcome was that the faculty was hopelessly divided, with a large element refusing to make a choice, so the School was left with its existing mixture of departments and centres. It was a powerful warning of the difficulty confronting leadership in academia. Consultation was essential but it was no guarantee of consent. As a member of Governing Body, I was also charged with leading a working party during this time on the School's external services. This provided an opportunity to review the initiatives that were being taken to develop fee earning programmes for special categories of student, as well as briefings and language training. Unsurprisingly, we recommended that the department be placed on a commercial footing with a business manager.

In the summer of 1989 Jeremy Cowan arranged for me to have an office in one of the School's rented properties – the Faber & Faber building on Russell Square, and I liked to think that I was sitting in T S Eliot's room. In this way I was able to meet all the heads of department before the start of the academic year as well as a number of other individuals who found their way to my room to unburden themselves. I was therefore well aware of the morale issue and of the desire for fresh leadership and I resolved to give an address to the whole faculty at the beginning of term – and also to provide tea afterwards so that it could turn into a social occasion. I maintained this practice of addressing the faculty at the beginning and towards the end of the academic year throughout my time.

After preliminary felicitations, I enlarged upon several topics. SOAS had just received a nasty shock from the first nationwide assessment of research rankings, where it had elected to be assessed on the basis of five area studies groups and had been rated a lowly 3 out of a possible 5. This was clearly a case for urgent remedial action as it affected the research grant. On finance, I signalled a concern over the future reliability of the special factor funding being received by the School and the consequent need to enhance normal funding by expanding student numbers, as well as fee income from the commercial courses. Fund raising needed higher priority. Lastly, I tiptoed round the issue of organisation and management in order to indicate a cautious and evolutionary approach to future reform. On a lighter note, I ended my remarks with an analogy drawn from Richard Strauss's *Capriccio* – with its play on whether words or music should have priority, and suggesting that the School's academic dilemmas could provide material for an opera. This left me with a challenge for the future and in every subsequent address I managed to incorporate a Wagnerian or other operatic analogy.

In 1990 the dominant financial problem was that SOAS had a student-staff ratio of around 5 to 1, when other research led universities managed 15 to 1 and rising. The consequence was that SOAS was not working the university funding fruit machine successfully, which was based on student numbers. Its academic problem was that, despite the introduction of modular degrees, too much of its specialised scholarship did not engage the interests of modern students and there was a reluctance to bridge the gap. The resolution of this puzzle was in part to master the dark arts of influencing Senate House, through whom all finance flowed, and – more importantly – in gradually devising a range of comparative degrees that made use of the rare scholarship in the school, but also appealed to modern students, through a range of comparative degrees in art history, literature, religious studies and, above all, in development studies. In my seven years at the School, student numbers were tripled to 3,000, including a large cohort of masters and other fee paying students.

In those early weeks I was also made aware of being under scrutiny from several distinguished persons with a special interest in SOAS: former professors Edith Penrose, Edward Ullendorf, Anthony Allot and others came to inspect me. A more comical incident involved Sir Hugh Cortazzi, former ambassador to Japan and chairman of the Japan Society. He took enormous umbrage at a satirical publication – in Japanese – by Professor Brian Moeran and demanded his removal, which of course was out of the question. Subsequently, Cortazzi became quite a friend and he played an active part in an award competition for businessmen learning Japanese.

London University provided a house for the heads of colleges, but SOAS was an exception. Jeremy Cowan lived in Dulwich and had seen no need for one. I also lived in Dulwich but took a different view – that it would be useful to have a private space near the School to meet and entertain colleagues. There was perhaps also another consideration: Ruth and I were both devotees of Wigmore Hall and Covent Garden and a Bloomsbury flat would be very convenient in the evenings. Senate House responded with some difficulty but they eventually came up with a small flat in Torrington Place, which turned out to be part of the former house of Christina Rosetti. As a result, we chose William Morris wallpaper and Ruth managed to acquire a copy of a cartoon of her. I made a habit of spending three or four nights a week at the flat.

The poor research assessment outcome provoked the School into providing targeted support for research, including reinstating sabbaticals, and enhanced monitoring by the Research Committee. An academic issue was also resolved: scholars are best rated in relation to their core academic discipline. The next research assessment in 1992/93 was submitted on a departmental basis rather than area centres and SOAS emerged in a much more favourable light with ratings of 4s and 5s.

The growing number of students also stimulated curriculum reform in order to simplify the plethora of course options, but also to introduce new, and popular, degrees. Economics and Politics became separate departments, as did Art and Religion. Surprisingly, none of the colleges at the university recognised Development Studies as a degree subject before the 1990s. Following a university report, LSE decided that it was a subject for graduate economists only, but to my delight SOAS was the first to introduce it as an undergraduate degree. It seemed to me that the School was especially well placed to treat development as a process of social transformation where all the social sciences and humanities had a contribution to make in understanding why some societies were more successful than others.[110]

The other academic initiative at this time with significance for the future was to procure the transfer to SOAS from the Open University of Professor Laurence Harris to introduce a targeted distance learning

---

110 As I write, a new book by the Oxford professor Stefan Dercon. *Gambling On Development: Why Some Countries Win and Others Lose,* Hurst, 2022, addresses this issue and emphasises the crucial importance of the ruling elite committing to what he calls a development bargain.

degree, funded by Swedish aid, for finance officials in two countries transforming from Marxist orthodoxy to IMF clients – Mozambique and Vietnam. As it happened, I had known of Laurence Harris from 20 years ago when Ruth was on the economic staff of LSE at the time he graduated with great distinction. I was also chairman (inherited from Jeremy Cowan) of the university's external degree programme and rather frustrated at the lack of support it received. The opportunity to move into this field at SOAS was not to be missed and this initiative burgeoned into an important dimension of the School.

Some years later, I went to Hanoi to give out diplomas at a special graduation ceremony, wearing academic robes on a very hot afternoon. I learned something of the way that the war against the French and then the Americans had been conducted and then witnessed the lengthy celebration of Vietnam's national day. As with the Lord Mayor's Show, there was a procession of floats in front of the country's ageing leadership, presenting key moments in Vietnam's history and usually in opposition to China. But one episode related to the French colonial occupation, which was personified by a single comic figure on a bicycle wearing a solar topee and slinging a rifle.

Lord Maclehose retired in 1990 and the Governing Body set up a search committee for his successor that included Julian Wathen. After many weeks it held a meeting in my office to report failure to secure anyone from their list of prospects. What to do? I had a proposal. Sir Robert Wade-Gery had recently retired after being High Commissioner in Delhi, where I had got to know him on Standard Chartered visits. He came from a distinguished academic family and was himself a fellow of All Souls. The suggestion worked and I had a good relationship with him for the rest of my time. Wade-Gery was both conscientious and supportive and he used his diplomatic skills to good effect over the Brunei Gallery development, as narrated later. My only regret was that he had also accepted quite an onerous door-opening role in the City, which meant that my hopes for him with regard to fundraising were unrealised.

The new Education Act and the Conservative government's combative relationship with the universities meant that it was no longer appropriate for the Minister for Education to be associated with any one institution as the Visitor to SOAS and I was asked to make alternative arrangements. I had only recently undertaken a revision of the charter of the Royal Commonwealth Society involving consequential negotiations with the Privy Council office and its Secretary at that time, was an old friend from the Home Office, Sir Geoffrey De Deney. I took the opportunity to seek Geoffrey's advice over finding a new Visitor for SOAS. We reviewed a number of possibilities and then he suddenly came up with the name of Sir Geoffrey Howe, who had recently resigned as Foreign Secretary, precipitating the downfall of Margaret Thatcher, and was looking for new interests. It was an inspired idea and Sir Geoffrey Howe accepted with enthusiasm.

Howe very much approved of my desire to restore a sense of occasion and ceremony to SOAS. We started off with Honorary Fellows and so, instead of just writing a letter of appointment (as happened to me on being elected an Honorary Fellow of Oriel), we created an event that also happened to mark the School's 75th anniversary in 1991. It was a happy circumstance that the honorands included Lord Maclehose, Sir Peter Parker and David Khalili, the benefactor of a chair in Islamic Art. I had had a special gown made for the Visitor which was embroidered with Oriental and African symbolism. When colleges were for the first time allowed to hold their own degree ceremonies in 1993, I persuaded the City of London to present the School with a magnificent silver-plated mace, again with symbolic decoration and surmounted by a precious stone.

Two events in particular stay in the memory from these occasions. In 1994 one of the Honorary Fellows that year was His Imperial Highness Prince Takahito Mukasa, an authority on Mesopotamian archaeology, who had been a visiting professor twenty years earlier. On these occasions I arranged with the Music Centre for appropriate music from Asia or Africa to be played and this time the choice fell on Japanese temple drums. They were played to a compelling but syncopated rhythm as the procession filed into the Assembly Hall, with the result that – after a few steps – everyone seemed to have a limp.

Subsequently, Prince Mukasa invited me to Tokyo to visit his museum and I stayed with Sir John Boyd and Julia at the magnificent British embassy in Tokyo close by the imperial palace. Prince Mukasa had undertaken an archaeological dig in Mesopotamia before the war and he proudly showed me round the collections. I was then invited to tea and Sir John provided the embassy Jaguar for the short drive to the palace precinct, where I was received with much formality on arrival. I was ushered into a small drawing room for tea when the thinnest imaginable cucumber sandwiches were served as we discussed the museum and SOAS.

On a memorable occasion when SOAS was managing its own degree ceremonies, we had arranged for a Cuban salsa band to strike up at the end of the proceedings while the platform party filed through the auditorium. Here, the salsa rhythm was so infectious that Lord Howe and his procession gave every impression of dancing their way out, to the delight of the audience of parents and new graduates.

David Khalili had obtained a PhD in Islamic art at SOAS and had remained in contact with the School. His Iranian Jewish family had left after the revolution and commanded considerable wealth. Khalili himself was in the course of assembling an amazing art collection and commissioning leading scholars to publish lavish catalogue raisonné. He had very much absorbed from his time at the School an awareness that Muslims and Jews had a shared semitic cultural heritage and was an articulate exponent of this view, and a consequence was that he had no problem in assembling a leading collection of Korans and examples of Islamic culture. He soon became the focus of a campaign to endow a chair of Islamic Art, which was successful and the first occupant was recruited from the British Museum.

As a result of getting to know Khalili, I became aware that he had played a key part in setting up a museum of Islamic Art for the Sultan of Brunei. This led to a thought that the Sultan might be open to a proposal to finance an Islamic art centre at SOAS, as it was known that he was minded to do something significant in Britain. Khalili explained that the first step was to get to know the Sultan's *homme d'affaires*, who was the gatekeeper to his charitable purse. Major Hanbury and his right-hand man Major Pusinelli were two former cavalry officers who had originally been responsible for introducing the Sultan to polo, which became a consuming interest. They had been seconded from the army to help develop Britain's relationship with this small country on the tip of Borneo, where Shell had developed an enormous natural gas field. Christopher Hanbury had a nose for spotting charlatans and he was currently dealing with a bogus architect who had got the Sultan's ear as a Muslim convert and had secured some kind of promise to design a mosque in Britain. I was put in touch with the man, with the idea that the SOAS project might take the place of the mosque. We had several meetings which revealed his unsuitability for any involvement; meanwhile Hanbury was persuaded that SOAS would provide a more suitable outlet for the Sultan's charity than another mosque.

A concept was refined for a building that would incorporate a substantial exhibition gallery and auditorium, together with three floors of academic offices, and the university was persuaded to allocate land opposite the SOAS building that was currently occupied by wartime prefabs. All this took a lot of tortuous discussion and negotiation, but we eventually reached a point where a £10,000 scale model was created and Sir Robert and I accompanied it to the London residence of the Sultan in Kensington Palace Gardens. We had an audience, standing round the model in his drawing room, that lasted all of ten minutes, when the Sultan agreed to sponsor the development. The sum mentioned on the day was much less than the final cost of £10 million, but the whole amount was generously provided. The Brunei Gallery was officially opened in the autumn of 1995 by the Princess Royal in her capacity as Chancellor of the University, but the Sultan did not attend the ceremony. With the agreed closure of the road between Malet Street and Russell Square running between the Brunei Gallery and the main School building, SOAS now had a rather elegant, newly tree lined, pedestrian precinct that has been much appreciated by students.

There were two unexpected events associated with the development of the Brunei Gallery. When transferring the building land to SOAS on a long lease, Senate House had quite forgotten about an undertaking given to the Bedford Estate that its approval would be sought for any new building work by the university abutting onto Russell Square. Lady Tavistock decided to make an issue of the matter, although building work was already in progress, and a legal nightmare threatened. My initial démarche was rebuffed and Sir Robert then stepped in. It so happened that he had got to know the Tiarks family when serving in the Madrid embassy and he was able to flatter Henrietta Tiarks (as she had been) with family reminiscences. His other tack was a heavy emphasis on the diplomatic sensitivity of the Brunei connection to HMG. Over several meetings a face saver was negotiated whereby London University would affix an engraved apology to the Russell family on the completed building, which reads:

The University of London hereby records its sincere apologies that the plans for this building were settled without due consultation with the Russell family and their Trustees and therefore without their approval of its design.

The plaque became a popular tourist snapshot in subsequent years, and Lady Tavistock had her tease.

The other matter was more tiresome. When the Brunei Gallery project went ahead without him, the bogus architect started legal proceedings against me personally and the Sultan's representatives, claiming that there was a breach of contract with himself and that he should have been appointed as architect to the building. Fortunately, Major Hanbury agreed to meet all the legal costs. The plaintiff conducted his own case and it dragged on expensively for many years before its final dismissal.

The School's financial relationship with the Universities Funding Council was a constant worry because of the lack of both clarity and certainty over future levels of funding. The awards usually came after the commencement of the relevant academic year and were subject to arbitrary reductions. Other universities received their grant in two ways, partly for teaching (and based on student numbers) and partly for research (guided by the research assessment evaluation). But SOAS received a block grant that also took account of the national status of its library and its specialised languages. In 1990/91 the School was provided for the first time with a breakdown of what it 'earned' under the standard criteria of teaching and research, to which had been added the 'special factor' grant of about £4 million, which accounted for more than half the total. It was a sobering revelation and I shared the picture in my Spring address to the staff –

'No-one guarantees fair play in real life. It seems to me that SOAS is being moulded into the pattern of a typical university, as defined by the formula treatment of T and R, and that no-one is going to pick up the pieces for us... We cannot wish this situation away, and we must devise measures to live within our resource grant and other recurrent income... Above all, we must not gamble on being rescued but instead ensure our own survival.'

I then spelt out that the school must continue to increase student numbers, fee income and research funding, as well as to find payroll savings.

In looking for savings, I had a cautionary experience. Following a two-day strategy meeting to produce an institutional plan, a consensus had been reached that the best way to achieve a decisive result on payroll saving would be to face up to abolishing a department that had few students and little interaction with the rest of the faculty. Such was the Linguistics Department in 1992, which had become highly theoretical in its research and divorced from the SOAS mission. However, its leadership was respected in the world of linguistics so that when I announced our decision there was an international uproar. I was inundated with emails and denunciations from around the world. It also emerged that procedures involving the closure of a department had not been correctly applied, which raised potential legal difficulties. I then faced a lengthy and gruelling meeting of Academic Board and had to concede defeat. Some long-standing fissures in the faculty had been exposed by the whole episode and one sad consequence was that my Pro-Director, John Wansbrough, who had promoted this solution, felt that he had to retire and he left at the end of term. We had been used to an agreeable daily consultation following his morning walk to the School from Islington, but after that Academic Board meeting he never spoke to me again.

SOAS was actually making significant progress in the vital metrics. Research income exceeded £1 million for the first time in 1991-2 and had doubled over three years. Over the same period student numbers had risen 45 percent to 1,500. Nevertheless, it remained essential to sustain pressure for continued special funding while these improvements were taking place. In early 1992 I was able to meet the chief executive of the Higher Education Funding Council for England, as it had now become, and learned soon afterwards that a task force was to be set up to review the methodology of the special funding to the School, and that I would be informed of its membership in due course. Some weeks later, I received a call from Senate House asking if I could, after all, come up with suggested names for the group.

I had met John Raisman, recently chairman of Shell UK, while at Standard Chartered and had been able to tell him that, while working in the Kenya Treasury, I had been the official designated to work on a study his father was undertaking for the Colonial Office on the financial relations between Kenya, Uganda and Tanganyika. I knew of John's interest in higher education and proposed his name, while colleagues in the School came up with two other names from academia, all of which were accepted. Thus, for the second time in my career I found myself involved with a Raisman Report. Subsequently, John and I were both involved for several years with the affairs of the British Empire & Commonwealth Museum in Bristol.

The Raisman Report was all that we could have wished in its robust language in support of special treatment for SOAS and the message was accepted by the funding council in an interesting way, although not adopting all the details when the 1993 grants were announced.[111] There was an exceptionally generous research allocation to accompany the non-formula grant (as it was now called). Overall, SOAS received a 12.6 percent grant uplift – well ahead of most institutions – making up for previous harsh treatment. The fact that so much had been done by the School over the previous three years to increase student numbers and fee income meant that, far from being 100 percent special funded, this element would now only account for 26 percent of total grant. It was still critically necessary, of course.

Standing on Our Own Feet

During the 1990s the federal university had to loosen its bonds, under strong pressure from the larger colleges, to be seen as universities in their own right. SOAS was able to benefit from these developments which, to me, had striking parallels with the unwinding of the colonial empire and the emergence of independent nation states, with all their trappings. We did not aspire to own an airline, but the prospect of having our own currency – SOAS examined and awarded degrees – was a different matter. To begin with, the school was allowed to run its own degree ceremonies and award fellowships. I supported enthusiastically the creation of our own rituals and regalia, as already noted, and music appropriate to our cultural reach in place of Handel and Brahms. Inaugural lectures for new professors were reintroduced, wearing academic dress (where I was pleased to don my B.Litt hood at last), to celebrate the scholarship of the school and the enhanced research ratings now being earned.

---

111 *Report of the Working Group on SOAS*: HEFCE, January 1993

1993 was a watershed year, due to the Raisman settlement and following the School's success in dramatically raising student numbers, fee earnings, research grants and its research rating. However, this increased business also required a transformation in the way that the School managed its affairs. Led by the Pro-Director, Bob Taylor, and the Deans there was a complete overhaul of undergraduate and masters degree programmes and of academic administration, including the important establishment of a graduate school with dedicated accommodation. At the same time, the School had to prepare for the devolution from Senate House to the colleges of examinations for the London degree and the procedures for appointing readers and professors. The government, meanwhile, was insisting on university-wide appraisals of teaching quality while continuing to impose mandatory efficiency savings. In the social science and humanities departments the student-staff ratio rose to 15:1, while still only 6:1 in the language departments. Three years earlier the overall School average had been 5:1. A new financial contribution analysis demonstrated that, notwithstanding the Raisman settlement, there was still a large cross-subsidy to the staffing of the language departments.

Matching reforms in the School's administration were also introduced, with the recruitment of experienced individuals to fill the posts of finance officer, registrar and School secretary.

The contribution of non-traditional teaching programmes had become quite significant. Mention has already been made of the distance learning degrees; another was the matriculation diplomas which were dominated by Japanese women students for whom special chaperone arrangements had to be made on arrival from sheltered backgrounds back home. During their year in London they visibly blossomed and the final award ceremony was a great occasion for showing off. It was my duty to present the certificates and at my last ceremony in 1996 something unprecedented happened. As the first diplomate paraded across the stage to collect her certificate there was a hush, and then a roar, since she had leant forward and kissed me on the cheek as I shook her hand. This created a dilemma for the others, and for me – should I kiss them all? Most preferred to scuttle forward, seize their scroll and run for it.

My last three years were very much pre-occupied with the adaptation of the School to its emerging status as a small self-governing university increasingly standing on its own feet, which included a revision of the SOAS charter. Premises developments loomed large as a result of its growth, and here the new School secretary, Frank Dabell, proved to be a godsend as he had a special interest and skill in property matters. SOAS took delivery of the Brunei Gallery in 1995, it leased and renovated properties on Russell Square, completed an addition to its main building and embarked on its first wholly owned student hostel. Frank Dabell played rugby, rode a Harley Davidson and was something of a *bon viveur*. He, Bob Taylor and I would quite often peel off for lunch together over a bottle of good wine to mull over school affairs, or meet after hours in my office for a pink gin.

Amidst more earnest events, some more entertaining ones stay in the mind. SOAS had a relationship with Chulalongkorn University in Thailand as part of a broad engagement with Thai culture. On one occasion, a retired member of faculty was awarded the Order of the White Elephant by Princess Sirindhorn at a ceremony in the Thai embassy. She had serious academic interests and fostered the SOAS relationship. There was a memorable occasion when she presented a complete gamelan suite of gongs to the Music Centre and herself participated in a recital in the senior common room, seated on the floor with the other players. This created a protocol dilemma for the Thai diplomats present who were supposed to place themselves literally below royalty. There was a resulting spectacle of crouching diplomatic staff around the room endeavouring to show proper respect.

The visit of the Dalai Lama to SOAS was another special occasion and was a tribute to the standing of Tibetan studies at the School. He addressed a packed assembly hall of students, staff and special guests and, as I recall, openly reflected on the possibility that China might prevent a successor being evolved in the traditional way, as seems to be happening. Afterwards, he took tea in my office and, corny to relate, one had a very pronounced feeling of being in the presence of a holy man.

More amusing was a gift orchestrated by the Indian High Commissioner, Dr Singhvi. He wished to present to SOAS a bust of the Tamil philosopher Thiruvaluvar, author of the Tirukkural in 500 AD. We duly selected a position in the entrance hall, but what arrived some months later was a life size bronze seated statue weighing half a ton.

A new site was found under a tree by the library and a presentation ceremony took place, complete with an ode by William Radice, lecturer in Bengali, and the School's poet laureate.

I had formed the view that my term at SOAS should not exceed ten years, and was rather influenced in this by the contemporary example of Margaret Thatcher's problems after she decided to continue for more than ten years. However, my decision to retire in 1996 after only seven years was driven by a personal consideration. I had unwisely fallen into a romantic relationship with a divorced senior member of the faculty and this threatened to compromise both my effectiveness and her career and I came to the conclusion that retirement was the solution. Ruth was then unaware of the true reason, but having retired from full time employment herself, she was supportive.

The appointment committee to choose my successor started work in autumn 1995 and in due course selected a distinguished American economist, then in California, who had previously headed an Oxford college. Unhappily, his wife took strongly against the SOAS accommodation, and perhaps did not wish to move back to England anyway. She persuaded her husband to renounce the appointment, to general embarrassment. At this point I became involved because the other names on the shortlist were not wanted. Sir Tim Lankester was permanent secretary at the Ministry of Education and had just lost his job as a result of the merger of his department with the Ministry of Labour. I had got to know Tim in his Treasury days when he had been seconded to the IMF in Washington and then went to head the Department for International Development. It was agreed that I should sound him out and indeed he was interested in the SOAS post. The rest is history.

My time at SOAS ended on a high note when I was appointed KCMG in the birthday honours in 1996 'for services to education'. It so happened that I was the senior honour recipient that June day and was therefore the first person to be presented to the Queen by the Lord Chancellor in the ballroom at Buckingham Palace. Before the ceremony, two courtiers took me to a side room so that I could rehearse kneeling on the stool and walking backwards afterwards from the royal presence, in order to set a good example to those following. I was touched on the shoulder with the ceremonial sword and the Queen placed the handsome order of St Michael & St George on its ribbon round my neck and I found

Degree day at SOAS. In the office. Visit of Dalai Llama

Award of Hon. Fellowship: Lord Howe and Sir Tim Lancaster. At Buckingham Palace

that she had been briefed about my roles at the Royal Commonwealth Society and the Royal African Society. Ruth, Robert and Martin were in the audience and I was then able to join them and listen to the rest of the ceremony. It was quite touching to listen to the long list of citations for MBE and OBE and to be reminded of the tremendous amount of devoted work that takes place in Britain with charities and in everyday life. After the ceremony we posed for photographs outside Buckingham Palace and then had a celebration luncheon at the Ritz.

Among the congratulatory letters was an irreverent reminder that I would now have to pay more for domestic services, and also that the initials stood for Kindly Call Me God as well as for Knight Commander of the Order of St Michael & St George. The Order has its own chapel in St Paul's Cathedral and there is an impressive annual service in the cathedral for members of the Order. Over time, I have become one of the more senior members and have now qualified for a brass plaque in the chapel.

The key transformation during my seven years at SOAS was that the School had been substantially – but by no means entirely – weaned from complete reliance on special funding, by showing that it could earn its way by teaching students and securing research grants like other universities. The faculty had been rebuilt to over 200 academic staff and 46 Asian and African languages were still on offer. A distinctive feature of the student body was the high proportion (around 40 percent) of graduate students, where the rich offering of one year masters programmes was very attractive. The interest of many young people in the developing world was a motivating factor in coming to SOAS and it gave a distinctive feature to the student body. Looking back over those years I am conscious of two regrets over matters that could have been progressed more actively.

Throughout its existence SOAS had an unsatisfactory balance in its language teaching between learning a language as a basis for scholarship on the one hand, and intensive language instruction mainly for vocational purposes. It was not until the post-Raisman period of curriculum reform that serious thought was given to establishing a separate language teaching centre, but there were divided opinions as to how closely linked it should be with the faculty and the matter dragged on for years. I regret that I did not engage with this important weakness more decisively, although Ian Brown's penetrating centenary history of the School brings out well that the strong opinions on the matter were hard to reconcile.

My other regret was a failure to professionalise fundraising. I had signalled it as a priority on arrival, but the necessary staffing for an effective unit was the casualty of financial stringency at a time when there was marked antipathy to any increase in administration costs. Oxbridge was showing the way in its intensive cultivation of alumni from the moment of graduation, as well as in its ability to home in on major prospects. We did have our successes with the Brunei Gallery and two endowed chairs, but on looking through a list of 'might have beens' I have a feeling that some of them could have been turned into achievements with more assiduous attention. The difficulty was that one had to incur significant staffing costs without assurance of results.

One of the successful fundraising initiatives caused me some problems. The Saudi ambassador in London cultivated academic contacts and one of the SOAS faculty attended his majlis regularly. From this emerged the prospect of a benefaction to the School and I became actively involved. The outcome was the endowment of a King Fahd Chair in Islamic Studies. To my astonishment, instead of being congratulated at this achievement I found that I had stirred up a hornet's nest. The faculty's links were mostly with Persian studies, modern Iran and the Shia branch of Islam and there was deep suspicion of Saudi Arabia and the influence of its puritan Wahabi/Sunni religious leadership. There was pressure to renounce the gift and it was only headed off by my agreeing to establish a new vetting procedure for approving prospective benefactors. It was a cautionary experience that other universities have since had to grapple with, including LSE and Oxford.

Another cautionary experience concerned fundraising for the library, where there was much concern that, even with special funding, SOAS was not purchasing enough new publishing, especially from China and Japan. I had a bright idea to sell a valuable Persian manuscript that had come to SOAS almost by accident, being tucked into an atlas that was part of a bequest from a diplomat's library many years ago. My view was that it was an isolated treasure that should more appropriately form part of a large collection of Persian manuscripts. Sotheby's advised that it might fetch £600,000 at auction. However, when I sought authority to sell the manuscript for the benefit of the library there was strong objection from the faculty and the proposal had to be abandoned. De-acquisition is a sensitive subject for all institutions with legacy treasures, but a blanket refusal to dispose of items is too simplistic, and I still regret this decision. I had to deal with a much more difficult circumstance several years later in connection with the British Empire & Commonwealth Museum, as narrated below.

I wonder sometimes whether more might have been accomplished to enhance the status of SOAS as *the* national centre for Asia and Africa. There is an element of fantasy in such speculation, given the financial exigencies of the time and the heavy workload; nevertheless, there were several interesting flirtations that had potential to enhance the School's position by forging links with learned societies and their journals. When I arrived at SOAS the School already hosted and edited a famous journal, *The China Quarterly*. There was some anxiety at the time over its continuation and I was asked to give reassurances to this end. The episode stimulated me to engage in a prolonged attempt to persuade the Oriental Society (which was then experiencing accommodation problems) to relocate to SOAS, along with its distinguished library and journal. Sadly, academic politics got in the way of a sensible project and it lapsed.

Another flirtation was with the Royal Society of Asian Affairs. Its journal was aimed mainly at a lay audience and the membership had a large diplomatic and overseas career character. Several members of the SOAS faculty were members and the journal and the society would have benefitted from closer links with an academic institution, but it was not to be. In 1994 I was invited to give the society's annual lecture and chose to research the circumstances that led to the foundation of SOAS.[112] It was a convoluted story and had much to do with a belief that those administering the empire should have a knowledge of its languages and cultures, but combined with concerns in official quarters that Germany seemed to have a deeper knowledge of the societies comprising the British Empire than was the case in England. Professor John Peel was more successful when he brought the office and journal of the International African Institute to the School.

---

112 'Knowledge and Power: The Study of Asia', Michael McWilliam. *Asian Affairs* Vol XXVI February 1995

The Royal African Society

My one success in this field was with the Royal African Society, with which I already had a long connection before coming to SOAS. The society dates from the imperial heyday, with the monarch as its patron. At its centenary in 2001 a celebratory volume was published and a reception held at Buckingham Palace.[113] The society publishes a journal, *African Affairs*, and it holds open public meetings on matters of current interest. In the post-war period a tradition had developed that Barclays DCO and Standard Bank would stand behind the society with an annual grant and also in providing key officers. In the mid-70s the society's president was the chairman of Barclays DCO, its chairman was Julian Wathen and the treasurer was one of their general managers. As soon as I became a general manager in 1974, Julian arranged that I should be appointed treasurer in order to re-engage Standard and I remained an officer of the society for the next 30 years until retiring from the chair in 2004.

At the time of joining the RAS council there was much concern over the society's secretary, Mercy Edgedale, who was an energetic anti-apartheid activist who had lots of connections with exiles from southern Africa. As a charity, the Royal African Society was precluded from taking a political stance and there was concern that the society's funds might start being used to support anti-apartheid activities. The solution was to set up a separate charitable trust to hold its reserves. Later on, this became a useful repository for gifts, but meantime the secretary relationship became increasingly strained and a parting had to be arranged. This was all quite time consuming.

The RAS was one of the charitable organisations that nested in the Royal Commonwealth Society's rookery in Northumberland Avenue so that it needed a new home when its redevelopment got under way in 1989. I had just arrived at SOAS and was able to arrange for the society to be given an office there. This proved to be something of a life saver in that, apart from the accommodation, SOAS gave the society a ready-made audience from the students and faculty for its open meetings. Apart from engaging in a Privy Council exercise to modernise its constitution, I addressed three main issues after becoming chairman in 1996 in succession to Sir Michael Caine, chairman of Booker. These

---

113 *The British Intellectual Engagement with Africa in the Twentieth Century,* ed. Douglas Rimmer & Anthony Kirk-Greene. Macmillan, 2000.

were the society's relationship with academia through the African Studies Association; the arrangements for editing and publishing *African Affairs* with Oxford University Press; and the appointment of an executive director.

As its name implies, the African Studies Association (ASA) was a UK-wide network of academics with a research interest in Africa. It held a biennial conference and the membership subscription paid for the services of an organising secretary. By tradition, members had a discounted subscription to *African Affairs* which had the unintended consequence that joining the ASA was cheaper than joining the RAS. After much haggling, it was eventually arranged that the RAS would handle the administration of both organisations and ASA members would receive *African Affairs*. Although still a 'cheap' way to the journal, the RAS now received a tangible contribution to its administrative overheads and had strengthened its link with Africa scholarship in universities.

The publishing arrangements with OUP were re-negotiated by Mel Balloch, the Standard Chartered manager who I had persuaded to become treasurer. OUP regarded *African Affairs* as something of a flagship journal and were keen to fold it into the new electronic data bases that had become available. The financial arrangements were also improved and the resulting profits were critical to any wider ambitions for the society. The editorial control of *African Affairs* was in the hands of a small coterie. The journal had become outranked by several newer academic journals while not really succeeding as a communication to lay readers with an interest in Africa. I had only limited success in improving matters, but the first step was to secure that academic articles would be refereed as was customary elsewhere. Another was to organise explicit 'briefing' pieces on topics of current concern. The missing element, in my view, was a clear strategy as to what the journal stood for, with the result that its contents were somewhat unpredictable, ranging from sociological studies to contemporary politics, to history, depending on the current editor.

The council of the society was gradually refreshed and this had the interesting consequence of creating pressure for a leadership post to direct its affairs in place of a committee of council. The first attempt to appoint a director was a disaster and my fault. He was a retired district commissioner from Zambia who had no standing with the academics and only a limited vision for the society and I had to bring the appointment to an end. Next time, I struck gold on discovering that the Africa editor of *The Economist* was looking for a change. It needed quite a courtship, but Richard Dowden came on board and transformed the influence and effectiveness of the RAS over some ten years, including an initiative to set up and service a Parliamentary group on Africa at Westminster.

When the project for Asia House was in its formative stage, SOAS was consulted and we took a rather sniffy view of the venture, arguing that the situation was unlike New York where there was a successful Asia House as there were already well-established societies in London covering all of Asia. I have wondered since whether a more positive attitude might have achieved a domicile at or linked with SOAS, and a resulting closer association with business in Asia.

Closer to home, the break-up of the federal university raised questions over the future of the so-called Senate Institutes, one of which – the Institute of Commonwealth Studies – already had close links with SOAS. The sensible solution would have been to integrate it with SOAS, especially its specialist library. But neither side managed to look beyond immediate problems: the history department held a poor view of ICS staff (other than its director who shortly moved to a chair at the School); and Senate House declined to facilitate the financial transition. The future of the School of Slavonic and East European Studies was also in question as it had failed to build up a student body in the days of expansion and was not financially viable. The 'fit' with SOAS related to its coverage of the Silk Road states of the former USSR, and there were extensive discussions, but again Senate House was unprepared to help with the financial aspect and SSEES was eventually dissolved into University College.

Finally, there was an intriguing possibility with the Overseas Development Institute. It was an early example of what would now be called a think tank, funded by corporate and institutional funding and closely linked with the Department for International Development. I had served on its council for several years. ODI could have complemented our development studies initiative nicely, but this time it was the economics department that disparaged ODI staff and the discussions fizzled out for want of a longer vision of the possibilities.

In 1986, while still at Standard Chartered, I was invited by the Economic Social & Research Council (ESRC) to sit on a panel to evaluate a £1 million funding bid to establish a new research centre in Oxford that was the brainchild of the economist Paul Collier. The Centre for the Study of African Economies (CSAE) was approved and was the largest ESRC project up to that time. Collier had been at Trinity and Nuffield and then was an economics lecturer at Oriel before becoming a fellow of St Antony's. He had formed the ambition to make Africa the focus of cutting edge economics research and this turned out to involve developing new data sets and econometric analysis on labour markets, risk perceptions, the study of trade shocks, trade policy and investment risk. It also led him to an influential role as a policy adviser. Years later, as Director of SOAS, Paul Collier invited me join the centre's Policy Committee in 1995, where I was rather pleased to find that its chairman was Richard Smethurst, the economist who was on the Monopolies Commission enquiry into the takeover bids for Royal Bank of Scotland, and who had issued a dissenting minority report in favour of the bids being allowed to proceed. Smethurst was a master of the intricate politics of the university and greatly helped the centre to become firmly established. A couple of years later he decided to give up the chairmanship and I was invited to succeed him. I held the post for fifteen years.

The Policy Committee was not a management committee, but rather a group of advisors and a sounding board for the director, with members drawn from the university, from NGOs, from the business world and individuals with special knowledge of Africa. The most important Oxford issue in the early years was the relationship of CSAE with other social science disciplines and, especially with Queen Elizabeth House and development studies. Paul Collier felt quite strongly that its distinctive contribution lay in it being an economics research unit within Oxford's recently established free standing economics department. He was ready to forge research links with other social scientists and centres on specific issues and that the centre should be au fait with the research methodology and insights of other disciplines, but this was not to be confused with becoming a multidisciplinary centre or a centre of African studies. The Policy Committee endorsed this position, although it was a teasing issue for several years. This debate resonated with me at SOAS, where the tension between academic discipline and area studies was a hot issue. When Oxford eventually established an African Studies masters programme, CSAE was in a position to contribute from a position of strength.

After I had joined the board of the Commonwealth Development Corporation, I was able to arrange for Collier to give a talk to the board and this led to CDC sponsoring the centre's 1998 conference, 'Investing in Africa'. CSAE enabled CDC to have a more sophisticated understanding of the way in which its project investments in Africa contributed to improving the climate for private investment, and of the important distinction between social and intrinsic returns. When I retired from the chairmanship of the Policy Committee in 2012 I was presented by Paul with one of the centre's publications, *The Oxford Companion to the Economics of Africa*. That autumn I was elected an honorary fellow of Oriel and I felt sure that a prompt had come from him.

During its first 25 years CSAE had evolved from an ESRC funded research project into an internationally recognised centre of economic research on Africa and of policy advice. It had established a leading *Journal of African Economics* and its economists were a notable feature of the university's economics department. Of particular significance has been the centre's energetic involvement in explaining Africa's poor economic record and in identifying the elements of a better policy environment, and then gaining currency for its views. One of its important initiatives was the African Economic Research Consortium that linked African universities and ensured a flow of D.Phil students to Oxford. Paul Collier himself was an indefatigable innovator and policy advisor and a formidable fundraiser; it was unsurprising that at the time of my retirement he was on the move himself to a chair at the Blavatnik School of Government and a more prominent public advisory role.

After a career in the City, SOAS certainly left its mark on me. There, one had been in an environment of corporate authority and discipline, where senior management decisions were implemented down the line. SOAS was not like that. Consultation was everything and building consensus was crucial. I used to compare it with tribal gatherings where everyone had their say until a consensus emerged. I found the change both liberating and character changing. I must acknowledge too that it was within the socially tolerant environment of SOAS, where there were several unconventional liaisons, that I started a relationship that nearly wrecked my marriage. I reflect on this in chapter 12.

The experience of working at SOAS helped me to live with differing points of view and alternative ways of tackling issues; one could say that it encouraged tolerance. Since then, I have been much involved with three charities, each of which had unusual problems, and I have been conscious that I would have been of much less use to them without the prior experience of SOAS. In my final graduation day address I sought to share my feeling about the School with the new graduates –

> '... I feel that SOAS has changed my perceptions of the world and of myself. Perhaps this is true of you too. The human comedy of life here is enriching and enlightening: the quality of the gossip is marvellous; the diversity of character is extraordinary; the mismatches between intellect and personality are cautionary. This all has Shakespearian potential, don't you think?... You – we – have emerged with a feeling of some achievement from the SOAS experience and are different persons from when we first came here. I am confident we will have a shared affection for the School which will grow over time. Perhaps on your behalf I could voice thanks to the faculty who have created this remarkable world of SOAS.'

THE COMMONWEALTH DIMENSION

9. ROYAL COMMONWEALTH SOCIETY

I first became involved with the Royal Commonwealth Society on returning from Kenya in 1961 when I was working in its great library on Saturday mornings to write a chapter on the subject of the settler contribution to Kenya's post-war economic policy for a *festschrift* to be presented to Margery Perham, at the instigation of Kenneth Robinson. He then persuaded me to become a member of the library committee, which led to membership of council, the finance committee and more general involvement in the society's affairs, especially after I had got to know the redoubtable Betty Owen who was responsible for the public affairs activities of the society at that time. Nearly fifty years later there was still a special job to do for the society.

The Royal Commonwealth Society – originally founded as the Colonial Society in 1868 – had imposing premises on Northumberland Avenue, with a substantial meeting hall and – unlike the Pall Mall clubs – it had long been open to women members. Its library housed probably the largest collection on the countries of the Commonwealth. Its membership was drawn from those working around the colonial empire and Commonwealth and there were strong affiliated societies in Canada, Australia and New Zealand, especially. The society provided office accommodation for the Royal African Society and for the Victoria

League for Commonwealth Friendship and several other organisations. The meeting hall was a favoured venue for public figures from the Commonwealth and for ministers speaking on these topics. The essay competition for schools around the Commonwealth was a well-established institution. The RCS was the lead society in organising the annual Commonwealth Day service in Westminster Abbey, which Her Majesty the Queen always attended.[114]

Altogether, the RCS combined the attractions of a London club and a current affairs society on the evolving Commonwealth. However, by the 1980s there were serious and growing problems concerning its viability and future prospects. The large membership numbers were deceptive, since many of them were retired people who made little use of the club facilities; the building was old and in need of modernisation; its leadership was poor. I had become a council member in the mid-70s and a deputy chairman in 1982; sadly, I have not retained any papers from that period to remind me of detailed events.

By 1987, and despite my responsibilities at Standard Chartered, I had become much more concerned and involved in the deteriorating position of the RCS, as its treasurer. Sir Michael Scott, the secretary general, had a rather limited perception of his role (more secretary than general) and was due to retire in 1988. It was also evident that the Chairman, Sir Peter Gadsden and former Lord Mayor of London, had collected a bauble but was not really prepared to give any attention to the RCS. Meanwhile, membership was declining, the building was getting shabbier, and the move to an outside catering contract was not making money for the society as intended. The problems were visible to anyone who looked, but no one seemed prepared to grapple with them.

Towards the end of the year, I became involved in a ginger group, or caucus, comprising council member Peter Searle, the UK head of an American charity, which had rented an office in the building and Pru Scarlett, who had succeeded Betty Owen to run public affairs and who was strongly committed to the society. We evolved two initiatives.

---

114 A centenary history of the society was published in 1968: Trevor Reese -*The History of The Royal Commonwealth Society 1868-1958*. Oxford University Press, 1968

The Commonwealth Trust

First, I persuaded a firm of management consultants, Spicer and Oppenheim, to review the management organisation of the society pro bono and I struck lucky in that George Thiel was assigned to the task and he became thoroughly absorbed in the future of the society. I was subsequently able to use him as a major catalyst of change. The other development was a renewed attempt to forge a link with the Victoria League where I was given a mandate by Council to lead discussions. The Victoria League had sold its own building and was now renting space in Northumberland Avenue. There was a previous history of an attempted amalgamation in the 1970s when Sir Michael Parsons was chairman, but negotiations had collapsed ignominiously. However, there was a feeling that a fresh attempt should be made and that this might now be easier in view of the imminent retirement of the powerful secretary general of the Victoria League, Sylvia Barnett, as well as of Sir Michael from the RCS council.

The situation was then transformed by my departure from the bank in March 1988. I noted in my diary, 'What I should really do is to volunteer to work there until the new Secretary General is installed, but I am not sure I am ready for that yet.'[115] And two days later, 'The urgent need is to establish some executive authority in the RCS as a precondition for implementing anything. If the Executive Committee is agreeable, I feel I should volunteer for 3 or 4 months.' On 14 March the Council appointed me executive deputy chairman. Thus, within a fortnight of leaving Standard Chartered I had a challenging assignment that gradually became a full-time job; it was only with some difficulty that I was able to escape from it at the end of December that year.

Although the main task was to find a way of linking the RCS with the VL so that the resources of the two societies could be combined, this could only be accomplished with a new organisation and management. In the meantime, there was a need for urgent remedial action notwithstanding collapsing finances. By the end of May the main elements of a strategy were in place.

Taking the last point first, it seemed essential to me to improve morale with some visible improvements even though it meant using up much of our remaining reserves. The symbol chosen was the renovation of the

---

115 Diary, 8 and 10 March 1988

ladies' loos in time for the AGM, along with some other redecoration, and to announce that the antiquated lifts would be replaced. A related aspect was growing dissatisfaction with the management of the club's services by the catering contractor: standards were poor, financial results were deteriorating and there was a worsening relationship with the liaison committee of council members. Peter Searle got his teeth into this aspect and arranged for a catering consultant who came up with a devastating critique of the situation. I concluded that the club should resume management of its operations and set about head hunting for a manager. I gave formal notice of terminating the contract at the end of July, having first found Jethro Lee-Mahoney from the Wig and Pen Club.

These initiatives then led me into trouble with a member of council, John Dove, who for years had been responsible for all building works and maintenance and who also had a personal friendship with the head of the catering contractor through his livery company. Responsible is the wrong word, since Dove took responsibility for nothing and interfered with everything, and had seemingly watched the decline of the society's fortunes with equanimity. He disapproved of the changes and made difficulties for some time thereafter. The situation illustrated a not-untypical problem for societies and charities where there has been a weak executive and unclear authority and where council members get involved in administration without being accountable. As a long standing member of council I was also somewhat culpable for failing to raise an alarm sooner at the deteriorating situation.

The catering consultancy report pointed out that large sums by way of trade discounts had been wrongly withheld that should have come to the society. When challenged, Sutcliffe were unresponsive so I obtained authority to litigate, claiming £150,000. Eventually an out of court settlement was reached.

George Thiel's consultancy assignment, like all good exercises of its kind, was in part aimed at getting the RCS to redefine its purpose and to understand the ingredients of success, into which a reformed management structure could be fitted. The existing system could scarcely have been better targeted on failure once things had started to go wrong. The RCS is a club with a difference – the difference lying in its objects as an educational charity with its essay competition for schools around the Commonwealth, public affairs programme, research library.

In order to sustain these charitable activities, the club side needed to generate a significant surplus from its members and other revenue. Yet this crucial element had been handed over to a catering company without being given full marketing discretion, or any incentive to maximise revenues. The liaison committee was a nagging body without defined responsibility. During Michael Scott's time the executive committee of council had gradually become the management, yet none of its members had any accountability for what happened; they could switch off between monthly meetings, even supposing they attended every time. Scott acted as secretary to the committee and not its implementer and considered himself excluded from club matters. The public affairs and library were supervised by deputy chairmen and bypassed Scott. He took only a cursory interest in finance because that was the Treasurer's job. In short, there was a great yawning hole at the centre of the society.

Unsurprisingly, Thiel had concluded that there must be a clear line of executive authority from a chief executive flowing to the three main areas of public affairs, administration and membership revenue and club services, each of which should have a manager. This was more radical than it might seem because it meant that the society would resume responsibility for club services; that the public affairs and library would be brought back under the oversight of the chief executive; and that there would be someone responsible for finance and administration and management of the premises. Council would have to stop playing at management and be prepared to resource a management team.

Earlier in 1989, Thiel and I had toyed with a bursar post as an interim solution and with the caterers still in place. But the catering report and my sudden availability led to the more radical solution of my stepping into the chief executive role on an interim basis. I held a strategy session in late April to refine the proposals with the three deputy chairmen, together with Pru Scarlett and our consultants. It took the rest of the year to get a new structure in place, with Lee-Mahony starting in September and a new chief executive in the following January. During this time there were major negotiations with the Victoria League.

In April Sylvia Barnett made an imaginative proposal that instead of struggling to merge the two societies with all the legal and emotional complications this implied, why not sponsor a new trust – the Commonwealth Trust – through which all activities would be channelled? I seized on the notion and developed a paper which included an additional proposal that the Victoria League should make a £500,000 investment in the Northumberland Avenue property in order to provide a source of finance to modernise the building. The next move was for Thiel to incorporate the scheme as an intrinsic part of his report, so that it could be presented with the endorsement of Spicer & Oppenheim to the councils of both societies. In parallel with this, I wrote a lengthy policy paper bringing all the threads together to take through Council (and also made available to the Victoria League).

During May the scheme was accepted by the RCS council, but there were unexpected upsets on the VL side. At their special council meeting the proposal was only carried on a split vote and there was strong reluctance to put up any money. Fortunately, I knew the Victoria League president – Sir Zelman Cowan – who was provost of Oriel where I was already working with him on a college fundraising project, so I was in a position to exert some influence behind the scenes.

Sylvia Barnett suddenly resigned in late May and Major General Sir Roy Redgrave took on the secretary general role on a volunteer basis and drove through the proposal. It was some time before the story emerged that Sylvia Barnett had been up to her neck in financial malpractice – borrowing VL funds for her own use, charging enormous expenses, and paying her daughter large sums for public relations. Something like £80,000 had gone adrift. As she came from a well-known City family it was decided to try to recover the sum through the family route and it worked. It also emerged that a member of the society had been suspicious for several years and had badgered the Charities Commission. However, when the Commission wrote to Sir Zelman its letter was twice intercepted in the office by Sylvia Barnett and it was only when the Commission wrote to him at Oriel that the balloon went up. The Charities Commission took a severe view of the matter and for some time they put pressure on Lord Maclehose and the council to make good the funds personally. It was a cautionary warning that accepting a charity trusteeship had real responsibilities attached to the role.

The whole episode was a great shock for the Victoria League council, but it had the beneficial effect that attitudes towards the RCS and the proposal for a new trust changed completely. Sir Roy Redgrave became a great ally in bundling everyone along at top speed. The society was wound down to a shell, apart from the student hostel, and by the end of the year the office was ready to be given up and one remaining member of staff absorbed. The postponed AGM of the society was quite a tense affair as members probed for details, but the key resolutions were supported and a City grandee, Sir John Prideaux, who had been involved in the earlier discussions, was complimentary from the floor.

The AGM of the RCS in June 1989 also had its complications. Under its elaborate procedures it was not possible on this occasion to seek formal approval for setting up Commonwealth Trust. However, it was an opportunity to do a selling job, the more especially as members from branches in Canada, Australia and New Zealand were in town for the week. I made lengthy presentations to them on the whole package of changes. It was gratifying to find that they were very supportive of the changes for grappling with the management of the society and that they agreed with the logic of the new trust. It was clear that the RCS had strong roots in the white Commonwealth. The Canadian team was outstandingly the strongest, ultra-loyal to the Queen, with several lively branches across the country, and wanting to have a meaningful link with London. The New Zealanders were earnest small-towners and the Wellington branch pulled off a coup by persuading the council to hold a meeting there in 1990, following the Commonwealth heads of government meeting.

Australia was represented only by its national president from New South Wales. This branch was in disarray and, as far as one could gather, had become insolvent (it was technically an unlimited company). The national president was trying to promote various solutions which would involve guarantees from the RCS in London but he was undermined by a branch member who appeared on the scene determined to expose him. This disorderly scene was partly resolved after a visit to Australia by a member of our council, after which the RCS agreed to participate in a guarantee, but it was not eventually required.

One of the more interesting complications in promoting the new Commonwealth Trust was the extent of royal patronage in both societies. The RCS enjoyed the patronage of the Queen, Queen Elizabeth the Queen Mother, and the Duchess of York as Grand President, who took quite an interest and came to several events. For several years I received Christmas cards showing the progress of her children. The Victoria

League also had the Queen Mother as patron and Princess Margaret as President. There was concern amongst some older members that the new trust was in some way *lèse-majesté* and I made sure that the private secretaries were kept abreast of developments.

After Sir Peter Marshall became chairman at the end of August, we made a round of visits to the private secretaries and our visit to Clarence House was memorable. We were shown upstairs to the office of the private secretary who was of the same vintage as the Queen Mother. Afternoon tea was served by a guardsman in this overfurnished room which was dominated by an enormous screen decorated with nursery figures that came from his Scottish baronial mansion.

At the special members' meetings in September we had managed to arrange for a message from Princess Margaret commending the new trust to be read to the Victoria League meeting and likewise one from the Queen at the RCS one. Her private secretary also told us that the usual probationary period would be accelerated so that The Queen could become Patron of Commonwealth Trust early in its life.

Ruth's hopes that I could lead a quieter life in the year before starting at SOAS were dashed by the demanding situation at Northumberland Avenue and by the need to extricate myself from executive responsibility for the affairs of the RCS before the end of the year. I still needed to recruit and install the new management team and complete the legal processes for the formation of Commonwealth Trust. She had decided to retire from the School of Hygiene as she was not getting on with its new director and this was stressful for her, not least because his predecessor was ill with terminal cancer.

The political difficulty in forming Commonwealth Trust was to avoid nostalgic entanglement with the constitutions of the founding societies. In this I was greatly helped by Michael Bowers of the law firm, McKenna, who strongly advised in favour of simplicity and general enabling powers. Although Commonwealth Trust had been proposed as the name early in the summer, I continued to refer to New Trust for as long as possible in order to keep down the emotional temperature. The most difficult issue was to avoid saddling the trust with an elaborate governance system as the RCS had been saddled with, and for which there was strong pressure. With Bowers' authoritative help I got through a structure that left all powers with the board of governors. He came up with a shrewd proposal that greatly calmed the nervous in both societies, namely that the RCS and VL nominate a slate of governors who together would constitute a majority of the board. In this way the founding societies would control Commonwealth Trust, and would avoid creating a sorcerer's apprentice that might spirit away their assets.

The need to keep the RCS and VL alive in membership terms was procedurally tricky because it required a dual membership concept, whereby a member of, say, RCS when renewing membership would also apply to become a member of Commonwealth Trust. This then met the Companies Act requirement that members should apply to subscribe to the new corporate entity – a company limited by guarantee.

Following approval by both councils, the actual incorporation of Commonwealth Trust had its own excitements, bearing in mind that we were racing against the clock in order to get out membership renewal forms in the name of the trust in November 1989. The first set of final documents was blown off the pillion of the motor bike courier and was eventually ransomed off a building site labourer. Companies Office in Cardiff was on a go-slow and then one of its officials decided to question our right to use the word Commonwealth. I got onto Sir Peter Marshall and, in his capacity as Deputy Secretary General of the Commonwealth Secretariat (and with the threat of the Foreign Office in the background) he put on a splendid act which did the trick and a message arrived during the November council meeting saying that all would be well.

Throughout the year, the deal I had worked on was based on the assumption that RCS and VL were equal founding parents of Commonwealth Trust and that they should contribute equal strength to the new governing body. Sir Peter Marshall as the first chairman was counterbalanced by Sir Zelman Cowan as president. Other realities were somewhat different. As already noted, the VL office was wound up quickly; this was possible because nothing was really happening there. The famous hospitality arrangements for students from the Commonwealth (which I had benefitted from at Oxford) had largely faded away, as a new charity was performing this function. Only the London student hostel was bustling and successful. The 3,000 members of VL on inspection proved to be a chimera, since fees were nominal and there was negligible revenue. Only a few hundred of their members joined the new trust. However, the society was sitting on £800,000 of investments and the hostel property was thought to be worth some £3 million. The RCS had about 6,000 paying members plus 2,000 life members and virtually all of them joined. The RCS had negligible financial assets, but owned the freehold of 18 Northumberland Avenue and a great library.

David Thorne and Redevelopment

As soon as I was confident that the Commonwealth Trust project would fly, I started the search for a director general and used a firm of head hunters that had done good work for Standard Chartered. Andrew Rait agreed to take on the assignment for a nominal fee and we went into the market before the summer holidays of 1989. By September we had an impressive shortlist of five; recent or about to retire general managers of both BP and Shell, the finance director of British Rail, an admiral and a general, and each of them had long preliminary talks with me. By interview day the oil men had dropped out as the job was a bigger challenge than they had anticipated. Although he was not my first choice, it emerged during the discussion that Peter Marshall strongly preferred the general so I quickly swung the committee behind Sir David Thorne. He had only retired from the army in the spring, having been head of infantry, and was ready to start on 1st January. I thought he was behind the others in intellect, but the qualities of commitment and man management ability were immediately apparent and, even better, he was completely sold on the grand strategy of exploiting the property potential of Northumberland Avenue, along with a determination to preserve the Victoria League's hospitality tradition. I was soon confident that we had made a major catch.

I had deferred progressing a finance appointment in the summer, partly for economy reasons and partly because the accountant, Ray Castle, was very busy on taking back the club administration and working on the next budget, and I was not confident that we needed two senior posts. It was a bit of shock therefore when he came to me in October to say that he had decided to resign with effect from February to take a job in the country. However, it cleared the way to recruit a finance director and Castle had shown no interest in being considered for it himself. Using head hunters again, we had a large field to choose from of experienced men in their early fifties and two very strong ones. David Thorne was a member of the selection board but found himself outnumbered over the choice, so I adjourned the meeting to allow both candidates to have further talks and it was then not difficult to confirm the selection of David's preference of Alan Skeyte, who could also start in January. Within a few days of all this, Castle had a severe stroke and lost the power of speech. The planned lengthy handover was washed out and, instead, Skeyte, arrived in January to a scene of some financial disarray.

After taking up my appointment as Director of SOAS in October 1989 I effectively gave up the executive element of my deputy chairmanship, although David Thorne did not arrive until January. In practice, David and I were in close contact for many months as he took up the reins and engaged with the redevelopment issues. The RCS had moved into an operating loss and the only guarantee of solvency was the valuable freehold. Our analyses indicated that the society should be viable providing a modernisation programme was implemented. But the more we examined what needed to be done the more it became clear that a total redevelopment was indicated, and this could only be affordable by surrendering part of the site. We talked to several potential advisers – surveyors, developers and merchant banks – and eventually appointed County Natwest, who were prepared to work on an expenses only basis until a solution was found and completed, when they would receive 1 percent of the value created.

A three-pronged strategy was evolved: a redevelopment project entailing partial disposal of the site to a French hotel company and the construction of a new club and meetings facility for the society; a fundraising campaign which raised £3 million to purchase the RCS library and donate it to Cambridge University, thereby relieving the society of a substantial annual cost while ensuring that the valuable collection remained in the public domain; and £1 million was provided by the Victoria League by purchasing a percentage interest in the property. Finally, temporary quarters were found for the administration in New Zealand House. All this involved a stupendous amount of work by David Thorne over the next seven years under the chairmanship of Sir Peter Marshall and then Sir Oliver Forster. My job at SOAS was itself demanding and in 1992 I decided that I must resign the deputy chairman role at the RCS. I only resumed active engagement with the society towards the end of 1996 after my retirement from the School.

Chairman

In October 1996 I was elected chairman of the RCS on the retirement of Sir Oliver Forster and held the post for the next five years until 2002. In the previous year there had been a sad development when the Victoria League council decided to withdraw from Commonwealth Trust. There had always been an element on its council that opposed the link-up with the RCS and, with the departure of Sylvia Barnett and Lord Maclehose, its views prevailed and the council decided to revert to a purely social role managing just its student hostel in London. The separation was fraught since David Thorne took a strict line over the fact that the VL had purchased a percentage share in 18 Northumberland Avenue (in the expectation of its increasing value) rather than making a specific loan. Independent valuation advice revealed that this percentage was at that time worth less than the £1 million invested, and David stuck to his guns.

Demolition of No. 18 took place in 1996 and construction got under way on the dual-purpose new club and small hotel. Great care was taken to secure a prominent place for the Commonwealth clock, which had been the most striking artefact in the old building. David Thorne had secured a slot with Buckingham Palace for an official opening of the new premises by the Queen in June 1988. On the day, it fell to Ruth to accompany the Duke of Edinburgh on an inspection of the building and I escorted a lady in waiting. As the royal party progressed an Australian didgeridoo performer got under way in the gallery with its characteristic burping notes. The Duke turned to Ruth with a twinkle:

'Is there something wrong with the new air conditioning?'

The RCS traditionally has the responsibility for arranging the Commonwealth Day service in Westminster Abbey, when the abbey is filled with schoolchildren, representatives of Commonwealth organisations and with Commonwealth diplomats. It requires a major feat of organisation, which is made more complex by an evolving tradition of ecumenical participation, together with musicians from the Commonwealth and other performers. Such an event is perhaps only made possible by the special status of Westminster Abbey as a 'royal peculiar'. At the start of proceedings there is a welcome line at the west door and then a procession wends round the abbey and to the choir stalls led by the chairman and lady of the Royal Commonwealth Society, with the Queen at the rear. This order is reversed at the conclusion of the service. It is quite a splendid occasion. In the evening of Commonwealth Day the Secretary General holds a grand reception at Marlborough House. One year, as Ruth and I were processing out a girl in the front row of the nave gave her a deep curtsey, which was touching.

In the autumn of 1997 Britain was due to host in Edinburgh the biennial Commonwealth Heads of Government meeting, or CHOGM, for the first time in twenty years, marking its 40th anniversary. It was also the year in which the RCS was re-launching itself in its original name and with the completion of the redevelopment of its home. David Thorne was determined to maximise the opportunity for the RCS and a huge effort was made to this end. A Commonwealth education pack was distributed to every school in the country and, at his instigation, the non-governmental dimension of the Commonwealth was given official recognition for the first time, with the RCS assigned the role of organising a Commonwealth Centre at the Assembly Rooms. Around 100 non-governmental organisations took stands there for a week and there was a full programme of workshops and conferences in the three meeting rooms. 22 heads of government visited the centre, including the prime minister, Tony Blair.

The meeting was also notable in other ways. For the first time the Queen took part in the opening ceremony and made an admired speech. The ceremony was very much in the mode favoured by the new prime minister, with music, dancers, video screens and a vigorous speech by Tony Blair himself. In contrast to Margaret Thatcher, he was much more positive about the role of the Commonwealth. It was the first CHOGM with an explicit theme to the discussions, resulting in the Edinburgh Economic Declaration of commitments.

Earlier in the year, the RCS held its international meeting in St John's, Newfoundland. It was arranged to coincide with the arrival there of the reconstructed sailing ship, *Matthew*, in which John Cabot had sailed from Bristol 500 years ago. Her Majesty the Queen was there to greet its arrival. The *Matthew* was delayed by adverse conditions as the loyal crowd on the quayside awaited its arrival on a freezing cold June morning, with icebergs floating in the sea. The RCS organised a tea time reception in honour of Her Majesty, for which we had brought from London the collection of Commonwealth flags used for the abbey ceremony, so that they could be paraded by the Canadian branches on the arrival of the royal party. On being handed the flag of Mozambique, which had just joined the Commonwealth following its support for the anti-apartheid struggle in South Africa, the recipient burst into tears at being handed such a revolutionary banner, so I quickly substituted the Union Jack for her to carry instead.

The prospect of holding CHOGM in Edinburgh in 1997 provoked a burst of intellectual activity in Britain, reflecting on the record of the modern Commonwealth and its ongoing role. The Foreign Affairs Committee of the House of Commons undertook an enquiry and published voluminous evidence. The RCS naturally submitted a paper and published a pamphlet aimed at Edinburgh, as did Chatham House and the FCO itself.[116] This introspective momentum was maintained into the following CHOGM in Durban, which instigated a High Level Review to report to the next meeting in Australia, and for which the RCS collaborated with a think tank on a study, as well as organising a symposium on the issues.[117]

All these studies celebrated the emergence of a network of states that had emerged from the former empire and had found mutual benefit from preserving and enhancing the multiple ties of language, people links and shared experience, business and professional associations. To this end a Secretariat had been established in 1965 to foster these associations, but without treaty formality and thus in marked contrast to what was emerging in Europe. The practice of biennial meetings between heads of government, and with the urging of Commonwealth enthusiasts, had led to the emergence of a body of Commonwealth doctrine around the centrality of democracy and associated human rights as defining the Commonwealth, especially arising from the CHOGM meetings in Singapore in 1961 and Harare in 1991. Although South Africa had left the Commonwealth in 1961 there was a powerful body of opinion that the Commonwealth – and especially Britain – could and should exert pressure to bring about the end of apartheid

---

116 *Economic Opportunities for Britain in the Commonwealth,* Katherine West. RIIA, 1995. *The Future of the Commonwealth,* Foreign Affairs Committee. HMSO, 1996. Vol1 Report, Vol II Minutes of Evidence & Appendices. *Britain and the Commonwealth,* FCO, 1997.
117 *Reinventing the Commonwealth,* Kate Ford & Sunder Katwala. Foreign Policy Centre, 1999. *A Future for the Commonwealth.* Report of the Commission on the Commonwealth, 2001. *A New Vision for the Commonwealth,* Commonwealth NGOs, 2001. *Report to Heads of Government,* Commonwealth High Level Group, 2002. *A UK Response to the High-Level Review of the Commonwealth.* RCS, July 2000

there. The happy and celebratory outcome was that when the desired transformation eventually occurred the new South Africa under Nelson Mandela re-joined the Commonwealth.

However, these developments took the Commonwealth down a perilous path towards becoming something of a rules-based community, and therefore carrying implications of external monitoring and even sanctions for lapses. It led to members that were subject to military coups having to leave the Commonwealth, and also to the creation of the Commonwealth Ministerial Action Group at the Auckland CHOGM in 1995. It also gave rise to hypocrisy and cynicism when there was failure to confront anti-democratic behaviour by authoritarian governments, for example in Kenya and Uganda. The most blatant instance was at the Nigerian CHOGM in 2003, when several African governments refused to endorse the suspension of Zimbabwe.

The Commonwealth has been on stronger ground in building up the profile of the many civil society organisations (over 80 of them) that foster collaboration between its members, especially those that seek to engage young people across the Commonwealth. The RCS essay competition for schools is the original exemplar, but there are now numerous other initiatives focussing on young people. The problem they all have in common is finance: the rhetoric is always forthcoming, but funding has not flowed so readily. The Commonwealth Foundation has been the umbrella organisation fostering civil society links and it could clearly play a larger role if so resourced.

Having seen the efforts of civil society organisations to make a mark in Edinburgh, Durban and Brisbane, I came to doubt whether CHOGM meetings, where they struggle to get meaningful recognition, are the best forum for them. It prompts a comparison with the annual meetings of the IMF, which I attended as a banker. The annual IMF meeting is ostensibly a gathering of finance ministers and central bankers, but it is attended by hoards of commercial bankers and the occasion leads to fruitful interaction between the two parties. The bankers had deep pockets and were able to resource the week with functions and special meetings and serious business is done. At CHOGMs, by contrast, the civil society groups have difficulty in affording their attendance (I paid my own way on these occasions) and they were almost literally listeners at the door. Few heads of government had much interest in interacting with them. It does not seem to be the right forum for the unofficial Commonwealth, except perhaps for those of the host country where they have an opportunity to put on a show to alert their domestic audience. Such an event would not necessarily have to be held simultaneously with the CHOGM.

Ruth and I paid visits to the Guernsey and Jersey branches in successive years and toured all the Australian branches in 2001. It was a strange experience. We met fervent supporters of the royal family, deeply conservative and not much interested in the affairs of a modern multi-racial and multi-cultural Commonwealth; yet they were all doing their bit for the RCS essay competition. In contrast to this, the international meetings of the RCS held in London and occasionally overseas brought the active elements of the society together and were worthwhile gatherings. We held such a meeting in Malaysia in 2000 that was addressed by the prime minister, Dr Mahathir, and was attended by delegates from twelve Commonwealth countries, and included a group of David Thorne Bursary young people. The conclusion I draw is that the organisation and management of civil society initiatives is a task for dedicated professionals, funded by whoever supports them and is not readily appropriate for a membership club, except at a rather amateur level. The RCS has had to learn this lesson painfully and, in effect, to transform itself into a youth-centred non-governmental organisation. In this it has been successful.

Reflecting on the way that the Commonwealth has evolved over some 30 years in which I had an interest in its affairs, I have come to the view that it suffers from unrealisable expectations from its most ardent fans and that this has obscured a more fruitful way forward for the longer term. The fan club constantly yearned for more resources for an enhanced Secretariat, more 'political will' from Commonwealth governments, a strengthening of its identity as an institution and of its authority over members in governance matters. This led to frustration at the slow progress in satisfying these aims and, as already noted, to hypocrisy and cynicism from others. This is not to deny that there were significant achievements in establishing widespread acceptance of democratic government as a core Commonwealth value, but expectations were generated that democratic values and standards could both be established and enforced everywhere and that the Commonwealth was on the way to becoming a rules-based entity. My view now is that this is not the right path over a longer perspective of relationships between Britain and the Commonwealth.

As an alternative model I think we should look to the so-called Special Relationship between Britain and America and also to the way that France fosters La Francophonie. In the post-Brexit world Britain should continue to invest in its Commonwealth relationships – diplomatically, through the British Council, education links and civil society – and do this through a web of bilateral relationships. It would be up to individual Commonwealth countries to put what they wished into their relationship with Britain and other Commonwealth members. Most would want to have a special relationship with the UK, but only selectively with each other. There would be no need for a formal structure of CHOGMs and the Commonwealth Action Group and the underlying bossiness of rules and monitoring would lapse. If a Commonwealth member fell under military rule or populist dictatorship this would doubtless have bilateral consequences, but the issue of 'membership of the Commonwealth' would not arise.

The Commonwealth would be seen as an association of anglophone countries with historic and contemporary links. The UK would still have a national interest in investing in these relationships disproportionately because it would enhance its status as a member of the Security Council, but also in terms of building support for global issues of concern: climate change, terrorism, drugs, migration. The association would be anglo-centric and analogous to France's Francophonie, and it could have similar periodic jamborees. The Commonwealth Foundation would still have a meaningful role, but the Secretariat would shrink to a modest facilitating role, and could be located other than in the UK.

David Thorne had agreed to serve for ten years as director general when he joined the RCS in 1989, but as the date approached he wanted to stay on longer. I had a firm view that we should stick to the original agreement, as I had done with the headmaster at Cheltenham College. David had done a superb job in managing the redevelopment and with the RCS role at the Edinburgh CHOGM, but he did not have the right temperament for leading a revived club or the ambitions over public affairs and there was need for a fresh approach. In point of fact, he was no longer a well man and, sadly, prostate cancer rather soon carried him away.

There was an impressive list of applicants for the job and Peter Luff was appointed. He had been active in the European Movement and was full of interesting ideas on how the RCS could reach into multi-cultural London and he set about the task energetically. It had also become apparent that we needed to make a fresh start with public affairs and say farewell to Pru Scarlett, although missing her large network of Commonwealth contacts. Sadly, Peter Luff found the leadership role a bigger challenge than he had anticipated and within a year had taken himself off to another assignment.

We then appointed Stuart Mole, who had been the runner-up. He had had a lengthy career in the Commonwealth Secretariat and had managed the private office of the Secretary General, Emeka Anyaoku, with great success. Stuart was in many ways a natural for the role: a conscientious and fluent administrator with an engaging personality and wide-ranging Commonwealth contacts. But the RCS challenged him severely on two fronts. As a manager Stuart found it difficult to deal with poor performers and instead tended to cover up for them and take on tasks himself, with resulting overload. Secondly, he saw his task as coping with the here and now, largely as a dealt hand, and was curiously unable to give strategic leadership.

This became a serious problem for my successor as chairman, Baroness Ushar Prashar. Like me, she hailed from a Kenya background, and she had made a name for herself with the Runneymede Trust, and was especially successful in raising public funding support. Barely a year after I had completed my term in 2002, Ushar contacted me with a request to re-join Council in my capacity as a vice president in order to drive an exciting initiative to acquire the adjoining Barclays Bank premises and integrate it with the club, with a view to providing a members' bar and social room, a 200 seat lecture theatre, administration offices and more.

The Extension Project

The bank premises had been acquired by a property developer with a view to creating luxury West End flats; nevertheless, quite extensive discussions had already taken place with the RCS by the time that I came back onto the scene in early 2004. The Treasurer, who might have been expected to take the lead, was a cautious Scot who was determined not to be placed in a position of personal responsibility for any transaction, and this accounted for my involvement. Having studied the papers, I attended a council meeting in late March and persuaded it to take a decision in principle to negotiate with the developer, pending a special meeting in April; in the meantime I offered to arrange briefing meetings for Council members. This was the start of an onerous assignment that eventually matured in another royal opening by the Queen in June 2006.

In financial terms, there was a choice either to purchase the accommodation for £6.5 million, or to enter into a lease and incur fitting out costs. The former was unaffordable and the latter would entail rent of £275,000 and provisionally estimated fitting out costs of £2.3 million and a bank loan. Council was quite divided over the wisdom of such a bold move. There was an element that did not wish to engage at all; another focussed on the risks of incurring rental and loan costs; a third felt that the RCS was being too ambitious; and finally there were those who felt that this was a unique opportunity to enhance the members' club and to create a distinctive Commonwealth venue in central London. I was tasked with presenting the rental option to Council and, when it was approved, with chairing a steering committee to progress the project to completion. In other words, the optimists, who hoped to build a new active membership and to enhance the current affairs role of the society (we called 'a Chatham House for the Commonwealth') won the day.

After difficult negotiations, a lease was signed in June 2004 and preparations commenced on detailed design work for adapting the former bank premises and linking it to the main building. The next 18 months were a gruelling experience for all concerned. The difficult site and specification kept yielding costly surprises and the problems were compounded by project management weaknesses. The quantity surveyors had difficulty in keeping on top of all the issues, which led to periodic crises and calls to replace them. The situation was made worse by our retaining the same design consultants as we had used for the main redevelopment, who were both temperamental and overstretched. All this placed enormous pressure on Stuart Mole. I aligned with him against the critics, taking the view that, having embarked on the project, we just had to find ways through the many difficulties and make our chosen agents perform. The main contract was approved in March 2005 with an indicated total project cost of £3.6 million, after a number of cost-saving simplifications. There were several further alarms, but this control figure was essentially achieved by completion. However, the final financial cost was more onerous when account was taken of significant related costs outside the core project, including lost income from the delayed completion.

The RCS now had a truly impressive club and meetings facility which became increasingly popular as a functions venue. And we were honoured, once again, with an official opening by the Queen. We were especially proud that Tony Blair twice held 'offsite' meetings of Cabinet members at Northumberland Avenue. While the London economy was booming the outlook was favourable, but it changed dramatically after the 2007/8 financial crash as functions events melted away. The cost of loan servicing and rent then became a serious problem and strategic issues became pressing.

As with many charities, the governance of the RCS found itself exposed when confronted with existential problems: people had given their time to Council and joined its staff on underlying presumptions of a well-established going concern. Ushar Prashar had substantial parliamentary responsibilities and was not in a position to devote executive time to the society, although she was the person most acutely aware of the big issues. Her deputy, Richard Bourne, was a former journalist and Commonwealth enthusiast, but was loath to shoulder responsibility within the society. The genial ex-Shell treasurer, Roger Davidson, was of similar ilk, as already noted. Stuart Mole was an able administrator but a poor manager and was totally absorbed in keeping the show on the road, rather than questioning where it was going. With the benefit of a longer perspective, it was unfortunate that the extension opportunity arrived when it did, as it pre-empted strategic issues about the compatibility of a club membership organisation with an evolving think tank role and it absorbed energy and resources at a critical time. In effect, there was an assumption that the RCS would go on doing what it had already been doing, only on a grander scale from its rejuvenated premises. For this, I must shoulder responsibility for failing to address the matter after the retirement of David Thorne.

Soon after her arrival, Ushar perceived the strategic void, although she was enthusiastic about the possibilities of the extension project, and she wanted to involve me both in this and in redefining a strategy for the RCS. At lunch with Peter Marshall and myself in April 2004 she expressed frustration at the lack of strategic purpose in the RCS: its activities were too disparate and it lacked credibility as a source of policy thinking; the high profile of the club mitigated against taking the society seriously on substantive Commonwealth issues. Ushar was finding it virtually impossible to engage Stuart on issues of strategic priority and to separate him from the here and now of keeping things moving. Some 18 months later Ushar was talking of resigning out of frustration and I noted in my diary –

'All this looks ominous. An open confrontation would show that Stuart has little support in Council, which he has not handled well and he would have to resign. Two final years of sullen compliance would not be good either. It is hard to fathom why he seems so opposed to building up the public affairs role of the RCS, except for his sentimental attachment to the string of minor activities involving Youth, Commonwealth Day, inter-faith, etc. I very much fear that we are in for a regime change. If this is the case, we must keep Ushar in the chair and get in a good deputy chairman soonest.' (10 Jan. 2007)

What was the strategic problem? Reading over my diary notes of the period, the issues become clearer, but perhaps one can also understand the reasons for not getting them articulated better at the time and acted on.

The fundamental problem was that the RCS was a members' club that had ambitions to be influential beyond its immediate membership, both on public affairs issues and as an agent of social cohesion in the Commonwealth. Perhaps because this dual role had evolved incrementally over a long time, the RCS never faced up squarely to the financial implications of sustaining it.

As a members' club the society faced an existential challenge with the end of empire, since people from Britain were no longer going abroad to live and make careers in the former colonies in large numbers, while those who had done so and were now retired were not a lucrative source of income for the club over and above their country membership fees. The failure to address this issue in the 1970s and 80s by making Northumberland Avenue more attractive to members now resident in England had serious consequences for future viability. Instead, the society's leadership at the time was focussed on public affairs and the apartheid issue and the club went into decline.

By way of contrast, the Royal Overseas League, which had a very similar original membership, improved its accommodation and increasingly presented itself – with success – as a London club for country members. Against this background, the great redevelopment project in the 1990s had a fatal flaw in that its motivating force was not the interests of existing members, since residential accommodation and a members' lounge were given up in favour of meeting rooms and a restaurant to produce a very contemporary facility. Presuming on the loyalty of its historic membership base, the RCS was in reality turning itself into a club and functions venue for a metropolitan, multi-cultural London. This was not an impossible reorientation, and the extension project strongly reinforced its credibility, but it required much more sustained marketing and priority than was actually made available, if this was to be a sustainable success.

The RCS had a miscellaneous collection of ancillary activities: the schools essay competition, Commonwealth Day Observance at Westminster Abbey, carol service at St Martin's in the Fields, youth initiatives and meetings and the public affairs programme. They all required staffing, money and management time and were the focus of attention and ambition for enhancement. They were mostly funded by the society, but were supported by elements of opportunistic financial support. The hard question that was never pressed home was whether these civil society, educational and cultural initiatives could be independently funded and, if so, who by. Put another way, was there a genuine demand for these out-reach activities such that an independent party would be prepared to underwrite them? Somewhat putting words into her mouth, I think it was Ushar's view that most would fail such a test and should be abandoned. Much later, and well after my time, the RCS has discovered a role with youth initiatives that is properly funded.

The big question was whether the RCS was capable of evolving a role as a think tank on Commonwealth related issues, to become – as I had put it to Ushar – the Chatham House of the Commonwealth. She was greatly intrigued and was, indeed, in a position to facilitate such a development in Parliament, but to her great frustration, nothing was achieved as it would have involved replacing an ineffectual staff public affairs manager.

This was a pity. From the sidelines, I tried to promote two possibilities without success. One would have been to service a parliamentary group on the Commonwealth at Westminster (as had been done successfully by the Royal African Society). Another would have been to bring the Commonwealth journal, *Round Table*, into the orbit of the society and to revitalise it. *Round Table* had a distinguished past, linked with Lord Milner's role in South Africa, but now languished with a minute circulation as the by-product of a coterie of Commonwealth specialists who met occasionally as The Moot. Its articles were not refereed, as was now customary in academia, and it had no academic standing.

The upshot of all this was that the RCS was trying to do too much, both as a membership club and as an influential NGO, and stretching its resources too thinly. Time passed. The onset of the financial crisis fatally undermined the viability of a lively, metropolitan club. Within the society, the governance and management situation became increasingly strained by 2007. Without narrating all the details, the problems encountered do illustrate some more general issues in the charities sector. I had more than a ring side seat in that I had been brought back onto Council by Ushar in 2004 initially to drive the extension project, but then to be one of a small group assembled by her to grapple with wider issues. I helped to articulate the policy issues and was also an intermediary-cum-conciliator with Stuart Mole. All the time there was doubt over the ability of council and management to agree on the way ahead and implement it.

Peter Marshall was frustrated over the lack of support from Mole in his fundraising efforts. Ushar was frustrated over his reluctance to prioritise the theme of Chatham House of the Commonwealth. Stuart himself was increasingly overworked – he had nine direct reporting relationships, all of which were taken conscientiously. Then, there was an unexpected glimmer of light: Stuart married and became a father less than two years before his retirement at the end of 2008 when he would be 60, and he requested to move to a four-day week in the office. This changed the dynamic and it became possible for me and a colleague to push through a management reorganisation and also to get the club side organised as a separate business with its own board. Finally, and with his legacy issues in mind, Stuart agreed at last to prioritise public affairs and to downgrade or eliminate several educational and cultural activities, although actual progress was slow. By the time that I retired from Council in June 2008 plans were in train for a new chairman and a new director, and Ushar had agreed to fulfil the role of president.

The experience of these five years brought home forcibly that charity trustees are not executive directors (apart from receiving no remuneration). In practice they are very much in the hands of the management, notwithstanding their formal power to change it. This tends to mean that matters have to become quite critical before action is taken. Moreover, and perhaps especially with long established ones, charities tend to accumulate loyal, long service individuals who are resistant to change and maybe are no longer effective in their jobs. Parting from them is often politically impossible, so one awaits their retirement. The RCS would have needed a radically reformed council membership if it was to tackle its problems more robustly than it did.

Interim Chairman

2008 should have marked the end of my active involvement with the RCS, especially as I was engaged with two new interests in the west of England, Cheltenham Festivals and the British Empire & Commonwealth Museum. More personally, Ruth was dying of cancer at home – with all the caring implications this implied. A rotation of agency nurses came day and night, who also had to be catered for. The day before she died in March 2009, I received an early morning phone call from the new public affairs manager who was in a state of some hysteria – as it seemed – and was purporting to be a whistle-blower contacting me as the previous chairman of the RCS about my successor.

It took several subsequent phone calls and meetings to clarify what was going on. It appeared that the manager was a somewhat unstable personality and there had already been doubts about his handling of meetings. At a recent conference held in Cyprus he had behaved badly and had been dressed down by the new chairman. Before speaking to me, the man had already unburdened himself to Chris Nonis, the deputy chairman, about alleged sexual misconduct and had also associated the new director in his charges. This was both potentially embarrassing and dangerous for the society. On learning what was afoot next day, the chairman – to his credit – resigned with immediate effect in order to distance the RCS from himself. After consulting council members, Ushar asked me to step into the breech as acting chairman until another appointment could be made, which I agreed to do. Proposed by Nonis, this was confirmed at a council meeting. I was conscious of history repeating itself in that, eleven years previously, I had responded to a similar urgent call to fill a chief executive role, pending the recruitment of David Thorne.

What might have been a fairly straightforward assignment turned into a somewhat bizarre experience that lasted for most of that year. I formed the view fairly soon that this was not a whistle-blower issue so much as a revenge drama, involving a shared lover. The work-out was far from simple and it also became a cautionary tale of how an unexpected event can destabilise an otherwise typical body of trustees. To illustrate, over the seven weeks to the end of April my diary records 54 entries relating to the affair.

I had not yet met the new director, Danny Sriskandarajah, who followed Stuart Mole. He was a Rhodes Scholar born in Sri Lanka who had been recruited from a think tank where he had been responsible for important work on migration. His wife, Susanne, was also a former Rhodes Scholar from Trinidad and now a human rights lawyer. Danny represented just the bright intellect that the RCS needed and had clearly been recruited as a change agent. He was showing himself to be a resourceful manager, but also beginning to ruffle some traditional feathers. An alarming development now was that several council members were all too ready to swallow a scurrilous story put about by the self-appointed whistle-blower over his recruitment. There was much picking over of the process of recruitment both of Danny and of the chairman by those who had not been involved, and one consequence was that I agreed to institute an advertised search using head -hunters for the next chairman.

The most worrisome of the doubters was Nonis himself, who not only believed the allegations but was also exercised by Danny's provenance from a left-wing think tank. It cannot have helped either that Nonis came from a prominent Burgher family in Colombo and was a supporter of the Sri Lanka president, Rajahpraksa, who was waging a ruthless campaign against the Tamil separatist movement, whereas Danny came from a Tamil professional family. Nonis worked himself into a state of hostility towards Danny, using every opportunity to thwart and undermine him. This spilled over to myself and I had several uncomfortable meetings at which he deployed his medical experience to impugn Danny as well as attacking my role, since it had become evident that I was an admiring supporter of Danny's efforts to reform the society and grapple with its problems.

This change in our relationship was quite a surprise in that over several years Chris Nonis and I had become friends and he had sought my involvement in his business life. He was a medical doctor by profession, but was no longer in practice as he had taken over the chairmanship of the family business on his mother's death in 2005. Mackwood was a traditional eastern agency conglomerate, with a range of business lines and tea estates. The Nonis family had purchased the agency business in the 1950s and then the estates as well on denationalisation in 1996. I had met Mrs Nonis senior over arrangements for a tea tasting event held at the RCS when I was chairman and she wanted to associate me with plans to develop the tea business. Chris was keen to implement his mother's wishes and the consequence was that I became a director of Mackwood in December 2006.

For the next two years I was closely engaged in its affairs, mainly to advise on the development of a tea museum at the company's tea centre in Nuryellia, where a start had already been made using an old tea factory. With my Kenya tea background, this was a very interesting assignment and I visited the estates and experienced the striking winding drive from Colombo up to the tea highlands, staying in one of the traditional bungalows. The terrain was much more precipitous than Kericho and the output of the estates much lower, but the labour force comprised long-settled Tamil families from India. Nonis then used me as an adviser on numerous other business proposals. The problem was that, although full of imaginative ideas he was hopelessly disorganised on anything to do with priorities and implementation. Right at the start, I flew to Colombo in December 2006 on a business visit, only to be confronted on arrival that I was to be the principal speaker at a lavish reception celebrating Mackwood's 140th anniversary. I immediately had to set about researching and writing a praise speech – with much editorial intervention.

Over the next two years I put in a lot of effort in devising the scope of the museum project: the opening up of the Ceylon highlands, the arrival of tea companies from Assam after disease had wiped the earlier coffee economy, the technical development in manufacture and location of historic machinery, the social life of Nuryellia with its club and race meetings, and finding a distinguished curator. But by late 2008 it had become clear that Nonis's newer enthusiasms had taken precedence and the project faded away, as did my role. Ironically, the one concrete outcome of my association with Mackwood was to facilitate a special tea event at Cheltenham Music Festival in 2008, whereby the company sponsored a tea tasting afternoon combined with the performance of operatic highlights. The event went well, despite much aggravation over the details and in getting the sponsorship payment out of the company. I was never paid anything for my two years' involvement, other than the costs of two visits to Sri Lanka.

Reverting to the scene in London, several council members became suspicious of the new director's reformist intentions for the RCS and were the more ready to believe that his appointment had a hidden agenda. There were also outright sympathisers of the 'whistle-blower', who was actively fanning the flames, but also others who thought he should be dismissed forthwith. The situation began to be resolved when we were able to clarify with a barrister that the formal conditions for a whistle-blowing case had not been met, and it was further helped when the man resigned, having found another job. However, he then commenced a grievance complaint accompanied by a demand for a large payment, which had to be processed formally before being rejected. The issue finally boiled down to a haggle over a token payment that was still not finally settled at the year end. My characterisation of the whole affair as a revenge drama was not far off the mark since, eleven years later, the man surfaced with tabloid allegations against Sriskandarajah and the RCS upon Danny's appointment as head of Oxfam, but this time involving myself as well. I was doorstepped by a journalist from the *Daily Mail* with a concealed microphone and the incident was only closed down with the help of lawyers.

The chairmanship issue was resolved in September. Notwithstanding an interesting shortlist produced by the head hunters, the clear winning candidate was a recent addition to the RCS council – Peter Kellner – who was best known for his role in creating the You Gov polling organisation. His Viennese Jewish background gave him a unique perspective on the Commonwealth, coupled with much experienced common sense.

Meanwhile, Sriskandarajah was grappling with the deteriorating financial position of the club and the stark realisation that there was little prospect, on current ways of business, of it being able to service its rent and loan service burdens. The emerging and uncomfortable conclusion was that the RCS had to get out of property ownership and the hospitality business if it was to survive, and that it should make its future as a Commonwealth NGO with membership support. During these months there were exploratory talks with the Overseas League and the English Speaking Union, and with hotel investors, but the future direction of travel was clear.

The 2009 CHOGM was held in Trinidad and I agreed to go with the RCS team (at my own expense) as a final engagement. It was not a good CHOGM from the standpoint of NGOs; officious security arrangements excluded us from the opening ceremony, the Secretary General's reception and the Queen's reception, while the distributed venues made for transport difficulties. However, Sriskandarajah had obtained backing from the Foreign & Commonwealth Office for an ambitious survey project to find out what young people from around the Commonwealth thought of the organisation and the report of '*The Commonwealth Conversation*' was presented by Peter Kellner at a well-attended press conference and there was a special BBC programme with the participation of the foreign secretary.[118] It was an impressive demonstration of what could be done by the RCS when it got its act together. However, the document ruffled some traditional feathers on the council and I was ostentatiously disinvited from the Round Table dinner and the follow-up meeting in England, even though I had not been involved in producing the report.

In contrast to this, Danny's in-laws threw a splendid party at their house in Port of Spain and, on another evening, Danny took me to a traditional steel band yard party for which the island is famous, with dancing and delicious finger food. Trinidad is close to the coast of Venezuala and it has a remarkable bird population. I was able to visit a bird sanctuary one day and also to witness the memorable sight of red ibises flying in to roost on their chosen tree on a creek; in the fading light it was like a Christmas tree being lit up.

---

118 *Common What? Emerging Findings of the Commonwealth Conversation*, RCS, November 2009. *An Uncommon Association A Wealth of Potential,* Final Report, RCS, March 2010.

After the meeting, I had arranged to go to Grenada, staying in a cottage opening directly onto the beach. Ruth had died in March and I wanted to spend a week reflecting on our long marriage and its storms. I spent the days writing what forms the basis of my Portrait of a Marriage chapter and going for long walks and swims.

Association of Commonwealth Studies

In 1995 the Commonwealth Secretary General set up a Commission on Commonwealth Studies to examine the scale and range of Commonwealth studies in universities and to make recommendations. Under the chairmanship of Professor Tom Symons of Trent University, Ontario, the commission established a large advisory panel and invited submissions. The full commission convened once before issuing an interim report to the Auckland CHOGM and met once again before issuing its final report in June 1996.[119] The report is a discursive document. Somewhat ignoring its terms of reference, it did not provide an authoritative account of the state of Commonwealth studies in universities and gave only an impressionistic account. The report makes an eloquent case for Commonwealth studies as a distinct academic activity, but singularly failed to address how they might fit into university degree programmes, or to acknowledge the contentious issue of discipline versus area studies. One is left with the impression that the commission was more interested in research and policy than in degree syllabuses. More seriously, the commission addresses itself to governments rather than to university vice chancellors in its appeal for priorities and resources.

One specific recommendation from the report that was implemented was to set up the Association of Commonwealth Studies as an informal network, whose convenor was Tom Symons. It sought to embrace a range of individuals and institutions with an interest in the subject. There was no formal entity or funding, but Tom Symons was an accomplished networker and he was successful in arranging several conferences with an impressive attendance list at Cumberland Lodge in Windsor Park.

I was first invited to the 2007 conference whose theme was 'Educating the Commonwealth About the Commonwealth'. Cumberland Lodge is

---

119 *Learning from Each Other: Commonwealth Studies in the 21stCentury.* Commonwealth Secretariat, 1996

an elegant country house with a conference facility that is dedicated to education and the Commonwealth. At the business meeting afterwards to which I was also invited, the chaotic administration of the ACS was very apparent and I spoke of the need for an institutional link. It was also apparent that Tom had his eye on me for the future. He came over to London the following June and asked if I would take over the chairmanship and stabilise the organisation. I agreed to do so, but failed to notice that Tom did nothing to formalise the matter.

I set to with a will and worked hard over the next two years to achieve a solution whereby the ACS was linked to an institution, rather than floating in space. My first idea was to explore a link with the Association of Commonwealth Universities, which was responsible for administering the Commonwealth Scholarships scheme – graduate scholarships funded by Commonwealth governments at their respective universities. There were already some 30,000 alumni of the scheme and efforts were currently being made to give more coherence to this network. I outlined a proposal whereby the ACS would become a manifestation of the Commonwealth scholars alumni and a visible outreach of the ACU itself. Biennial conferences would be partly themed meetings and partly reunion occasions. The idea was predicated on securing financial backing from the Commonwealth Foundation and it preserved the notion of a membership association – now to be greatly enlarged. Initial enthusiasm from Mark Collins at the foundation and from John Kirkland who ran the scholarships scheme gave way to doubts that the foundation could provide continuing support, and there was also a realisation that the ACU itself was something of a virtual body with little in the way of administrative substance.

In October Mark Collins suggested another approach: why not envisage the ACS as a conference convenor with a policy bias, whose gatherings the foundation would be able to support as individual projects? During the following year this idea was worked on and I produced another document that still envisaged a link with the alumnus network, but this time basing the operation on the Institute of Commonwealth Studies at London University, where an able new director, Philip Murphy, had been appointed. The scheme was endorsed. It envisaged three sponsoring partners – the Association of Commonwealth Universities, the Commonwealth Foundation and the Institute of Commonwealth

Studies, with the latter taking responsibility for organising a conference in autumn 2010 on a self-funding basis through an attendance fee. The chosen theme of the meeting was 'Citizenship and the Commonwealth'. A decision was taken to drop the ACS name and replace it by The Commonwealth Conference, and a successful meeting was eventually held at Cumberland Lodge.[120]

Perhaps naively, I presumed that a sustainable solution had been found and that the Institute of Commonwealth Studies would integrate meetings of The Commonwealth Conference into its forward thinking, with another planned conference in 2012. Sadly, this never happened. Looking back over this episode, it is clear now that the Association of Commonwealth Studies never had robust foundations and that the solution which I promoted was also fragile. As already noted, Tom Symons' report lacked rigour and the ACS had no substantive links with universities in the Commonwealth. What Tom Symons really wanted was periodic and genial gatherings of Commonwealth scholars and others, and he had the persuasive powers and personality to achieve several such occasions. As regards my efforts to institutionalise the ACS, the departure of Michael Collins from the Commonwealth Foundation removed a vital support cog, but the decisive factor was that the Institute of Commonwealth Studies made no attempt to repeat the event.

There was an unresolved dilemma at the heart of the ACS idea which may go some way to explaining this. If the conference meetings were to be policy oriented, then this was really a project for a think tank. The Institute of Commonwealth Studies had ambitions in this direction, but it never consolidated such a role after a promising start. The alternative would have been to focus on the community of scholars sharing this specialised Commonwealth interest, rather like the African Studies Association and Africa. This would have entailed a quite different orientation of the Institute to forge links with universities in the Commonwealth and examine the scope for teaching and research in this field. The Institute did not have this kind of capability either, as exemplified by the Commonwealth Conference project.

---

120 *Educating About the Commonwealth*, Conference Report. RCS, 2003

10. BRITISH EMPIRE & COMMONWEALTH MUSEUM

The idea for a museum devoted to the history of the British Empire originated with John Letts. He had played a leading role in the establishment of the National Railway Museum in York and in the founding of National Heritage, and had gone on to run the Folio Society and the Trollope Society. He then turned his attention to creating a museum of Empire. In 1986 a charitable trust, Museum of Empire and Commonwealth Trust was registered. John Letts secured the early support of the noted patriot Sir Jack Hayward (often referred to as 'Union Jack Hayward) and also of the Railway Heritage Trust. The new trust was granted a 99 year lease of Brunel's railway station terminus at Temple Meads in Bristol in 1989. A distinguished body of trustees and patrons was assembled and a fundraising campaign was launched to restore the Temple Meads building and to prepare it as a museum. Work was commenced in 1993 and a museum director, Gareth Griffiths, was appointed in 1995. A campaign to solicit objects for the museum by donation or loan got under way, with the assistance of a Friends organisation led by the former diplomat Sir Nicholas Barrington. An approach to the Heritage Lottery Fund (HLF) was prepared. It had already supported several new museums in the run up to the millennium. Despite employing consultants to prepare the bid, the trustees were slow to finalise the application and by the time it was submitted, HLF had moved on to other priorities and the bid failed.

In my capacity as chairman of the Royal Commonwealth Society, I was approached by Nicholas Barrington to become a trustee of the museum in 1997 in order to foster collaboration between Commonwealth organisations in Britain. Sadly, this vision was frustrated by lack of interest both by Mole at the RCS and by Griffiths, the museum's director, both of whom felt that they had more urgent priorities. However, I became keenly interested myself in the museum and it was a pleasure to find that one of my fellow trustees was John Raisman, who had been so helpful to SOAS.

In 1999 Dame Margaret Weston was appointed chair of the museum and she immediately injected fresh vigour into preparations for the public opening. She had been director of the Science Museum and was actively involved in several other museums, having notable success in securing public funding for them. By early 2000 £3 million had already been raised from trusts, companies and individuals and the restoration work had been substantially completed, although fitting out the exhibition galleries had still to be funded. I became closely involved with Margaret Weston in plans for the opening and was appointed deputy chairman, which proved to be a difficult role.

Margaret had an immense capacity for work and wanted nearly every detail to come through her, which led to constant nagging of the director and second guessing of his decisions. Just because she wanted to be involved in everything, Margaret had very little sense of organisational structure or assigned responsibilities. One consequence was that she was not alert to the risks posed by poor management information reporting, or of unclear accountability. During 2000 I became increasingly exercised over the financial viability of the museum as it juggled two complex issues.

The first was the management of the restoration and opening programme, where the museum had been successful in obtaining grants from the Railway Heritage Trust and English Heritage, as well as a loan from the Arts Heritage Fund. The conditions for drawing these moneys in relation to the works programme were demanding, while the museum only had access to a modest and nearly fully used bank overdraft facility. Some of the clerical work was done by a part-time person in

Bristol, but control was exercised by the Treasurer from his home in London. Management information was sparse and tardy and the audit was delayed.

The other issue was operating viability. From 1995 the museum had a salaried director and he began to build up a core staff to process accessions, administer fundraising, arrange events, and keep track of the works programme. The aim was to open the museum to the public in 2002, the year of the Queen's Golden Jubilee, which required that galleries would have to be fitted out and curated and the staff complement upgraded to achieve this. These costs had to be met from donations initially. It was clearly desirable to develop revenue as quickly as possible, which would in turn require investment and attention focussed on a shop, a café and commercial letting of surplus space. This was all quite challenging for a body of non-executive trustees, all of whom had other responsibilities, but it also placed a heavy burden on the director, who was essentially a one-man band.

Jack Hayward made a large gift in 2000 which was a galvanising event; even the occasion for it was dramatic. He had made one of his rare appearances at a trustees' meeting from his home in the Bahamas and, while I was giving a sobering account to trustees of the financial challenges facing the museum, he took out a cheque book, wrote a cheque, and passed it along the table towards the chair, causing a stir along its passage until it reached Margaret Weston, who then read out the number: £1 million.

In June that year I arranged a meeting with Gareth Griffiths and Margaret Weston to review the situation. It was clear that the financial administration of the museum was not fit for purpose, with a part-time clerk and the treasurer trustee in Clapham, who controlled the bank accounts and made up the statutory accounts. We agreed that the financial management needed to be moved to competent hands in Bristol and the bank relationship moved there as well from London. The refurbishment project at Temple Meads was financially complex in that it entailed retrospective claims on the two funders and the loan provider, while managing to operate within the overdraft facility limit. There was no cash flow plan in place to track future payments, nor offset arrangements with the bank to reduce interest charges. In this situation, there was a real risk that the Hayward gift would be drained to meet on-going running costs, as had already happened to an earlier major gift. An element of controlled 'leakage' from the Hayward gift was inevitable since the opening could not take place unless the preparation costs, including some new posts, were incurred.

I was still worried in August and expressed the fear that we might have a version of the Millennium Dome problem on our hands, i.e. just enough funds to open the museum at the beginning of 2002, but then unable to run the institution as there was a large prospective recurrent deficit. The museum lacked a credible business model of how it could operate as a going concern once it was open to the public. I went to meet Margaret Weston at her home one day to discuss the situation. She decided that a special meeting of trustees be convened in September so that everyone understood the financial uncertainties and the measures needed to improve matters, and to agree a strategy to underpin a business plan. I then prepared a paper 'Defining a Business Plan for the Museum' in the name of Weston and myself for the September meeting. This had the effect of getting trustees to focus in much more detail on the number and complexity of the tasks ahead.

Unfortunately, Weston then left for an extended visit to museums in Australia and I came under pressure to arrange another meeting to progress matters. I decided to convene one at the end of November, shortly after Weston's return, and distributed another paper detailing the matters that needed to be dealt with leading up to the opening in 2002. To my surprise, she took great umbrage at this initiative and seems to have concluded that I was seeking to displace her. The meeting was difficult and our previously frequent and close communications ceased, and thereafter Weston dealt exclusively with Gareth Griffiths as far as she could.

Over the turn of the year I decided that the only way to clear the air was to leave the field and to resign as a trustee. I wrote to Margaret, resigning with immediate effect. This caused some consternation to my colleagues, but I was adamant. As a result, for nearly three years I had no involvement in the museum's affairs. During this period Margaret Weston had successfully supervised the preparations for opening the British Empire & Commonwealth Museum (as it was now called) in 2002, and she and Griffiths deserved their congratulations for achieving this. The official opening was performed by the museum's royal patron,

Princess Anne, who made an excellent speech and subsequently retained a keen interest in the museum. The occasion was notable for a splendidly politically incorrect speech by Sir Jack Hayward. On Margaret's retirement, John Raisman became chairman and he pressed me to re-join, which I did in March 2003 and was appointed vice chairman.

17 galleries had been created and an academic panel set up to advise on the presentation of exhibits and their narrative, led by Professor Peter Marshall, the former Rhodes professor of imperial history at London. It was quite a delicate exercise to strike a balance between the celebration of empire while showing an awareness of its darker side, and there were some pointed exchanges between the director and trustees over the labelling of exhibits. Perhaps inevitably at that time, there was more emphasis on celebration.

An impressive oral history archive had been created and an education department set up. Contributions to the collections had flooded in from families with connections to the Empire: objects, costumes, photographs, books; some as gifts and others on loan. The most momentous gift came early in 2003 when the Commonwealth Institute in London donated its entire collection to the museum, following the decision of its trustees to close the Institute, sell its premises, and turn itself into an educational research charity based in Cambridge. Unfortunately, this deal had been negotiated without any provision for financial support, with the consequence that most of the collection was never formally accessioned and remained in store, which led to much subsequent difficulty.

The museum had a small shop and a café. It had let an area of the building as a children's creche and, more importantly, the former Passenger Shed had been transformed into a space that could be let for large functions – it was the largest venue in Bristol. All this contributed to revenue. However, Margaret Weston had failed to pull off the transforming deal that she had identified as essential at the outset, namely to secure recurrent funding from the government as a national museum. Some £5 million had been raised to set up the museum, but its operating expenses received no support from government and had to be covered by commercial revenue and further donations. On re-joining the council, there was a pronounced sense of déjà vu to re-encounter an air of financial crisis.

With the euphoria of the official opening behind him, Griffiths set about filling out the mandate of the museum: developing the education department's outreach to schools; encouraging university researchers to work on the archive collections; soliciting new archive donations – notably the successful bid to inherit the collections of the Commonwealth Institute as it closed; and working up the potential of the substantial photographic and film records. A development committee was established under my chairmanship and Judith Egerton recruited to lead it (and also to become Gareth's effective deputy). Another committee was set up to plan the further development of the Temple Meads site and architects were commissioned to produce a master plan. As a member of the finance committee I was intimately involved in all this and also as John Raisman's 'man on the spot', albeit from twenty miles away.

The need to increase self-generated revenue was evident to all, but it was also clear that the over-riding priority must be to pursue Margaret Weston's original aim of securing regular public funding of the museum. Political support was sought from former prime ministers Callaghan and Major, and from Blair, but the main focus had to be on the Department of Culture, Media and Sport (DCMS) and its minister, Tessa Jowell. She visited the museum in April 2003 and John Raisman's follow-up letter spelt out the need for £400,000 a year of core revenue funding. The minister's reply was discouraging, 'I do not think it will be possible to offer direct support from the Department', but the museum was encouraged to access specific department programmes. With a change of minister to Estelle Morris, another attempt was made the following year, combined with a concerted campaign of supportive letters. The minister commissioned a report on the viability of BECM, which concluded that the museum's collections met the criteria for national status, but it was concerned at the heavy dependence on donations to sustain its activities and doubted whether this could be relied upon indefinitely. In short, there was recognition that the current business model was not sustainable, but the report failed to endorse our request for regular public funding. The minister confirmed that core funding was not on offer. One is tempted to wonder whether a shift in public opinion towards empire was playing a part.

Both the report and the minister's letter referred to the desirability of BECM coming within the orbit of Bristol Galleries and Museums, while acknowledging that this was not currently likely due to other commitments. There was a catch-22 with DCMS in that the museum needed to qualify formally as a national museum, but this required a significant increase in staff posts that could not be afforded unless the museum was assured of public funding. A trustees' meeting in March 2005 finally acknowledged that core public funding was not going to be available.

The museum had set up a sizeable education department that was receiving much praise. Its aim was to fill the gap left by the closure of the Commonwealth Institute and to establish a national role. Britain had hosted a Commonwealth Education conference after the Edinburgh CHOGM in autumn 2003 and it was a logical follow-up to try to get the Department for Education and Science to become a sponsor of the museum's education outreach, especially as the National Curriculum had just included a Commonwealth component. An encouraging meeting was held with the minister, Charles Clarke, in January 2004, but the department was unable to take on the envisaged role and another funding prospect came to nothing.

There was a particular frustration over the closure of the Commonwealth Institute and its trustees' plans to realise the substantial capital value of the property in order to establish an education research institute in Cambridge. Although its collections were donated to Bristol, no funds were offered to assimilate and curate the material and, it seemed, no consideration had been given to allocating any of its capital proceeds to the museum as the legacy holder of its collections. I drafted a letter for John Raisman to send to the chair, Judith Hanratty, proposing that the trust establish a £6.5 million endowment of the education programme and that it make a £3.75 million grant towards the master plan development. This evoked a rather odd reply to the effect that the Commonwealth Education Trust (as it was now called) was unable to support a project 'disproportionately for the benefit of the UK', although the same could have been said of the Commonwealth Institute; instead, it was going to set up a Centre for Commonwealth Education in Cambridge. This plan had already evoked much criticism from people concerned with Commonwealth education and it was further complicated when English Heritage, under Sir Neil Cossons' chairmanship, had listed the Commonwealth Institute building in South Kensington so that it could not be demolished as proposed, and the

Commonwealth Education Trust had failed in its attempt to have the building de-listed. Subsequently, this led to problems for the museum after Neil Cossons became chairman of trustees.

The full implications of no public funding of the museum were not fully digested at the time, although the numbers were stark enough: the budget projections through to 2006 included large annual deficits of c.£400,000 that were supposed to be covered by fundraising, notwithstanding all the plans to increase operating income. Optimism was sustained by several factors. First, Jack Hayward stepped in twice to balance the books, and there were hopes that he might still make the big gesture that would solve all problems. Second, a number of superficially attractive major funding sources were pursued, but they all faded away. Third, the museum was receiving good support from the Sainsbury Linbury Trust, the Garfield Weston Foundation and the Esme Fairbain Foundation, which sustained optimism.

In 2004 a master plan had been commissioned to optimise the potential of the Temple Meads site. It envisaged a capital spend of around £27 million. At that time the surrounding area was due for major redevelopment and meetings were held with the regional development agency and Bristol Corporation and this led to plans being formulated for an application to the Heritage Lottery Fund. We were advised to apply to its South West regional body rather than to London and to scale down the bid to fit a project of around £10 million. The process was then overtaken by a separate drama over Lottery funding for the proposed Slavery exhibition, noted below, and this bid was never progressed. However, the need to maximise income from the site remained and this was a constant preoccupation of those years: to enhance the café, improve facilities for functions letting and open up additional areas, including the extensive vaults. It eventually gave rise to a train of thought that perhaps the museum itself should be relocated so as to maximise commercial potential and produce a viable business model.

With hindsight, I and other trustees were too reluctant to face up to the harsh logic of operating a museum without core public funding, and we were not hard headed enough to see that the commercialisation of the Temple Meads property would not of itself deliver a solution. Reliance on a perpetual flow of donations to balance the accounts was a fantasy. We were buoyed by the enthusiasm and energy of the director and by the support and good reviews from academia and fellow museums.

To his credit, Griffiths began to think about another model for the museum: to turn it into an academic institution under a university umbrella. An exploratory meeting with Bristol University was friendly, but not followed up properly, even though the vice-chancellor was a trustee. (There was a similar discussion with the vice-chancellor of University of West of England). Money was the obvious difficulty, but no one thought at the time of realising the capital value of Temple Meads as part of a solution.

The possibility of the British Empire & Commonwealth Museum coming under the umbrella of Bristol Museums – as eventually happened eight years later – had been mooted by DCMS, but was not a runner at the time for two reasons. First, Bristol was already in receipt of major Lottery funding for the new Museum of Bristol and was fully engaged with this project. Second, our museum was something of a cuckoo in the nest, as it had come to Bristol, not by invitation, but by courtesy of the donation of the Temple Meads property by the Railway Heritage Trust, and it was an avowedly independent museum venture. The early trustees did not discern a need to place it within the family of Bristol museums. It also has to be noted that Gareth Griffiths was himself a loner by temperament and his relations with the corporation and the other museums was prickly more than collaborative.

The bicentenary of the abolition of the slave trade by Britain in 1807 called for a special exhibition and it was known that the Heritage Lottery Fund would be entertaining proposals from several centres to mark the event. The presence of the museum in Bristol and the historic involvement of the city with the slave trade made it a natural candidate for one of the national exhibition venues and in early 2005 Griffiths formulated an £800,000 bid to the Lottery Fund. A decision was due by the end of the year and detailed planning commenced. I received an outline in November of 'Empire and Slavery – 400 years of Forced Labour and its Legacy' and was horrified by its tone and content.

The horrors of the slave trade, in which Bristol had been much involved, were naturally to be exhibited along with the achievements of the abolitionist movement. But I was concerned by the notion that the slave trade had a lineal descendant in British colonial administration a hundred years later with examples of recruited indentured labour and forced labour for public works. I was also worried about a proposed final section on slavery's supposed legacy in Britain as the source of colour prejudice, and raising issues of atonement and reparation. There was no reference to the descendants of the abolitionists – British people working for native rights and welfare in the colonial period and for poverty alleviation and humanitarian causes in the post-independence era; or of the paradox of the large voluntary migration to Britain from the Caribbean, Indian sub-continent and Africa. Fortunately, the academic advisory panel was also critical and a more balanced outcome was prepared under the title 'Breaking the Chains'.

The difficulty with an exhibition of this kind was that visitors would bring to it current experiences, attitudes and ethical values and could have difficulty in recognising, let alone sympathising, with the behaviour and beliefs of an earlier era. An outstanding example was that Wilberforce, a hero of the Abolitionist movement, was still adamant that slaves were property and that the abolition of slavery (as opposed to the slave trade) required financial compensation to owners.

With no prior warning a letter was received in early December from the Lottery's regional office informing Griffiths that the funding bid had been rejected outright, and offering by way of explanation concerns over the financial situation of the museum. No such concerns had been raised in preliminary meetings. Tough letters were written to the regional and national chairs of the Lottery Fund, and MPs were alerted. Bristol Corporation was taken aback since the exhibition was integral to its own plans to mark the anniversary. A disturbing political explanation emerged. The Lottery officials had supported the bid and the rejection came from the South West council members, who were heavily weighted towards Devon and Cornwall. There appears to have been both an anti-Bristol feeling and a blimpish disapproval of the rationale for such an exhibition, and there was a very weak chairman. However, the rejection was a done deed and there followed a great scrabbling around to find a face-saving solution, since the Lottery wanted there to be a Bristol component to the national celebration, which also involved Liverpool, Hull and Greenwich.

The answer proved to be for Bristol Corporation to front a revised bid, which was submitted in May 2006. This had the merit of making explicit the partnership between museum and corporation and it also enabled a large saving in VAT costs. In September a grant of £770,000 was approved, but funds were not released until January, which caused considerable problems for work in progress and the corporation made £150,000 available to meet urgent bills. The formal opening of 'Breaking the Chains' had to be put back twice, but it was eventually performed by the Princess Royal to much acclaim in April. I still felt that it rather leaned on the side of imposing contemporary judgements on events of long ago, but the anti-slavery movement was well represented and there were many striking exhibits, including important loans from the British Museum.

By way of a footnote in order to make a link with my Mocatta chapter, I approached Henry Jarecki to ask if he would consider supporting the Slavery exhibition and possibly sponsoring one in the British Virgin Islands. He spoke to the chief minister and an immediate consequence was that arrangements were made for his daughter to come to the museum on a work placement for two months at the beginning of 2007. This was followed by her mother coming to England for the official opening of the Slavery exhibition. Griffiths prepared an outline proposal for an exhibition 'Learning about Our Past' and was then invited to the BVI, where Henry pulled out the stops and Gareth addressed a meeting of the cabinet. Sadly, the project then faded away as a result of local elections. Henry himself flew in to Bristol in his plane on the way back from meetings in Jordan on his charity that rescues endangered scholars, and wrote a cheque for $20,000 by way of apology.

John Raisman was due to retire as chairman in 2006, but agreed to stay on until the end of the year while successor discussions continued. Our target was Sir Neil Cossons, Chairman of English Heritage and a former Director of the Science Museum, who was due to retire in March 2007. He was interested, but discussions were protracted – partly on account of arrangements for his own succession, although he agreed to become a trustee of the museum forthwith. The outcome was that I was asked to bridge the gap as chairman between the end of 2006 and whenever Neil Cossons could take over. This proved to be a more open-ended commitment than expected because his appointment at English Heritage was extended to September 2007, and then Neil himself had commitments to fulfil. The result was that he did not take up the chair until summer of 2008 and I filled the role for a very demanding eighteen months.

The opening of the slavery exhibition in April 2007, on top of all the other issues, put enormous pressure on Griffiths and the management of the museum became a concern of the trustees. This was heightened when the head of fundraising announced that she was leaving to take up another post, since she had become a key figure and was, in effect, Gareth's deputy. I concluded that we needed to appoint a formal deputy. Our first attempt was a failure, but by the end of the year an effective person whom Griffiths found had been installed and we were back on track save for recurring financial worries.

The more that we studied the numbers, the more difficult seemed the prospect of achieving operational viability on the Temple Meads site in Bristol. The museum had to charge an entrance fee to visitors, unlike national museums that received a direct grant, and it was hard to envisage how visitor numbers in the West Country could be dramatically increased beyond 40,000 without massive marketing and a succession of events in the museum. The site itself – at the main Bristol terminus – had considerable commercial potential, but only with the benefit of large capital expenditure. Griffith's thoughts turned increasingly to the idea of moving the museum to London, where there was the tempting prospect of the now-closed Commonwealth Institute site. Bridging the two locations was some creative thinking from Gareth over what might be called a virtual museum: using the collections to put on special exhibitions and conferences at other locations. Its feasibility was demonstrated with a travelling exhibition 'Administering Empire' in association with the Colonial Service pensioners' association, and an impressive conference held at Kings College, London that was the prelude to an ambitious plan for an exhibition on the Palestine Mandate.

The financial pressures forced our hand and at its meeting in June 2007 the trustees reached two important conclusions: first that the museum was not viable in its present configuration at Temple Meads, so that it should vacate the site in order to obtain maximum value from its development potential, and second that it should investigate the possibility of moving to London, and especially to the Commonwealth Institute site. At its next meeting in October it was agreed that we would close to the public in the autumn of 2008 and relocate to London when a suitable site was found.

Meanwhile, agents were appointed to advise on the sale of Temple Meads and a guide price of £8 million was indicated. However, the international financial crisis in 2008 badly affected the property market and the responses from developers were disappointing compared with earlier expectations. The only two serious bidders were indicating £4.5-5.0 million, but the trustees were now set on a path. Over the next three years to the end of 2010, we endeavoured to keep four balls in the air: first, to maintain the profile of a museum that was still in business in some way; second, to search for a new home in London; third, to sell the Temple Meads site in order to provide an endowment for the future; and lastly, while the property issues dragged on, there was the challenge to maintain its commercial revenue from lettings in order to meet on-going expenses, as well as to fund museum activities.

Sustaining the museum's activities at Bristol entailed making the photographic collections and certain special archives available to researchers. Thus, there were projects on the colonial film archives with the Film Institute; on the aerial survey maps of Africa with Oxford; research for the Palestine Mandate exhibition; and on the Rhodesian Army archives with UWE. This last arose from the removal of the archives to South Africa at the time of independence on security grounds and held secretly there until they were brought to England. A lengthy courtship by Griffiths resulted in them coming to the museum and I attended the handover by former Rhodesian army officers.

The first serious discussions in 2008 for a London home related to the former Commonwealth Institute site in Kensington. The local authority planners were supportive as was the MP, Malcom Rifkind, but the redevelopment was by then in the hands of major property developers and we lacked sufficient financial credibility, notwithstanding supportive noises from the Sainsbury Linbury Trust that had already backed the museum in Bristol. The Design Museum was the eventual cultural partner, with the benefit of generous support from Sir Terence Conran. During the year Griffiths got wind of a huge project involving Berkeley Homes and Southwark Council for housing development next to Tower Bridge that was to include a cultural centre as part of the proposed public benefit. He drew up an impressive proposal and the museum was selected as the preferred candidate in March 2009. This involved granting rent and rates free occupation of some 30,000 sq.ft., including a shop and café. A year later Southwark was still undecided whether to go ahead with the main scheme.

Back in Bristol, the dire state of the property market had resulted in the deferral or abandonment of several large projects. The only two developers who had shown serious interest in Temple Meads came up with complex proposals whose import was to minimise their risk and immediate capital outlay while promising future 'uplift' on very contingent terms. As chair of the finance committee, I spent much time evaluating these proposals and helping Griffiths with his discussions. At the end of 2008 it was decided to reject both developers' proposals and to continue to manage the facilities in house. This did not prevent one of them continuing to proposition us during the following year and it was not until early 2010 that agents were appointed to manage the facilities on behalf of the museum.

Meantime, the budgetary situation was a constant worry. Despite severe cost cutting, it proved impossible to avoid annual deficits and cash flow problems. The bank overdraft had been increased to £250,000 and it was a struggle to stay within it. In October 2008 trustees were informed that the finance committee had agreed a budget item to raise £25,000 from the sale of duplicate books and equipment, which triggered a discussion on de-accessioning and it was minuted 'It was agreed that the sensitivity involved was such that the Director should prepare a list of potential items and put it to the Exhibitions Committee for approval.' This was never done and was to have fateful consequences.

During 2009 there were numerous and complicated discussions over the possible arms-length management of the Temple Meads facilities, without any conclusion, and the Southwark prospect also went very slowly, so the museum was in a kind of limbo. The only important activity related to the proposed exhibition on the Palestine Mandate, where Griffiths was successful in raising funds to finance the research. We also had a meeting together with the Board of Jewish Deputies to brief them and, hopefully, to allay fears of bias and to seek ideas for possible Jewish financial support. Nothing concrete came of this.

In April 2010 an antiques dealer who had moved to Australia contacted Neil Cossons and another trustee to inform them that New Zealand items from the former Commonwealth Institute collection were being offered for sale by a London dealer. On being asked about this, Griffiths denied that they could have come from the museum and proffered alternative explanations, with the result that Neil wrote a put-down reply. However, the dealer had also informed the Commonwealth Education Trust (CET) who took the unusual step of contacting Scotland Yard without informing Neil. The police eventually reported that no crime had been committed. However our relationship with CET became tense (and not helped by Neil's earlier role over the listing of the Commonwealth Institute galleries) and he and I had an uncomfortable meeting with the combative chair, Judith Hanratty, who had an assiduous investigator who kept coming up with information we knew nothing of.

Cossons became increasingly frustrated at Griffiths' refusal to take the problem seriously and to provide a comprehensive account of events as other pieces of information kept coming to light, such as that payments by the dealer to the museum for items that he had de-accessioned and sold had been entered into BECM's accounts as donations to the Mandate exhibition. I summarised the situation to Neil in the following note on 8 December –

'There has been exposed to us a very casual standard of custodial administration of the collections, or at least of the Commonwealth Institute collection. This would have been explained in part by financial stringency, but it suggests that the museum has been very exposed to the risk of items disappearing. It highlights the importance of an audit of the collections and related procedures. Apart from gifts to the museum, there is the aspect of items purchased for the Slavery and Mandate exhibitions, and the Royal Loan collection. The disposal of material through the Barrett dealership has epitomised the lack of professional standards, lack of supervision, lack of documentation, lack of follow-up when queries were first raised a year ago, and since; the loss of records.'

By now we knew that at least one item from the Commonwealth Institute collection had been sold through a dealer, while two other items he bought had included a loan item from the Royal Collections but he had returned them to the museum when the investigations started.

A disturbing aspect of all this was what seemed to be an element of deliberate trouble-making by several participants. Hanratty had instigated an aggressive lawyer's letter before making any effort to clarify issues at trustee level and there appeared to be a personal animus against Cossons; allegations had been made against Griffiths of seeking personal gain and of making further disposals; and outside parties had been briefed, including the New Zealand authorities. Finally, there was the puzzle of Griffiths' own behaviour throughout the whole affair: dismissive, disengaged, and apparently uncaring of the dangers to his position as Director. Was it cover-up or shock?

At the trustees meeting in December 2010 the director was censured for his handling of matters and instructed to bring about significant improvements in collections management. He made no comment. I wrote to Griffiths afterwards urging him to acknowledge error and his resolve to address the problems, but there was no response. Everyone was reluctant to draw the worst conclusion as we were all too conscious of our dependence on Griffiths to manage the move to London, and especially with regard to the forthcoming Mandate exhibition.

Against the background of continuing pressure from Hanratty, a devastating piece of information came to hand: the recently deceased Lord Caldecote had lent two pictures and some naval memorabilia to the museum and the family were tidying up his estate and had been unable to get any response from Griffiths about these items. Accordingly, they wrote to Cossons who quickly established that the pictures had been sold at Christie's over a year before and the proceeds again entered as donations towards the Mandate exhibition. At that point I wrote in my diary on 11 February –

'My feeling is that we have to make a swift and complete break with Gareth – without any negotiation over severance terms, or resignation.'

Cossons quickly endorsed my view and events moved quickly. The situation had now been transformed, but taking action was procedurally complex and we had to proceed carefully having regard to the possibility of an appeal to a tribunal. Cossons was about to go to an important Unesco meeting in Japan and I was left to implement matters. Without rehearsing all the details, Griffiths failed to attend the disciplinary hearing; nevertheless, the meeting took place and reviewed the evidence. It concluded that he had abused his position as director by selling items from the collections without authority and forfeited the trust that goes with that position. A decision was taken to dismiss him with immediate effect. I agreed a firm letter with the lawyers, removing their expressions of regret, appeal consequences if successful, reference to health and access to his office, and it was dispatched by special delivery on 17 February.

The dismissal of the director of the museum led to several testing problems and Cossons and I were in almost daily consultation in the following weeks. He took on the external relations issues with the Charities Commission, the minister, Commonwealth Education Trust, Southwark Council, where his great experience of the museum world was invaluable, while I concentrated on financial matters and especially the difficult relationship with our bankers, Royal Bank of Scotland. The other key trustee was John Smith, chairman of the Friends – who made himself available on almost a daily basis to keep staff together and operations going, especially with the education programme to sustain our charitable status, where he lent £15,000 to enable it to continue.

Our first step was to halt expenditure and plans for the Mandate exhibition. It emerged that Griffiths' bizarre fundraising actions had all been to finance research for this exhibition, to the tune of several hundred thousand pounds. The costs of actually mounting the exhibition had yet to be addressed and it was clear that the whole project had to be put on ice. This meant that the curator would have to be made redundant, and she was Gareth's partner. The separation was contentious.

It was also apparent that we could not, in good faith, continue to pursue a relocation of the museum to Southwark. As it happened, the council had concluded that it could not, after all, offer rent and rates-free accommodation (which had been a key requirement); also, our own assumption of realising a substantial endowment fund from the sale of Temple Meads had become unreal. On both grounds it was clear that we could not go ahead with a move and we formally withdrew in July.

As to Griffiths himself, there was a major question as to whether criminal fraud was involved, and we had the Charities Commission on our backs. Cossons and I made depositions to the Avon & Somerset police, who decided that there was a serious prima facie case that should be pursued. The investigations took all the rest of the year, with elements of 'Mr Plod' to contend with. The final outcome, when we were summoned in January 2012, was both a disappointment and something of a relief. The police decided not to bring a criminal prosecution due to uncertainty of success in a situation where the proceeds of 'crime' had not been for personal benefit, but for the Mandate exhibition. We were told that the trustees had good grounds to pursue a civil action with police support, but the informal advice was to doubt whether an elderly and distinguished body of trustees would have the stomach to go through with what would probably be contentious proceedings. They would have been costly and there were negligible prospects of financial recovery. The matter was allowed to lapse.

In all this, we had been amazingly fortunate in keeping pretty much out of media attention (helped by the drawn-out police enquiry), until the issue had become somewhat stale. There was a tiresome BBC episode in August, but it could have been a great deal worse.

While all this was going on, we had to maintain income from Temple Meads and find a new chief executive to manage operations and to pacify a nervous bank. We appointed an energetic man who specialised in 'turn around' business challenges, and almost immediately John Mott began to make a positive impact on letting income. Unfortunately, problems soon developed as well. Mott devised a five-year plan to turn the museum into an outreach education charity, using a virtual museum concept. He promoted this aggressively to trustees, including demanding that they contribute personally to a big fundraising campaign, and he successfully sold his plan to the bank. He also supported a proposal that Royal Bank took a stake in the Temple Meads property as a condition of further loan support.

Mott quickly came into conflict with Neil and myself, as we had reached quite different conclusions over the future of the museum. The matter came to a head in October when Mott demanded that Neil and I resign as a condition of his continuance as chief executive, which inevitably led to his exit. He took the finance manager with him and he had also poisoned the well at Royal Bank. This left us with a severe management problem which we were lucky to resolve quickly as our Bristol accountant trustee found an excellent finance replacement and then we were be able to bring back Judith Egerton, the former fundraiser, as chief executive. She had been working at another museum in Bristol and now saw us through the final phases with great good sense and efficiency.

Our problem with Royal Bank of Scotland was that the museum was already close to its overdraft limit when the crisis hit us, and it needed more headroom to enable it to augment its revenue opportunities, as well as meeting exceptional costs. The bank had initially been encouraged by Griffiths' replacement, but were now concerned by his departure. More seriously, the museum then became a victim of Royal Bank's subsequently notorious Business Restructuring Group, which proceeded to displace our local bank manager and take charge of the relationship. We had an urgent need for additional overdraft accommodation of £80,000, but the bank was obsessed by an imperfection in their security arrangements, and matters were endlessly prolonged. The situation was the more urgent in that there was a looming risk of insolvency, which we had to take very seriously. The eventual solutions involved first, granting the bank a direct charge over the Temple Meads property in place of an existing charge over the lease on the property. In agreeing to this, we demanded as quid pro quo an additional £150,000 increase in the overdraft. Secondly, the bank stipulated that the additional overdraft be subject to joint and several personal guarantees by each of the trustees.

Rather amazingly, I was able to persuade trustees to agree to the guarantees, after an elaborate presentation of the procedure and risks. The bank had also indicated that it wanted to participate in any uplift on disposal of Temple Meads over its very conservative valuation, but this was resisted. The bank had earlier forced the museum into an interest rate swap on its loan, with an onerous break clause, and then proposed to charge eye-watering fees for the new transactions. In a weekend phone call I eventually managed to cut a deal on the fees, but had no luck with the interest rate swap costs. As a footnote, some three years later Royal Bank went through an elaborate process of contacting former customers of the Business Restructuring Group proposing compensation. In our case, I had the satisfaction of eventually securing the payment of £273,000 in compensation for imposing inappropriate financial transactions on its customer, and this was added to our legacy dowry.

While these pressing matters were being addressed, there was an underlying preoccupation and debate: was there still a future for the museum? Neil and I fairly soon came to a negative conclusion; in my case financial considerations were uppermost, but Neil saw more clearly that sources of funding for the museum had been irretrievably compromised and that the responsibility of the trustees was to safeguard the collections rather than the museum as an institution, and especially to avoid if possible their piecemeal breakup. A range of theoretical options was put to the trustees in June 2011, but there were already indications that Bristol Museums and Galleries could be the solution. This was a remarkable piece of good luck, since there had been no interest from national museums and keeping the collections in Bristol had great attraction. With the constructive engagement of the director of the Bristol Museum, Julie Finch, and of a leading city councillor, Simon Cook, this solution gradually took shape and by the autumn it was agreed to be the way forward. However, its achievement rested on our being able to sell Temple Meads in a still difficult property market and discharge all our financial obligations with the proceeds. If we were lucky, there would be a residual dowry to give to Bristol for conserving and using the collections.

When Old Temple Meads, as we now called it, was first put on the market in 2008, the hope was that we might raise up to £8 million for the property. However, the financial crisis put paid to such optimism and the only serious contenders were making highly qualified offers of £4-5 million, with a core cash proposal of around £3 million and any uplift depending upon the success of the development. As already noted, these negotiations were terminated. Returning now to the market in 2011, our priorities had changed: there was no longer a need to realise a large endowment fund and, instead, our need was for a speedy transaction with a reliable counterparty that would enable the museum to clear all debts and compensation obligations and – hopefully – leave something by way of a dowry to pass on to Bristol to support the collections. The number that would achieve this was £3 million.

Fortune smiled on us when, in August 2011, Neil mentioned that Railtrack might be a purchaser and he had a contact. He had become aware that Railtrack were proposing to electrify the main line from Paddington and that, at Bristol, this would mean acquiring part of the Brunel property. A meeting took place in October and by the end of the year the outline of a deal at £3.1 million was on the table. The actual transaction turned out to be complicated due to the involvement of the Housing and Communities Agency and Bristol Corporation, who both had an interest in the site. Eventually, a sale was completed in March 2012 at £3.1 million, in which Bristol Corporation became the owner of Old Temple Meads and Network Rail had an option on part of the site for its purposes. This cleared the way for us to make plans to arrange for voluntary liquidation of the museum, although it took another 18 months to achieve this objective.

The most immediate problem was to complete the audit process and to establish what was missing from the very incomplete records, and then to resolve claims in respect of items that had been wrongly sold. The item that had caused all the fuss in New Zealand was eventually repurchased from its new owner at the auction price and presented to the government. The Caldecote pictures and items that had been sold through Christie's to a museum abroad led to paying compensation to the family (with a contribution from Christie's). A bargain was struck with the dealer who had been allowed by Griffiths to purchase numerous items. And so on. Several official archives were found new homes.

The Commonwealth Education Trust and its combative chair continued to foment trouble for us, in particular over a notion that she had an obligation to write to all Commonwealth governments with an account of what had happened, and thus opening a door for the return of objects and possible restitution payments. There was a testing meeting, with lawyers in attendance, which I went to in place of Cossons, following which the various demands were gradually whittled down by our legal advisers and the threat went away.

A potentially more difficult situation arose when a new individual at the Charities Commission took over the file and was minded to dig deeply into what had happened, coupled with warnings about the potential personal liability of trustees. Neil dealt with this in masterly fashion and this issue also died away.

Eventually, in October 2013, we were able to hold meetings to place the museum formally into voluntary liquidation and responsibility for final sorting out was assumed by the liquidators. There was confidence that they would be able to distribute over £500,000 by way of dowry to Bristol Museums & Galleries. This was subsequently enhanced by the compensation payments from Royal Bank amounting to £273,000. This was made possible by receiving £3.1 million from the sale of Old Temple Meads. Some £1.5 million was needed to discharge bank debt and the closing down expenses and compensation payments amounted to over £1 million. This satisfactory outcome meant that the trustees had been able to preserve the integrity of the collections and place them into professional custody: all the costumes, photographs, memorabilia and oral histories had been kept together as a unique collection of material to illustrate Britain's imperial experience.

Although Bristol Museum received a handsome dowry to maintain the collections, and it had ample storage facilities, there was no longer a dedicated gallery available for a permanent exhibition of items drawn from them. Financial stringency on the corporation also meant that Bristol did not have either the curatorial resources to mount regular presentations drawn from the collections. My regret over the closure is that we trustees failed to anticipate this problem. We were an elderly and somewhat exhausted body by this time, and Neil had another assignment awaiting him. With hindsight, we should have tried to revive the Friends of the Museum as an interest group, and we could have segregated part of the dowry to funding a programme of events around the collections and the imperial story.

Old Temple Meads had originally been sold to the museum for £1 and over the years £5.6 million had been raised and spent on creating the galleries and turning the building into a museum, so this cost was not recouped by the sale. The only public funding received by the museum towards capital costs was £189,000 from English Heritage, and there was a ticklish moment when English Heritage started moves to reclaim this sum. The museum had received £770,000 from the Lottery Fund towards the costs of the Slavery exhibition, but no public money towards its operating costs. The finance manager calculated that over the 25 years some £10.4 million had been contributed by trusts and individuals in support of the museum (including the capital contributions).

Writing now in the wake of the treatment of the Colston statue in Bristol, of BLM and the woke environment, one has to wonder what would have happened had there still been a British Empire & Commonwealth Museum at Temple Meads. Donors can perhaps draw some comfort from the knowledge that the collections have been preserved and that a time may come when they can contribute to understanding the social history of empire in its last years in the twentieth century.

I was closely involved with the British Empire & Commonwealth Museum over some 16 years and sometimes reflect on whether matters could have turned out differently. Having failed to secure public funding from the outset, the museum was perhaps fated from the outset. Nationally funded museums have to offer free entry to the public, which makes life hard for private museums that are dependent on entrance fees as a key revenue stream, assuming they are without a major endowment. Wonders were achieved in setting up the museum, but it was crippled without an assured base income from government. Yet the times were unpropitious for public funding of a museum of empire. A museum of Commonwealth (inheriting the mandate of the Commonwealth Institute) would have had better prospects and it is a real regret that this line of thinking never had purchase due to the personalities involved. In a fantasy world I could envisage a situation in which Britain's commitment to the Commonwealth was given expression in an institution that combined the historical perspectives of our museum, the educational links of the Commonwealth Institute and youth and think tank initiatives of the Royal Commonwealth Society.

Griffiths remains a sad enigma, as he did so much that was admirable. However, unauthorised disposal of pieces from a museum – whatever the motive – is a capital crime in the museum world. It was the immediate cause of the closure of the British Empire & Commonwealth Museum, but I think it is now clear that the institution was already doomed.

11. COMMONWEALTH DEVELOPMENT CORPORATION

I first became aware of the Commonwealth Development Corporation (CDC) when standing as the Labour candidate in a mock general election at Cheltenham College in 1951. I was faced with jibes about the fiasco of the Gambia Eggs Scheme that was one of the early ventures of CDC, newly established by the Attlee government. Then, at Nuffield and working for Arthur Gaitskell on his Gezira book, I quickly found that he had been appointed to the CDC board and was hugely supportive of its agricultural schemes involving smallholder farmers. One heard much of the powerful chairman, Lord Reith, and its equally formidable general manager, William Rendall. It was unsurprising, therefore, that when I was job prospecting in the autumn of 1961 I should have sounded out Arthur Gaitskell about a job with CDC. He arranged for me to be interviewed and I was seen by the head of project appraisal, Peter Meinertzhagen (and future successor to Rendall), who was keen to have me, and then by Rendall himself. He was unimpressed by my Kenya Treasury experience and economist background and regretted that I was not an accountant. However, I was offered a job as a management trainee at my Kenya salary, which I then had the temerity to turn down in favour of Samuel Montagu.

In my final years at Standard Chartered I occasionally mused that it would be interesting to be appointed to the board of CDC, but I was aware that its main banking relationship overseas was with Barclays and, indeed, Peter Leslie was appointed chairman of CDC in 1989 in succession to Lord Kindersley. It was a pleasant surprise, therefore, in 1990 to receive a visit at SOAS from Peter to seek agreement to my name going forward to the Foreign Secretary to join the CDC board. I was to be a member of this remarkable organisation for an extended period of nearly seven years.

The Commonwealth Development Corporation had been set up by the Labour government as an agency to promote economic development in the colonies. Initially, the priority was to augment Britain's supply of non-dollar foods. Under Reith and Rendall it had acquired operational independence from Whitehall (and politicians) and a widening development remit and was much admired internationally for its achievements. However, the Tories had always been suspicious of this public agency for impinging on the realm of private enterprise. There were threats of privatisation under Margaret Thatcher; additionally, relations with the aid ministry were often strained for being outside its bureaucratic control. This background made for an interesting time that reached something of a climax when CDC was nominated for partial privatisation as one of the early actions when Tony Blair became prime minister.

On retiring from the board (and from SOAS) in 1996, and with its 50th anniversary imminent in 1999, I offered to write a short history of the corporation. The 30,000 word text reached page proof stage, along with numerous illustrations in place, when the chairman, Lord Cairns, decided that publication was politically inexpedient, due to the controversy around the partial privatisation, and the project was binned as a corporate venture. However, I was given permission to write a history of CDC under my own name, with full access to archives, and this was eventually published in 2001.[121] During this time, I became increasingly critical of what was happening to CDC. It is touched on at the end of the book, but I carried this forward in a more public arena for several years. This provides the theme of this chapter.

Having been given access to the archives, I found that most of the

---

121 Michael McWilliam, *The Development Business: A History of the Commonwealth Development Corporation*, Palgrave. 2001

historic files had been transferred to microfilm in order to save space. This involved using an enormous piece of equipment to read the microfilm and to photograph key pages. In this way I built up quite an archive myself. CDC's machine eventually broke down and the management was reluctant to replace it, so I rented a machine myself and had it installed at our weekend cottage in the Cotswolds. A sad sequel to all this is that when CDC moved from its offices in Bessborough Gardens, its then management decided not to retain the microfilm (and perhaps other) records. It seems therefore that my history has had unique access to CDC's own records, apart from Rendall's own account of the first 25 years.[122] There will, however, be material in government files and The National Archives that duplicates CDC records.

Not long after I joined the board, the Department for Trade & Industry instigated a referral of CDC to the Monopolies & Mergers Commission (MMC) under its rubric to investigate the cost and efficiency of public corporations. Such enquiries have a tendency to raise wider issues, as Leslie presciently noted, and this happened. Re-reading my account of those proceedings some twenty years later, it is noteworthy that, writing as an insider who was familiar with the policy debates, the reader is guided through the various issues and made aware of their significance.

John Eccles, the general manager, was a strong chief executive, intellectually self-confident, and he did not hesitate to engage robustly with the MMC. He was in the process of transforming CDC's management culture to make it more pro-active and accountable and was not to be deflected. The MMC was astonished to discover that CDC had no executive directors and that the board had delegated its executive authority to the general manager. This arrangement had been devised by Lord Reith in order to shield management from political interference; the argument being that politically appointed executive directors would lead to ministers having to answer to Parliament on individual investments ('bedpans in Shropshire' as with the National Health Service). It took several years (and after Eccles' retirement) before the matter was resolved by conceding the point.

CDC was contending with an unsympathetic Tory ministry, where the question – Why keep CDC? – was far from an academic one. CDC

---

122 *The History of the Commonwealth Development Corporation 1948-72*, Sir William Rendell. Heinemann, 1976

wanted to remain a public corporation and in this it succeeded, both with the MMC and with the government's response to its report. Eccles had been careful not to be doctrinally opposed to the introduction of private capital; however, his preference was to continue to receive funds from the aid programme but also to be authorised to borrow commercially (which the Treasury adamantly opposed). Rather than trying to win over the Overseas Development Administration (ODA) to his point of view, Eccles moved into confrontational mode with the department and one consequence was a diminishing allocation of aid funds over several years, to the point of CDC actually having to make a net contribution to the aid programme. An informal working dinner was held prior to the monthly board meeting, where these political issues were openly rehearsed, and where the aim often was to mobilise directors behind the general manager in his battles with Whitehall.

Eccles was succeeded in 1994 by an executive from Shell, Roy Reynolds, and Lord Cairns was appointed chairman on Peter Leslie's retirement in 1995. Two important consequences flowed from these changes. Internally, a strategic review introduced the concept of prioritising 'turning point' economies and of being able to demonstrate 'additionality' in CDC's investments; also the portfolio was reorganised under three new heads: managed businesses, financial markets, and the investment portfolio. Reynolds inherited a growth mind-set for CDC whereby access to new funding (whether from the aid programme or external borrowing) was deemed an essential ingredient, and this became a critical factor in what happened next. Externally, there was a marked improvement in relations with ODA and with Westminster under the new leadership.

A notable instance of the changed atmosphere occurred when the Commonwealth Secretariat sought CDC's advice on what to do about a failing initiative to set up a privatisation fund for the Commonwealth. CDC advised that the proposal should be recast into a fund that would invest in the private sector in Commonwealth emerging markets, managed by the corporation. This was endorsed by Commonwealth Finance Ministers in 1995 and the new financial markets division of CDC set up an initial $65 million Africa fund that was launched with ceremony by Nelson Mandela at Marlborough House in 1996. Similar funds were then launched for South Pacific, South Asia and the Caribbean, totalling

$209 million in all, of which 40 percent was contributed by CDC. It was an important demonstration that CDC had the reputation to attract other investors to its chosen projects, although it was less impressive as an exhibit of Commonwealth solidarity since Canada, Australia and New Zealand declined to get involved, as I analysed in an article for *The Round Table*.[123]

The election of a Labour government in May 1997 and the appointment of Claire Short as minister of the re-named Department for International Development (DFID), transformed the scene for CDC. A solution was discerned for the funding problem of raising additional capital by a government decision to introduce private capital into CDC under the novel concept of Public-Private Partnership, of which Claire Short became a passionate advocate. Tony Blair made the announcement in October to capture a headline on the eve of the Edinburgh CHOGM, and well before its implementation had been thought through. The announcement was not well received by the press and those interested in development aid and I became one of the more prominent critics of what was happening. Essentially, there was concern that pressure to meet the financial returns that would be demanded by private investors would prevent CDC from undertaking many projects of development value in poor countries, especially in agriculture and if they would take a long time to mature.

I had retired from the CDC board at the end of 1996 and was busy working on my history of the corporation and I became increasingly concerned over the implications of the new semi-privatisation policy. The issue dragged on for four years before a solution was reached in 2002 and modified in 2004. All the twists and turns are not for this narrative, but looking over my papers, a few reflections seem worth making, after setting the scene.

The Public-Private Partnership announcement on CDC was the first privatisation move of the Blair government and the House of Commons International Development Committee decided to hold extensive hearings in 1998 and published a report on the situation. The hearings were notable in that CDC and DFID were still trying to work out how to implement the decision while the committee was in session. Legislation

---

123 'The Commonwealth Private Investment Initiative', Michael McWilliam, *The Round Table*, October 2002

then followed to turn CDC into a public limited company in which the government held a golden share in the equity and there was a built-in development mandate. The first accounts of CDC in this new form were for the year 2000. The International Development Committee revisited the scene in 2002, by which time it had become clear that the semi-privatisation was not going to work as the rate of return on the overall balance sheet of assets was far below what new equity investors would accept. This was duly acknowledged in November when an alternative solution was announced, whereby CDC would remain as a wholly government owned company with its assets held in an investment subsidiary, while the management of the assets would be the task of a separate business. This management company, Actis, was then privatised in January 2004 in a management buy-out with an initial term contract to manage the remaining CDC assets.

I first engaged with the situation by giving evidence to the International Development Committee and by publishing an article on its report.[124] The issue was then taken up by a City think tank, the Centre for the Study of Financial Innovation, that was critical of the government's plans, and I participated in several meetings and was then commissioned to write a pamphlet that was published in March 2000.[125] My history of the CDC was published in 2001 and I had managed to insert an epilogue that was critical of the government's move and suggested a different approach. Subsequently, I gave a talk to the Royal African Society and presented papers to conferences at Edinburgh University, a conference in Oxford held by its Centre for the Study of African Economies, and at a meeting at the Overseas Development Institute. The broadsheet press became interested and there were three critical pieces in *The Economist*, *Financial Times* and *The Times* in 2001 and 2002.

Why was the Public-Private Partnership so controversial and why was the eventual outcome still unsatisfactory to its critics?

In the first place, Public-Private Partnership was a panic response to an artificial problem. CDC was blocked by the Treasury from accessing the commercial loan market and blocked by DFID from access to new money from the aid programme and the solution was deemed to be to introduce

---

124 'The Future of the Commonwealth Development Corporation', Michael McWilliam. *The Round Table*, January 1999

125 *Reinventing the Commonwealth Development Corporation under Public-Private Partnership*, Michael McWilliam. Centre for the Study of Financial Innovation. March 2000.

private equity capital.[126] This was actually unnecessary since CDC had by then the ability to generate around £200 million a year from its own cash flow of investment income and realisation of mature investments and it did not really need access to new funding in order to pursue an active investment policy. It had soon become apparent that it would not be feasible to attract private capital to invest in CDC equity until a track record had been demonstrated of acceptable rates of return. The historic obligation on the corporation had been to break even and, although recent results were much better than that, it was far from meeting what was now defined as requiring a return of 20 percent for new investment. The implications of adjusting to this new regime, as implemented by the new chief executive from Goldman Sachs, were profound.

It was evident that there would have to be a wholesale reorganisation of the balance sheet to lose loan assets and exit from low return investments, and that this would take several years to achieve. It also resulted in substantial cost cutting on staff numbers and closure of offices and hence a reduction in CDC's expertise and presence on the ground. Most importantly, new investment business would have to meet much more demanding financial standards and the sectors invested in would be narrowed. As these policies were implemented it became apparent that CDC was losing country specific and specialist knowledge and hence ability to manage a wide portfolio of projects, which led first to outsourcing the management of its funds that invested in medium sized business to the Norwegian aid agency in a vehicle called Aureos, and eventually to a complete retreat when the management company, Actis, was privatised. By 2002, the penny had dropped that God and Mammon could not be reconciled through introducing private equity investment in CDC, but that it would be possible to associate private equity in special purpose funds and in selected individual projects. Of the left-behind sectors, CDC made clear that most of its agricultural investments would have to go, and also investment in infrastructure, although new proposals would still be entertained if they met the financial criteria.

What emerged by 2004 was that CDC had become an investment

---

126 The Treasury's stance was politically motivated and did not withstand serious scrutiny; as was DFID's refusal to make available new aid funds, which was seen to be even more specious when the aid programme was enormously enlarged.

company with a large pot of capital controlled by DFID. This capital could then be allocated to selected mangers – initially to Actis, but in due course to other managers and to new special purposes. In contrast to this solution, I had been advocating the retention of CDC as a wholly owned public sector corporation that still retained project management capability, but with a more sophisticated understanding of what constituted development value, and deriving support from the aid programme on ancillary features such as related infrastructure and aspects of appraisal.

The widespread discomfort over this transformation of CDC stemmed most notably from its reputation for direct involvement in agricultural projects, especially in Africa, and to the realisation that this aspect of its operations was to be downgraded and largely eliminated by disinvestment. This sentiment was exacerbated by the anti-capitalist bias of the aid industry: NGOS and most academic specialists, who did not readily embrace the arguments for investing in the private sector as a legitimate aspect of promoting economic development. From a later perspective, it strikes me that there was a joint failure by DFID and CDC itself to address the intellectual issues more thoroughly and to show how CDC could contribute to rural development strategy in poor countries in a way that would raise living standards there, pending development of alternative occupations. My involvement with Paul Collier's Centre for the Study of African Economies at Oxford had alerted me to the analytical argument that the social returns on an investment could be notably higher than the intrinsic economic return, which gave a different complexion to enhancing rural livelihoods, and I had drawn attention to this in my pamphlet. I was especially disappointed, and critical, that DFID was unwilling to contemplate associating aid programme funds with CDC, when it had no such reservations about supporting favoured NGOs. It was a pity too that CDC's management did not try harder to reach out to what one might call the aid lobby, or indeed to achieve a better understanding within DFID of its developmental role. I myself could have made more effort to talk directly with DFID; instead, I was seen as a public irritant.

PORTRAIT OF A MARRIAGE

12. RUTH

The chapter on Kenya in the 1950s records my roller coaster courtship of Ruth and the early months of our marriage life in Nairobi. We both had challenging jobs in the transition period to political independence and we both enjoyed life to the full. The George Delf episode was buried, as I have noted, yet it was an extraordinary experience for both of us. In breaking off her romance with me, Ruth was not in character by allowing herself to become pregnant, yet she still turned to me for help and I then responded in the manner I have narrated. We should have treasured this reconciliation – maybe even laughing about it, rather than burying it as we did, I now feel.

There was another strange episode while Ruth was working at the Ministry of Agriculture: a district commissioner had been seconded there and he became infatuated with Ruth. She found this flattering initially, but the situation threatened to get out of hand and one day Ruth told me what was happening. I telephoned this much senior man and told him to lay off, and we then took a day's leave to drive to Nyeri to The Outspan hotel to talk things over. Would that I had been so pro-active later on.

My rapid advancement at Standard Chartered in the 1970s had a domestic cost. I was completely absorbed in my job, often bringing work home and at weekends and also doing a great deal of overseas travel, and I failed to notice that Ruth was feeling underappreciated. I was conscientious over domestic responsibilities and with the boys, but I was not sufficiently recognising the difficulties she was facing in trying to develop a career of her own while still being the anchor parent. There was an implicit assumption that my career had precedence, even though our decision to leave Kenya when we did and not to join Barclays Bank's international management cadre was heavily influenced by Ruth. She had once told me that as a child she had wanted to be a boy and dressed in trousers, which was perhaps some indication of her determination to stand on her own feet and make a career, even as a married woman, which indeed she did.

I had a pronounced feeling as I shot up the bank hierarchy that Ruth was somewhat jealous of my success, when set against the struggle she had to secure interesting jobs that were compatible with school holidays. Although she was rather successful too, the glamour and rewards were with me. My ambition swept us along and she gamely played her role, although she never wanted to live up to the status of a senior bank wife that my advancement made possible and we always lived well within our (rising) income. Part of the difficulty was that my peers were some ten years older than me and their families were well past school age, so were much freer to enjoy the perquisites of those days of overseas business travel with accompanying wife and customer entertaining in the West End.

One morning in 1979 during the silver crisis caused by the Hunt brother squeeze on the silver market when I was ordered to fly immediately to New York by Concorde, as I have narrated, I left a note at home on my way to the airport and was away for two or three days. I have a faint recollection of a rather tense phone call with Ruth while I was in New York. Returning in the evening I came into an empty house and to a note that she had decamped earlier to stay at the Royal Commonwealth Society. Looking in the waste bin, I found a torn-up suicide note –

'M

This is your birthday present – your freedom.

Sorry about the mess.

Please have me cremated and if possible scatter the ashes on the mountains in Seefeld.

Lebwohl'

I managed to get through to Ruth on the phone to say that I was on my way up to town. We spent the night in an uncomfortable single room and returned to Dulwich the next morning. I cannot recall now the detail of our conversation, except that Ruth told me that she could not face up to hanging herself in the linen cupboard or cutting her wrists. My trip had been the last straw for Ruth, who had become increasingly exercised by my absorption in my job (by then I was deputy managing director and in line, but not certain, to succeed Peter Graham). Although normality was ostensibly restored, I failed to reflect seriously on the causes for this extraordinary episode and, if anything, tended to think that it – and other occasional outbursts – were rather unreasonable behaviour and best glossed over in the course of an increasingly busy life. However, I kept the suicide note as some kind of warning, I suppose, of a dark side to Ruth's psyche.

Annus Horribilis

In November 2002 – six years after retiring from SOAS – I arranged to visit Glasgow for a few days to research the records of James Finlay for the book I was proposing to write on the history of the Kenya tea industry. One morning shortly beforehand the postman delivered a letter for me while I was out marked Glasgow National Opera and Ruth had an instinct to open the envelope; she found that it contained tickets for two. She then looked in my diary and noticed the BA flight number and a phone call confirmed that two tickets had been booked. It took 48 hours before Ruth confronted me at Sunday breakfast in our Idbury cottage. We had a terrible scene and were both crying by the end as I had to acknowledge a long term – nine years – relationship with a professor at SOAS, Lisa Croll, and that we had planned three nights together in Glasgow. Ruth demanded that I break with her forthwith and we returned to London, where I phoned Lisa and told her that our relationship must end. In a bizarre development, Ruth insisted on coming to Glasgow with me and on the first night she demanded sex as I did it with Lisa, which of course was impossible.

In what follows, I have printed Ruth's and Lisa's letters in italics and my diary in quotation marks.

Friday 13 December, 2002
Michael

As you find it so much easier to understand things if they are written down, I have decided to explain to you in writing how I see our situation.

It is common ground between us that for many years our marriage has been incomplete. For all our interests in common, love of family etc., there has been a lack of sex and physical affection – 'love' in that sense. Naturally, we blame each other for this. I felt that as you advanced in Standard Chartered your job took over your life and I existed only as an appendage – someone to minister to your domestic and sexual needs. In my defence, I did try on several occasions to express my resentments but you appear either not to understand or not be willing to address the issues. Finally, as in any case you were not fulfilling my sexual needs, I decided to call it a day. No doubt you saw things differently and blame me for the breakdown in our physical relationship.

Although our relationship was not all it might or should have been, I came to terms with it. I considered myself fortunate to have a good husband whom I admired and trusted and with whom I shared so many activities and interests. I thought that was a pretty good basis for a marriage. So many couples grow apart, particularly if the husband is successful as you have been, and I didn't feel that happened to us. I did not know, nor did you ever indicate to me, that you were seriously sexually frustrated. I had always regarded both of us as not very highly sexed – and in all honesty I still think that.

Anyway at SOAS you were seduced and soon the missing dimension was restored to your life. Apparently you were not sufficiently in love to want to break off our marriage. At the same time you allowed yourself to be loved and as long as no-one knew about your illicit affair you were able to enjoy it without any qualms. But then, inevitably, it began to impact on your job. However, instead of ending the affair as being incompatible with your position as Director, you ran away from the situation by taking early retirement. From that moment on, whether or not you were aware of it, you had sold the pass. By giving up the job you no longer had any real reason not to continue the affair and it was an easy matter for Lisa to revive it. What hurts of course is that deceiving me was never a real issue. You were merely concerned to keep the affair secret from me.

When I found out, you sought to justify yourself by saying that you had always told Lisa that marriage was not on the cards. But she must have believed this would change, otherwise she would have given you up. And if you had genuinely tired of the affair (as you would have me believe) she would have sensed that she was on the way out. In point of fact this autumn she was rapidly gaining ground and I am convinced that you were planning to make your future double life easier by encouraging my one day a week 'baby sitting' for Anne.

I understand that life for you was more complete with Lisa than without her and that there is now a hole which you are looking to me to fill. It is a nice idea that, having been honest with each other, the outcome will be a more deep and complete relationship. But it is not that simple. I had become used to our relationship and was contented. Until 4 weeks ago I believed you were too. Now I am devastated, subject to violent swings of mood and uncertain what I want to do next. It is surely unreasonable to expect that what I now know will strengthen our relationship? Your willingness to deceive me in order to have a more fulfilled life seems to me to be a more extreme version of your earlier willingness to ignore my needs in order to pursue your career. Moreover I suspect that your present attitude to me is based more on feelings of guilt and shame than love. Nor am I sure that you are free of Lisa. That will only be so when you are able to meet her face to face and be indifferent to her. So there is a lot for both of us to sort out and I hope we can do it honestly. There is no point in building up a pretence relationship based on false emotions.

I had fondly believed that we were all set to have a contented old age together. That is now in tatters and what will take its place I honestly don't know. I suppose only time will tell.

Ruth

This was a penetrating missive that hit home in several ways and it formed the basis of many fraught discussions in the following weeks. The first point about sexual frustration was all too true as Lisa's passionate involvement with me had been a revelation. What surprised me was Ruth's assertion about herself, given that it was she who had first refused conjugal relations some fifteen years before and the incident in Seefeld was engraved. The deception charge hurt as I had kidded myself that one could live a dual life as a caring husband without Ruth knowing that I also had a mistress. Lisa had the disconcerting habit of referring to herself as 'No 2 wife' following Chinese custom (she was an anthropologist of China). I had become aware of the falsity of my position and several times tried to end the relationship with Lisa, but then responded once more to her importunity. In short, I had failed to acknowledge that this was an unstable situation that would culminate in a crisis.

In the following weeks there were almost daily post mortems, with violent swings of mood as we reconstructed the past and tried to understand what had happened to each other. It was a painful and revealing process and, for the first time since childhood, I was often reduced to tears. So what did we talk about? To begin with – progressively – there was a formidable charge sheet, as Ruth went over her diaries of the last nine years and reconstructed events, and revived old hurts. Thus: at our 40th wedding anniversary party I had failed to make a special reference to Ruth in my welcoming remarks; on getting my KCMG I had never explicitly thanked Ruth for her support; I had not dedicated my CDC book to Ruth, which she saw as a deliberate slight, given that Lisa was mentioned among the people thanked (the book was dedicated to the staff of CDC); I had confessed to overnight trips to Oxford, Edinburgh and Paris, as well inviting her to the SOAS flat; having told Ruth that I had several times tried to break with Lisa, but had then resumed the relationship at her insistence, and that I had precipitated early retirement from SOAS to make it easier to make a break, Ruth repeatedly questioned why I was still having an affair with Lisa six years later. Surely it meant that I had a deep dislike for her? Actually no.

All this led to more emotional charges: that it was self-deception and dishonesty to pretend that one could maintain a marriage in good order and have a mistress; that I demonstrated a profound moral failure to appreciate the enormity of my behaviour to Ruth; that having shown such weakness in failing to stop the affair, it was certain that I would be a repeat offender, whatever I said now. Ruth felt keenly that she had been deprived of sexual enjoyment after she terminated conjugal relations between us and had resisted her 'opportunities' because she thought I was loyal. She referred specially to a just resisted seduction by our Idbury architect and to her ten-year intense but platonic relationship with Gordon Smith, the Dean of the School of Hygiene (without realising its irony). It all added up in her view to an acute sense of a wasted life that I had difficulty in arguing against as I thought of all the good times we had had together.

On 26 January there was a long evening of recriminations and at midnight Ruth asked me to sleep elsewhere. So I took my pillow and duvet into the study for a restless night. About two, I was aware of a light in our bedroom for a while. Ruth did not follow me into the bathroom in the morning and I could see she was still sleeping. I breakfasted alone and at 8.30 I went to remind her that we had an appointment across town at 10. She mumbled something and I sat on the floor. 'I took 18 pills, why aren't I dead?' This was to be a recurring theme throughout a long day at University College Hospital, and it so alarmed the doctors that they resolved that Ruth would have to be sectioned under the Mental Health Act and placed under close surveillance. In the event she agreed voluntarily to go to a psychiatric hospital.

There was plenty of time for introspection. Despite my external reputation of being quite tough in dealing with people, I was really very weak minded when confronted with Lisa's strong personality and had caved in completely, without regard to moral consequences. It had been rammed home that my ambition and self-absorption in my career at Standard Chartered, and indifference to Ruth's morale, had been the prime cause of her unhappiness. Ruth had hoped that SOAS would be different, but once again I plunged totally into the new academic role (and was knighted for it). She had been saved by Gordon Smith while I was still at Standard Chartered, but not since. I now acknowledged that I had been very unwilling to talk out our problems and had deliberately adopted a stance of preferring silence, in the mistaken belief that least said soonest mended. But the result had been to bury them. Our investigation of the past had helped me to understand myself much better and hearing all Ruth's unhappiness had made me desperately contrite and to love her more deeply than ever before. But how was I to overcome Ruth's sense of betrayal and alienation?

I decided to talk to our neighbour, Sanda Carciog – a characterful and worldly Romanian lady now living on her own whom we had got to know quite well. Over a whisky she told me about her own problems with her late husband from whom she had separated, but that she herself had had several affairs. When I told her that I was thinking of seeking psychiatric help she recommended that I talk to the plastic surgeon whose consulting rooms were on the ground floor (and who treated Ruth before we came to Portland Place) and whom we had met at bridge with Sanda. I phoned him that evening and he invited me to go round straight away. He told me that he and his wife had been under an analyst who they both admired and she offered to phone him and arrange an appointment.

The Huntley Centre at St Pancras Hospital was an alarming place: all locked doors and really disturbed patients, and made worse by the fact that Ruth was under constant supervision in case she tried to commit suicide again so that conversation was difficult. After Robert and Martin went to see her together they immediately went into action to find a private hospital. Nothing in town with supervision capability, but they settled on The Priory at Roehampton and Ruth was speedily transferred there. They came round to see me about six for a drink and a rather strained review. In the following days Robert and Martin were fantastic – taking it in turns to spend many hours each day with Ruth, but also phoning me because she did not wish me to visit her. Instead, I wrote her daily letters. After a week, Ruth was released to go to stay with her cousin Lisa and Victor Gersten, but continued to see the consultant psychiatrist. She then demanded that I remove myself to Idbury so that she could return to our apartment on her own.

I went to see Dr Michaelopolis at the psychotherapy department at Barnes Hospital for the first time on 29 January – the first of 13 weekly visits, after each of which I made a note of our discussion. He started by explaining that suicide is not something that others do to you; it is a uniquely personal decision. The pretext may be thought to be particular events, but it is likely to be much more complex in origin. From my narrative he fastened onto the unintended hurts to Ruth and the way I had taken her for granted too much. He stressed that it was important to be observant of her feelings and above all to be very honest in our relationship. He probed why I wanted to stay with Ruth and whether I would go back to Lisa if free to do so. I pointed to 40 years of shared life and to my real regard for her, and that mutual support and companionship would be all the more important as we got older. I said I was assuming that there would first be a reconciliation so that we could re-establish some genuine intimacy, but that if this was rejected and I left on my own I probably would go back to Lisa, which led him to wonder whether I was being honest with myself. Perhaps, just still confused.

In reflecting on our situation, I composed a letter to Ruth, which was never posted. Its opening paragraphs reflect the state of my feelings –

'Tomorrow, we see a new psychiatrist together, Sylvia Milton, and I wonder how she will help to rebuild a bridge between us. The gap seems too wide at the moment.

'You are still so angry with me and intent on unearthing every more detail of my relationship with Lisa so that you can have more ammunition to fire at me. I resist because it only seems to make everything worse and you call this deceit. But an affair obviously entailed deceit, otherwise I would have been seeking divorce. Deceit was sustained just because I did not want to leave you or directly hurt you, and I always made it plain to Lisa that if it came to the crunch you were the person I loved in the true sense and to whom I had loyalty and commitment. And this is what happened. Of course it would have been better if I had terminated the affair – as I had intended – when I left SOAS and it is all much worse that it was still on-going when you discovered it. As I have said many times, I am relieved that it is over now, I am truly sorry for the pain I have caused you, and my only wish is to re-build our relationship – to show my love to you and to win back some regard for me.

'In our last two conversations your anger seemed tinged with hatred and you were in denial over the enjoyment we had in each other's company in the last six years since I left SOAS. If there is no underlying regard, how can there be forgiveness and a search for a new life together? Unless there is some indication from you that you want this to happen our prospects are pretty hopeless.

'It is a coincidence – and surely a happy one in the circumstances – that my last public roles of any consequence will wind out this year. The RCS chairmanship has already gone; the RAS succession process is already in train; I am nearing the end of my final stint on the ODI council and finance committee; even chairing 82 Portland Place Ltd will go soon. This will leave only the British Empire & Commonwealth Museum and my African tea book project. What this surely means is that we will now have time for each other and to do new things together, and for me to try to repair the damage I have perpetrated. Will you come with me?'

Ruth's psychiatrist arranged that the two of us should be seen by a sex therapist colleague, Sylvia, for several sessions. At these meetings Ruth was very angry and outspoken and any reconciliation seemed over the horizon. She then cancelled the joint meetings, but continued to see Sylvia herself. In mid-March I wrote to Sylvia: 'such hard things have been said now and such a cruel personality has been on display that I no longer wish to live with this person. I have been saying goodbye to the Ruth that I loved. What was unthinkable in January now beckons: a return to Lisa, openly.'

Another joint meeting was then arranged later in March, which started off on a positive, even cheerful, note until Ruth suddenly said, 'I have decided to divorce Michael, but I want this to be a civilised parting.' Sylvia was gob-smacked and I was gutted – so much the opposite of what I had been preparing for.

Before this happened I had written a brief note to Lisa in February to inform her of the suicide attempt and also to say sorry for the hurt I must have caused her. I endeavoured to explain my motives in my diary: 'It is in reaction to being totally ostracised by Ruth and the fear that this is but a prelude to separation and divorce... So the letter is a kind of contingency plan – to tell Lisa what has been going on, to apologise for the hurt I have caused – and to raise just the possibility that all is not over between us. Is this exploitive? I hope not, because I know that Lisa really loved me, although Ruth asserts that she was just being manipulative.' By strange coincidence Lisa wrote to me on the very same day, so that our letters crossed in the mail. Hers was a generous and inspiriting missive, especially the paragraph:

If I have a farewell gift for you it would be to ask that you try to think of your own sweet self more kindly and gently by remembering two things. Firstly for all those years you really, really tried to do your best not to hurt anybody, including your family. Perhaps I know this more than anyone else – how you hoped and tried as far as possible to respect the wishes of those around you and at the same time look after your own needs. You are probably questioning the validity of your own needs for warmth, respect, love and passion, and denying you ever had any. Michael, my sweet, when I met you, you were like the desert and I was always so pleased for you that you had chosen somebody who would respect and not take undue advantage of those needs, which were so obvious to all around you – even those who disapproved professionally. Although you had great difficulty in overtly acknowledging those needs to yourself they, rather than pride, possession, and property, are indeed the oxygen of life, and that it is part of the human condition to be so nourished. One interpretation of the last ten years may be that you were so nourished that you were able to give to others in such an open, relaxed and genuine way, and thus paper over very considerable cracks. As you know, I always thought I was part of your solution and not the problem. Although I cannot judge the effect of this within your family, your own reports and certainly the observations of others in other parts of your life, suggest that they observed a major change in your demeanour and really like you, and this was so especially in recent months when your own happiness was visible and widely commented on.

I then met Lisa a couple of times to review the situation and I tried to explain that, notwithstanding our mutual attraction and pleasure at seeing each other again – 'I have not yet made the irrevocable decision and could still go the other way if Ruth really wanted this – however unlikely.'

I went on to explain that I was, in a way, in mourning for my marriage and Lisa was very understanding. These exchanges were in the background at the fateful meeting when Ruth made her announcement.

These developments were related to Dr Michaels (as I called him) in our weekly sessions. He kept probing the sincerity of my expressed wish for reconciliation: 'You are not getting any younger. You've got a life to lead as well.' He urged me to take things more slowly, both to minimise the risk of another suicide attempt, and not to hurt Lisa again. He had liked a letter I had sent to Ruth in February, which included: 'Just as I shared responsibility for your suicide attempt with its more deep-rooted causes within you (and I am not seeking to deny that I provoked it), so you should also recognise that you were a contributing cause to my starting an affair after over 30 years of marriage. Unless we can both recognise this and share a desire to re-connect with our 'original' selves, then there will not be any proper reconciliation and we would be better off living apart and trying to get over bereavement for a lost marriage with a new life of some kind. You need to understand that I would make every effort to make this new beginning work, but there would have to be wholehearted reciprocity on your part. At the moment I get the impression that you cannot contemplate such a possibility, and maybe Sylvia would say that it is too early to consider it. But the weeks go by.'

I had my last meeting with Dr Michaels at the end of April when he opined that Ruth was still a long way from being able to take a mature view of what had happened by drawing a line and accepting that there was good and bad in both of us and working to re-establish a relationship. And he quoted from memory Shakespeare's sonnet 138 – 'When my love swears that she is made of truth/ I do believe her though I know she lies.' Reflecting on these meetings, I wrote, 'I find it quite hard to know what my true feelings are in answer to his probing. I am sure he has helped me to understand Ruth better, but my fluctuating behaviour does not look good in retrospect. Yet, it is through talking to Dr Michaels that I have come to understand that Ruth is the person that I really love and want to restore relations with, despite all the difficulties.'

After Ruth's announcement, we both saw divorce lawyers and the process of financial separation got under way. We still met almost weekly, usually at Idbury, and these were not easy occasions as Ruth remained very angry in herself. On her birthday in July I sent her a birthday card and compared myself to Penelope at her tapestry with me in my Cotswold garden. There was no comment and I reflected: 'Is this how marriages end? The internal ache becomes calloused over by the pre-occupations of living, and the details of each other's lives are gradually lost, and how the other feels.' We had one major difference when Ruth insisted that Paddock Cottage be sold, whereas I was assuming that this would become my home, and I was obstinate for a while before giving in. Ruth went to South Africa in August with her friend Janet and I made a tea research visit to Kenya. The autumn was difficult as we headed towards divorce and I resumed relations with an all too eager Lisa. At Christmas, Ruth took herself alone to Venice on an art tour; I was not welcome by the family so moved into Lisa's circle. At New Year we went to Guana

Island, which was not an outright success although Henry Jarecki was very hospitable and understanding.

On 6 January I received an extraordinary letter from Ruth:

It has taken a long time, perhaps too long, to come to terms with your betrayal, but at last I am able to forgive you and to contemplate resuming our marriage, if it is not too late. I realise that I cannot offer you Lisa's heady mixture of sensuality combined with mothering. But if what I am capable of giving you is enough, I would like to feel that we could live our remaining lives together harmoniously, surrounded by family and friends... in my heart of hearts I believe we would both be happier having a positive life together rather than continuing this negative life apart.

I immediately caught the next train to London and we had dinner together and the process of reconciliation began. There were hiccups, but our course was charted. I reflected on the past tumultuous year in my diary: 'I suppose what I have never clearly articulated to myself, let alone to others, is the tension between the conventional side to my character and the darker wilder side which occasionally bursts out. The respectable side is the public school head boy, chief executive, SOAS director, RAS chairman, model family man. But the wilder bit has always been lurking – risk taking, flirting with the unconventional, sexually adventurous in spirit! It showed itself over my life from time to time: an unconventional head boy; dilettante tastes as an undergraduate; liberal politics in Zambia; out of ordinary friends in Kenya; Henry Jarecki; the unorthodox defence against the Lloyds Bank bid; some of the friendships at SOAS, and above all the affair with Lisa. It goes with a responsiveness to slightly outrageous ideas and behaviour, a willingness to 'have a go', adventure. But perhaps it also goes with undue self-regard and insensitivity to other people's interests and reactions.'

Lisa

The parting with Lisa on the day after I received Ruth's letter was painful, but decisive. I did not see her again until nearly four years later when she was ill with cancer. At the urging of Jonathan Taylor I went up to London one day to have lunch with Lisa at her home where she was out on remission, and then drove her back to University College hospital for treatment. We managed to have calm conversation and to achieve what Lisa would term 'closure'. She died not long afterwards.

I first became aware of the name Lisa Croll about two years after taking up my appointment as Director of SOAS, when there was a problem over appointing a new head of the department of Anthropology. I found that there was a puzzling lobby in favour of an amiable but academically undistinguished lecturer and I was keen to get stronger leadership into the department and began to investigate alternatives. The name of Lisa Croll was put to me – a relatively new member of the permanent faculty, but someone who had been associated with SOAS for many years as a part-time teacher. One of those I consulted was a professor who (unbeknown to me) was just ending a major affair with her and he advised against the name. In the event another professor in the department agreed to take on the headship.

However, I now became aware of this attractive and dynamic person, and I enjoyed opportunities to chat to her. She was a social anthropologist of China and very much a liberated woman. She had admirers amongst her male colleagues as well as intense friendships with several women. Then, during a research trip to Beijing she had a fall and injured her foot and coincidentally I had an operation to remove a toe as a result of an accident many years ago, and this provided a further excuse to chat. I was soon better, but Lisa's injury turned into a dangerously unpleasant disorder of her nervous system and she was consigned to the Hospital for Nervous Diseases in Bloomsbury. Several colleagues took turns to visit her and I thought to do likewise. Lisa fastened onto my visits, urging frequent repeats and in no time we were holding hands.

On day release from hospital we had supper together and kissed passionately on parting. She came to the SOAS flat one evening, where I spent three or four nights a week, and there was more kissing and fumbling. Perhaps the next occasion was her house in Highgate, with passionate love-making. An intense affair followed, accompanied by floods of tears, emotional reproaches and reconciliations. The occasion for all this intensity was always to do with some slight – a changed rendezvous, unwillingness to come into the open in front of colleagues, refusal to contemplate breaking with Ruth. But at the same time there was much fun and endless talk about SOAS, to which Lisa was deeply attached. She knew the dynamics of the place like no one else I talked to and was enormously helpful to me over learning to handle the academic staff. And all this came against a background in which Ruth had refused to sleep with me for over five years.

Lisa was a New Zealander from a churchy family, but unsupportive of an academically inclined daughter. She married an academic engineer and had two children, and then Jim was appointed to a chair at UCL and they came to London. However, their marriage went cold and Jim took up with a wealthy divorcee and Lisa and he separated, though still remaining friendly and meeting up at birthdays, Christmas etc. Lisa then had this affair with a colleague at SOAS, which was supposed to lead to marriage, but he drew back and went off with a Korean researcher instead (and married her). Lisa openly and often said that she would wait for me and was happy to be my mistress meantime. My response was always that I had no intention of leaving Ruth. I realise now that Lisa was counting on our relationship becoming public sooner or later, and that would be her moment of opportunity. She was endlessly resourceful in devising ways to meet and she kept looking for ways for us to be away together – and they eventually came along. We went to Paris about four times in connection with my investment trust board meetings; twice to Edinburgh for the Royal African Society; twice to Hong Kong; twice to Oxford; once to South Africa for the Royal Commonwealth Society. Sometimes I paid for the fare, sometimes Lisa was able to link the trip with one of her research assignments. Naturally too, she wanted tangible tokens and there was a gold bracelet for her 50th birthday and eventually a ring.

This was all very compromising and yet I knew I ought to break off the relationship, despite its thrills and the real enjoyment of her company. Actually, I did so on two occasions – lasting a month or two, and I felt liberated. But something would happen and we would be back again – with endless recriminations and analysis. I eventually decided that the only way to escape would be to leave SOAS and retire early i.e. after only seven years in post at age 63. There was much surprise from the Chairman and colleagues, but I stuck to a line that with SOAS doing well it was important to revert to more traditional academic leadership. Also, the contemporary example of Margaret Thatcher could be adduced that staying for ten years was probably too long. Having set the wheels in motion I had to see it through, although in 1996 I was more involved with Lisa than ever, and she more than anyone ensured that I had a good send off from the School.

Thus, my attempts to break with Lisa were pathetically inadequate as I headed for the inevitable domestic crisis. Looking back over the ten years of the affair, there was one aspect that only Lisa and I knew for sure: in many ways I had become a much nicer and more tolerant person in that time – 'comfortable within my skin' as Lisa would put it. And I know that I made hugely greater compensating efforts with Ruth and the family, and we had some great holidays together in that time. None of this excuses the pain I caused Ruth when she found out, but I think we had a happier relationship in the 90s on account of what Lisa did for me, which needs to go into the reckoning somewhere.

Lisa came from a milieu where it was not an outrage for people to change partners during a lifetime – not in a frivolous 'Happy Valley' way, but because of evolving careers and personalities, and to accept that if two people found happiness together this was something to be accommodated and even celebrated. But I suspect this attitude treats too lightly the pain caused to the losing party. I think Ruth was right to be outraged that Lisa had a determined strategy to 'get' me. Where she was wrong – I feel – was not to recognise that she could have done more to put things right between us. Such an analysis presents me as a passive agent between two powerful women – and there is force in this. However – late in the day though it was – Ruth eventually did the brave thing in proposing that we get together again, and I was right to seize that moment. It is deeply ironic that both Lisa and Ruth should die of cancer within five years. But Ruth was the one who most needed support from me and I was more than happy to provide it. Lisa dedicated her last years to SOAS as deputy Principal and it is fitting that a memorial fund was set up in her name, to which I contribute.

Indian Summer

2004 was a year of readjustment and reorganisation of our lives. Having divided our income and capital in half, we sold Paddock Cottage as agreed and I purchased Yew Tree Farm in Brimpsfield, near Cheltenham, and Ruth bought a flat in the Barbican. The arrangement was that she would spend the week in London where I would join her for concerts and other joint events and then she would come to Gloucestershire at

Together again

Lisa

the weekends. She was on permanent anti-depressant medication which made her calmer and more controlled, but one knew that underlying emotions were still strong and only mastered by a strong effort of will, and every now and then there was an outburst. Ruth's focus was mainly on her new life as an 'independent' woman in London, with her circle of women friends that she assiduously cultivated. We started a limited amount of entertaining again where she did the cooking in London and I was the chef at Brimpsfield, unless we were entertaining. And so – to outside eyes at least – normality had been restored, albeit with a somewhat hollow centre.

In the autumn of 2004, disaster struck. Ruth had had treatment before for colon polyps, but the check-up this time revealed colon cancer and the need for a major operation. A kind friend of hers opined that I was the cause of this development. Ruth was referred to one of the star surgeons of the day – Professor Sir Ari Darzi at St Mary's, who was the pioneer of keyhole surgery. However, to his astonishment Ruth elected to have a traditional operation in order to make sure that everything was removed, as she put it. It was deemed a success and I moved into the flat for twice a day hospital visits and for the immediate convalescence.

Ruth wanted to have a winter holiday in the sun and, with the help of Abercrombie and Kent, we chose an exclusive resort in Kenya in the mangroves down near the Tanzania border, only reached by small plane from Mombasa. The break was good for both of us. While there, the owner flew us to Diani for a day's visit to the Foster brothers at the Sand Island home, which their parents had acquired in the 1930s. The house was full of hunting trophies and old photos and we had a good reminiscence over the good old days. In June 2005 we went to Austria to the Schubertiade festival at Schwarzenberg, which was a wonderful combination of morning walks in the mountains and afternoon concerts, and Ruth got her strength back and put on weight. I noticed an increased sense of insecurity over novel situations, travel arrangements and clothes but this was counterbalanced by hyperactivity with her women friends. Our old family friends were delighted that we were back together again, although I thought I could detect a reserve in some quarters, as Ruth had worked hard in 2003 to secure total commitment to her cause.

In the next two years we had two more grand safari holidays, as well as trips in Europe. On the safari in southern Tanzania there are memorable photos of Ruth being carried piggy back over a river when the 4x4 could not get through and others crossing a river on a rope pulley; we then went to see chimpanzees by Lake Tanganyika and witnessed an ambush fight between the chimps and copper tail monkeys. I still had commitments as chairman of the British Empire & Commonwealth Museum and of Cheltenham Festivals and was quite busy. Would I have got closer to Ruth without them? I have my doubts. She did not really want me around in London during the week, unless we were going to a concert or something similar, and the flat was arranged very much to suit her. Yet, I could, and should, have devoted more attention to her needs, although this was hard to do against the background of no tactile contact – hand holding, arm in arm, a hug. I could see that she exerted charm and appeal to men when she wanted to; it was just that I did not qualify for this kind of attention.

Thus passed four years. Whether they could have been a prelude to a happier phase as we approached our golden wedding anniversary, one will never know because fate struck again. But the experience of the final year suggested to me that the answer would more likely than not have been in the affirmative.

Towards the end of 2007 we planned another African safari in the new year, but Ruth's hip had become painful and, on visiting a consultant, urgent replacement was advised and the trip was cancelled. The operation went well and Ruth was making an excellent recovery and diligently did her exercises. However, I had noticed a persistent dry cough throughout this episode. Although ignored by the anaesthetist, I persuaded Ruth to go and see her GP. She was immediately whipped up to Barts hospital for an X-ray and lung cancer was diagnosed. A biopsy was undertaken and this established that the tumour was a secondary infection from the original bowel cancer. This was bad news, since the consultant explained that further outbreaks were likely and that Ruth probably only had another year of life. She took this news with extraordinary courage and equanimity – at least outwardly. The consultant was a chemotherapy specialist and the options were discussed frankly. Ruth refused surgery and chemotherapy: she felt that there was no quality of life in the latter and, as the consultant conceded, it would only have offered the prospect of a few extra months at best. There followed a dangerous lung infection when she nearly died, and then a course of radiotherapy which shrivelled the tumour. Ruth was soon back to her old routine of staying in the Barbican during the week and I would go up to town by train so as to drive together to the Cotswolds for the weekend.

The prolonged hospitalisation sequence over two months threw me into major caring mode, and naturally it drew us closer together. I was able to do things for Ruth and be with her in a way that no-one else could do. The consultant believed in total straightforwardness if the patient could take it, and Ruth clearly could do so. Thus, she knew the prognosis and digested it. She became quite introspective and uncommunicative, not wanting to share her thoughts with me, and she showed enormous courage in facing up to her fate. It did not lead to her wanting to make peace with me openly, but at the same time she realised that she was becoming increasingly dependent on me, since she had determined that when the time came, she wanted to die at Yew Tree Farm, which had become home for both of us.

Ruth had the nice idea of bringing all the family together for the last time in summer 2008 at a holiday location and, after much research, we settled on the Palais Hotel in Biarritz for a fortnight. It was a fabulous establishment, which made up for indifferent weather and everyone made great efforts to make the stay memorable. During that year Ruth took two extraordinary initiatives, unbeknown to me at the time. First, she decided to make detailed arrangements for her own funeral, visiting the Cirencester undertaker and devising the order of service with a humanist to officiate. She had also been thinking about our 49th wedding anniversary, realising that we would not be able to celebrate a golden wedding and in September she wrote me the following letter –

Dearest Michael

What I am about to tell you was intended to be a surprise, but keeping a secret for several months has become too difficult!

I have commissioned Matthew Taylor to compose a string quartet in celebration of our marriage. It is a present for you which I hope you will treasure as much as I have treasured our marriage – notwithstanding the odd blip! It is also a big thank you for the loving care with which you have looked after me during the worst of my illness.

The plan is that the Salieri Quartet will give the first performance of the quartet on 5 March next year in the Barbican Conservatory at a party for our family and friends. I know it is not our 50th anniversary, but as it is uncertain that I will be around by March 2010 I wanted to get on with it. If I am gone by next March the event, if you so wish, might also be regarded as a celebration of my life.

As you know, I want just a small private cremation in Cheltenham, with family only, and no memorial of any kind. I have left an envelope with my wishes spelled out in more detail, to be opened when the time comes.

For now, with all my love Ruth xxx

This letter was the strongest indication yet that Ruth had managed to heal the past, and it gave us something very positive to look forward to. Matthew Taylor had played at our silver wedding celebration – the 'boy next door' from Kennington days, who was now a composer and music teacher. His wife was a member of the Salieri string quartet.

And then, one day in early December when Ruth was due to come to Yew Tree Farm for the weekend, she phoned at breakfast time to say that she did not feel well enough to drive. I immediately set off to fetch her and she never saw London again. I took her to Cheltenham's A&E on Monday and while she was being X-rayed the duty doctor opined that it might be a brain tumour. Ruth was kept in hospital for four days and the oncologist confirmed that the cancer had spread to her brain and that life expectancy could now be measured in weeks. Ruth was supremely brave about it. She was firm that she wanted to die at home and this was accepted. After Christmas we went together to talk to my GP when she explained that she did not want any artificial life prolongation and he pledged full support, saying that they would gradually increase the morphine dose so that she would experience no pain as her metabolism gradually closed down.

In the New Year we played a little bridge and saw the family as much as possible. I was introduced to the British Nursing Association and began to use their services if I had to go out for any length of time. Special kit was produced by the NHS and there was a splendid district nurse to give medication. One day we had a day of comedy when snow was falling and the district nurse could not get through in her car. Our GP summoned Martin to meet him at the pharmacy, where he instructed him on how to make up the morphine dose and administer it and change the drip, saying that in his time in the South African Defence Force they often had to empanel auxiliaries in an emergency. The district nurse happened to phone the pharmacy soon afterwards and learned what was going on. Horrified at the idea of a layman administering a class one drug, she commandeered a 4x4 vehicle and steamed over to Brimpsfield, where Martin's potion was poured down the drain and she administered her own.

A week later I went upstairs to help Ruth to come down to lunch when she collapsed on me at the top of the stairs and we tobogganed down the full flight, head first and with Ruth on top of me. My head hit the corner of the wainscot and bled profusely; in addition there was something seriously wrong with my left knee. We lay there for a bit until I managed to crawl to a phone and tell Martin that we were in difficulties. He had the wit to phone the doctor who called an ambulance. It was snowing again as we were both loaded into the ambulance which fortunately was able to get through to Cheltenham – the last one that day. Ruth had bruised ribs and was kept in hospital for two nights. An X-ray revealed no broken bones so I insisted that Martin take me home, although I was only able to crawl upstairs. Once home, Ruth was put to bed and never walked again.

The support services were impressive. The district nurse came daily to renew steroid and anti-nausea medication and adjust morphine, while the GP called weekly as well as in several emergencies. Every morning and evening a 'continuing care' person under the district nurse called to wash and change Ruth, and every evening a 'twilight' nurse phoned to enquire whether a visit was needed. Meanwhile the British Nursing Association carers came from 8am to 1pm and another to sleep over. These women had varying experience and motivation, but would change Ruth in need (she had become incontinent) and would help around the house with washing, cleaning and ironing. We rather took to a doughty Welsh girl, Jessica, but also admired Margaret (from Zimbabwe), Ginnet (from Ethiopia), Gill and Linda. I was kept extremely busy and this was aggravated by still having an extremely painful leg, with an insecure knee joint. I pushed Ruth's meals up the stairs on a tray, one step at a time, and it was difficult to be helpful when the nurses weren't there. (After it was all over, I went to a physiotherapist who referred me for a scan which established that my internal ligament had snapped and there was other damage. I then had keyhole surgery and several months of physio treatment to get back to normal).

Ruth was adamant that our concert and party should go ahead on 5 March even though she would not be able to attend it. When the Salieri Quartet heard that Ruth would not be able to come up to London they made a wonderful proposal to visit Brimpsfield and play Matthew's composition in our home. This they did and we had the marvellous experience of sitting with the score and listening to their performance from the next room for an hour – truly something to treasure. His Seventh String Quartet is a delightful composition, with a texture reminiscent of Mendelsohn. Matthew had arranged to record the concert and make a CD.

I went up to London for the evening to welcome our 64 guests for the concert and dinner and said to them: 'It was very much Ruth's wish to bring together all her friends who had been so supportive during the difficulties of recent years, and to go ahead with this evening, whether or not she could manage to be present. Sadly, she is not well enough to be here tonight. It was to be her way of saying thank you, but also to provide an occasion to remember her by. Her thoughts are very much with you all this evening, and she wished me to stress that it has been planned as an occasion to be enjoyed.'

On 9 March Ruth deteriorated with phlegm in her throat and new medication was prescribed. A hospice nurse was produced to sit up that night. She was better the next day, but unconscious and heavy breathing. No food. A hospice nurse came again and at 3.30 am she roused me to say that Ruth's breathing had changed. I sat with her as she quietly expired. It was 11 March and Anschluss Day in Austria in 1938 and 70 years since her parents resolved to leave Vienna for England.

The sad thing in those final weeks was that Ruth never wanted to talk about us; she was essentially withdrawn and seemingly indifferent to me as a person and husband, so we never really managed to say goodbye. Quite tough. It is hard to know how much it might have helped had we been better able to talk. I think Ruth died painlessly, but not altogether peacefully, and it is heart breaking that I was unable to be more than a super carer in those last months.

In Celebration

Sitting on a Caribbean beach for three days in the autumn of 2009, after attending the Commonwealth heads of government meeting in Trinidad with the Royal Commonwealth Society, I sorted through diary notes and letters that I had brought with me and endeavoured to write an unvarnished account of our marriage, not only to record what we had learnt about each other in the annus horribilis, but also to recall how we had enriched each other over nearly fifty years. I have drawn on this account in this chapter and I close it with something of a celebration of a treasured relationship.

Ruth's background of Viennese Jewish culture had fascinated me from the outset, and she often remarked that I was more interested in it than she was. Her own memoir of her early life records the story of the family's belated escape from Vienna in 1938. Her family were well to do and cultured; their house was designed by a leading modern architect – down to the furniture and light fittings; their glass and silver was from the artists of the Secession; there were prints and drawings by Klimt, Liebermann and Slevogt. Ruth spoke German at home to her parents and therefore retained colloquial command of the language all her life – albeit with a limited, domestic and childish vocabulary, as she put it. Ruth's mother was cultured and vivacious; her father was a shy lawyer (aged 45 when she was born) who never had a proper job after coming to England.

Ruth and I met up with her parents in Vienna on our way back from Kenya in 1961 and we saw all the family haunts and sights of the city, were taken to the opera and the Spanish Riding School, to Demels, to the Kahlenberg. Unsurprisingly, Ruth had an ambivalent attitude towards modern Austria and the continuing, barely suppressed anti-semitism that is still so common. Austria was much more reluctant and tardy over providing compensation for expropriated wealth than Germany, but Ruth's parents did receive compensation for their house in the 1970s, and Ruth derived considerable satisfaction in doggedly pursuing other claims that became available during the last ten years. She invariably gave the proceeds to charity.

Notwithstanding this, we started having regular holidays in Austria after the boys were off our hands – and made much more enjoyable by Ruth's ability to speak German with a Viennese accent. Then, as a banker, I was eventually in a position to authorise the opening of a branch of Standard Chartered in Vienna. This involved a number of high profile visits, always staying at the Sacher Hotel (in the days when it still refused to accept credit cards) and becoming friendly with senior

Austrian bankers and the Central Bank. In turn this led to visits to the Salzburg Festival and, one memorable year, to the Opera Ball. We were twice in Vienna for the New Year – the second time at the Millennium, with *Die Lustige Witwe* at the Opera, New Year's Day at the Koncerthaus and *Taffel Spitze* lunch at the Sacher.

Music was a huge shared interest and pleasure for us both – concerts, opera and a large record collection to listen to on evenings after supper. Before meeting Ruth I had a somewhat austere music taste, including Indian classical music. Ruth introduced me to Mahler, to German lieder, Richard Strauss. We discovered a mutual fascination with Wagner and I worked out once that we had been to eleven complete cycles of *The Ring*, including two in Beyreuth. The first was in 1986 after defeating Lloyds Bank's hostile bid for Standard Chartered. Our branch manager in Hamburg managed to buy tickets off the South African consul in Munich. We stayed for a week at the gourmet Gasthof Feiler about 20k from Bayreuth, and could intersperse country walks between the four performances. It was the first showing of the Solti/Peter Hall Ring, a naturalistic conception in contrast to the prevailing 'koncept' tradition. So, the Rhinemaidens were nude in a real tank, the Valkyries descended from the sky in a fearful swoop, there was a great dragon and a huge conflagration at the end. But there was a Siegfried disaster – the East German butcher's boy with a golden voice (Goldberg) couldn't learn his part in time despite frantic coaching by Solti, and a repertory replacement had to be brought in at the last minute. A friend of mine from the *Sunday Times* was writing a book about the whole production, so we heard all the gossip. In the long dinner intervals we were placed at a table with a French baron and his sister – a piece of old Europe, they came to Bayreuth every year and stayed with cousins in Regensburg. It was frightfully hot, but in those days Bayreuth was still smart as only Germans can be: evening dresses, jewels and just a small permitted cushion to relieve the rigours of hard wooden seats. Recalling the opening E flat horn calls at the start of *Das Rheingold*, as one embarks on that incredible journey, brings a lump to my throat as I write. Who can fail to identify part of their own life story with Wotan's family saga?

Through my position at the bank we enjoyed some fifteen years of privileged musical experiences – at Covent Garden, the Coliseum, Glyndebourne, Salzburg, Bayreuth and other sites. Before the days of the redevelopment of the Floral Hall at Covent Garden, Ruth would make superior sandwiches on Wagnerian evenings, served with double Scotch. Ruth had a much stronger interest in the visual arts than me, except for my quirky liking for Oriental and African culture, and she took the lead over visits to exhibitions and museums. In retirement this became a major activity, and every year Ruth would study the prospectuses to decide what course to take at Birkbeck or City Lit. The courses also encompassed literature and a two-year diploma in garden history. I was able to benefit from some of the garden visits and took the photographs to illustrate her essays.

Ruth agreed to start a family after we came back to England. She was not a natural lover of babies and small children and, for a start, she couldn't produce enough milk, so we were into bottles, which was my job at night time, as well as changing nappies. We had a nanny from the start. My recollection is that, as small children, Robert and Martin were more closely bonded to me than to Ruth; it was my bed that they crept into in the early mornings. Later, Ruth was much more involved and it was she who focussed on Robert's dyslexia and arranged remedial treatment. Once at boarding school, Ruth was the weekly letter writer. Her post at South Bank Poly meant that she had roughly coincidental vacations with school holidays and was able to devote huge effort to holiday activities.

Ruth had a better trained intellect than mine, with strong reasoning powers. We had both read economics at university, but she was in a superior league and won a prize at UCL as the outstanding student of her year. I retained a keen interest in macroeconomics and policy and this was always material for lively argument. Latterly she found me too opinionated. Ruth was determined to be recognised for her intellectual abilities, though she was not above using her charms in the office. She overcame much adversity in carving a career. As already noted, Ruth had to resign from the Colonial Service on getting married and could only be employed as a temporary civil servant, yet was appointed to the same rank as me. She had to establish credibility at LSE to be appointed head of the research department and then administrative secretary of the economics department. She made her mark at the National Economic Development Office and was then an economic adviser at the Ministry of Housing. Then there was the switch to becoming a teaching economist and finally the challenge of being appointed School Secretary at the London School of Hygiene and Tropical Medicine for ten years.[127]

A common feature of Ruth's several career jobs was that they nearly all ended on a sour note with a significant personality clash. This happened in Nairobi, and then at LSE where, after the death of Ely Devons, she fell out with his successor who engineered to terminate her appointment. At Neddy, after a successful period under Bonham Carter's directorship, she again fell out with his successor and the appointment came to an end. At South Bank the same happened, and again at the School of Hygiene after Gordon Smith's retirement. Ruth had an uncompromising sense of what was right and wrong, which perhaps did not sit easily with bureaucratic life and, I think, was at the root of her showdowns. She was most probably well justified in her stance in each case, but a sequence of jobs that ended in a breakdown of relationships also indicated a rigidity in her character make-up that could be hard to live with.

It is striking that Ruth had several intense relationships with older men who were also in authority over her and, perhaps, this had something to do with not having the experience of a young father. I think of Carey-Jones in the Kenya Ministry of Agriculture, with whom Ruth worked on the bids for World Bank support for the first settlement schemes. Then, at LSE Ruth became close to Ely Devons and was emotionally drained by his illness and death. There was Maxwell Smith at the South Bank Poly, and most of all was her ten-year relationship with Gordon Smith, Dean of the School of Hygiene. They were both seriously in love, Ruth eventually told me, but she refused to break up the marriage and, being her, kept the relationship platonic. There was also an affair with our architect at Paddock Cottage, but again it was held within bounds – just. Of course, I only learned of all this during our post-mortem sessions.

Why did Ruth marry? Perhaps in the end she was not resilient enough. She had a need for a pal, but perhaps not for a loved partner. Ruth could have had a more brilliant career if she had not wanted also to have children. However, I believe she was too lacking in self-confidence to have stayed single, although she would undoubtedly have been highly successful if she had carried this off. The fact was that she did want a family (though not enjoying the baby years) and proved

---

127 Appointed in 1980.

herself a wonderful mother as the boys matured. Thus, I think her optimum life style would have been with a less successful husband (and certainly a more caring one!), with herself as the main breadwinner and matriarch. In effect, perhaps, a reworking of her parent's circumstances, where Suzi was the dominant personality in the Arnstein family, with Fritz as very much a background figure. Fritz never worked again as a lawyer after coming to England, and had not much enjoyed being one in Vienna, and was content to be a 'gentleman'. They had very little money from salvaged investments, but Suzi managed to become agent for an Austrian lace manufacturer for a number of years. It is hard to say how much this background affected Ruth, but I think her mother's role was an important influence on her character.

My ever-more-demanding banking career had a marital cost. I did a lot of overseas travel, although there were occasional state visits with Ruth as consort. She did not enjoy this role, or do it well, as she felt no natural sympathy with expatriate wives and their problems. Meanwhile, travelling on my own left Ruth to run the house and family. She would blow up periodically and subject me to long emotional harangues on my neglect of herself and the family and on my career preoccupations. I never knew how best to handle these scenes: to argue back only made things worse; to stay silent (my usual line) put a chasm between us. This led up to the awful occasion with the torn-up suicide note in 1979.

For someone who was so attractive, Ruth was very insecure over clothes and went through great agonies of indecision over what to wear for special occasions and how to do her hair. On the latter she eventually came to the rather formidable answer of a French pleat for special occasions. Rather late in the day, Ruth found someone who would 'dress' her for Standard Chartered occasions, and this led to some impressive outfits that she would never have had the courage to choose for herself. Essentially, Ruth derived no enjoyment from clothes shopping as so many women do. In the last five years she was happy to move into 'granny' mode and not to mind too much, especially as she let her figure go and decided to enjoy food and an evening Scotch.

Ruth learned the Austrian cuisine from her mother and was a good cook. She followed recipes meticulously, and was not one to improvise. As a serious hostess, she kept careful records of dinner party menus and guest lists, and I inherit a formidable card index, starting with translated

Austrian recipes. Before our marriage I was also quite a cook, but then stopped completely for forty years, which was perhaps a mistake. I had to start cooking again in 2003 when I was rusticated to Idbury. Subsequently, a pattern evolved that Ruth would be responsible for catering in the Barbican (where she rarely cooked just for herself), and I would be responsible at Yew Tree Farm (where it is a point of honour to produce a proper meal), except for family occasions in the country when we both might contribute. In her final illness Ruth much enjoyed being looked after in this way. Throughout our family life Ruth never had to do housework or ironing and this continued at the Barbican. Meanwhile I was the family washer-up, handyman, and above all gardener.

Boarding school had taught Ruth to have a go at most things – lacrosse, swimming in the sea at Bournemouth, tennis – although she was not naturally athletic, having flat feet and a lifelong problem with varicose veins. She had no aptitude for dancing, especially modern free styles, having no rhythmic sense. This was a shame as I liked dancing, so we were not great party types. We played tennis in Kenya and with the boys until she pulled a muscle on holiday in France aged 40, and we gave up the game. Neither of us were downhill skiers, but she gamely agreed to take up *langlauf* skiing when winter holidays became feasible after the boys left school. We enjoyed about six winter holidays in Austria until she once again hurt her leg and we stopped.

We both learned to play bridge from our parents, but Ruth was by far the better player. In turn we taught the boys when they were 10 and 12 and for several years we had a family foursome on holidays. Both Robert and Martin later played for their university. In recent years Ruth played weekly at the Acol Club with her friend Janet, and was chairman of the Barbican Bridge Club, and we even began to play some social bridge in the Cotswolds. We were both keen readers. Ruth read contemporary literature more widely than me, and I perhaps had a more intellectual bent. Together, this gave us plenty to talk about. Ruth was out of sympathy with my interest in Virginia Woolf and Bloomsbury, and with Byron. One summer she read the whole of Proust and I read *Decline and Fall* (Low's abridgement).

Our real recreation came to be walking, in the Cotswolds at weekends and the focus of our summer holidays. We went to the Austrian alps every year in the 1980s and until we bought Paddock Cottage in 1993. Seefeld in

Ruth. The Arnstein village. In the Tyrol. Kenya coast

Banana girl. In Namibia. River crossing

the Tyrol became our favoured destination, with a self-catering flat with Frau Zorzi. We bought all the walking maps of the region and would aim to drive to the starting point of our day's expedition by 10 am, with a picnic lunch on our backs, unless we planned to reach a mountain café after a two or three hour hike, and with a different route back to the car. Sometimes we had to huff up a mountain; others there might be a cable car at the start. On several occasions we took a train and walked back to the car. Once we stayed overnight in a mountain hut. Then back by late afternoon to a bath, rest, strong Scotch and supper, either at home or out to a restaurant.

Ruth was prepared to be an adventurous traveller, without having any special enthusiasm for wildlife, birds and botany as I had and we had some memorable safari trips. In Namibia we went tentless camping with friends, with a retired South African special forces officer as guide. In Kenya we did a walking safari down the side of the Rift into the Senguta Valley, followed by fly camping in a small plane. In Tanzania we did a camping safari to see the Serengeti migration. The reward always was to finish up on the Indian Ocean to recuperate and relax. At heart she was a cultured, metropolitan loving Londoner, wanting the stimulus of theatre, concerts, galleries and friends. The country was for weekends and holidays and family. This was behind our original strategy to retire in Mayfair, while retaining a country cottage. Out of the horrors of 2003 a real divergence of priorities emerged: Ruth as a town dweller wanting only a weekend retreat in the country, whereas I was a countryman and gardener, responding strongly to nature, while still wishing to retain some metropolitan stimulus. Luckily, we could afford the Barbican and Brimpsfield and the best of both worlds.

Being the wife of a Standard Chartered executive was not Ruth's best thing and she hated this role. So official visits were not a priority, in contrast to my colleagues' wives who relished it. Nevertheless, we had some memorable visits and Ruth was ingenious in creating alternative itineraries. I have already mentioned Independence Day in Delhi, the Green Revolution workshop in Kenya, the lectures at Lagos University and the ship launch in Japan. Ruth disliked bankers' small talk and seized any opportunity to raise the level of discourse. She was truly an interesting person to talk to for those who were not frightened off – usually the wives. Indeed, she had a gift for friendship and a talent for inspiring confidences from others, both men and women, being both sympathetic and discreet. In the last years she had a large circle of women friends plus two bachelors, who also gave her much needed support. I could not help contrasting this with my own situation of having reached my mid-seventies without accessible long term friends. Part of my problem was that being top dog at Standard Chartered and at SOAS made it quite difficult to develop genuine friendships with colleagues, on account of the status relationship. It is genuinely lonely at the top.

After Ruth retired from the School of Hygiene in 1990 (as I was about to start at SOAS), she determined to continue working, but this time in a voluntary capacity. After a short stay with the Alzheimer's Society, Ruth joined the Parkinson's Disease Society and did an important job in allocating research grants for several years, until she fell out with its clubby hierarchy. She then took up gaining extra-mural degrees at Birkbeck – especially a diploma in garden history, and she also made a serious effort to upgrade her French by taking lessons with a French schoolteacher friend. She was determined to be intellectually active and she had something of a horror of mental deterioration. This led also to a commitment to a daily crossword puzzle and, later, to weekly bridge at the Acol Club with Janet Langdon. When I retired from SOAS, Ruth was in full spate, while I continued to be busy with CDC, the Royal Commonwealth Society and Royal Africa Society and a directorship of investment funds at Indo-Suez and Barings. Although there was no intimacy in our relationship, we were good pals and also enjoyed a great deal of opera and concert going. At this time, I was also leading a double life with Lisa. Paradoxically, being fulfilled sexually in my relationship with Lisa made me much more attentive and solicitous to Ruth in our domestic life. She suspected nothing, which contributed so greatly to the shock when she eventually found out.

Ruth became an outstanding Oma figure within the family, by dint of application and empathy and love. She had a close relationship with both Robert and Martin all the way into their mid-forties over their careers, wives and personal problems. She worked hard to win the confidence of her daughters in law and was sad that Jane did not want to have a family of her own, while Anne was a constant enigma. Ruth predicted that there would be a divorce after she died and this happened. She was always thinking up ways to bring the family together and to anticipate needs. It was her idea to make advance distributions of capital to Robert and Martin to help with their housing, and also her idea to take over the last three years of Cheltenham school fees to relieve pressure on Martin (and to adjust wills). It was Ruth's idea to celebrate the millennium by taking the family to Guana Island for ten days, and to do the same in 2008 to Biarritz – knowing it would be the last such gathering. I feel certain that it was concern for the interests of the family that led to her proposing our reconciliation.

Ruth was very loyal to her friends, but she could be unforgiving of perceived lapses of conduct, which made her intolerant of those she did not approve of. The main casualty so far as I was concerned was Richard Stein, my closest City friend from Montagu days. We saw a great deal of him while he was a bachelor, but when he eventually married by breaking up a colleague's marriage, Ruth never forgave him and our friendship lapsed. Walter Elkan, whose crime was to refuse to take sides during our annus horribilis, was another casualty, but this friendship was retrieved. Ruth devoted a huge amount of attention to her own friends, making sure that they met regularly as well as keeping in touch by phone. She was attentive to their needs and in thinking up things to do together: concerts, films, theatre, exhibitions, outings. They were mostly single women, of course, with Janet Langdon as her closest friend, dating back to Neddy days. It always struck me as a strange relationship, as Janet was not at all musical or intellectual, but she was a terrific networker and, latterly, a bridge partner. I felt that she was a malign influence during our year of separation, since she was so much the beneficiary and did not really approve of our reconciliation. In the last five years I often felt myself an outsider.

This feeling was most acute during Ruth's last year, when she knew that she was under sentence. She became withdrawn and pre-occupied and was quite reluctant to talk about our life together, or to look back to happier days. I wrote up forty years of family accounts, which I thought might trigger off some such conversations. But no. Six months after she had made all arrangements, I was told about her funeral plans and handed the dossier. Likewise, I was only informed of the imaginative arrangements she had planned for our (almost) golden wedding anniversary after they were completed – in a letter. This was all quite saddening, because it only seemed to emphasise that she only saw me as a (much appreciated) carer.

Ruth embodied some puzzling contrasts. There was the brainy economist and capable administrator, determined to prove that she could have a career. There was the very attractive woman who enjoyed exerting her charms, but was nevertheless quite inhibited and 'correct' when men tried to follow through. There was the very conscientious mother and family conscious matriarch. Somewhere inside there was a very insecure person who needed a strong supporting partner. There was the good friend, but also the slightly frightening figure with determined moral standards. There was the wife who, despite some dalliances, reacted violently when she found herself betrayed – first with attempted suicide and then with a vengeful separation. Yet she finally declared a truce and a desire to re-establish a marriage basis. Ruth seems to have been genuinely surprised by the way that I looked after her during the last year. She was appreciative too, but not to the extent of feeling able to forgive, to reconcile or to explore the possibility of renewed mutual affection.

It was our personal tragedy that Ruth and I failed to establish a mutually loving relationship, despite all the interests and attitudes that we shared and the many good and happy experiences we had together. I am thankful however that we had the last five years together and succeeded, I hope, in repairing much of the damage of the past. None of this should detract from the friendship and enjoyment she gave to so many others, and the feeling that all those who knew her can all share that we had been privileged to know and love a person of rare qualities.

HEIMAT

13. FROM KENNINGTON
TO BRIMPSFIELD

It is not hard to understand how an ancestral home, owned by generations in a family, and with its surrounding district can have an important influence on a person's outlook on life. Something of the same sentiment can also operate even in the absence of such an obvious link. Even with multiple residences over a long life there is a particular resonance about some of them that carries on long afterwards because of its associations with significant periods and events in one's life. These homes exert a kind of magnetic force so that even if there is no desire to return to them, there is still a tug of sentiment. For myself, I have welcomed the opportunity to revive memories in this way and have been able to revisit homes in Kenya, Zambia and Oxford before settling in England.

For expatriates working in the colonies, Home had a particular connotation of returning to Britain every few years on home leave. The expression was common too with Kenya settlers. Home was a somewhat mythical England that glossed over the often-inconvenient realities of having to stay with relatives and rented accommodation. For me, Home had a different meaning. Having been shipped off to Cheltenham College at the age of 13 and only returning to Kericho once in five years, Home was an idealised Kenya childhood that I have tried to recapture in the opening chapter of these memoirs. The connotation of Kenya as heimat was reinforced for me by the experience of living again with my parents for six months in 1952 before going up to Oxford. They were still intending to retire in Kenya at that time and I had inchoate ideas of finding a career there. As it happened, I did join the Kenya Treasury at a time when British policy still envisaged a full career in the Colonial Service. And when Ruth and I married we seriously considered buying a house in Nairobi in 1961. Our 'home leave' that autumn broke the spell that Kenya would really be our home on a long-term basis. Yet my internal compass still pointed in that direction and accounts for my joining Standard Bank and for other subsequent interests. Even now, when meeting new people, I usually contrive before long to introduce the Kenya connection.

Although Kericho – and Kenya more generally – has a special place in my psyche, other homes over the years also loom large, and this chapter attempts to link them to the wider picture. I start with 137 Rosendale Road, Dulwich, having already described our return to England and our first rented home in Kennington.

It had been a bit of a shock on joining Standard Bank to discover that office hours still included working on Saturday mornings, unlike in the merchant banks and stockbrokers. However, a more pleasant discovery was that I was immediately eligible for a 100 percent house loan at a privilege rate. We started house hunting and by the spring of 1967 had found a double-fronted Edwardian house with a 90ft garden in Rosendale Road, West Dulwich. There was no central heating and the house needed major modernisation, but we paid the asking price of £6,700 and ran down our savings to pay for the improvements to reach a final cost of just under £11,000. Unlike my new colleagues at Standard Bank, I had no skills in home improvements and we relied on a friend who was trying to establish herself as an interior designer to propose bold colours and wallpapers. We bought our first washing machine, but not a television set until the man on the moon landing several years later. Meanwhile I worked energetically to create an attractive garden. Many young couples, like us, put huge effort into their first home and I am reminded of this as I write, as my granddaughter Olivia and her husband are busily engaged in doing up their newly purchased home, preparing walls for painting, reorganising the kitchen and bathroom and so on.

West Dulwich was in the early stages of gentrification, although our immediate neighbours were 'old Dulwich': a local government clerk who was married to the daughter of missionaries in Nigeria on one side, and on the other a colourful widow and her daughter. Mabs Bone died and the house was acquired by a Bahai family from Tanzania, while the daughter married an Italian language teacher and bought a nearby house where they suffered the tragedy of their baby son drowning in the garden pool. A rising star in the Treasury moved in nearby and David and Jill Hancock became long standing friends. The Foreign Office was represented by the Arbuthnots where Dulwich was their base between postings. An entrepreneurial couple on the other side of the road dealt in 'antiques' from a stall in Bermondsey market and were playing the housing boom by moving twice in the neighbourhood in our time. A writing couple moved in; Tim Green wrote an authoritative annual survey of the gold market and several years later he was commissioned to write a celebratory history of Mocatta & Goldsmid for its 300th anniversary so we had plenty to talk about. There was also an IT consultant and a company secretary and his picture restorer wife, all in neighbouring houses. It was the days of reciprocating dinner parties and Ruth was a good cook, with a repertoire of Viennese dishes. We were all bringing up young families and had promising careers, but no capital to speak of except that our houses were increasing in value.

Our second son, Martin, had been born while we were in Kennington so at the time of our move he still needed a nanny, while Robert was ready for primary school. Finding and affording domestic help so that Ruth could pursue her own career interests was a major preoccupation in these years. Our move meant that we lost our nanny from Hackney and Beryl was followed by two misfit mother's helps. One of these girls had an alternative life and one weekend she disappeared without warning. After a couple of days we reported her missing to the police, just at a time when a woman's body had been found on a local golf course. I had the surreal experience of being subjected to a long interview by two detectives playing hard cop and soft cop, with a view to ascertaining whether I could be a suspect. It turned out that our girl had been on the spree with a boyfriend and had to be dispensed with. We then found unflappable Julie who was with us for several years. She walked the boys to and from Rosendale Infants School and Primary School each day while

Ruth was at work. We then moved to cheerful Austrian au pair girls, organised by a friend who worked for the Anglo-Austrian Society. Robert was quite dyslexic and was having difficulty in keeping up until we were able to arrange for intensive remedial coaching and then transferred him to a local day prep school with small classes.

In 1967 Ruth had moved from LSE to the National Economic Development Office as Secretary of the Little Neddy for the building industry, which she was able to do on a part-time basis. She eventually authored a major report on the industry, which formed the basis of a transfer to the Ministry of Housing where my Nuffield contemporary, Ian Byatt, was the economic adviser. From thence she moved again to an economics lectureship at the South Bank Polytechnic (as it then was) in the department that trained building surveyors. It was a great advantage to move to the academic year timetable as this roughly overlapped with school holidays, and I could take leave from the bank to cover gaps. Perhaps because we both had jobs, all the more effort was made to spend time with the boys. I read to them in bed every evening while Ruth was preparing our supper, and weekends were family oriented with activities, including regular visits to Ruth's parents in Swiss Cottage and the possibility of a row on the lake in Regent's Park. Another boy from school virtually lived with us and this was also a boon.

We had the benefit of a holiday home after 1962 as my parents had purchased a cottage in Oakridge Lynch pending the resolution of their planning application to build a house there. We were able to have our summer holidays there for several years when the children were small and we got to know the Cotswold countryside well during our daily picnic outings. They eventually left Kenya in 1968 to retirement in their newly built house. In June the following year my father had a severe heart attack while staying with us in Dulwich; there was a repeat in November which was fatal. He was 65. It was sad that he had such a short enjoyment of retirement in his beloved Cotswolds, and sad too that the modern treatment of coronary disease was not yet well established. He had suffered from angina pains for years, but nothing was done about it. Margaret stayed on at Stream for five years and we became much more frequent visitors.

Ruth's mother died of leukaemia in 1970 and was a sad loss. Suzi and her circle of Jewish émigré friends from Vienna opened a window into

Our sand castles. Cotswold picnic. Sports Day with Robert and Martin. In uniform

a world of music and culture that fascinated me, while her worldly-wise understanding of people's foibles was a stabilising influence. She had been very reluctant to leave Vienna in 1938 and they almost left it too late. Having moved to London, however, she had no desire to return to Austria after the war. The family had been on holiday in Bournemouth in late summer 1939 and, on the declaration of war, rightly feared internment. Suzi went to see the headmistress of Wentworth School and asked her to take six-year-old Ruth as a boarder, which she agreed to do. Ruth was at the school for the next twelve years and was a star pupil and was clearly a protégée of Miss Bourne ('I was her war effort,' Ruth used to say). A happy consequence of all this was that Miss Bourne had kept in touch with Ruth and in 1970 she offered us a summer holiday home in the chalet on her brother's farm near Sidmouth in Devon, where we went for four years. The sand on Sidmouth beach is very fine and we perfected a style of sand castle building that drew admiring onlookers.

One year we arranged to spend the day at Budleigh Salterton at the spot where the River Otter enters the sea. Robert wanted to fish from the opposite bank of the river to where we were picnicking, which involved a walk upstream to a foot bridge and back. When I returned to our base and looked over the river, Robert was nowhere to be seen. I went back again and failed to find him. It then occurred to us that he might have tried to wade across the river at its mouth, but the tide was now coming in. Panic. After a desperate search we went to the police. It turned out that Robert had been frightened from his fishing perch by a dog and began to retrace his steps but took a wrong turning. The police eventually picked up a small boy with a fishing rod on the far side of the village wandering along a lane and brought him back to us. This drama had a happy ending, but one comes to appreciate later how fortunate we were that we experienced no major upsets as the children grew up.

My rapid promotion in the bank (I was an assistant general manager by 1971) enabled us to make the major decision in the summer of 1972 that we would be able to afford boarding school education for the boys. We went to see the headmaster of Cheltenham College and he recommended one of its feeder prep schools, Beaudesert Park, which was in a position to take both Robert, aged 10, and Martin, aged 8, in September that year. The school was only a few miles from Oakridge Lynch where my mother had stayed on at Stream, which was an added attraction. Like all parents, we were in tears as we drove away from dropping off the boys for the first time that autumn, but convinced nevertheless that we had made the right decision. Beaudesert was still run by members of the founding family at that time and had a happy atmosphere. The boys settled in well and we got to know the local hotels on fortnightly Sunday lunch visits. They became rather good letter writers from the discipline of having to write a Sunday letter on weekends we were not visiting, and they made up lost ground scholastically and coped adequately with common entrance in due course.

During the seven years we lived at Rosendale Road our income had doubled and we had managed to save as well; this was very much helped by negligible holiday expenses. At Rosendale Road we had mounted the housing ladder just as house prices had started their upward spiral. We had established a lifestyle of working parents and the beginnings of boarding school education and we lived pretty modestly.

Ruth's father stayed on in the Swiss Cottage flat, but we had growing concerns over his ability to manage on his own. After his spinster sister died he began to have domestic accidents, including one night stuck in the bath, and it became clear that we should make a home for him. This meant a larger house. We realised that we could not afford to move north of the river on the basis of the value of Rosendale Road so we started looking around Dulwich in early 1974, just as 1 was coming up for promotion again to be a general manager. This led us to 24 Alleyn Road, a six-bedroom family house c.1880 that had just been extensively modernised by a medical couple who had then decided to emigrate to America. The cost was £51,000. Rosendale Road realised £28,000, but leaving only £19,000 after repaying the outstanding mortgage which left a substantial funding gap. We were able to contribute some savings, but it was quite a struggle to persuade the bank to lend the balance of £28,000 as an interest only mortgage. This was the largest staff house loan it had made up to that time and it needed the personal approval of the chief executive after lobbying him in the loo one day.

We had decided to make a ground floor suite for Fritz on one side of the house and to move the drawing room to the first floor by amalgamating two bedrooms. The builder who had looked after us in Rosendale Road did the transformation that summer, mostly while we were on holiday in Denmark. Sadly, Fritz died in late 1975 after living with us for little more than a year. The fine furniture and possessions that had amazingly been shipped safely from Vienna in 1938 had now became an integral part of our home and a reminder of what Suzi used to refer to as 'the good old days'.

Rounding off the family background, while we were on holiday in Denmark in 1974, I received a telegram from my mother – to the excitement of the local post office staff in Blokhus, Jutland – announcing her marriage to Hugh Thomas. Hugh was one of her oldest friends who had come out to Kericho shortly before my father and rose to become the Superintendent of James Finlay's estates. His wife had died some 15 years previously. Margaret had found life quite difficult on her own and Hugh had been courting her assiduously, so it was very welcome news that she had decided to team up with him. They bought a bungalow overlooking the sea at Emsworth in Sussex and had ten very companiable years together until Hugh's death in 1984. Margaret lived for another six years in Emsworth as a spirited eighty-nine-year-old almost until the very end.

The family links with Kenya and Vienna had now been severed and we were now on our own, so to speak. The pre-occupations of our 28 years in Dulwich centred on our careers and on bringing up the boys, from nursery school through to university and their first jobs and then marriage.

We had moved up in the world by moving closer to the centre of Dulwich. On one side was a banker from Barclays and on the other a business psychologist with a theatre producer wife; there was a City law partner opposite, a dentist and a man with a successful business. It was less neighbourly than Rosendale Road, but for the Queen's silver jubilee the road was closed and there was a splendid street party with children's races and barbecued food. Robert and Martin had stayed up late the night before making dozens of carnation blossoms out of red tissue paper which were hung in a great garland from an upper window and from a cherry tree in front, and they won a prize for festive decoration. These were years of prosperity for us, although we never lived up to our income. This was partly because we were not living in a competitive social environment, but one dominated by civil servants, professional people and academics, and partly because we both had demanding jobs.

It was customary at the time for Standard Chartered senior

executives to make an annual visit accompanied by wives to one of their overseas territories. For our visit to Nigeria in 1976 Ruth had managed to arrange an invitation to give several lectures at Lagos University on housing finance. It was situated on the far side of the lagoon from the bank residential area and there were horrendous morning traffic jams at that time, with the result that on each occasion she arrived late, which was tough. The tensions among the executives did not make this a very enjoyable visit and Ruth did not find it easy to tune in with the expatriate wives. In truth they did not have an easy time, as they were precluded from paid employment and living conditions were challenging. I noticed over the following years that, with the introduction of annual home leave, more and more bank wives in the African banks stayed in England as grass widows.

Robert left Cheltenham in 1980 as head of his house and with a place at University College, London to read economics after a gap year. His last year at college had not been a happy one for a strange reason. The headmaster instituted a drive against boys drinking in Cheltenham's pubs and, as head of house, Robert endeavoured to enforce this against a determined group of pub crawlers, and with a feeble housemaster in the background. Things reached such a pitch that Robert had to be taken into safe custody in the private side of the house in his last term.

Martin's last year at Cheltenham was also unusual. He could not abide the same feeble housemaster and was threatening to leave school early. I talked to Richard Morgan, the headmaster (being president of Council at the time) and he came up with an imaginative solution: he arranged for Martin to be a lodger with a charming and interesting woman, as a day boy for the year. One of the incidental benefits of the arrangement was that she had a sloppy Labrador and Martin overcame his very real fear of dogs. Martin was also offered a place at UCL to read geography after a gap year. Both boys had felt strongly that, after being 'banished' to Cheltenham for their schooldays, they wanted to go to university in London, and UCL was where Ruth had been. After their first year in halls, I purchased a flat for each of the boys to share with fellow students and this eventually provided each of them with an equity pot to buy their first house on getting married.

With the boys coming to the end of their schooldays, Ruth felt that she could resume a full-time job, particularly as the set-up at South

Bank was no longer so enjoyable. The post of Secretary (head of the administration) at the London School of Hygiene and Tropical Medicine was advertised in 1980 and Ruth was appointed, holding the post for ten years.

The City was a magnet to university graduates at that time as foreign banks poured into London and the domestic institutions prepared for Big Bang. On graduating in 1984 Robert was hired by Sumitomo Bank as a trainee dealer, and there he met his future wife Jane – another graduate hire from Manchester University. Martin, likewise, turned to the City but wanted to go into corporate finance and was taken on in 1986 by the new merchant bank established by NatWest – County Bank, where he met his future wife Ann.

The 1985 quinquennium saw my City career reach its climactic conclusion, first with the defeat of the hostile bid from Lloyds Bank where I was widely seen as playing a decisive role, and then with my ousting from the bank less than two years afterwards, followed by my move to academia. Yet it was also a time of momentous developments in the family, which had to be balanced somehow with the more public events. I was doubtless buoyed to an extent by the drama, but it was more difficult for Ruth and there were costs. Although there were compelling reasons for stepping in to run the Royal Commonwealth Society in 1988/89, as I have narrated, it was a mistake in domestic terms to have taken on such a demanding assignment in that interregnum before going to another challenging job at SOAS. From Ruth's point of view, there was no let-up in work pressure apart from our holiday trips. I would like to think that if there had been a more relaxing year I would have devoted more to our relationship, but I am not confident that I possessed that degree of emotional awareness at that time. She did not get on with the new director of the School of Hygiene and decided during the year to retire in 1990, and then she was much upset by the death of his predecessor, Gordon Smith, from prostate cancer. The two family weddings were also stressful in their way as Ruth had put a lot into her relationship with the boys.

I was a local resident member on the trust that owned Dulwich College, the Alleyn schools and Dulwich Picture Gallery. I persuaded the ex-Colonial Service administrator to allow me to hold our silver wedding event in the picture gallery in 1985. It was the first time that the gallery was let for such a purpose, which comprised a reception, a concert and a dinner (catered and brought to the gallery by the Standard Chartered chef). The concert was memorable for being provided by musical friends: Cyril Erlich's violinist daughter had formed a string quartet and they played Mozart's K465 quartet. Matthew Taylor from Kennington was now a music scholar at Cambridge and he played Brahms (and he features again at the end of Ruth's life). Our friend Mary Craig sang Richard Strauss's *Zuignung*, amongst other songs. And Robert gave a magnificent speech that revealed unexpected depths of feeling.

Alleyn Road was the operations centre of our busy lives, but neither of us became emotionally attached to the house as the place where we wanted to end our days. This feeling was reinforced once Robert and Martin were married with homes of their own, but more particularly from 1990 by my having a weekday residence in Bloomsbury. The SOAS flat greatly facilitated our concert and opera visits and gave rise to the thought that perhaps we should retire to central London, the better to enjoy its cultural life. The alternative was to live in the country and perhaps have a London pied-à-terre.

Knowing what came later, it is difficult to look back over our life together in the SOAS years. l know that l made great efforts to sustain a 'normal' relationship and in some ways l succeeded too well. We really enjoyed our summer holidays in Austria, especially having found a flat in Frau Sorzi's house in Seefeld that we rented three years running, and we really got to know the surrounding walks and mountains.

While on holiday in Austria in 1992 we explored the possibility of buying a house there, but concluded instead that we should look for a weekend cottage in the Cotswolds. We spent every weekend that autumn visiting Cotswold properties trying to reconcile ease of communications, good location, garden potential and affordability. We discovered and liked ldbury in West Oxfordshire near Stow on the Wold and made two unsuccessful bids for a house there. Then, finding ourselves sitting next to Edmund and Suzi Dell at Wigmore Hall one evening – and knowing that they had a cottage there – we mentioned our search frustrations. They told us that the owners of a neighbouring cottage were planning to move and l decided to write a cold-call letter to them. We struck gold, exchanging contracts in April 1993 for a delayed completion in October, while they moved house.

A royal visit. At Idbury

Robert and Martin and family

Hiking in Austria

Paddock Cottage was a former dairyman's cottage that had been modernised and extended and, above all, it had a fabulous view. We paid the asking price and were able to have Martin and the grandchildren to stay straight away. We soon had ambitious plans to replace an old pigsty shed with a Kenya-style guest house or pavilion. We celebrated its completion with a splendid outdoor catered lunch party for about 30, seated at a long table overlooking our wonderful view. Idbury now became the focus of our domestic life and we found that it was a sociable community, very much led by a writer couple, Neil Philip and Emma Bradford. Paddock Cottage abutted a bare-subsistence farm owned by a brother and sister and farmed by her characterful son, fathered by an Italian prisoner of war. The farm was acquired piecemeal by Teresa Stopford-Sackville, who lived at Idbury House and soon turned the property into a livery stable for hunters. Some years later, I persuaded her rather reluctantly to sell an adjacent copse with a pond to add to Paddock Cottage.

Having a country cottage meant that we went there every weekend and this pushed Dulwich further into the background. We then lent the house to Martin and Ann for six months while they sold their house preparatory to a move to Gloucestershire. These developments crystalised our decision to sell and to buy a flat in Mayfair as our main residence. The sale was quickly achieved and we put our belongings into storage and moved into the SOAS flat as our temporary home. In the event it was two years before we were able to move into our new London home: a top floor flat in a handsome 1920s building in Portland Place. It was in a rundown condition and needed extensive modernisation. In retrospect we rather went over the top on the project, with Gerald Moran as Pied Piper coming up with a series of imaginative proposals involving cherry wood shutters and doors, beautiful marble and two amazing bathrooms and a superb kitchen.

82 Portland Place was a community of 24 apartments in a street that was reminiscent of a Paris boulevard ending in a Nash crescent facing Regents Park, and the BBC and Langham Hotel at the southern end. Our neighbours were cosmopolitan with several who had been there a long time. There was also a younger business couple, Donald Rushton and Penny, who became good friends. He quickly passed over chairmanship of the management committee to me, before they moved to Japan for

a while. A few years previously the man who was then running the committee had stolen all its reserves and the other members were so embarrassed that they never pursued him through the courts, although Barclays had made a partial restitution on account of negligence. As a result, there was no sinking fund and any works had to be financed project by project through a supplementary service charge. This was already very high, since only 24 flats had to support the porterage and cleaning. The building was of an age when some significant expenses loomed for the lifts, electrical and services. Securing agreement for such works was quite a diplomatic challenge and I got to know the other residents through these negotiations.

We were at Portland Place for seven years before changing circumstances led to a decision to sell the apartment. Our original intention had been to extend the lease, or convert to freehold, but two things changed our minds. In the first place, there was little enthusiasm for a joint approach with other owners, while the de Walden estate was not cooperative as its policy was to gain increased control over properties on the estate. Secondly, we learned that there was a distinct possibility that de Walden would be able in due course to add another floor to No. 82, which would be particularly disruptive to the two top floor flats. We also realised that we had become increasingly attached to our Cotswold home and also that the family was migrating that way. Robert and Jane bought Brambles Farm in Fifield – within sight of Paddock Cottage – in 1998, while Martin was planning to send James and Olivia to Cheltenham College (which involved them moving to Painswick in 2003). This led to a major reversal of priorities: we now saw Paddock Cottage as becoming our main home with a view to finding a pied-à-terre in London.

We put our apartment up for sale in 1992 and after some false starts sold it a year later and just about recouped our original outlay.

In retirement, we took the view that, while we were fit enough to enjoy the experience we would indulge in some adventurous holiday travel, especially in Africa. Other people's travel reminiscences can be a bore and I will content myself with one: a walking/flying safari in northern Kenya in 1999. We set off like a 19th century expedition with 14 donkeys and their armed Samburu minders, down the steep side of the Rift escarpment into the Senguta Valley. There were campfire reminiscences with Black Label scotch in hand from our guide before we turned in to our tent that was tactfully located a little way from the main camp. I awoke in the middle of the night to the sound of a lion grunting some inches away. I plucked up resolve to leap up with a great shout to discourage it and to raise help, only to discover that the 'lion' was Ruth snoring in the next bed.

We then had a small plane to fly to the shore of Lake Turkana, near the famous Leakey excavation which we visited. Our pilot guide said that we must catch our supper of tilapia and made to wade out waste deep into this crocodile infested water. I declined to follow him so was fixed up with a rod and float to fish from the shore, with the benefit of a seaward breeze. The float was a blown-up condom. Our next stop was the Chalbi Desert. When the pilot came down to land he discovered that the desert was a sheet of water and he had to search for some higher ground near a village and we slept under the wings of the plane.

We marked the millennium with considerable panache, starting with a visit to Vienna with friends to see in the new century. In February, we treated the family to a holiday on Guana Island[128] where Olivia celebrated her 9th birthday. In March we marked our 40th wedding anniversary with a dinner dance and then re-traced much of our honeymoon route by motoring to the Riviera and round the coast to 'our' hotel in Santa Margherita, before going to stay with Dulwich friends in their lovely hill-top villa in Umbria.

The sale of Portland Place coincided with my annus horribilis. All our residence plans were then in disarray and 'Heimat' was a sick joke. But the divorce did not happen and we began to rebuild our relationship. Ruth wanted to see more of her women friends, attend lectures and follow art appreciation courses. I had started serious research and writing on tea (with visits to Kenya in 2003 and 2004) for what eventually became a book on the Kenya tea industry, *Simba Chai*.[129] But I was also much involved with the Royal Commonwealth Society and the British Empire and Commonwealth Museum.

Ruth never took to the village community, but liked country walks and the garden, yet when she developed secondary cancer and was given a year to live she chose to end her days at Yew Tree Farm. It is an attractive small farmhouse set in about two acres, and it enabled us to

---

128 Owned by Henry Jarecki.
129 We bought a flat in the Barbican and Yew Tree Farm in Gloucestershire.

have a bedroom suite each and another for visitors. A small barn is fitted as a guest cottage. The large garden is a satisfying challenge.

Ruth's decision to come to Yew Tree Farm to die – rather than to go to hospital, or ask me to look after her in the Barbican flat – was momentous for me. It was a powerful signal of recognising that we had found 'home' at last and wanting to be there in her last months. To begin with, we were able to go for short walks together and she appreciated the garden. And then after the accident on the stairs she was confined to her bedroom. Neighbours in the village were very supportive in the final weeks and increasingly one felt part of a community and *heimat* had renewed meaning.

14. JOINING IN

After Ruth's death, I decided to rent a flat in Marylebone so that I could continue to go to Wigmore Hall concerts and I went up to London most weeks for a night or so. Coming back by train one day to Kemble I met up with a friend, Peter Martin, and during our chat he told me about an old friend of theirs who had been abandoned by her husband and suggested that I might like to invite her to a concert one day.

I duly made an email proposal to Thalia for a concert at Wigmore Hall with supper beforehand. She accepted for 16 December and I only managed to secure return tickets for the Ingrid Flitter recital on the morning of the concert. Thalia had not dressed up for the occasion, while I had announced that I would be wearing a bow tie and was sitting at the table when she walked in. She was immediately easy to talk to as we began a striptease of mutual history. It turned out that she had also read PPE about seven years after me and that we had several friends in common. Also, that she had three children by her first husband and seven grandchildren and had then been married to Jonathan Stone for thirty years. We met next in mid-January at another concert at St Martin in the Fields and travelled back on the No. 13 bus, parting again on the doorstep. Matters developed rapidly thereafter and Thalia's children became aware that she had acquired a 'special friend' and were delighted, while I hesitated to tell Robert and Martin until I had finally proposed on 15 May. The next day we went to lunch with the Martins and I asked Peter to be best man.

Our engagement announcement in *The Times* prompted the *Daily Telegraph* to make contact and then to write up a story in the Mandrake Diary.[130] We saw no reason to delay a wedding, other than preparation time, and decided to get married in the autumn at the Hinde Street Methodist church that Thalia had been attending. She abandoned a planned trip to Namibia but wanted to go ahead with attending the decennial Oberammergau festival in Bavaria with her church group in September. We decided to make it a kind of pre-honeymoon, which was quite complicated. I was added to the festival ticket, but made my own way by car to meet Thalia at Munich airport. She dropped out of the several-day preparatory sessions with the group while we drove on to Seefeld, where I was able to introduce her to some of the lovely walks there. Unfortunately, she had bought new walking boots that were too small and acquired two black toe nails as a result. The Oberammergau performance was most impressive, with an enormous community cast, including livestock. Afterwards we had two days' leisurely drive back to England and then the final wedding preparations.

Thalia had decided that the family men should wear kilts which caused quite a stir. For the ceremony, she took charge of the hymns and readings and I chose the music, which included a short song recital: Beethoven's *Ich liebe dich*; Brahms's *Wie bist du meine Konegin*; Richard Strauss's *Zueignung* and finally *Where e'er you walk* from Handel's *Semele*. Hinde Street had a charismatic Brazilian minister who looked like paintings of Jesus and he made quite an impression on everyone. After the reception (with bagpipes) we spent two nights at the Ritz and we bought an eternity ring. Back at Brimpsfield we held a neighbours' party to symbolise joining the village community, and then in February flew to Guana Island as a guest of Henry Jarecki.

To begin with, Thalia and I maintained an active presence in both London and in Brimpsfield – in effect we were country weekenders. While in London we went to music events, Thalia was a member of an art appreciation group, while I played bridge at the Carlton Club and became

---

130 When the Wigmore Hall celebrated an anniversary in 2010 and there was a Radio 3 programme by Christopher Cooke, chairman of the Cheltenham Music Festival, he wove our engagement story into his narrative.

chairman of Bryanston Square Trust that was responsible for the garden in the square. This brought us into contact with some neighbours, as did the fact that No. 9 was part of a management company covering five houses and I was soon actively involved. The Trust organised an annual garden party, which were quite grand affairs – catered by the Hyatt Hotel. In the Queen's golden jubilee year I arranged for the planting of a memorial tree – *Paulownia Tormentosa* – and led singing of the national anthem at the party. In the 200th anniversary year of the Trust Thalia and I wore Regency costumes for the occasion. We toyed with buying a larger flat to give us more entertaining space, but Brimpsfield began to beckon more strongly.

In the village, Thalia became a member of the parochial church council and of the village hall committee and was elected chair of the WI for three years, until the branch was closed. I became chair of the garden society and when the village hall was granted a once a week pub licence (there being no village pub) I helped complete funding of the project. More recently I have been elected a parish councillor. We have made changes to Yew Tree Farm to make it a joint enterprise, with a greenhouse for Thalia's cactus collection, incorporating the trap shed into the house to provide Thalia with a study of her own, and absorbing many of her pictures and other treasures. The Covid 19 lockdown has not been a bad experience for a village like ours. With everyone at home one has actually seen more neighbours for a 'garden gate' chat than previously, and people have been solicitous of others' welfare.

My involvements with the Royal Commonwealth Society, the British Empire & Commonwealth Museum and Cheltenham Festivals came to an end, but I was invited to be a founding member of a new society modelled on the London livery companies, the Honourable Company of Gloucestershire. It was the inspiration of Sir Henry Elwes, the Lord Lieutenant, and has the imaginative aim of promoting the interests of the county in culture, sport, social welfare and business. A separate charitable trust was formed to which all members have to make an annual contribution. Very soon, I was asked to take responsibility for developing the Arts & Heritage dimension and joined the Court for several years. I put a lot of effort into this, so that it became the most active of the company's committees. Perhaps the most interesting venture was the creation of a prize fund for Gloucestershire libraries to reward initiatives by the county's libraries to stimulate book reading. The idea came from Jonathan Taylor, who had been chairman of the Booker Prize for many years, and we managed to persuade the Honourable Company to be the nominal sponsor of the David Vaisey Prize and won the support of the Gloucestershire library service and a range of supporting parties.[131] It is perhaps not unconnected that Gloucestershire has been one of the few counties in England not to have closed a library during the squeeze on local authority funding.

On reaching 80, I decided to set up a small trust to complement annual gift aid donations and transferred £200,000 to it, with a plan to distribute the whole fund over the following ten years in roughly equal instalments to the educational and charitable bodies that I have been involved with. Thus, Cheltenham College, Oriel, SOAS, Cheltenham Festivals, the Honourable Company and a number of Gloucestershire causes have received regular support over the succeeding years.

In these ways Thalia and I have become increasingly drawn into country life in the Cotswolds and to the friends we have made there, so that London became marginal to our lives. We mutually concluded that Brimpsfield is the place where we wish to end our days, but there remained an anxiety over eventually becoming housebound and needing care. An unexpected solution then presented itself. A neighbour in the lane became ill with cancer and died rather quickly, leaving an impoverished widow in a partially modernised house that was attached to a ruined cottage that he had never got round to incorporating into his own house. The property was put on the market when he became ill and did not sell. We suddenly realised that this could be a solution to our own anxieties: to purchase the house and modernise it and hold it as a rented investment against the day when we might want to install full time carers to look after us. To the immense gratitude of the couple, we agreed to purchase the property at the asking price before Mike died. Subsequently, we integrated the two cottages into a four-bedroom house and let it.[132]

Although I have lived in many homes during the course of my life, I think I have always had a desire to identify strongly with each one of

---

131 David Vaisey came from a modest agricultural background in Gloucestershire and was a scholarship boy to Oxford and joined the Bodleian Library where he became its distinguished head.

132 We have recently sold the house in favour of an alternative solution: to add a bedroom to the small barn close to the house so as to make a guest cottage/carer's home.

Engaged. Guana Island honeymoon

85th birthday family gathering. Summertime

them, of wanting to personalise a home, to make a garden, to relate to neighbours. I think of my shared bachelor quarters at Mufulira Copper Mines where I had shipped out all my books from England to give character to my bedsit; of the guest cottage in Nairobi where I tried to improve the surrounding garden patch; of the little garden I created in Kennington and of my first attempts at DIY redecoration while listening to Wagner; and then of the much more ambitious efforts at home making and gardening in Dulwich and the cultivation of neighbours in a suburban street. Settling at last in Gloucestershire and Brimpsfield has added another dimension, almost of manifest destiny. Both my parents were Cirencester born, and then there was Cheltenham College, not only for me but also my sons and grandchildren. Summer holidays when the boys were small entailed endless picnics and a growing familiarity with the highways and byways of the county, and this has been reinforced by the more recent weekly excursions with my gents' walking group. Both my parents had a deep love of the Gloucestershire countryside and especially its flora, which has been passed on to me. I know where to go to look for butterfly orchids and bee orchids, pasque flowers and herb Paris.

An added bonus was the discovery that Thalia was born in Cheltenham and that she has happy memories of staying with her grandparents in their historic house outside Gloucester where King Charles I stayed during the siege of Gloucester.

Good health in old age is a blessing and I have been so fortunate. At Cheltenham I used to get up at 6.30 for a cold shower, skipping and yoga exercises, and I have kept up a morning exercise routine ever since. A stint seems to have settled an irregular heartbeat, an episode of arteritis a few years ago was alarming at the time, my weight is the same as thirty years ago and elderly joints feel arthritic in winter but do not prevent gardening and country walks. One forgets the names of acquaintances and of garden flowers. One apparent consequence of advancing age is a reduced curiosity, or urge to have new experiences and to see new places. I do not watch television, but read a lot and listen to music. Home seems best, especially if one has the good fortune still to be sharing it with a loved wife and companion.

Writing this memoir has entailed revisiting long ago events and experiences and poring over old diaries and papers. And then I think of my mother who resolutely refused to dwell on the past and lived for the present and what comes next. I think she had a good attitude to make the most of life as it is and not to dwell too much on past glories and might have beens. However, writing these chapters has made me speculate on some of the turnings and opportunities that were not followed at crucial moments in earlier years. What if my appointment to a lectureship at Makerere University had not been blocked? Would I then have followed an academic career and perhaps married Cherry Gertzel? What if we had stayed on in Kenya until independence and after, perhaps then joining the World Bank in Washington as international civil servants? If I had joined Barclays DCO instead of Standard would I have had the same glittering career and would Ruth have stayed with me on the inevitable overseas postings? What if the SOAS opportunity had not been there? Given that I was resolved to leave the City, I might have struggled to find a satisfying new role. And what if Peter Martin had not been in matchmaking mode to introduce me to Thalia? I return to the comment in the preface, that there are moments in life to seize opportunity and to make one's luck. I think that Thalia and I both had a sense of serendipity in those early meetings, a sense that our stars were congruent and the omens were benign. We have been so fortunate to find safe haven together so late in our lives.

Thalia

ACKNOWLEDGEMENTS

My grateful thanks to Sharon Zink of Jericho Writers for diligent editorial advice and to Andrew Chapman of Prepare to Publish for seeing the book through the press. Any remaining infelicities are down to me.

Thalia has been a constant encouragement to write these memoirs and, more importantly, she has been the beacon that led to *Finding Home*.

INDEX

African Congress, 84, 86

Africa Private Enterprise Group
Dinner for Tambo and Mbeki Nov.
1985, 226

Association of Commonwealth Studies
Symons Report, 325
Seeking a partner, 326ff

Barber, Tony. Baron Barber of
Wentbridge. Chairman, Standard
Chartered
Proposing deputy chairman, 213
Receptive Lloyds bid, 239
Retirement, 241
Referee for SOAS, 264

Big Bang legacy, 256ff

British Empire & Commonwealth Museum
Appointed trustee 1997, 330
Resignation and re-appointment as
vice chairman, 332-3
Slave trade exhibition, 337
Museum items on the market, 342
Director dismissed, 344
Royal Bank of Scotland dispute, 346
Decision to close museum, 347
Dowry to Bristol Museums, 349

Capricorn Africa Society
Contributor to newsletter, Equinox,
80
Northern Rhodesia political party, 82

Centre for the Study of African
Economies, 291

Chase Manhattan Bank
Shareholding in Standard Bank, 170
Strategy with Standard Chartered,
174
Visit to New York, 178

Cheltenham College
Cheltondale House 1946, 27
Eliot-Smith, 31
Head boy ambition, 32
College Council 1977, 39, 41
Morgan, Richard, 40, 42
150th Anniversary, 43
Wilks, Peter, 43-4

Christian Council of Kenya
The Economic Development of
Kenya, 122

Commonwealth
Oxford special subject, 48
CHOGM 1997 and 2009, 309, 324

Reflections, 311ff and 351
Commonwealth Development
  Corporation
  Job interview 1963, 153
  Appointed to Board 1990, 354
  Writing the history, 354
  Eccles v. Whitehall, 355
  Public Private Partnership, 357ff
Commonwealth Institute
  Closure and collections gifted to
  museum, 334-5
Constitution Party
  See Capricorn Africa Society
  Launch of party, 82-3
  Appointed Mufulira agent, 86
  1987 Convention 89
Frankel, Prof. Herbert
  Thesis supervisor, 53
  Member East Africa Royal
  Commission, 56
Gaitskell, Sir Arthur
  Research fellowship, Nuffield
  College, 57
  Appointed as research assistant, 57
  Gezira Cotton Scheme, 57-8
  Visits to Khartoum and Gezira, 58, 62
  Nationalism and partnership 63
  Nairobi dinner party, 116
Galpin, Sir Rodney
  Institute of Bankers conference, 180
  Doubts on independence of
  StanChart, 241, 245
  Banking Act Inquiry, 245
  Supports Amex bid approach, 250
  Bank of England letter to board, 252
  Appointment as executive chairman,
  253
  Disposal strategy, 254
Gertzel, Prof. Cherry
  Visit to Makerere, 118ff
Glyn-Jones, Eleanor
  Research secretary to Margery
  Perham, 52
  Makerere meeting, 95
  Mufulira visit and after, 95-98

Graham, Sir Peter
  Groups strategy conference 1975, 201
  Deputy chairman proposal, 213
  Recommend as chairman, 242
  Broadbent Jones assignment, 248
  Assessment, 255
Gulf
  Regional general manager 1977 and
  report, 200
Heimat
  Kimugu, Kericho 1933, 6
  45 Courtenay Street, Kennington
  1963, 167
  137 Rosendale Road, Dulwich 1967,
  402
  24 Alleyn Road, Dulwich 1974, 407
  Paddock Cottage, Idbury 1993, 411
  82 Portland Place, Mayfair 1996, 415
  Yew Tree Farm, Brimpsfield 2004, 417
Hong Kong
  1980 visit report, 210
Hicks, Prof. Sir John
  Kenya visit and thesis examiner, 68
  Kenya Treasury appointment, 102
Howe, Geoffrey. Lord Howe of Aberavon.
  SOAS Visitor 1990, 274
India
  Regional general manager 1975, 197ff
Jarecki, Dr Henry
  Friend and advisor, 186
  Leeds Castle assessment, 220
  Johnson Matthey Bankers episode,
  224
  Guana Island
Kaptagat School
  Entered 1939, 14ff
  Chris Young's influence, 18
Kenya Treasury
  Post advertised, 100
  1958 appointment hiccups, 108ff
  Assistant secretary, 139ff
  Retirement, 142
Kenya Politics
  Lennox-Boyd constitution, 112-3
  Odinga rally in Kisumu, 114

Understanding Mau Mau, 124
Preparing for independence, 140
Ariel Foundation report, 146
Interview Sir Evelyn Baring for
Oxford colonial records, 149
Lloyds Bank
First bid approach 1982, 209
Bank of England sympathetic, 219
Bid announcement 1986, 233
Bid defeat, 234ff
Renewed interest, 241
Makerere University
Proposed economics lectureship, 102
Appointment, 108, and prohibition,
109
Major, Sir John
Joins my department, 187
Bank supported member of
Parliament, 188
Mboya, Tom
Post-Oxford meeting, 66
Equator Club dinner, 116
Dinner with Gaitskell, 116 and
Perham, 117
McWilliam, Michael Douglas. Career
dates:
Date of birth 21 June 1933, 3
Kaptagat School 1939, 14
Cheltenham College 1946, 27
Oriel College, Oxford 1952, 45
Nuffield College, Oxford 1955, 53
Mufulira Copper Mines 1957, 75
Kenya Treasury 1958, 107, 127
Samuel Montagu 1962, 154
Standard Chartered, principal market
research 1966, 173
"   manager business development
1969, 178
"   assistant general manager 1971,
180
"   general manager 1974, 188
"   senior general manager 1977, 200
"   deputy managing director 1979,
210
"   group managing director 1983, 211

School of Oriental and African Studies,
director 1989, 263
McWilliam, Margaret Helen
Family background, 5
John Brooke letter, 137
Corporate wife, 138
Married Hugh Thomas, 408
McWilliam, Douglas Sydney
Family background, 5
Joins Brooke Bond, 3
Career: producer cartel 17, tea
controller 17, director 20
Resignation, 133-4
Secretary Tea Board, 143, 167
Death 404
McWilliam, Ruth
First meeting, 126
George Delf, 128
Engaged, 130, and married, 132
Ministry of Agriculture, 141
LSE post, 170
National Economic Development
Office and South Bank Polytechnic,
404
London School of Hygiene &
Tropical Medicine 410
Portrait of a marriage, 363ff
McWilliam, Martin Frederick
Date of birth 7 November 1964, 168
Cheltenham College, 409
First job 410
McWilliam, Robert Douglas
Date of birth 6 September 1962, 167
Cheltenham College 409
First job 410
McWilliam, Thalia, Sybil
First meeting, 410
Marriage, 420
Midland Bank
Deal options 1984, 219
Renewed discussions 1985, 227
Clydesdale offer 1987, 246
Mocatta & Goldsmid
Standard Chartered purchase 1974, 184
Jarecki association, 186

1978 silver crisis, 204
Mufulira Copper Mines
  Approach to Prain, 73
  African Personnel Department,75
  Mine club race incident, 81
  50 Club, 82
  Resignation, 103
  Visit as banker, 105, 197
Nigeria
  Induction tour 1967, 176
  Regional general manager 1974, 188
  Nigerian chief executive, 189
  A minority shareholder 1976, 193
  Board conflicts 1981, 211
Nkumbula, Harry
  Ndola meeting 1958, 90
  Kansuswa meeting, 91
Nuffield College, Oxford
  Research studentship 1955, 53
  Deferral of thesis, 57
  Kenya Tea Board conditions on
  thesis, 64
  Thesis resume, 66ff
  Simba Chai publication, 69
Nyendwoha, Sarah
  Meeting at Oxford, 49
  Uganda meetings, 65, 119
Oriel College, Oxford
  Arrival in 1952, 45
  East Africa Association, 46
  Switch to PPE, 47
  Honorary Fellow, 54
  Rhodes Must Go, 54
Prain, Sir Ronald. Chairman Roan
  Selection Trust
  Application for a post, 73
  President Cheltenham College
  Council, invitation to join, 39
  Mufulira post-mortem, 101
Publications (in text chronology)
  Central African Examiner, 80, 82, 86
  Equinox, 80,83
  Africa South, 81
  East African Economics Review, 143,
  144, 145

Simba Chai: The Kenya Tea Industry,
144
Journal of Commonwealth Political
Studies, 145
The World Today, 147
Economic Development and Cultural
Change, 148
Essays in Imperial Government, 149
History of East Africa, 149
Banking in the 1980s, 220
Asian Affairs, 287
The Development Business – History
of the Commonwealth Development
Corporation, 354
Round Table, 357,358
Reinventing the CDC and Public
Private Partnership, 358
Rake, Alan
  Editor, Drum East Africa, 120,122
  Ghana visit,163
Raisman, John
  Chair of HEFCE Review of SOAS, 278
  Chair British Empire &
  Commonwealth Museum, 332
Rhodes Must Go, 54
Royal African Society
  Council member 1974, 288m
  chairman, 1996, 288
  Relocation to SOAS, 288
  Reforms, 289ff
Royal Commonwealth Society
  Council member 1975, 297, chairman
  1996, 308
  Viability concerns, 288 and executive
  role 299
  Commonwealth Trusts 301ff
  See Victoria League
  David Thorne appointed, 306
  1997 CHOGM, 309-11
  Commonwealth reflections, 312-3
  Strategic issues, 316-9
  See Commonwealth
  Whistle blower, 320
  Danny Sriskandarajah appointment,
  321

Institutional refocus, 324
Royal Bank of Scotland
    Merger offer and Monopolies
    reference, 208
    Repercussions of failed deal, 209
    Williams & Glynn proposal, 209
    Share purchase manoeuvres, 218-9
Samuel Montagu
    Job interview, 154
    The changing City, 157
    Visit to West Africa, 162
    Venture capital and EED, 165
School of Oriental and African Studies
    Appointment, 263-4
    University funding model and SOAS,
    271, 277
    Brunei Gallery, 275ff
    Raisman report, 279
    Retirement decision, 282
    Expansion ambitions, 287-90
    Appraisal, 285, 292
South Africa
    Induction tour 1976,176
    Board appointment sensitivity, 206
    Apartheid strains, 208
    Bank of England concerns, 221
    Disinvestment, 247
Standard Chartered
    Recruited 1966, 170, 174
    Induction tours to West, South and
    East Africa, 176ff
    Merger steering committee, 179
    Diversification investments, 181
    Devolution philosophy, 215, and
    federalism, 220
    See Royal Bank of Scotland
    Union Bank purchase 1979, 202
    Midland Bank, 219, 227, 246
    See Graham
    See Galpin
    See Lloyds Bank
    Corporate good citizen in Africa, 228
    Independence declarations, 211, 232
    Board divisions, 239
    Banking Act Inquiry, 245
    American Express approach, 249
    Departure March 1988, 253
United Kenya Club, 121
Vasey, Sir Ernest
    Intervention on Treasury
    appointment, 110
    Resigns as Minister of Finance, 113
    Invitation to join Tanganyika
    Treasury, 130
    Obituary 133
Victoria League
    Possible link with RCS, 299
    Commonwealth Trust joint
    sponsorship, 301
    Unequal partnership, 305
Wade-Gery, Sir Robert
    Chairman SOAS Governing Body, 273
Wathen, Julian
    Accra meeting, 163
    Offer to join Barclays DCO, 169
    Career influence, 171
Zambia
    Regional general manager 1974, 194
    Preparing for a Zambian chairman, 194
    President Kaunda, 230

Lightning Source UK Ltd.
Milton Keynes UK
UKHW012016250123
415976UK00003B/38